A Ved Mehta Reader

BY VED MEHTA

Face to Face

Walking the Indian Streets

Fly and the Fly-Bottle

The New Theologian

Delinquent Chacha

Portrait of India

John Is Easy to Please

Mahatma Gandhi and His Apostles

The New India

The Photographs of Chachaji

A Family Affair

Three Stories of the Raj

Rajiv Gandhi and Rama's Kingdom

A Ved Mehta Reader: The Craft of the Essay

Continents of Exile

Daddyji

Mamaji

Vedi

The Ledge Between the Streams

Sound-Shadows of the New World

The Stolen Light

Up at Oxford

Remembering Mr. Shawn's *New Yorker*

A Ved Mehta Reader
The Craft of the Essay

Ved Mehta

Yale University Press
New Haven & London

Designed by Rebecca Gibb. Set in Garamond type by Keystone Typesetting, Inc. Printed in the United States of America by R. R. Donnelley & Sons.

Mehta, Ved, 1934–
A Ved Mehta reader : the craft of the essay / Ved Mehta.
p.   cm.
ISBN 0-300-07189-2 (cloth: alk. paper)
ISBN 0-300-07561-8 (pbk: alk. paper)
I. Title.
PR9499.3.M425A6   1998
824—dc21
97-39079 CIP

A catalogue record for this book is available from the British Library.

The paper in this book meets the guidelines for permanence and durability of the Committee on Production Guidelines for Book Longevity of the Council on Library Resources.

10   9   8   7   6   5   4   3   2   1

TO ELEANOR GOULD PACKARD

Author's Note

❦

When I was invited to select some pieces for the "Reader," I was confronted with an awkward task. I had published twenty-one books over forty years, and a good many of them were so different from one another that some of my readers had difficulty believing they had been written by the same person. Indeed, I have always enjoyed experimenting with different genres and forms, and have had a dread of repeating a performance, so no sooner did I try my hand at one kind of writing than I felt the need to move on. There was also a complicating factor, which was that I grew up in India, America, and England, and because my subjects were drawn from all three countries they gave my various books different tones and colors, for one cannot write about Calcutta in the same manner that one would write about Oxford, nor can one write about Oxford in the same manner that one would write about New York. I would have much preferred to have someone else do the selecting, but when I mentioned this to a friend of my publisher he said that that kind of honor was generally reserved for authors who were dead.

My first attempt at selection was a failure. I tried to cram into the book as many different kinds of my writing as I could, including autobiography, biography, travel, politics, reporting, opinion, history, and fiction, on the theory that variety should be the guiding principle. The result seemed to lack focus and coherence, and, since I had been determined to publish whole pieces rather than just bowdlerized, truncated fragments, the book as a whole seemed overlong and unwieldy, its only virtue being that it exemplified my motley background and changing interests. In the end, I settled on a simpler and more manageable guiding principle: to give the reader just a sample of a number of my books as an introduction to my writing and as a teaching aid to young wordsmiths.

V.M.
Stanford, California
February, 1998

Contents

❧✦❧

Lightning and the Lightning Bug

In 1956, when I was twenty-two, I graduated from Pomona College, in California, and went up to Oxford. There I started working for a second bachelor's degree, for in those days the best way to take full advantage of what Oxford offered and to enter into the stream of English life was to work for an undergraduate degree at the university. I was reading history, and was required to write one or two essays a week and to submit them to the scrutiny of my tutors, most of whom were world-class scholars. While I was reading aloud to my tutor in the history of the Middle Ages one of my first essays, having to do with the Anglo-Saxons, he stopped me just after I had used the word "motivation," and asked how it was that I tended to reach for jargon when a good English word was to hand.

"But everyone uses 'motivation,'" I protested.

"Jargon is imprecise, and encourages weak thought," he said. "A careful writer would use a word like 'impulse.'"

Until then, I had thought I was a tolerably good writer, and had believed that after working over a draft several times I was able to say what I wanted to say. Indeed, before going up to Oxford, I had completed an entire book, an autobiography, much of which had been set down two years earlier, in the course of a summer. But I was so deeply in awe of Oxford and its tutorial system, and so impressionable, that my tutor's questioning of one infelicitous word had the effect of unravelling my confidence in my writing even as it began to sensitize me to the nuances of language. For some time thereafter, whenever I wrote a sentence for an essay I would read it as my tutor might, and would conclude that almost everything was wrong with it. I was reminded of an accomplished pianist friend of mine who was then undergoing intense psychoanalysis and had become in the course of her treatment so self-conscious that she could scarcely play a five-finger exercise. But I felt sure that, just as her treatment contained the promise of her becoming a better pianist, so my Oxford education contained the promise of my becoming a better writer. The road, however, turned out to be a long and arduous one—and to stretch far beyond Oxford.

I recall how daunting were my first steps along that road: what they led me to was a chaos of randomly assembled materials that had to be subjected first to the elusive formulation of ideas and then to the untamable nature of language itself. I was constantly tempted to put off writing. There was always more to read, more to reflect on. I found I had first to decide what, exactly, I wanted to say, even if in the course of writing I should find myself saying something totally different. (All ideas grow and develop as one writes, I learned, since one's memory expands through the process of association.) Nevertheless, having that initial idea, though it might be only the germ of one, enabled me to overcome the terror of the blank page. So as not to feel constrained or constricted, I would write what I came to call a "vomit draft," in which I would pour out everything I could think of without worrying about sense or grammar. Then I would start the process of revision— cutting and shaping my thoughts, which would help me learn what, if anything, I knew about the subject. As I pressed on with my essay, I would try to come up with the most telling arguments or examples to buttress whatever point I was making. To locate them required me to interrupt the writing and go searching through many books. In time, I learned to find my way around indexes and tables of contents, and around library catalogues as well. Sometimes I would put aside the essay and return to it later, casting a cold eye on it. The process as I describe it here may sound simple, but, as every student knows, it is turbulent and involves a lot of angst.

I remember that I was struck by the elegance and lustre of many of the essays written by my English contemporaries; compared to their essays, I realized, my best efforts came across as dull and lame. (In England, writing well in one's chosen subject is the foundation of a good education.) Before long, I discovered that many of the undergraduates I admired had developed their writing style as schoolboys by imitating the styles of great authors or, if they were studying to be classicists, by translating Latin or Greek prose or verse into the style of a contemporary English author, or vice versa. Sometimes these students wrote with a certain archness and artificiality, but the best of them wrote with facility and a grace of expression adapted to the subject at hand. To cultivate ear and eye, some of them would play a game that consisted of picking out characteristic passages from authors ancient and modern and seeing who could identify them. I tried to play the game, too, but, because my knowledge of classical texts was either shaky or nonexistent, I was hopeless at it.

I confided my doubts about my schooling to my tutor in the history of the Middle Ages, and he said that he thought I needed to read more widely. I told him that since the age of fifteen, when I first started speaking English (I'd grown up speaking Punjabi), I had done little besides read—and that, like many foreigners for whom English was not their mother tongue, I was an autodidact.

"Ah," he said. "But have you studied what makes one author's work different from another's?" He explained that for any piece of writing to prove finally effective and memorable depended on its author's having found the right voice and the right style. For the study of these matters, he directed me to the "Oxford Book of English Prose," a selection of choice morsels by mostly British authors culled and introduced by Sir Arthur Quiller-Couch and published in 1925. It was a feast: Chaucer, Shakespeare, Milton, Swift, Samuel Johnson, Lamb, Coleridge, Jane Austen, De Quincey, the Brontë sisters, Melville, Dickens, Matthew Arnold, Shaw, and many others. Over the next months and years, I returned to the book again and again. Genius being, by definition, inimitable and transcendent, the selections certainly didn't encourage me to attempt any such feats but, rather, made anything I did attempt seem insipid. Many might find a study of the works of genius useless, because it might stop them from ever trying to write. They would do well to go their merry way and, like Walt

Whitman, discover their inner resources on their own. How often have I met a mother who told me that her daughter wrote beautiful letters and would write a book if she could only find the time. Perhaps so. But, in my experience, for every natural writer there are ten or more writers who have to labor over their craft. Mark Twain once said, "The difference between the *right* word and the *almost* right word is the difference between lightning and the lightning bug." Even so, it is hard to imagine Mark Twain—a great writer who made a virtue of seeming artless—studying the great masters of the past.

I myself found that over time I had been helped by my study of the masters. Because I could savor only a few pages of the "Oxford Book of English Prose" at a sitting, I dipped into the volume whenever I had a little time, reading and rereading a selection to ponder its tone and cadence, its diction and imagery, its movement and structure. It gradually became clear to me that well-wrought sentences from different authors had a distinctive logic and beauty, which could no more be tampered with than could the authors' signatures. Unquestionably, no two writers were alike, yet it took me a long time to discern just what stylistic characteristics made every writer different from every other and then to put those differences into words.

The precision and finish of prose became a passion with me, and I was led on to grammar books, most notably Fowler's "Modern English Usage," and to full-length essays not only by authors in Quiller-Couch's anthology, which didn't include anything published after 1914, but also by twentieth-century authors: by Virginia Woolf, of whose ardent prose it may be said, among other things, that it launched a whole new way of thinking and writing; by Edmund Wilson, who encapsulated in sinewy prose the life, work, and critical value of great authors as if no one else had ever written about them; by V. S. Pritchett, who never wrote a book review that didn't contain an unexpected image; and by E. B. White, whose homey yet elegant turns of phrase made you think that no one could convey, for instance, the feel of the day better than he could.

My first, autobiographical book, entitled "Face to Face," which was written before I went up to Oxford, was published in 1957, just after I completed my first year there, and by that time my writing style—indeed, my whole consciousness—had gone through such changes under the pressure of writing and rewriting my essays that I could scarcely bear to acknowledge authorship of it. It seemed prosaic, and the story seemed to be carried along more by the nature of the material than by the force of the style. Perhaps as a result, my second book, "Walking the Indian Streets," published three years later, when I had graduated from Oxford and was doing further study at Harvard, seemed to err in the opposite direction: style seemed to overshadow substance. It did, however, get me started on my vocation, because in the course of working on it I met William Shawn, the editor of *The New Yorker.* The meeting began my long and happy relationship with the magazine: it lasted twenty-seven years, until the end of his editorship, in 1987, and resulted in the publication of that book and of sixteen others as pieces in *The New Yorker.* Shawn himself edited almost all of them, and in the course of working with him I absorbed his—and, by extension, his magazine's—principles of good writing, which were, as best I can sum them up, clarity, harmony, truth, and unfailing courtesy to the reader.

Like many other students and writers, I owe a debt of gratitude to my mentors—along with the literary masters I read—for teaching me much about writing. In the mid-nineteen-eighties, when Shawn's departure seemed imminent, and I was no longer able to count on making my living just from writing, as I had done during most of my adult life, I myself taught writing at half a dozen colleges and universities. It is a truism that writing can't be taught the way history or physics can, so I was pleasantly surprised at how much progress was made by those of my students who were open to suggestions, were attentive readers, and were patient during the various stages of writing and revising. Still, the best I could do as a teacher was to help students, in Emerson's words, "bear the fruit they were meant to bear," for, ultimately, the voice that is best suited to both beginners and pros is the one that comes most naturally to each group. It may take years to know what that voice is, but when one finds it, there is a shock of recognition. Of course, any writing, whether occasional or frequent, and whether hasty or enduring, requires one to stick to one's last as a lifetime apprentice. So it is that some forty years after I published my first book I am still struggling with words and sentences, drafts and alterations.

The eight nonfiction pieces collected in this volume all appeared first in *The New Yorker,* between 1961 and 1993, and, later, with one exception ("Naturalized Citizen No. 984-5165"), as individual chapters of as many books. (I have reprinted them as they appeared in their final book form, without trying to update or doctor them. Although I wrote them to be read at any time, not surprisingly they have a period flavor.) Although what I wrote during those years was intended to become part of some larger whole, each piece was also intended to be free-standing. Shawn published entire books by me and by other writers serially, always insisting that each piece had to be, like everything else in the magazine, independent, self-contained, and self-explanatory. (In publishing entire books, he was following a tradition not only of his predecessor, Harold Ross, who founded *The New Yorker,* but also of editors of nineteenth-century periodicals. This system was the opposite of that followed by some present-day editors, who instead carve out material from books on the brink of publication and shape teaser articles from them.) Nevertheless, these eight pieces are examples of literary journalism, and such journalism has a long lineage in English. One of the first English journalists was Joseph Addison (1672–1719), who in 1711, with Sir Richard Steele, founded *The Spectator*—a London daily that contained only one piece per issue—and wrote a good deal of it himself. His place in English letters is clearly spelled out by what Samuel Johnson has to say about him: "He has restored virtue to its dignity, and taught innocence not to be ashamed. No greater felicity can genius attain than that of having purified intellectual pleasures, separated mirth from indecency . . . of having taught a succession of writers to bring elegance and gayety to the aid of goodness."

Shawn, in his own way, resembled Addison, because Addison's pieces in *The Spectator* and the pieces that Shawn published in *The New Yorker* belong not only to journalism but also, in a broad sense, to the more distinguished and more inclusive literary form known as the essay. The term *essai,* meaning "attempt," was first used by the French writer Michel de Montaigne (1533–92). "Could my mind find a firm footing, I should not be making essays, but coming to conclusions," he writes in "On Repentance." "It is, however, always in its apprenticeship and on trial." His essays—on repentance, on idleness, on the imagination, on the education of children, on friendship, on cannibals, on smells, and on experience, among other topics—were often written as self-portrayals. "Others shape the man; I portray him," he writes, "and offer to the view one in particular, who is ill-shaped enough, and whom, could I refashion him, I should certainly make very different from what he is. But there is no chance of that."

The essay had its greatest flowering in England. Growing out of the literary and philosophical essays of Francis Bacon in the late sixteenth century and the autobiographical essays of Abraham Cowley in the seventeenth, it became with Swift—perhaps the most acerbic practitioner of the form—an instrument of satire, as a means of reforming society, in the eighteenth, and came into its own in the nineteenth, when it dealt with a great variety of subjects by such writers as Coleridge, Lamb, Carlyle, De Quincey, Macaulay, and Mill. Their style was forged in an age when men of letters were trained in Greek and Latin. During their school years and then at the universities, they all read the same texts, they all belonged to a community of readers, and each of them consciously sought to cultivate an individual voice. They specialized in what today we would call "opinion," yet their opinions were often expressed in grandiloquent styles, based on the works of their predecessors and their contemporaries. "Is not the principal and most famous branch of modern learning that of learning to understand the learned?" Montaigne had written. "Is not this the common and final purpose of all studies? Our opinions are grafted one on another. The first serves as a stock for the second, the second for the third. We thus climb the ladder, step by step; and hence it is that the man who has mounted highest has often more honour than he deserves; for he has only raised himself by the height of one inch on the shoulders of the last but one."

Sometimes Montaigne's man didn't raise himself at all, because his foothold was on rungs of opinion only, and opinions, by their very nature, are idiosyncratic and slippery. For instance, not only Johnson but also Pope, Thackeray, and Macaulay made extravagant claims for the genius of Addison, with Macaulay going as far as to compare him to Shakespeare and Cervantes. Yet Virginia Woolf, in her book entitled "The Common Reader," dismisses Addison as "a writer of the second class," who had "little to give us." She maintains that what writers such as Addison liked is no longer what readers in the modern period like. "As the charm of their writing depends much more upon taste than upon conviction," she writes, "a change of manners is often quite enough to put us out of touch altogether. . . . [Addison] was extremely fond of saying that men ought not to be atheists, and that women ought not to wear large petticoats. This directly inspires in us not so much a sense of distaste as a sense of difference." Whether we read Addison's admirers and detractors for the sheer pleasure of their writing or because we agree with their opinions, we may in the end come away learning more about the writers themselves than about Addison.

In our century, the form of the essay has been so thoroughly transfigured as sometimes to include no explicit opinion whatever but, rather, to consist of a combination of implicit opinion and reporting—in fact, to encompass almost any kind of nonfiction writing. Moreover, whereas many earlier essays tended to be expository, short, and formal, and often made an appeal to the intellect, the essays of our day tend to be personal, long, and informal, and often make an appeal to our emotions. (James Baldwin's "The Fire Next Time" comes to mind.) Indeed, in Ross's and Shawn's *New Yorker*, narratives of fact and quoted speech were considered superior to pieces expressing explicit opinions, as if facts were precious and opinions cheap. The magazine categorized its variety of essays with such rubrics as "Profiles," "A Reporter at Large," and "Onward and Upward with the Arts." The form, however, has all along been so elastic that the term "essay" can accommodate almost any kind of writing.

One of the authors in the "Oxford Book of English Prose," Arthur Clutton-Brock (1868–1924), distinguishes poetry from prose in this way: "If the cardinal virtue of poetry is love, the cardinal virtue of prose is justice." Quiller-Couch offers an improvement upon this unquestionably worthy nineteenth-century definition: "I should prefer 'a high compelling emotion' to Mr. Clutton-Brock's 'Love,' however widely interpreted, as the virtue of Poetry; and Persuasion rather than Justice as the first virtue of Prose." Quiller-Couch's gloss certainly has a more contemporary ring. He goes on to offer a further refinement of his definition, this time distinguishing literary prose from the words dashed off in a penny-a-liner: "The Newspaper Press admits to-day a portentous amount of that Jargon, or flaccid writing to which flaccid thought instinctively resorts. But literature, I repeat, is memorable speech, recording memorable thoughts and deeds."

Much memorable speech is to be found in the eight pieces gathered here, but memorable in a different way, perhaps, from what Quiller-Couch had in mind. I should explain that my procedure for research and writing has been to choose a subject that for one reason or another I had some interest in, to immerse myself in books about it, and then to supplement what I had learned from them by arranging extensive interviews with their authors or with people who knew or had known them. In previous centuries, the conversation of notables found its way into the memoirs, journals, and correspondence of their contemporaries, but the notion of formal interviews was unknown. (No one would have thought of interviewing Coleridge, for instance; people simply read his books.) The interview as a method of exploration came into its own in our day, through the explosion of newspapers, magazines, radio, films, and television. Even so, as late as 1960, when I wrote about philosophy (the first piece in this volume), my idea of interviewing philosophers in order to explore their recondite ideas was considered a heretical innovation. In conducting such interviews, and others, whether with the learned or with the unschooled, I tried to become the proverbial fly on the wall. I would arrive without specific questions in mind, and, after some amenities, I would just observe and listen, breaking in only when something said was unclear, and would underline in my mind what seemed to me salient remarks, so that I could later note them down. (I was reluctant even to take notes during an interview—not to mention tape-recording it—for I wanted the talk to be as natural as possible, without any distraction or encumbrance.) Whether a person I interviewed found my method disarming or nerve-racking, its result was that he often told me what was on his mind, rather than what was on my mind. I came away with an impression of the person which, combined with my reading and substantiated by talks with collateral sources, had, I think, lasting value. But, of course, what eventually became a part of my essay was only a fraction of what I had read and heard, because a piece of writing has its own demands and logic.

Prose, like manners and dress, reflects its period, and our period is a democratic, Everyman's informational age, in which anything smacking of tradition, élitism, or pretension is suspect. When authors appear on television, we are apt to warm to them more readily if they wear sweaters and slacks than if they are formally clothed. Even language and dress distinctions between the sexes are blurring: men and women are both apt to be called "guys" and tend to favor unisex clothes. In the nineteen-fifties, when I first started reading seriously, my contemporaries and I could surmise from an author's prose style whether the author was male or female—or, rather, there were characteristics of style which we associated with one sex or the other. For instance, in those days everyone would have understood what was meant when the writer James Morris was said to have a feminine style: namely, that his style was lush, ornate, and finely embroidered. As it turned out, he himself felt that he had a female soul trapped in a male body, and in 1973 he underwent a sex change. (If one now looks up James Morris in the British *Who's Who,* the entry reads, "MORRIS, James; *see* Morris, Jan." Morris is perhaps the first writer to be entered under both a real male and a real female name.) The dual nature of Morris's identity may have been a harbinger of new literary trends, in which the yin and yang of yesteryear merge into one uniform—or, rather, unisex—style. Today, if I read an article without noting the author's name I often can't tell whether it was written by a man or a woman. Now that everyone is supposed to be like everyone else, and distinctions not only of sex but of degree and quality are blurred, any attempt at formal prose is hazardous. Indeed, the writing by contemporary authors which I read nowadays, with some possible exceptions, such as John Updike, is not set apart from conversational English. But this may not necessarily be a loss. Contemporary prose has an immediacy and a punchiness that reflect the fast-paced, technological character of our burgeoning mass culture. Ours is an age of supposedly "telling it like it is."

It would be difficult for me to characterize my own style or to place it in any particular tradition. If in my writing I sometimes come across as a bolder person than I actually am, that is because, like other writers, I freely adopt a persona as a way of organizing and presenting my material. Exactly what the persona is may frequently depend on the personalities of the people I am dealing with. For the rest, I keep in the forefront of my mind something that Bertrand Russell told me when I was working on the first piece in this volume. (I can't resist the temptation of recalling it here, even though the reader will come upon it again in the text.) Russell said that as a young man he wrote with difficulty—that he could recall having to revise his prose as many as ten times—and that he had developed his style by studying two models: Milton's prose and Baedeker's guidebooks. The Puritan never wrote without passion, he explained, and the cicerone used only a few words in recommending sights, hotels, and restaurants: passion was the voice of reason, economy the signature of brilliance. However prose is defined—as Russell's passionate "reason," as Clutton-Brock's "justice," or as Quiller-Couch's "persuasion"—economy of thought and language certainly makes it memorable, thereby according it the status of lasting literature.

A Ved Mehta Reader

ONE

A Battle Against the Bewitchment
of Our Intelligence

I've spent some happy years in Oxford, and to keep in touch with England I read her newspapers. I am most at home with the *Guardian,* but I also like to look at the correspondence columns of the *Times,* where, in an exception to the *Times* tradition of anonymity, the writers are identified by name and speak directly to the reader. I relish a contest of words, and the *Times* page of letters becomes for me a street where I can stroll each morning and see the people of England—lords and commoners—shake hands, spit at each other, and set off verbal barrages. I began taking this engaging daily walk during my undergraduate years at Balliol College, Oxford, and I've kept up the habit, whether I have found myself in Paris, Damascus, New Delhi, or New York. One autumn day in 1959, as I was taking my intellectual promenade, I met Bertrand Russell, under a signboard reading "Review Refused." "Messrs. Gollancz have recently published a book by Ernest Gellner called 'Words and Things,' " he said as he hailed me. "I read this book before it was published, and considered it a careful and accurate analysis of a certain school of philosophy, an opinion which I expressed in a preface. I now learn that Professor Ryle, the editor of *Mind,* has written to Messrs. Gollancz refusing to have this book

reviewed in *Mind,* on the ground that it is abusive and cannot therefore be treated as a contribution to an academic subject. Such a
partisan view of the duties of an editor is deeply shocking. The merit
of a work of philosophy is always a matter of opinion, and I am not
surprised that Professor Ryle disagrees with my estimate of the work,
but *Mind* has hitherto, ever since its foundation, offered a forum for
the discussion of all serious and competent philosophical work. Mr.
Gellner's book is not 'abusive' except in the sense of not agreeing with
the opinions which he discusses. If all books that do not endorse
Professor Ryle's opinions are to be boycotted in the pages of *Mind,*
that hitherto respected periodical will sink to the level of the mutual-
admiration organ of a coterie. All who care for the repute of British
philosophy will regret this."

I did care for the repute of British philosophy. It is, in a sense, a
dominant philosophy, with Existentialism, in the present-day world. I
had gone up to Oxford with the idea of studying it—British philosophy has its home there, and, indeed, is known generally as "Oxford
philosophy," even though its detractors, taking their cue from its so-
considered petty linguistic concerns, insist on calling it linguistic philosophy. However, just reading a few essays on philosophical subjects
to my tutor had made me realize that the linguistic inquiries then
being undertaken at Oxford had little connection with what I understood to be philosophy, so I immediately abandoned it and took up
history instead. Now I recalled that Gellner was a Reader in Sociology
at the London School of Economics, a home for angry intellectual
orphans, while Gilbert Ryle was Wayneflete Professor of Metaphysical
Philosophy at Oxford, from which he edited the extremely influential, eighty-five-year-old philosophical journal *Mind.* The notion of
an attack on Oxford thinkers interested me, and I dashed off a letter
to Blackwell's, my favorite bookshop, for Gellner's book. While I
waited for it to arrive, I impatiently read the subsequent issues of the
Times, eager to see Earl Russell's gauntlet taken up, preferably by Ryle.
It was. This important spokesman of the philosophical Establishment
replied four days after Russell's challenge. His communication was
terse, to the point, and full of references for diligent readers: "In the
book referred to by Earl Russell . . . about 100 imputations of disingenuousness are made against a number of identifiable teachers of
philosophy; about half of these occur on pages 159–192 and 237–265."

The shooting had just begun. An eighty-seven-year-old philosopher, out of humor with "a certain school of philosophy," had clashed with its standard-bearer, and neither of them lacked a retinue. The day after Ryle's note appeared, the *Times* carried a third letter under the heading of the week, "Review Refused," this one written by a correspondent named Conrad Dehn. "If the imputations are justified," Dehn argued, "this could not be a good ground [for Ryle's refusal to review Gellner's book], while if they are not I should have thought a review in *Mind* would provide an excellent, even a welcome, opportunity to rebut them." There was also a letter from G. R. G. Mure, the last of the English Hegelians and the Warden of Merton College, Oxford. He, too, was on the side of Russell. "In a tolerably free society," the Warden wrote, "the ban, the boycott, even the too obtrusively cold shoulder, tend to promote the circulation of good books as well as bad. One can scarcely expect that the linguistical Oxford philosophy tutors, long self-immunized to criticism, will now rush to Blackwell's, but I am confident that their pupils will." I was delighted that Mure had taken this occasion to speak out against any philosophical establishment; while I was at the university, the undergraduates used to say of the Warden that he couldn't declare his mind, because half a century ago Russell had demolished Hegel and since then no respectable philosopher had dared acknowledge himself a Hegelian openly.

On the following day, I found a letter from Gellner himself. "My book," the polemicist wrote, replying to Ryle, "does not accuse linguistic philosophers of 'disingenuousness.' . . . This word does not occur in it once, let alone one hundred times. It does attack linguistic doctrines and methods as *inherently* evasive. . . . This claim does not require (though it does not exclude) conscious dishonesty. . . . I am sorry to see Professor Ryle resorting to one further device, the exclusion of criticism as indecorous, and thus evading once again the substantive issue of the merits of linguistic philosophy." Gellner's letter left me baffled. I was still wondering whether Ryle had an excuse for not reviewing the book. My skepticism was not shared by a knighted gentlemen, Sir Leslie Farrer, private solicitor to the Queen, who appeared on the same page as Gellner. Sir Leslie defended the author of "Words and Things" with a sharp tongue. "Ridicule," he wrote, "is one of the oldest and not the least effective weapons of philosophic warfare, but yet we find Professor Ryle . . . speaking no doubt '*ex cathedra* on a matter of faith or morals,' propounding the dogma that making fun of members of the Sacred College of Linguistic Philosophers is mortal sin. True, Ryle's first description of Gellner was the word 'abusive' and his second that he 'made imputations of disingenuousness,' but those who read 'Words and Things' (and I trust they will be many) may agree with me that 'made fun of' is a more accurate description."

Sir Leslie was the sixth disputant in the Gellner controversy. In the first week of "Review Refused," the *Times* must have received many letters on the subject, but, of the six that it selected, five took the Gellner-Russell side. The *Times*' five-to-one support of Gellner indicated a confidence in him that, in my opinion, was not completely justified by his letter. Despite encounters with some worldly philosophers while I was an undergraduate, I did not associate public letter-writing with philosophers; I continued to think of them as Olympian sages. Now this bout in the *Times* shattered my view of their serenity. Instead of age and quiet wisdom, they had youth and energy and anger. I pictured in my mind all the philosophers in England racing to the *Times* office with their dispatches now that Gellner's book had given them an occasion for their precious pronouncements. The day after Sir Leslie's letter, the *Times* correspondence page was silent on philosophy, but the Queen's peace was broken the next day by John Wisdom, a Cambridge professor of philosophy, and "Review Refused," already a heap of pelting words, continued to grow. Wisdom's loyalty to Ryle was unquestioning, and resembled that of a cardinal to the Pope. "I do not know whether it was right to refuse a review to Mr. Gellner's book," he asserted. "I have not read it. Lord Russell's letter . . . carried the suggestion that Professor Ryle refused the book a review because it is opposed to Ryle's philosophy. That suggestion I believe to be false." Such a letter could hardly do much to advance Ryle's cause. But the next day—a Saturday—the Russell-Gellner brigade's secure position in the *Times* column was for the time being shaken by the charge of B. F. McGuinness, a Fellow of Queen's College, Oxford. His philosophical fusillade, though undramatic, was extremely effective. He began impressively, "Newman had to meet the following argument: 'Dr. Newman teaches that truth is no virtue; his denials that he teaches this are not to be credited, since they come from a man who teaches that truth is no virtue.' He described it as an attempt to poison the wells. A subtler form of psychological warfare has been discovered. You belabour your opponents for systematic disregard of truth and consistency, but you add later that there is no question of conscious dishonesty. Thus you can safely call them both knaves and fools. If they expostulate with your account of their views and practices, you reply: 'A typical evasion! . . . They would disown their own doctrines when criticized.' If you are charged with being abusive, your answer is: 'I have accused them of nothing but error!' In his letter . . . Mr. Gellner has even managed to use both kinds of riposte at the same time. The following are some of the phrases in his book that seem to me, in their context, tantamount to accusations of dishonesty: 'camouflage' (p. 163), 'evasion' (p. 164), 'pretence' (p. 169), 'spurious modesty' (p. 170), 'invoking rationalizations according to convenience' (p. 171), '[devices] to cow the neophyte into submission' (p. 186), '[refusal to avow an opinion because it] would ruin one's reputation,' 'insinuation' (p. 188), 'trick' (p. 189)." After this letter, I joined up with the minority—Ryle, Wisdom, and McGuinness.

The following Monday, a letter appeared from Kevin Holland, an undergraduate at Worcester College, Oxford. Holland pealed precedents of "imputations of disingenuousness," and he advanced as many facts in support of Gellner's position as McGuinness had advanced in support of Ryle's. "In the 'Philosophy of Leibniz' (1900), for example," he wrote, "Russell accused Leibniz of a kind of intellectual dishonesty. Forty-six years later, this charge was repeated in 'A History of Western Philosophy,' and Aquinas joined Leibniz in the dock. Ten years ago Professor Ryle published a book in which, 'with deliberate abusiveness,' he characterized a belief held by most ordinary people [that man has a soul in his body] as 'the dogma of the Ghost in the Machine.' In spite of their 'abusiveness,' these three books are regarded by many as philosophic classics." I put down the *Times* reconverted by the undergraduate to the Russell-Gellner position that a philosophical work could call names, heap curses on philosophers, and still deserve to be read. It might even turn out to be a classic. For me the battle was over—and the victory, as I now saw it, went to the majority. As for Ryle's indiscretion—the initial injustice—it was more than corrected by the wide discussion in the newspaper. When the book arrived from Blackwell's, I would read it and make up my own mind about its worth.

After a few days, when I looked at the *Times* again, there was a ponderous epistle, in dignified diction, from a Queen's Counsel, Sir Thomas Creed: "Socrates knew that a true philosophy thrives on blunt criticism and accusations. No one, however inept, who sat at the feet of the robust Oxford philosophers of 40 years ago was ever allowed to forget the scene when Socrates, taunted by an exasperated Thrasymachus with being 'a thorough quibbler,' with 'asking questions merely for the sake of malice,' with 'needing a nurse to stop his driveling,' implored his accuser to abandon his proposed departure from the discussion so that a problem might be further examined between them. So far from refusing review Socrates forced further discussion on the recalcitrant Thrasymachus. . . . Is Socrates forgotten in modern Oxford? Is Plato's 'Republic' no longer read? Many will hope that a purchase of Mr. Gellner's book will enable undergraduates to ask those awkward questions and make those accusations and insinuations of 'evasion,' 'camouflage,' 'pretence,' 'bamboozling,' 'trick,' which caused Oxford philosophy tutors of an earlier generation such unfeigned delight, a delight only exceeded by the relish with which they exploded the arguments of their accusers."

Next day, J. W. N. Watkins was in the paper. I knew something about him from the gossip of the undergraduates in my day, and pegged him immediately as Gellner's man. I had thought it was about time for someone to play the peacemaker, and Watkins' letter was a white flag: "Let all parties concede that 'Words and Things' is often impolite. But having conceded this, let us remember that etiquette is not the most important thing in philosophy. The best way for linguistic philosophers to repel Mr. Gellner's attack is to overcome their squeamishness about its indecorousness and get down to the rebuttal of its arguments." A few days later, Alec Kassman, editor of the journal published by the august Aristotelian Society, faced up to some questions that had been bothering me. His analysis proceeded in the measured rhetoric of an intellectual editorial: "The essential issue is not whether or not Mr. Gellner's book is meritorious; nor whether or not it is abusive; nor whether or not, if abusive, it is therefore unfit for review: it is a fundamental one of professional ethics and its gravamen is contained in one protasis in Earl Russell's letter: 'If all books that do not endorse Professor Ryle's opinion are to be boycotted in the pages of *Mind*,' etc. The charge, therefore, is one of dishonorable conduct in that Professor Ryle abuses his editorial powers so as to suppress criticism of his own views. Clearly, the allegation in general terms is rhetorical: it is more than sufficient if a single case be substantiated. The reply is a direct traverse—that the review was declined on the ground that the book was found abusive. Earl Russell flatly denies this: 'It is not "abusive" except in the sense of not agreeing with the opinions which he discusses' (. . . Professor Ryle's among others). He offers no opinion on the instances indicated by the editor. The moral case has not progressed beyond this stage save that many . . . evidently wishing to support Earl Russell, depart from him upon this critical point. They (for example, Sir Thomas Creed . . .) seem mostly to claim that the book may well be abusive and no less fit for review on that account. It is quite possible that the editor's claim that an abusive book does not deserve a review in *Mind* is ill-founded or injudicious. That, however, is a side issue, if in fact the view is one which he genuinely held and acted on. The accusation is not that he is unduly sensitive, or unwise, but that he is biased against any critic as such, to the consequent detriment of his journal. . . . He publicly rebutted the specific charge in some detail, and Earl Russell has not replied. It is about time that he did; the pages of *Mind* are available to illustrate editorial policy. The allegation is a disagreeable one, and as serious as could be made against a philosopher in Professor Ryle's position. If Earl Russell can sustain it, he should show this. If he cannot, he should say so, that the reputation of both editor and journal may be cleared. That is the heart of the matter."

Even though Mr. Kassman argued from a position opposed to mine—I was still sticking to the side of Russell-Gellner—I had to admit that he had succeeded in making the best possible defense for Ryle. I made up my mind not to look at any more letters from the philosophical combatants, but I could not help glancing at the succeeding issues of the *Times* just in case Russell should answer Mr. Kassman. Nineteen days after Russell had attacked the philosophical Establishment, he was back in print with a reply. "There are two different points at issue," Russell remarked, closing the controversy. "First, is anything in Mr. Gellner's book 'abusive'? Secondly, should a book containing anything abusive be, on that account alone, refused a review in *Mind?* As to the first point, 'abusive' is not a very precise word. . . . I cannot . . . 'reply' . . . since Professor Ryle has not given a single instance of a single sentence which he considers abusive. It is up to Professor Ryle to quote at least one passage which he considers abusive. This, so far as I know, he has not yet done. As to the second and much more important point, I do not think that a serious piece of philosophical work should be refused a review even if it does contain passages which everybody would admit to be abusive. Take, for example, Nietzsche's 'Beyond Good and Evil.' In this book he speaks of 'that blockhead John Stuart Mill,' and after saying 'I abhor the man's vulgarity,' attributes to him the invention of the Golden Rule, saying: 'Such principles would fain establish the whole of human traffic upon mutual services, so that every action would appear to be a cash payment for something done to us. The hypothesis here is ignoble to the last degree.' I do not accept these opinions of Nietzsche's, but I think a philosophical editor would have been misguided if, on account of them, he had refused a review to 'Beyond Good and Evil,' since this was undoubtedly a serious piece of philosophical work. I note that neither Professor Ryle nor anyone else has denied that the same is true of Mr. Gellner's book." Firmly turning his back on the philosophical Establishment, Russell stumped resolutely away, carrying most of the medals.

Through the fight over "Words and Things," I acquired a renewed and rather persistent interest in Oxford philosophy. Several English publications ran editorials about the conclusion of hostilities, and I read them eagerly, but they did not tell me very much about the philosophers working in England. The *Times* wrote its typical on-the-one-hand, on-the-other-hand leader. It said, on the one hand, that Gellner's book "caricatures its prey," and that his "barbs are not of the carefully polished kind." It said, on the other hand, that the caricatured philosophers "stick closely to their lasts" with "enviable academic patronage," and regard "philosophical problems as a sort of cerebral neurosis which it is their job to alleviate." The leader in the *Economist* was no more enlightening about the nature of this cerebral neurosis. "Why are modern philosophers hated—if they are?" it asked. "Hardly any of them, despite their other diversity, would claim that, as philosophers, they can tell us what to do. When other direction posts are falling down, philosophers are assumed to be the people who ought to be giving us directions about life. But if they cannot, they cannot." The tone of these two comments was fairly representative of the editorial voice of Britain's intellectual press.

Gellner's book, when it finally arrived, was equally unsatisfactory. It was passionate, polemical, and disjointed, and grouped disparate thinkers indiscriminately—this much was apparent even to a novice like me. The editorials had bewildered me by their opaqueness; Gellner bewildered me by his flood of glaring light, which prevented me from seeing through to the philosophers. At the time of the turbulent correspondence, I was living in America, but I decided that on my next visit to England I would seek out some of the philosophers and talk to them about their activities.

Some time later, I found myself in London. I wrote to three or four philosophers for appointments and started my researches into contemporary philosophy by approaching an old Oxford friend of mine, even though he is by no means the most unprejudiced person about. As an undergraduate, he read Classics and Greats, the English-speaking world's most thorough study of classical literature, language, history, and philosophy, and—Greats' concession to our age—modern philosophy. All the time he was working at philosophy, he hated it, but he did it as a job, and because he was naturally brilliant, after his Schools (the final degree examination) he was courted to be a professional philosopher at Oxford; he remained true to his temperament, however, and turned down the offer, deciding to sit it out in London until he spotted a good opening in Oxford classics. In the meantime, he has amused himself by composing Greek and Latin verses and prose, and turning the poetry of Hopkins, Pound, Eliot, and Auden into lyrics in the style of the Greek Anthology or of Vergil, Horace, or Petronius. Having been trained in Latin and Greek since the age of six, he reads the literature of these languages almost faster than that of his own country. This classical, or language, education is characteristic of almost all the contemporary English philosophers. Aside from his Victorian training, the most typically philosophical thing about my friend is that he constantly smokes a pipe—a habit that has long been the *sine qua non* of English philosophers. Over some mulled claret late one evening in his Chelsea back-street basement flat, he surveyed the subject of philosophy from the tremulous heights where it had led him, and he talked to me about it too frankly and unprofessionally to wish to be identified, so I'll call him John.

During their four years as undergraduates, the Greats men sit for altogether twenty-four three-hour papers, and John said he imagined that one-third of his time had been spent doing philosophy and preparing for examinations in logic and moral and classical philosophy. "The examination in classical philosophy was straightforward, since it meant, for the most part, reading the works of Plato and Aristotle," he explained. "For logic and moral philosophy we were supposed to do a certain amount of philosophical history, but in fact we did extremely little; we started by doing a tutorial on Descartes and followed it up by writing essays on Locke and Berkeley, and I believe we were meant to do a couple on Hume. But these historical people are just for exercise; they need not be brought into the exam. I never once mentioned them, and the examiners are really rather bored to have you do so, I think." John said that Greats men mostly read contemporary philosophers, because the philosophers at Oxford are concerned only with their own puzzles. They are not very much occupied with problems that interested earlier philosophers, even as little as forty years ago. John actually went into philosophical training when, after dabbling a little in the history of different schools, he read Ludwig Wittgenstein's "Philosophical Investigations" and two books of A. J. Ayer's—"Language, Truth and Logic" and "The Problem of Knowledge," both of which he had to work through several times, once making notes all the way. He was then turned loose on P. F. Strawson's "Introduction to Logical Theory" and "Individuals: An Essay in Descriptive Metaphysics." He read only the first half of "Individuals" and then skimmed the rest, because he couldn't make much sense of it. After Strawson, to John's great relief, came easier volumes, on ethics, by Richard Hare and P. H. Nowell-Smith. But the bulk, and the most important part, of his study was articles in issues of *Mind* and the *Proceedings of the Aristotelian Society*—the richest repositories of Oxford philosophy.

Since the main purpose of the Greats course is not to produce Professor I. Q. but to develop minds, John insisted that his handling of the Schools questions was more important than the list of books and articles he had read. Alas, once the results were published, as custom enjoined, all the Schools papers were burned, and John could reconstruct his brilliant answers only from memory. He considered his logic paper to be the paradigm, both because logic is the centerpiece of Oxford philosophy and because the principles of logic can be applied to other branches of the subject. Examiners therefore tend to read the logic paper with more care than any other. "Um," he began, recalling his paradigm, "there was a question I didn't do: 'Is my hearing a noise in my head as mechanical as the passing of a noise through a telephone?' The suggestion here is: Can our senses be explained away in mechanical terms? One that I did attempt but abandoned was 'Who is Socrates?'—the figure that people greeted when they saw it coming with the words 'Hello, Socrates,' or the person who was Socrates? You clearly can't answer, 'This is the body that went around with Socrates.' It's also not very nice to say, 'This is the body that went around *as* Socrates,' because it sounds as if it went around disguised as Socrates. Since I couldn't make up my mind about this, I couldn't write about it. But a stock old war horse of a question that I did complete was 'If I know that Y is the case, is it possible for me not to know that I know it?' And what I said about it must have been on these lines: To know that a thing is the case is not—this is very straightforward stuff—to have my mind in a certain position. If I know, for instance, that ice melts when the sun shines, this means that when the sun shines I don't go skating. In that case, it's perfectly possible that I don't consciously know that ice melts when the sun shines. But the question now arises of whether I know it unconsciously, and the answer is that it's possible never to have considered this. But to analyze it still further: Once you do ask yourself whether you know it unconsciously, can you give yourself the wrong answer? And I think the answer to this is— Now, I wonder what I said. Um. Well. Yes. The answer is that you sometimes say, 'I don't know whether I know it unconsciously; I don't know whether I really know it or whether I'm just guessing.' So far so good. But can you now go on to say, 'I thought I didn't know that ice melts when the sun shines, but then later on I found out I did'? My conclusion was that you could feel certain you didn't know it, and then when you *came* to it you found out you did. Take this example: Suppose they said 'Do you know how to tie such and such a knot?' and you said 'No.' And then when you were drowning they threw you a line and said 'Tie that knot on your life belt,' and you succeeded in tying it. When you were saved, they would say 'Well, you did know how to tie it after all, didn't you?' And you could say either 'Yes, I did know all the time, but I was certain that I didn't before I started drowning' or 'I just found out how to do it—it *came* to me when you threw me the line.'"

By now, John was so lost in philosophy that I couldn't have stopped him if I had wished to. He was puffing away madly at his pipe, and, without pausing, he went on to the next question on his logic paper. "My favorite in the paper, however, was the answer to another question: 'Could there be nothing between two stars?' All these Schools questions look very simple till you start thinking about them. What I said about this one was 'There are two senses in which there can be nothing between two stars'—which is always a good way of going at such questions. On the one hand, if there is strictly not anything between two things, then they are together, and if two stars are adjacent, then, clearly, they aren't exactly two stars—they're perhaps a twin star. On the other hand—and this was my second point—if I were to say to you, 'There's absolutely nothing between Oxford and Birmingham,' meaning 'There aren't any restaurants on the road,' or something of that sort, in this sense there isn't anything between two stars. A distinction thus emerges between nothing and *a* nothing, because when you answer the question 'What is there between two stars?' by saying 'There isn't anything between them,' you tend to think there is a nothing, a great lump of nothing, and there it is, holding the stars apart. This, actually, when you think about it, is nonsense, because you can't have 'a nothing,' which naturally led me to discuss the difference between space and *a* space. If you can't say that there's nothing between two stars, neither can you give much account of what there is between them. You tend to say there's a great expanse of Space, with a capital 'S,' and this is not very satisfactory, because the way you use the ordinary word 'space' is to say there is *a* space between my table and my door, and that means you can measure it, and presumably there is a distance between table and door that can be measured. Whereas if you say there is a great lump of Space, that's like saying a great lump of nothing or of time, which, of course, is misleading. My conclusion was that in the loose sense, in which there is nothing between Oxford and Birmingham, there could be nothing between two stars; that is, nothing you could give a name to, or nothing you thought it worth giving a name to, or nothing of the sort that interests you. But in the strict sense there can't be nothing between two stars, because if there were nothing between two stars, the stars would be on top of each other. How tedious, I agree, but I was just giving you this as an example of what Greats people actually do."

We poured some claret, and drank a toast to John's success with Schools and, upon his insistence, to his wisdom in putting the whole subject behind him. He reluctantly drank also to my researches into Oxford philosophy. From his paradigm answer I had received the distinct impression that Oxford philosophy was simplified, if accurate, mental gymnastics, or, at best, intellectual pyrotechnics. But I wasn't sure I had grasped the essence, so I pressed him for his own view, and for a definition. He twitched nervously, offered me some more claret, went into a sort of trance, and said puzzling things like "Philosophy at Oxford is not one thing but many things" and "Some of the philosophers there are in one sense doing the same thing and yet in another sense doing quite different things." And how the things they did were the same and yet different could emerge only by talking about the philosophers individually, and even then I was likely to get them confused. And although he didn't say it, he implied that the best thing for me to do would be to read Greats (of which, of course, modern philosophy is just a part) and, if possible, get acquainted with the philosophers themselves, as "people." He suggested meeting Gellner, as the man who had roughly broken the calm of Oxford philosophy; Russell, as a born controversialist who had served the mistresses of both science and art as no one else had in the twentieth century; Strawson, as an antidote to Russell ("Strawson is now far and away the most original thinker of what is often called the Oxford philosophy"); Ayer, as a brilliant thinker who had his pipeline from Central Europe and whom neither the Russells nor the Strawsons could overlook; Stuart Hampshire, as a philosopher with a civilized view of the whole subject—he had one foot in Continental thought and the other in the whole history of philosophy; and Richard Hare, who represented the impact of Oxford philosophy on morals—the rights and wrongs of living; and certainly one feminine philosopher, because women's invasion of the field was a sort of twentieth-century philosophical event. Then John went on to use what appeared to me English adaptations of Chinese proverbs, like "We are all squirrels in

cages and we go round and round until we are shown the way out."
And how was I to find my way out? We were back to reading Greats.
To such direct questions as "Is Oxford philosophy, like geometry,
suspended in a vacuum?" I received negative answers. "No," he said
once, "in one sense we have as much real substance as Socrates, Plato,
and Aristotle, and are even doing their sorts of things. But in another
sense . . ." I wanted to find my way back to the clarity and confidence
of his Schools answers, so I pried at his mind with ancient philosophers (who taught men, among other things, what to do and how to
live) for an opening. "Does each of the Oxford philosophers fancy
himself a Socrates?" I asked. "I have never seen them hanging around
street corners and athletic rooms, as Socrates did in Athens, with
unwashed aristocratic young men, to cheer philosophical disputations
and to jeer crowds of fools."

"You're mixed up in a difficult business," he said, pouring me some
claret. He went on to explain the connection between the ancients
and the contemporaries. "The idea of Greats philosophy," he said, "is
that after a few years of work—training in clear and precise thinking—
the high-powered undergraduate can unravel any sort of puzzle more
or less better than the next man. It makes a technique of being non-
technical." He smiled. "Like Socrates, we assume the pose of knowing
nothing except, of course, how to think, and that is the only respect in
which we consider ourselves superior to other people. For us—as, to a
certain degree, it was for him—philosophy is ordinary language (but
don't press me about this 'ordinary language'), and so, we choose to
think, it ought not to be a technical business. Although he did not
know it, Socrates, like us, was really trying to solve linguistic puzzles,
and this is especially true in the longer dialogues of Plato—the 'Republic' and the 'Laws'—where we learn quite a lot about Socrates'
method and philosophy, filtered, of course, through his devoted pupil's mind. Some of the Pre-Socratics, who provided Plato and his
master with many of their problems, were in difficulties about how
one thing could be two things at once—say, a white horse. How could
you say 'This is a horse and this is white' without saying 'This one
thing is two things'? Socrates and Plato together solved this puzzle by
saying that what was meant by saying 'The horse is white' was that the
horse partook of the eternal, and perfect, Form horseness, which was
invisible but really more horselike than any worldly Dobbin; and

ditto about the Form whiteness: it was whiter than any earthly white. The theory of Form covered our whole world of ships and shoes and humpty-dumptys, which, taken all in all, were shadows—approximations of those invisible, perfect Forms. Using the sharp tools in our new linguistic chest, we can whittle Plato down to size and say that he invented his metaphysical world of Forms to solve the problem of different kinds of 'is'es; you see how an Oxford counterpart of Plato uses a simple grammatical tool in solving problems like this. Instead of conjuring up an imaginary edifice of Forms, he simply says there are two different types of 'is'es—one of predication and one of identity. The first asserts a quality: 'This is white.' The second points to the object named: 'This is a horse.' By this simple grammatical analysis we clear away the rubble of what were Plato's Forms. Actually, an Oxford philosopher is closer to Aristotle, who often, when defining a thing—for example, 'virtue'—asked himself, 'Does the definition square with the ordinary views of men?' But while the contemporary philosophers do have antecedents, they are innovators in concentrating most of their attention on language. They have no patience with past philosophers: Why bother listening to men whose problems arose from bad grammar? At present, we are mostly preoccupied with language and grammar. No one at Oxford would dream of telling undergraduates what they ought to do, the kind of life they ought to lead." That was no longer an aim of philosophy, he explained, but even though philosophy had changed in its aims and methods, people had not, and that was the reason for the complaining undergraduates, for the bitter attacks by *Times*' correspondents, and even, perhaps, for his turning his back on philosophy.

Both of us more or less stopped thinking at the same time, very much as one puts down an intellectual work when thinking suddenly becomes impossible. "How about some claret?" both of us said. The decanter was empty. We vigorously stirred some more claret, sugar, and spices in a caldron and put the brew on the gas ring, and while we were waiting for a drink, we listened to a portion of "The Magic Flute." I felt very much like Tamino at the Temple of Wisdom, except that my resolution was sinking. The claret revived it, and, with curtains drawn against the night, I pressed on with my researches.

Talking with John, I came to feel that present-day Oxford philosophy is a revolutionary movement—at least when it is seen through the eyes of past philosophers. I asked him about the fathers of the revolution. Again he was evasive. Strictly speaking, it was fatherless, except that Bertrand Russell, G. E. Moore, and Ludwig Wittgenstein—all of them, as it happened, Cambridge University figures—"were responsible for the present state of things at Oxford." Blowing pipe smoke in my direction, John continued, "I think the aspect of Russell's philosophy that will be remembered is his logical atomism, which was proclaimed to the world in a series of lectures in 1918; the driving force of these lectures was a distrust of ordinary speech. He argued at that time that you had to get away from ordinary language (and disastrous grammatical errors of past philosophers—'is'es again), which did nothing but foster misleading notions, and construct a language on a mechanical model—like the symbolic logic of his and Alfred North Whitehead's 'Principia Mathematica,' published in 1910—that would in turn correspond to the logical structure of the universe. He thought that you could take any statement and break it up into its atomic parts, for each part would have a meaning, or a reference, or both. What he was trying to do was to build a formal logical system, so that you could do arguments and logic on computers. But it is now thought that, among other things, he confused meaning and reference, and also broke up sentences in a totally wrong way, and therefore his philosophy is considered to be mainly of historical interest."

By now, I felt very much as though I were inside a Temple of Knowledge, if not of Wisdom, and I asked John if he would like to tell me a little bit about Moore, too. He said he wouldn't like to but he would do it, because he supposed he had to. "Moore was a common-sense philosopher," he began. "Almost unphilosophically so. His most famous article was 'A Defense of Common Sense,' which was mostly concerned with morality. His common-sense view was, on the surface, very much like Dr. Johnson's: I am certain that my hand is here because I can look at it, touch it, bang it against the table. While he did distinguish between a naturalistic statement ('The grass is green') and a non-naturalistic statement ('God is good'), he held that we *know* both kinds of statements to be true by intuition. (Goodness was not naturalistic, like green, because it could neither be analyzed in terms of any basic qualities, like greenness or hardness, nor was it itself a basic quality.) On the question 'How do I know the grass is green or

God is good?' he agreed with most people, who would reply, 'Because I know it's so, and if you don't know it's so, too bad!' "

John said that Oxford people owed their faith in ordinary language and ordinary men to Moore. But it was Wittgenstein who made John puff furiously at his pipe. "There are two Wittgensteins, not one," he said. "There is the Wittgenstein of 'Tractatus Logico-Philosophicus,' published in 1921, and the totally different Wittgenstein of 'Philosophical Investigations,' printed posthumously, a quarter of a century later. I'm almost certain to give a misinterpretation of Wittgenstein," John went on humbly but vigorously, "but in the 'Tractatus' he was trying to find out the basic constituents of the world, and in a way his 'Tractatus' attempt was reminiscent of Russell's 1918 try. According to the first Wittgenstein, the world was ultimately made up of basic facts, and these were mirrored in language: accordingly, a proposition was a picture of the world. Now, basic facts were made up of basic objects and basic qualities. The basic objects were sense data—for example, a patch before my eyes, or a feeling in my leg. But these could not exist without having some definite quality. I mean, you could not just have a patch before your eyes—it had to be some definite color. And you could not just have a feeling in your leg—it had to be some definite sort of feeling. When you attached a particular color to the patch or specified the sort of feeling in your leg, you had basic facts, which language mirrored or could mirror. An example of a basic sentence that mirrored a basic fact was 'Here, now, green,' meaning that you had in front of your eyes a sense datum that was green. Just as the world was essentially built out of these basic facts, so language was essentially built out of basic-fact sentences. The business of the philosopher was to break down the complex statements used in language—like 'My wife sees a green table'—into its constituent parts. In the 'Investigations,' Wittgenstein completely gave up his 'Tractatus' ideas, and thought that philosophical perplexity arose because people abused the ordinary ways of speech and used a rule that was perfectly all right in its own area to cover another area, and so they got into a muddle; he thought that you could disentangle the puzzle by pointing out that they were misusing ordinary language. As he wrote, 'Philosophy is a battle against the bewitchment of our intelligence by means of language.' It was like showing, in his most quoted phrase, 'the fly the way out of the fly-bottle.' If in the 'Tractatus' Wittgenstein was like Russell, in 'Philosophical Investigations' he was like Moore, a common-sense man. Wittgenstein now thought that you couldn't ask what the structure of reality was; you could only analyze the language in which people talked about it. A lot of different types of structure were found in language, and it was impossible to assimilate them all under any one heading. He regarded the various ways of expression as so many different pieces in a game of chess, to be manipulated according to certain rules. It was quite wrong to apply the rules of one set of statements to another, and he distinguished several types of statements—for example, common-sense statements about physical objects, statements about one's own thoughts and intentions, and moral propositions. It was the philosopher's job to find out the rules of the language game. Suppose you had been brought up from a small child to play football. By the time you were sixteen, you played it quite according to the rules. You probably didn't know the names of the various rules or what, exactly, they said, but you never made a mistake about them, and when anyone asked you 'Why do you play this way, and not that?' you just said 'Well, I always have played this way.' Now, it would be possible for someone else to come along as an observer and write down what rules you were playing by, if he observed you long enough. Like the observer on the football ground, a philosopher should primarily investigate what the rules used for communication are."

Just when I thought I had absorbed all this, John said, "I hope I haven't left you with the impression that there is necessarily a firm connection between Russell, Moore, and Wittgenstein, on the one hand, and present-day Oxford philosophy, on the other. Some people would argue that the late J. L. Austin, in the fifties White's Professor of Moral Philosophy at Oxford, had as much to do with shaping thinking at the university as anyone else, including Wittgenstein. Also, you mustn't overlook the role of logical positivism in all this." John said he would prefer not to say anything about Austin, because he had very mixed feelings about him. But logical positivism—well, that was another matter. A. J. Ayer, recently appointed Wykeham Professor of Logic at Oxford, was the first Englishman to proclaim the principles of logical positivism to the English intellectual world. After his graduation from Oxford, in 1932, he went to Vienna and made the acquaintance of some of the most famous European philosophers—members of the so-called Vienna Circle—who had come together to discuss, among other things, Wittgenstein's "Tractatus." Ayer made his reputation for life by returning to England six months later and writing "Language, Truth and Logic," a tract of logical positivism. "If I may put it so," John concluded, with a smile, "he has pattered all around the kennel, but he's always been on his Viennese leash."

I knew it was getting late, but I asked John for a little more philosophy, for the road. We had some more claret, and before we packed up for the night, he quickly served up logical positivism.

The logical positivism of the thirties, I learned, was a skeptical movement. It claimed that any statement that could not be *verified* by sense experience was meaningless. Thus, all statements about God, all statements about morality, all value judgments in art were logically absurd. For example, "Murder is wrong" could only mean, at best, "I disapprove of murder," or, still more precisely, "Murder! Ugh!" What made a statement like "There is a dog in my neighbor's garden" meaningful was that I could *verify* it. If I went into the garden, I could see the dog, beat it with a stick, get bitten, hear it bark, and watch it chew on an old bone.

The room was thick with smoke by now, for John, in a very un-English way, had kept all the windows closed. Both of us were tired. He put on some coffee, and we chatted about this and that, after which, instead of trundling to my own lodgings, I dossed down on his sofa.

The next day, I hung around John's room, trying to sort out my thoughts after the injections of Oxford philosophy administered by the sharp mind of my friend, until the time came for me to call on Gellner, the first philosopher on my list. During the *Times'* siege of Ryle, I had been first pro-Gellner, then anti, then pro, but John had watched the whole affair with the detachment of a philosopher. He gave me a rationalizing explanation: Good editors were eccentric people, and potentates who ruled scholarly periodicals tended to be even more eccentric than their counterparts on popular magazines. Then he handed me a copy of G. E. Moore's autobiography opened to a passage about Moore's editorship of *Mind,* which made me shift my weight about uncomfortably on the Gellner-Ryle seesaw. "In 1920, on

Stout's retirement from the Editorship of *Mind,* an office which he had held since the beginning of the 'New Series' in 1892," I read, "I was asked to succeed him as Editor; I . . . have now been Editor for more than twenty years. . . . I think . . . that I have succeeded in being impartial as between different schools of philosophy. I have tried, in accordance with the principles laid down when *Mind* was started and repeated by Stout in the Editorial which he wrote at the beginning of the New Series, to let merit, or, in other words, the ability which a writer displays, and not the opinions which he holds, be the sole criterion of whether his work should be accepted. . . . The most noticeable difference between *Mind* under me and *Mind* under Stout seems to me to be that under me the number of book reviews has considerably diminished. This has been partly deliberate: under Stout there were a great number of very short reviews, and I have thought (perhaps wrongly) that very short reviews were hardly of any use. But it is partly, I am afraid, owing to lack of thoroughly businesslike habits on my part, and partly also because, knowing what a tax I should have felt it myself to have to write a review, I have been shy about asking others to undertake the task. Whatever the reason, I am afraid it is the case that I have failed to get reviewed a good many books which ought to have been reviewed."

After reading these honest words of Professor Moore—a good editor and a perfect gentleman, who was fanatical about avoiding prejudices—I went to see Gellner with an open mind. I got on a bus that would take me to his home, in S.W. 15, and an hour later I found myself on the edge of a middle-middle-class settlement where houses stood out sparsely, like so many road signs. Trucks and broken-down little cars sluggishly wheeled themselves through the growing suburbia carrying vegetables, meat, and a few people to the city. A man was standing in front of Gellner's house, holding a baby in his arms. It was Gellner. "Come in! Come in!" he said. Gellner (a man of thirty-four) proved to be dark, of medium height, and casually dressed. His hair was uncombed, and he had the air of an offbeat intellectual. We went inside, and he introduced me to his wife. He was reluctant to talk philosophy while his wife and the infant were in the room, so we chatted about this and that, and I learned that he was born in Paris of Czech parentage, spent his boyhood in Prague, and had come to England with his family just before the war.

When Mrs. Gellner took the baby upstairs, he diffidently pointed out twin tape recorders in a corner of the living room. "These Grundig machines produced 'Words and Things,'" he said. "The Memorette recorded my words and a secretary at the London School of Economics, thanks to this magical Stenorette, transformed my voice into typed copy." He spoke in a quick and rather harassed way, as though the tape recorders were at that moment catching his words on an ever-shrinking spool.

"I was going through the *Times* correspondence the other day," he went on. "I have kept a complete file of it. I was elated to find that most of the people lined up on my side."

As far as Gellner was concerned, I gathered, all philosophers at Oxford were more or less alike, since all of them were interested only in linguistic analysis. ("Oxford philosophy," he said, was a misnomer, since it grouped the philosophers by the setting of their practice, rather than by the linguistic method which they all shared in common.) Instead of regarding philosophy as an investigation of the universe—or knowledge as a sort of inventory of the universe ("There are more things in heaven and earth, Horatio, than are dreamt of in your philosophy"), to which wise men from the beginning of time had been adding—the linguistic philosophers handed over the universe to the students of the natural sciences and limited philosophy to an inquiry into rules of language, the gateway to human knowledge. They analyzed language to determine what could and could not be said and therefore in a sense what could and could not exist. Any employment of words that did not conform to the rules of dictionary usage was automatically dismissed as nonsense. "But I answer," Gellner said, "all words cannot be treated as proper nouns." To clarify his point, he read a passage from one of his Third Programme broadcasts: "The . . . reason why the dictionary does not have scriptural status [according to him, all linguistic philosophers use the Oxford English Dictionary as the Holy Writ of philosophy] is that most expressions are not [proper] names; their meaning is not really exhausted by the specification of their use and the paradigmatic uses that occur in the dictionary. Their meaning is usually connected in a complicated way with a whole system of concepts or words or ways of thinking: and it makes perfectly good sense to say that a word, unlike a name, is mistakenly used in its paradigmatic use. It makes sense to say this *although* we have not done any rechristening and are still continuing to use it in its old sense." He pegged the rest of his criticism on the practitioners of linguistic philosophy.

"Out of the bunch of Oxford philosophers," he said, "I suppose I have the strongest aversion to Austin, who in some ways typified the things I dislike about them most. I found his lecture technique a creeping barrage, going into endless detail in a very slow and fumbling way. He used this style to browbeat people into acceptance; it was a kind of brainwashing. The nearest I got to him was on some committees that we were both members of. I always took some trouble not to get to know him personally, because I disliked his philosophy and I knew that sooner or later I would attack him and I didn't wish to be taken as a personal enemy. With Austin, I had an impression of someone *very* strongly obsessed with never being wrong, and using all kinds of dialectical devices to avoid being wrong. He intimidated me with his immense caginess; like Wittgenstein, he never stated the doctrines he was trying to get across—or, actually, the crucial thing was stated in informal sayings, which never got into print. Thus he artfully shielded himself from challengers. To Oxford philosophers Wittgenstein, like Austin, is another little god who can do no wrong. They like Wittgenstein mainly because he gave up his achievements in the technical field and his power as a mathematical magician for the ordinary language of a plain man—or, rather, the kind of ordinary language that an undergraduate who has studied the classics in Greats can take to pieces."

Linguistic philosophers were thought to alleviate cerebral neurosis, Gellner said. To understand them, he believed, one had to turn to sociology, his present professional interest. "About the social milieu from which these Oxford philosophers arose," he went on rapidly, "I can say nothing except what I have already said in the ninth chapter of my book. On second thought, perhaps there is one improvement that, on the basis of my reading of C. P. Snow, I could have made in my chapter." Gellner said that had Snow's brilliant pamphlet "The Two Cultures and the Scientific Revolution" existed when Gellner wrote his book, he would have invoked it, for Snow's characterization of the two cultures was right up his philosophical alley. "The milieu of linguistic philosophers is a curious one," Gellner continued. "As Sir Charles, in his pamphlet, points out, there are these two cultures—a literary one and a scientific one—and traditionally the literary one has always enjoyed more prestige. But for some time it has been losing ground; technology and science have been taking its place. Only in Oxford has the literary culture managed to retain an unchallenged supremacy. There Greats still remains at the apex of the disciplines, and within Greats the brightest young men are often selected to become philosophers. But is there any intellectual justification for this self-appointed aristocracy? Is there any widespread theory that any-body can subscribe to as to why the Greats form of philosophy is the highest sort of activity? I say no. The literary culture would have perished a long time ago if it weren't for the social snobbery of Oxford and her self-perpetuating philosophers. Linguistic philosophy is nothing more than a defense mechanism of gentleman intellectuals, which they use in order to conceal the fact that they have nothing left to do."

Turning to his Stenorette tape recorder, Gellner asked me, "Would you like to hear something I was dictating this morning? It really sums up my position, and in a sense you could say it is the essence of 'Words and Things.'" I nodded, and he flicked a switch. "Philosophers in the past were proud of changing the world and providing a guide for political life," the voice whispered through the little speaker of the tape recorder. "About the turn of the century, Oxford was a nursery for running an empire; now it is a nursery for leaving the world exactly as it is. The linguistic philosophers have their job cut out for them—to rationalize the loss of English power. This is the sociological background which is absolutely crucial to the understanding of linguistic philosophers."

Gellner stopped the machine and said, "There you have my whole sociological analysis. Full stop. In 'Words and Things,' I used Thorstein Veblen for the sociology of the philosophers. If I were writing the book now, I would use Veblen and Sir Charles."

Gellner picked up a copy of *Commentary* from the coffee table and read me a sentence or two from its review of his book, which implied that he had written "Words and Things" because he had failed to get a cushy job at Oxford. "Dash it, job-hungry people do not write my sort of book," he said. "How nasty can you really get? As far as professional philosophy is concerned, 'Words and Things' ruined my future rather than secured it. I attacked the philosophical Establishment, and as long as the present philosophers remain in power, I will never have a position at an Oxford college. Whether I will be accepted again in philosophical circles remains to be seen."

Gellner offered to drive me back to the city. For transportation he had a small truck, which he used for getting to the London School of Economics when he missed his commuter train. We bounced noisily along the road, Gellner making himself heard intermittently over the engine clatter. He had more or less given up formal philosophy until the philosophers should once again address themselves to "great issues." While waiting for the change, Gellner was studying the Berbers of Morocco. He visited them now and again and observed their social habits. He considered himself a synoptic thinker—one who saw things as a whole, from the viewpoint of their ultimate significance. He was not a softheaded visionary, and his education at Balliol, traditionally the most rebellious Oxford college, had prepared him to battle with the philosophical Establishment for his unpopular views. He thought that with "Words and Things" he had galvanized men of good sense into taking his side.

Gellner left me reflective. I was sorry that my first philosopher should dislike his colleagues so much. I was sorry, too, that he should turn out to be a harassed man. But then I knew well that prophets are made of strange stuff.

Next day, I walked round to Chelsea to have a talk with Earl Russell at his house. He opened the door himself, and I instantly recognized him as a philosopher by his pipe, which he took out of his mouth to say, "How do you do?" Lord Russell looked very alert. His mop of white hair, swept carelessly back, served as a dignified frame for his learned and animated eyes—eyes that gave life to a wintry face. He showed me into his ground-floor study, which was sandwiched between the garden and the street. It was a snug room, full of books on a large number of subjects: mathematics, logic, philosophy, history, politics. The worn volumes stood as an impressive testament to his changing intellectual interests; they were wedged in with rows of detective stories in glass-fronted Victorian bookcases. "Ah!" he said. "It's just four! I think we can have some tea. I see my good wife has left us some tea leaves." His "ee" sounds were exaggerated. He put a large Victorian kettle on the gas ring. It must have contained little water, for it sang like a choir in a Gothic cathedral. Russell ignored the plainsong and talked, using his pipe, which went out repeatedly, as a baton to lead the conversation. Now and again he reached out to take some tobacco with unsteady fingers from a tin. When we were comfortably settled with our tea, he began interviewing me. Why was I concerned with philosophy when my life was in peril? I should jolly well be doing something about the atomic bomb, to keep the Russians and Americans from sending us all up in flames. Anyone might personally prefer death to slavery, but only a lunatic would think of making this choice for humanity.

At present, when he wasn't working on nuclear disarmament, he used detective stories for an opiate. "I have to read at least one detective book a day," he said, "to drug myself against the nuclear threat." His favorite crime writers were Michael Innes and Agatha Christie. He preferred detective stories to novels because he found that whodunits were more real than howtodoits. The characters in detective stories just did things, but the heroes and heroines in novels thought about things. If you compared sex scenes in the two media, in his sort of pastime they got into and out of bed with alacrity, but in the higher craft the characters were circumspect; they took pages even to sit on the bed. Detective stories were much more lifelike. The paradox was that authors of thrillers did not try to be real, and therefore they were real, while the novelists tried to be real and therefore were unreal. The things we most believed to be unreal—nuclear war—might turn out to be real, and the things we took to be the most real— philosophy—unreal.

The savior in him was eventually tamed by the tea, and the elder statesman of philosophy reminisced a bit about Moore and Wittgenstein, his Cambridge juniors, and said a few caustic words about today's philosophers at Oxford and Cambridge. "I haven't changed my philosophical position for some time," he said. "My model is still mathematics. You see, I started out being a Hegelian. A tidy system it was. Like its child, Communism, it gave answers to all the questions about life and society. In 1898 (how long ago that was!), well, almost everyone seemed to be a Hegelian. Moore was the first to climb down. I simply followed him. It was mathematics that took me to logic, and it was logic that led me away from Hegel. Once we applied rigorous logic to Hegel, he became fragmentary and puerile."

I asked if he had based his system of mathematical logic on the belief that language had a structure.

"No, it is not so much that I believe language has a structure," he said. "I simply think that language is often a rather messy way of expressing things. Take a statement like 'All men are mortal.' Now, that has an unnecessary implication when stated in words; that is, that there are men, that men exist. But if you translate this statement into mathematical symbols, you can do away with any unnecessary implication. About Moore—the thing I remember most was his smile. One had only to see it to melt. He was such a gentleman. With him, manners were everything, and now you know what I mean by 'gentleman.' To be Left, for example, in politics just 'wasn't done.' That was to take something too seriously. I suppose present-day Oxford philosophy is gentlemanly in that sense—it takes nothing seriously. You know the best remark Moore ever made? I asked him one time who his best pupil was, and he said 'Wittgenstein.' I said 'Why?' 'Because, Bertrand, he is my only pupil who always looks puzzled.'" Lord Russell chuckled. "That was such a good remark, such a good remark. It was also, incidentally, very characteristic of both Moore and Wittgenstein. Wittgenstein *was* always puzzled. After Wittgenstein had been my pupil for five terms, he came to me and said, 'Tell me, sir, am I a fool or a wise man?' I said, 'Wittgenstein, why do you want to know?'—perhaps not the kindest thing to say. He said, 'If I am a fool, I shall become an aeronaut—if I am a wise man, a philosopher.' I told him to do a piece of work for me over the vacation, and when he came back I read the first sentence and said, 'Wittgenstein, you shall be a philosopher.' I had to read just a sentence to know it. Wittgenstein became one. When his 'Tractatus' came out, I was wildly excited. I think less well of it now. At that time, his theory that a proposition was a picture of the world was so engaging and original. Wittgenstein was really a Tolstoy and a Pascal rolled into one. You know how fierce Tolstoy was; he hated competitors. If another novelist was held to be better than he, Tolstoy would immediately challenge him to a duel. He did precisely this to Turgenev, and when Tolstoy became a pacifist he was just as fierce about his pacifism. And you know how Pascal became discontented with mathematics and science and became a mystic; it was the same with Wittgenstein. He was a mathematical mystic. But after 'Tractatus' he became more and more remote from me, just like the Oxford philosophers. I have stopped reading Oxford philosophy. I have gone on to other things. It has become so trivial. I don't like most Oxford philosophers. Don't like them. They have made trivial something very great. Don't think much of their apostle Ryle. He's just another clever man. In any case, you have to admit he behaved impetuously in publicly refusing a review of the book. He should have held it over for two years and then printed a short critical review with Gellner's name misspelled. To be a philosopher now, one needs only to be clever. They are all embarrassed when pressed for information, and I am still old-fashioned and like information. Once, I was dining at Oxford—Exeter College High Table—and asked the assembled Fellows what the difference between liberals and conservatives was in their local politics. Well, each of the dons produced brilliant epigrams and it was all very amusing, but after half an hour's recitation I knew no more about liberals and conservatives in the college than I had at the beginning. Oxford philosophy is like that. I have respect for Ayer; he likes information, and he has a first-class style."

Lord Russell explained that he had two models for his own style—Milton's prose and Baedeker's guidebooks. The Puritan never wrote without passion, he said, and the cicerone used only a few words in recommending sights, hotels, and restaurants. Passion was the voice of reason, economy the signature of brilliance. As a young man, Russell wrote with difficulty. Sometimes Milton and Baedeker remained buried in his prose until it had been redone ten times. But then he was consoled by Flaubert's troubles and achievements. Now, for many years past, he had learned to write in his mind, turning phrases, constructing sentences, until in his memory they grew into paragraphs and chapters. Now he seldom changed a word in his dictated manuscript except to slip in a synonym for a word repeated absent-mindedly. "When I was an undergraduate," he said, sucking his pipe, "there were many boys cleverer than I, but I surpassed them, because, while they were *dégagé*, I had passion and fed on controversy. I still thrive on opposition. My grandmother was a woman of caustic and biting wit. When she was eighty-three, she became kind and gentle. I had never found her so reasonable. She noticed the change in herself, and, reading the handwriting on the wall, she said to me, 'Bertie, I'll soon be dead.' And she soon was."

After tea, Lord Russell came to the door with me. I told him about my intention of pressing on with my researches at Oxford. He wrung my hand and chuckled. "Most Oxford philosophers know nothing about science," he said. "Oxford and Cambridge are the last medieval islands—all right for first-class people. But their security is harmful to second-class people—it makes them insular and gaga. This is why English academic life is creative for some but sterile for many."

My first call in Oxford was at the house of Richard Hare, of Balliol, who, at forty-two, is one of the more influential Oxford teachers of philosophy. His evangelistic zeal for the subject consumes him. He is renowned throughout the university for his kindness, for his selfless teaching, and for writing an exciting book in his field, "The Language of Morals," published in 1952. He is also famous for his eccentric tastes, which I encountered for myself while lunching with him. When I arrived, he was sitting in a caravan—a study on wheels—in the front garden of his house, reading a book. He hailed me from the window, and said, "I find it much easier to work here than in the house. It's quieter, don't you agree?" He looked like a monk, though he wasn't dressed like one; he wore a well-made dark tweed jacket and well-pressed dark-gray flannel trousers—and he had his legendary red and green tie on. After talking for a few minutes through the door of the caravan, we went into the house and joined Mrs. Hare and their four children for lunch. I felt relaxed at his table. His children spoke in whispers and were remarkably well-mannered. His wife was douce and poised. I had been told that invitations to his country-house reading parties during vacations were coveted by able undergraduate philosophers at Oxford, and now I could see why.

At the table, we talked about Hare's interests. "I like music very much—it's one of my principal relaxations," he said at one point. "I listen in a very catholic way to all kinds of music. I deliberately don't have a gramophone, because I think it's better for one to catch what there is on the wireless instead of choosing one's own things. I take in quite a lot of modern stuff, although I don't enjoy it as a whole. I listen to it in the hope that one day I will. Also, on the wireless I have to listen to Beethoven. I'd never go and get a gramophone record of Beethoven. As a schoolboy, I liked him very much, but when the war began I was—as I think most of us were, or anybody at all sensitive—

very troubled by war and whether one should be a pacifist. And I can't explain why, but it suddenly became clear to me, listening to Beethoven and to Bach and comparing them, that as *food,* musical food, for anybody in that kind of situation, Beethoven was exceedingly superficial and insipid. But principally superficial. To be precise, it appeared to me one wintry day in 1940 that his music rang exceedingly hollow."

At the end of lunch, Mrs. Hare told us she would bring us coffee in the caravan, and I followed Hare to his wagon retreat.

I asked him if there was a key to linguistic philosophy.

"No," he said forcefully. "There isn't a method that any fool can get hold of in order to do philosophy as we do it. The most characteristic thing about Oxford philosophy is that we insist on clear thinking, and I suppose scientists and philosophers are agreed on what constitutes a good argument. Clear thinking, of course, is especially important in my own field of moral philosophy, because almost any important moral question arises in a confused form when one first meets it. But most of the undergraduates who come up to Oxford are not going to be professional philosophers; they're going to be civil servants and parsons and politicians and lawyers and businessmen. And I think the most important thing I can do is to teach them to think lucidly—and linguistic analysis is frightfully useful for this. You have only to read the letters to the *Times*—unfortunately I forget them as soon as I've read them, or I'd give you an example—to come across a classic instance of a problem that is made clearer for one, and perhaps would have been made clearer for the writer, by the ability to take statements to pieces. My own hobby is town planning. I read quite a lot of the literature, and it's perfectly obvious that immense harm is done—I mean not just confusion, academic confusion, but physical harm, roads being built in the wrong places and that sort of thing—because people don't think clearly enough. In philosophy itself, unclear thinking has led to a lot of mistakes, and I think it is my job to take pupils through these mistakes and show them the blind alleys in the city of philosophy. They can go on from there. Careful attention to language is, I think, the best way not to solve problems but to understand them. That is what, as philosophers, we are mainly concerned with."

I asked how, exactly, attention to language helped in understanding problems.

"Suppose I said, 'That chair over there is both red and not red,' " he replied. "This would make you say, 'That can't be right.' Well, I say partly it's the same sort of thing that would make you say 'That can't be right' if you wrote down 'fullfil,' spelled f-u-l-l-f-i-l. If you wrote down 'fullfil' that way and you saw it on a page, you would say, 'That can't be right.' Well, this is because you've learned, you see, to do a thing called spelling 'fulfill,' and you've also learned to do a thing called using the word 'not.' And if somebody says to you, 'That is both red and not red,' he's doing something that you learned *not* to do when you learned the word 'not.' He has offended against a certain rule of skill (if you like to call it that), which you mastered when you became aware of how to use the word 'not.' Of course, learning to use the word 'not' isn't exactly like learning how to spell, because it's also knowing something about how to reason. It's mastering a very elementary piece of logic. The words for 'not' in different languages are the same, but not quite the same; there are variations. For example, in Greek you've double negatives; you say, 'I have not been neither to the temple nor to the theatre." This is why Oxford philosophy is based both on simple reasoning and on exhaustive research into language—in this particular case, into the word 'not.' "

Hare's ideas about moral philosophy, I learned, were influenced by his experiences in Japanese prison camps in Singapore and Thailand, where all values had to be hewn from the rock of his own conscience. In the artificial community of the prison, he came to realize that nothing was "given" in society, that everyone carried his moral luggage in his head; every man was born with his conscience, and this, rather than anything in society, he found, was the source of morality. (As he once wrote, "A prisoner-of-war community is a society which has to be formed, and constantly re-formed, out of nothing. The social values, whether military or civil, which one has brought with one can seldom be applied without scrutiny to this very strange, constantly disintegrating situation.") Indeed, the rough draft of his first book, "The Language of Morals"—on the strength of which he was eventually elected a Fellow of Balliol—was hammered out in the grim and barren prison compounds. He went on to tell me that his present views, which were a development of his old ideas, were that ethics was the exact study of the words one used in making moral judgments, and that judgment, to be moral, had to be both universal and prescriptive. "This means," he explained, "that if you say 'X ought to do Y,' then you commit yourself to the view that if you were in X's position, you ought to do Y also. Furthermore, if you have said that *you* ought to do Y, then you are bound to do it—straightway, if possible. If you say that X ought to do Y but you don't think that in the same circumstances *you* ought to do it, then it isn't a moral judgment at all." In effect, let your conscience always be your guide. "If you do not assent to the above propositions," Hare went on energetically, "then you do not, in my opinion, really believe in any moral judgments. You cannot answer 'ought'-questions by disguising them as 'is'-questions." He admitted, however, that most of the philosophers at Oxford were not much interested in moral philosophy. For that sort of philosophy one had to go to the Continent and to Existentialism.

What was the relationship between Existentialism and British philosophy?

"The thing wrong with the Existentialists and the other Continental philosophers," Hare said, "is that they haven't had their noses rubbed in the necessity of saying exactly what they mean. I sometimes think it's because they don't have a tutorial system. You see, if you learn philosophy here you read a thing to your tutor and he says to you 'What do you mean by that?' and then you have to tell him. I think what makes us good philosophers is, ultimately, the method of teaching. But you ought to see Iris Murdoch about Existentialism. She's read the big books." He'd read only little Existentialist books, he said. He had no sympathy for people less good than Miss Murdoch who "let rip on Existentialism and use it as a stick with which to beat 'the sterile Oxford philosophers.' "

Was it possible to be a philosopher and have a religious faith?

Hare pointed out that some of the Oxford philosophers were practicing Christians. He went on to name some Catholics: Elizabeth Anscombe; her husband, Peter Geach (who, though he was not teaching at Oxford, was still "one of us"); B. F. McGuinness; and Michael Dummett. "If you wish to be rational," he went on, "you've got to look for some way of reconciling formal religion, science, and philosophy. I personally think you can reconcile only two of these things. As a philosopher, you can work out your own personal religion, which may or may not conform to what any particular church says, but I think it's slightly sophistical, say, to be a Catholic and then insist that

Hell is scientific. Some philosophers here think that they can serve all three masters, and the way they reconcile religion and science is revealing. They take the dogmatic attitude and call it 'empirical': 'When the bad go to Hell, they will *verify* the statement that the bad go to Hell.' So much for the scientific principle of verification! I think if you are a Catholic and are going to be a philosopher, you're almost bound to do one of two things. One is to stick rigidly to the formal kinds of philosophy—I mean mathematical logic, pure linguistic analysis, and that kind of thing. The other is to do ordinary philosophy—my sort—but with a distinct slant."

It was getting late in the afternoon, and I said I must take my leave. We went back into the house, so that I could say goodbye to Mrs. Hare, and she insisted on our taking another cup of coffee. "I hope your afternoon has been worthwhile," she said. "I have learned all the philosophy I know from reading the proofs of my husband's books."

Mr. Hare had been candid and informative. Like all good tutors, he was a little idiosyncratic and somewhat oracular but very approachable.

Next morning, I dropped in on Iris Murdoch. She, Elizabeth Anscombe, and Philippa Foot make up the squadron of Oxford's feminine philosophers, and they and Richard Hare make up the constabulary of moral philosophy at the university. Among her friends and students, Miss Murdoch has the reputation of being a saint, and she has no enemies. She's likely to go about without a thought for her dress and without a penny in her pocket, and this absent-mindedness perhaps has its source in her custom of living and thinking in two worlds—philosophy and literature—both of which she inhabits with facility and aplomb. Two of her engaging novels, "The Bell" and "Under the Net," I had read very recently, and I was surprised that a writer of such gifts should be only a part-time novelist. She greeted me at the door of her study, in Saint Anne's College, and I was immediately drawn to her. She had a striking appearance, very much like my image of St. Joan—a celestial expression cast in the rough features of a peasant, and straight, blond hair unevenly clipped.

I determined to steer my way to philosophy by asking her about her writing. "I do my writing at home, during vacations," she said haltingly. "I settle down with some paper and my characters, and carry on until I get things done. But terms I devote mostly to reading and teaching philosophy—I haven't written any philosophy lately. Yes, I do find time to read a lot of novels, but I don't think I trespass on my serious reading. No, I don't think there is any direct connection between philosophy and my writing. Perhaps they do come together in a general sort of way—in considering, for example, what morality is and what goes into making decisions." She had been an undergraduate at the same time as Hare and, like him, had read Greats, but, unlike him, she had come accidentally to professional philosophy. The aftermath of the war put her in touch with Existentialism. "I was in London during the war," she recalled, "and afterward went to Brussels to do refugee work. In Belgium, there was a tremendous ferment going on; everyone was rushing around reading Kierkegaard and Jean-Paul Sartre. I knew something about them from my undergraduate days, but then I read them deeply." She returned to England and Cambridge to study French philosophy and to look at English philosophy afresh. Wittgenstein had just retired, and she regretted very much that she had arrived too late for his lectures. His philosophy, however, still towered over the university, and she was led up to it by Professor John Wisdom, a disciple of Wittgenstein's, and Miss Anscombe, a pupil and translator of Wittgenstein's, whom Miss Murdoch had known from her undergraduate days.

I asked Miss Murdoch if she had ever seen Wittgenstein.

"Yes. He was very good-looking," she replied, feeling her way like a novelist. "Rather small, and with a very, very intelligent, shortish face and piercing eyes—a sharpish, intent, alert face and those very piercing eyes. He had a trampish sort of appearance. And he had two empty rooms, with no books, and just a couple of deck chairs and, of course, his camp bed. Both he and his setting were very unnerving. His extraordinary directness of approach and the absence of any sort of paraphernalia were the things that unnerved people. I mean, with most people, you meet them in a framework, and there are certain conventions about how you talk to them, and so on. There isn't a naked confrontation of personalities. But Wittgenstein always imposed this confrontation on all his relationships. I met him only twice and I didn't know him well, and perhaps that's why I always thought of him, as a person, with awe and alarm."

She stopped talking suddenly, and it was some time before she resumed. Then she said that she had some things in common, as a moral philosopher, with Miss Anscombe and Mrs. Foot. The three of them were certainly united in their objection to Hare's view that the human being was the monarch of the universe, that he constructed his values from scratch. They were interested in "the reality that surrounds man—transcendent or whatever." She went on to add that the three of them were very dissimilar. "Elizabeth is Catholic and sees God in a particular color," Miss Murdoch said. "Philippa is in the process of changing her position." As for herself, she had not fully worked out her own views, though sometimes she did find herself agreeing with the Existentialists that every person was irremediably different from every other.

Would she perhaps compare the moral philosophy in England and France, I asked, remembering Hare's comment that she had read the big books.

"Some of the French Existentialists feel that certain English philosophers err when they picture morality as a matter of consistency with universal rules," she answered. "The Existentialists think that even though you may endorse the rules society offers you, it is still your own *individual* choice that you endorse them. The Existentialists feel that you can have a morality without producing consistent or explicable rules for your conduct. They allow for a much more personal and aesthetic kind of morality, in which you have to explain yourself, as it were, to your peers."

As she talked on, it became clear to me that she was much more an intuitive person than an analytic one, and regarded ideas as so many precious stones in the human diadem. In contrast to Hare, she found it hard to imagine the diadem locked up in an ivory tower or, like the Crown Jewels, in the Tower of London. "Most English philosophers," she said, "share certain assumptions of Wittgenstein's and Austin's. You might want to look into them as persons. They were the most extraordinary men among us."

After saying goodbye to Miss Murdoch, I carried my researches on to Magdalen College. There I intended to draw out G. J. Warnock, who held one of the keys to the Austinian legend. This legend was as ubiquitous as the stained-glass windows, and it might be presumed to illuminate the dark room of Oxford philosophy, for J. L. Austin, who died a few months before I began my quest, had dominated Oxford in much the same way that Wittgenstein had dominated Cambridge. In the course of an Oxford-to-London telephone call, I asked John, "What was the source of everyone's veneration of Austin?" and he said, more analytically than unkindly, "Every cult needs a dead man." He likened the Austinian sect to primitive Christianity, though he added that he did not think the worshippers would ever be blessed with a St. Paul.

As it happened, I had attended one of Austin's lectures, just out of curiosity, while I was an undergraduate, and had been entranced by his performance. To look at, he was a tall and thin man, a sort of parody on the desiccated don. His face suggested an osprey. His voice was flat and metallic, and seemed to be stuck on a note of disillusion. It sounded like a telephone speaking by itself. The day I was present, he opened his lecture by reading aloud a page from Ayer's "The Problem of Knowledge." He read it in a convincing way, and then he began taking it to bits: "What does he mean by this?" He bore down heavily on Ayer's argument with regard to illusion—that you cannot trust your senses, because they are sometimes mistaken. He said that the passage about people's having illusions made this sound as if it were much more frequent than in fact it was—as if when people saw a stick in water and it looked bent, they were inevitably deceived into thinking that it actually was bent. Austin turned around to the blackboard and, leaning forward, drew a sort of triangle with a thin, crooked stick in it. He added a cherry at the end of the stick. "What is this supposed to be?" he asked, facing us. "A cocktail glass?" And he drew a stem and a foot, asking as he did so, "How many of you think it is a bucket?" He lectured in a deadpan voice, peopling the room with Ayer's deceived men, all of whom would take the glass to be a bucket. This was Austin's way of saying that no more people were deceived by Ayer's stick in the water than by the glass on the blackboard, that Ayer's argument about the fallibility of the senses was much less cogent than he made out, and that most of what the logical positivists called illusions were in fact a madman's delusions. I was told that Austin performed like this day after day, mocking, ridiculing, caricaturing, exaggerating, never flagging in his work of demolition, while the skeptical undergraduates watched, amused and bemused, for behind the performance—the legend—there was the voice of distilled intelligence. Austin's trenchant remarks on philosophers would make a small volume of cherished quotations, and among them would surely be a clerihew he wrote on the Harvard logician W. V. Quine:

> Everything done by Quine
> Is just fine.
> All we want is to be left alone,
> To fossick around on our own.

When I arrived at Magdalen, I found Warnock reading the bulletin board in the porter's lodge. He looked slightly younger than Hare, and was round-faced and rather tweedy; his appearance went with round-rimmed glasses, though he didn't have any glasses on. He was, however, wearing a rather nice, formal V-shaped smile. Yes, he was expecting me, he said, and took me straight to the Senior Common Room for lunch. Warnock was the custodian of Austin's papers, but we didn't talk about Austin right away. Once we were in the S.C.R., I asked him about the lightning attack he and Dr. David Pears, of Christ Church College, had made on Gellner and Watkins in a discussion on the B.B.C. Third Programme in 1957. After Gellner's polemical book appeared, some of his detractors had claimed that this broadcast had provided him with both the motive and the cue for writing it—that when the articulate Oxford pair defeated the less articulate Gellner and his satellite, Watkins, the defeat had made Watkins sulk and Gellner write. "I wish I'd known that that little rapping of the knuckles would lead to the big storm," Warnock said. "Gellner is a rather sensitive chap." I had not expected him to show even this much sympathy for Gellner, for I had been told that Warnock was one of Austin's two or three favorites, and I knew Austin was one of Gellner's main targets.

The lunch was a communal affair, an occasion for general conversation, and I was not able to draw Warnock out until it was time for coffee, when all the other Fellows settled down to their newspapers and we managed to find a corner to ourselves. Once I had mentioned Austin, Warnock needed no further urging. I just sat back and listened.

"Like Wittgenstein," he said, "Austin was a genius, but Wittgenstein fitted the popular picture of a genius. Austin, unfortunately, did

not. Nevertheless, he did succeed in haunting most of the philosophers in England, and to his colleagues it seemed that his terrifying
intelligence was never at rest. Many of them used to wake up in the
night with a vision of the stringy, wiry Austin standing over their
pillow like a bird of prey. Their daylight hours were no better. They
would write some philosophical sentences and then read them over as
Austin might, in an expressionless, frigid voice, and their blood would
run cold. Some of them were so intimidated by the mere fact of his
existence that they weren't able to publish a single article during
his lifetime."

Austin's all-consuming passion was language, Warnock went on,
and he was endlessly fond of reading books on grammar. He thought
of words as if they were insects, which needed to be grouped, classi-
fied, and labelled, and just as the entomologist was not put off by the
fact that there were countless insects, so the existence of thousands of
words, Austin thought, should not be a deterrent to a lexicographer-
philosopher. "Austin," Warnock said, "wanted philosophers to classify
these 'speech acts'—these promises, prayers, hopes, commendations."
In Austin's view, most philosophers in the past had stumbled on some
original ideas and had spent their time producing a few illustrative
examples for their theories, and then as soon as they were safely dead
other philosophers would repeat the process with slightly different
original ideas. This practice had frozen philosophy from the beginning of time into an unscientific, non-cumulative state. Austin
wanted to thaw the ice of ages, by unflagging application of the
intellect, and make philosophy a cumulative science, thus enabling
one philosopher to pick up where his predecessor had left off. "He
envisaged the future task of philosophers as the compilation of a
super-grammar—a catalogue of all possible functions of words—and
this was perhaps why he enjoyed reading grammar books so much,"
Warnock said. "He was extremely rigid in pursuit of details, and he
had the patience and efficiency needed for this difficult task. If he had
not died at forty-eight—he had cancer, you know—his detailed work
might have led to some beautiful things."

"Was Austin influenced by Wittgenstein?" I asked.

"Oh, no," Warnock said quickly. "In all of Austin's papers there is
no evidence that he ever really read him. I do remember one or two of
his lectures in which he read a page or two of Wittgenstein aloud, but

it was always to show how incomprehensible and obscure the Austrian philosopher was, and how easily he could be parodied and dismissed."

I was getting worried by the fact that I was supposed to admire Austin as a man, and said, "Were there some things about him that were human?"

"Oh, yes," said Warnock, with a smile that indicated a faint donnish disapproval of my question. "He was one of the best teachers here. He taught us all absolute accuracy."

I repeated my question in a slightly different form.

"He really was a very unhappy man," Warnock said quietly. "It worried him that he hadn't written much. One lecture, 'Ifs and Cans,' which appeared in the *Proceedings of the British Academy* in 1956, became famous, but it is mainly a negative work, and he published very few articles and, significantly, not a single book. He read, of course—an enormous amount—and the margins of everything he went over were filled with notes, queries, and condemnations. When he went to Harvard to give the William James lectures, in 1955, he took everyone there by surprise. Because he hadn't written anything, they expected his lectures to be *thin,* for they judged the worth of scholars according to their *big books.* From his very first lecture they realized that his reading was staggering. To add to his writing block, he had a fear of microphones, and this prevented him from broadcasting, like Sir Isaiah Berlin; this was another source of unhappiness. He took enormous pride in teaching, but this began to peter out in his last years, when he felt that he had reached the summit of his influence at Oxford. Toward the end of his life, therefore, he decided to pack up and go permanently to the University of California in Berkeley, where he had once been a visiting professor and where he thought he'd have more influence as a teacher. But before he could get away from Oxford, he died."

Warnock was in the middle of straightening out and editing Austin's papers, and he told me there were scores of bad undergraduate essays that Austin had written for his tutor at Balliol. "These essays were of little value because his philosophy tutor set him useless subjects," Warnock said. It was probably his education at his public school, Shrewsbury, rather than at Balliol, that got him his Firsts, the Magdalen tutor thought. Besides the bad essays, his papers included only two sets of lectures—one on perception, the other the William

James addresses. But both of them were in note form, and would not total much more than eighty thousand words when Warnock had finished turning them into sentences. Warnock was worried by his task of filling out his master's lectures. If, by some miracle, the Austin-Warnock composition did add up to a hundred thousand words, then the publishers might be persuaded to bring out the work in two handsome volumes. Otherwise, there would be only one posthumous book, along with the few published articles, as a record of Austin's genius. (Some time later, the Oxford University Press brought out a small book, "Sense and Sensibilia," by Austin, reconstructed from manuscript notes by Warnock.) There were, of course, his many devoted pupils, and *they* would commemorate him.

Austin's family life, I learned, had been conventional. "He married a pupil, and had four children," Warnock said. "He was a good husband and a good father. His daughter, now eighteen, is about to come up to Oxford; his elder son, who is seventeen, is going to do engineering. The third child, a boy of fourteen, is very clever, and is about to go up to my school, Winchester. He talks and looks very much like Austin, and we have great hopes for him. The youngest child is a girl."

It was time to go, and as Warnock walked out to the porter's lodge with me, I asked him a bit about himself. Unlike most of the other philosophers about, he had not read Greats straightway. He had done P.P.E.—a combination of modern philosophy, political science, and economics—before going on to a year of Greats and a prize fellowship at Magdalen. He had been very fortunate in having Sir Isaiah Berlin, now Chichele Professor of Social and Political Theory, for his tutor, and also in having a philosopher for his wife. She and Warnock had together managed the Jowett Society (for undergraduate philosophers), and they had decided to get married after they were officers emeritus. He was writing a book on free will—one of the oldest chestnuts in the philosophical fire. His parting injunction to me was to see Strawson. "He'll be able to tell you some more about Austin," he called after me, waving.

I walked back to my old college, where I'd been given a guest room, to pick up my mail, and was delighted to find a letter from John, who had an uncanny gift of never failing me; he seemed to sense my questions before I could put them. Just as Oxford philosophy, in his words, "made a technique of being non-technical," John made a technique of helping his friends without apparent effort. It cheered me up to find out that his impatience with philosophy did not extend to his friend's researches. He said that I shouldn't miss seeing Strawson. "He not only is the best philosopher in the university but is also unrivalled as a teacher of it," John wrote. "He's discovering new stars in the philosophical firmament." Austin, he went on, had his equal in Strawson; indeed, at one meeting of the exclusive Aristotelian Society, *crème de la crème* of all philosophical societies, Strawson had roundly defeated Austin in a disputation about Truth—a truth that Austin had never acknowledged.

Next day, I waited for P. F. Strawson, Fellow of University College, Oxford, in his Senior Common Room. Strawson, who is considered by both undergraduates and his colleagues to be the most high-powered and creative philosopher in England, arrived just a little late and greeted me apologetically. He had blue eyes with what I took to be a permanently worried expression, and, at forty-one, looked like an elderly young man. At lunch, I asked him to tell me a little bit about himself, which he did, in a modest fashion that by now I had stopped associating with philosophers. He had been schooled in Finchley, a suburb of London, he said, and he had read Greats about the same time as Hare, Miss Murdoch, Miss Anscombe, Warnock. His career, like theirs, had been interrupted by the war, the close of which found him teaching in Wales. "I didn't know what provincialism was until I got there," he said. He had been delighted to get an appointment to Oxford, partly because Oxford had more philosophy in its curriculum than any other university. This, he explained, was the reason that a philosophy planted in Cambridge had flowered at Oxford. Cambridge now had only two eminent philosophers—John Wisdom and R. B. Braithwaite—while Oxford was swarming with them. Without the buzz-buzz, there would be no philosophy, he said; the university would be a hive minus the honey.

After lunch, as I climbed up the steps to his room, I felt I was leaving the Oxford of lost causes behind me—the way he moved suggested subdued confidence. We sat by the window, and for some time, as we talked, I was aware of the acrobatic motions of Strawson's legs, which were now wrapped around one of the legs of a writing table and now slung over another chair. We talked about other philosophers as so many birds outside preying on the insects that Austin had dug up for them. I felt I'd reached the augur of philosophy. On the window sill were lying the proofs of an article called "Philosophy in England," which was stamped " *Times Literary Supplement,* Special Issue on the British Imagination." Strawson admitted that he was the author of the anonymous piece, and while he went to telephone for some coffee, I glanced, with his permission, at the first paragraph:

An Australian philosopher, returning in 1960 to the center of English philosophy after an absence of more than a decade, re-marked on, and regretted, the change he found. He had left a rev-olutionary situation in which every new move was delightfully subversive and liberating. He returned to find that, though the subject appeared still to be confidently and energetically culti-vated, the revolutionary ferment had quite subsided. Where there had been, it seemed to him, a general and triumphant movement in one direction, there were now a number of individuals and groups pursuing divergent interests and ends, often in a relatively traditional manner.

When Strawson had returned to his chair, I asked him whether he agreed with the Australian philosopher. He said he did—that "the view of the Australian philosopher was essentially right." For a fuller statement of his own conclusions, he modestly directed me to the summary at the end of his article:

Even in the heyday of the linguistic movement, it is doubtful whether it numbered among its adherents or semi-adherents more than a substantial minority of British philosophers. It was associ-ated primarily with one place—Oxford—and there it centered around one man—Austin—its most explicit advocate and most acute and wholehearted practitioner. Its heyday was short. When a revolutionary movement begins to write its own history, some-thing at least of its revolutionary impetus has been lost; and in the appearance of "The Revolution in Philosophy" [by A. J. Ayer, W. C. Kneale, G. A. Paul, D. F. Pears, P. F. Strawson, G. J. War-nock, and R. A. Wollheim, with an introduction by Gilbert Ryle, 1956] . . . and of G. J. Warnock's "English Philosophy since 1900" (1958) there were signs that eyes were being lifted from the imme-diate task, indications of pause and change. Indeed, the pull of generality was felt by Austin himself, who, before he died, was beginning to work out a general classificatory theory of acts of linguistic communication. It is still too early to say what definite directions change will take. In spite of the work of Ayer, who never attached value to the linguistic idea, and who, in his most recent book, "The Problem of Knowledge" (1956), continued to uphold a traditional empiricism with unfailing elegance and skill, it seems unlikely that he or others will work much longer in the vein. There are portents, however, of a very different kind. One is the appearance of a persuasive study entitled "Hegel: A Re-examination" (1958), by J. N. Findlay. Hampshire's "Thought and Action" (1959), with its linking of epistemology, philosophy of mind, and moral philosophy, is highly indicative of a trend from piecemeal studies towards bolder syntheses; it shows how the results of recent discussions can be utilized in a construction with both Hegelian and Spinozistic affinities. Strawson's "Individuals" (1959) suggests a scaled-down Kantianism, pared of idealism on the one hand and a particular conception of physical science on the other. The philosophy of logic and language takes on a tauter line and a more formal tone in the work of logicians who derive their inspiration mainly from Frege. Finally, some of the most successful work of the period has been in the philosophy of mind; and it seems reasonable to suppose that further studies will follow upon Ryle's "Concept of Mind" (1949), Wittgenstein's "Investigations" (1953), and Miss Anscombe's "Intention" (1957) and that, in them, Ryle's explicit and Wittgenstein's implicit suggestions of systematization will be refined and reassessed. The Australian philosopher had reason enough to claim that he found a changed situation. When knowledge of this fact of change finally filters through to those who habitually comment on the state of philosophy without any significant first-hand acquaintance with it, reactions of complacency may be expected. In the anticipated face of these it is worth reaffirming that the gains and advances made in the dozen years which followed the war were probably as great as any which have been made in an equivalent period in the history of the subject. A new level of refinement and accuracy in conceptual awareness has been reached, and an addition to philosophical method has been established which will, or should, be permanent.

I wanted my augur to divine in more detail the flights of the philosophical birds, and asked him to tell me what was next.

"Fifteen years ago," he began, with a nod to the past, "we were perhaps over-confident, and dismissed the problems of the great thinkers of the past as mere verbal confusions. It was right after the war, and we were mesmerized by Wittgenstein and Austin." Some were still under their spell, he continued, but within the last five years most had wandered out of the magic circle.

"Was the Russell and Gellner charge of sterility in philosophy applicable, then, only to the first decade after the war?" I asked.

He thought so, he said, adding, "They are thinking of things like Austin's Saturday mornings." He went on to tell me that these meetings admitted only Fellows, no professors or others senior to Austin. Austin and his pet colleagues whiled away their Saturday mornings by distinguishing shades of meaning and the exact applications of words like "rules," "regulations," "principles," "maxims," "laws." "Even this method, sterile with anyone else, was very fertile with Austin," Strawson said, "though apparently not for Sir Isaiah Berlin and Stuart Hampshire. Sir Isaiah didn't last very long, because the whole approach was uncongenial to him, and in any case his genius lay in breathing life into the history of ideas. Most of the other brilliant philosophers, however, turned up regularly." This was perhaps what gave Oxford philosophy some sort of unity in the eyes of its critics, Strawson thought, but they overlooked the fact that on weekdays Austin did encourage (with results) people to do research in perception—in psychology and physiology. "Even on his Saturday mornings, toward the end of his life, he was coming around to more general sorts of questions," Strawson added, waggling his feet on the table. He then echoed a sentiment I'd heard again and again at Oxford: "Austin was one of the kindest men in the university." He went on, "As for the present, we are now rediscovering our way to the traditional way of doing philosophy. Ryle is composing a book on Plato and Aristotle, Warnock is reworking the problem of free will, and I'm writing a little volume on Kant." Thus, everything was now in ferment, and he imagined that the future might hold a philosophical synthesis chiselled and shaped with linguistic tools.

Strawson's scout brought in some coffee, and both of us sipped it gratefully. I spent the remaining time piecing together Strawson's intellectual biography. He spent the early fifties writing "Introduction to Logical Theory," in which he tried to explode Russell's theory that formal logic was the road to a perfect, unmessy language. Logic was simple, and ordinary language was complex, Strawson maintained in this work, and therefore neither could supplant the other. But it was really his "Individuals," published in 1959, that contained his present views. He devoted the second half of the fifties to working out the distinctions presented in "Individuals." "In my 'Individuals,'" he said, "instead of analyzing the language, I ask what the necessary *conditions* of language are. Like Kant, I reach the conclusion that objects exist in space and time, and that our language is derived from *them,* rather than the objects from the language. This enables me to state that the concept of a person *precedes* the idea of mind and body— that we think of a person, which includes mind and body, *before* we think of either mind or body. Through this concept of persons I solve the old dualistic problem—how mind and body, if two separate entities, can interact on each other. I answer that I can think of myself as an *objective* person—which subsumes both mind and body—when I postulate the existence of other persons. In my view, people's existence is objective in the same sense that, for example, this table is hard. It is hard because everyone agrees that it is hard, and it does not make any sense to say 'This is not so,' or to ask whether it is really hard. But if everyone had a different opinion about whether this table was hard or not, the fact of the table's hardness would, for that very reason, cease to be objective, and one would have to speak in some such terms as 'I have the peculiar sense of this table.' If people had peculiar senses of the table, it would deprive the table of existence. This argument holds for existence generally. For the existence of anything would be a private experience if people didn't agree about it. In my 'Individuals' I establish that agreement about the hard table is tantamount to saying that the table exists. But the sort of objectivity we ascribe to the hard table we cannot quite ascribe to pain, for example, because people do not agree about other people's pain, and people do not feel pain all at the same time. If they did, we should be able to talk about pain in the same way that we talk about the hard table. Nonetheless, I am able to establish that pain is objective."

By now, his legs were completely entangled with those of the hard table, but it was quite clear to me that he was one thing and the hard table another, and that both of them (hard table more than he) were objective. It was also quite clear to me that if men were no longer just clockwork machines, or Pavlov's dogs with ivory-tower bells ringing for their intellectual food, then metaphysics (or the mind)—which until the publication of Strawson's "Individuals" Oxford philosophers thought they had discarded forever—was now back in the picture. With the edifying thought that I had a mind in some sense as objective as my body, I took my leave of the scaled-down Kant.

I returned to my college and found John in its buttery; he had come up to consult some classical manuscripts in the Bodleian Library. Once beer was served, we settled down on a bench in a corner.

"I don't really want to talk *your* subject," John said, smiling, "but my curiosity has got the better of me."

"I've just come from Strawson," I said. "He explained to me his notions about mind and body, but I did find them difficult. What do you think about them?"

"As I told you in London," he began, reluctantly but good-humoredly, "I only skimmed the second half of 'Individuals.'"

"Yes, yes," I said. "Go on."

"The ideas contained in 'Individuals' have a very long history," John said. "Without going into all of it, you know that in the thirties Wittgenstein talked a lot about the problem of mind and body. His pupils kept elaborate authorized notes, which were only recently published as 'The Blue and Brown Books.' It was during his lifetime that Ryle brought out his 'The Concept of Mind,' which galled Wittgenstein very much, since it contained many of his unpublished ideas. Ryle had reached most of his conclusions independently, but this did not assuage old Wittgenstein, who had allowed himself to be beaten at the publishing game."

John swallowed some beer and then fumbled in several pockets for tobacco, pipe cleaner, and matches. As he filled his pipe, he blew a question in my direction: "Would you like to know something about 'The Concept of Mind'?"

I said I would, especially since Ryle, for personal reasons, was unable to see me. "Well, it is a great work and has had enormous influence," John said. "In this book, Ryle talks about the question 'What is knowledge?' and also talks, more significantly, about what he calls, or, rather, what he caricatures as, 'the dogma of the Ghost in the Machine.' " The behaviorists, he went on to explain, had maintained that there was no mind but only a body—Pavlov's dogs—and that all statements supposedly about the mind were covertly about the body. For them, thinking came down to merely a movement of the larynx, for when you think, you can feel your throat move, as if you were talking to yourself. Ryle became convinced that the behaviorists had not conquered the classic problem of the mind and the body, and went on to ask the classic question of how one gets from the mind to the body—how the two halves meet. When I feel a pain, how do I get, say, from the pinched nerve ends to sensing a pain; or when I am revolted by a bad smell, how does, say, the sulphur applied to my nostrils find its way to the inside of my mind? In "The Concept of Mind," Ryle, like the behaviorists, dismissed the commonly held theory, formulated by Descartes, among others, that the human person consists of two halves, the mind and the body, the body being material, or visible, audible, tastable, touchable, and smellable, and the mind being spiritual, or invisible, inaudible, untastable, untouchable, and unsmellable. He caricatured this dualism as the Ghost in the Machine. The Ghost-in-the-Machine men thought that when one said "I feel a pain" or "I see a flash," one was referring to a private mental act; such acts, unlike the movements of the body, were not verifiable except by the person who performed them. "Ryle, agreeing with the behaviorists, said that in fact we know perfectly well whether other people want things and hate things and know things," John continued. "You tell whether someone knows something by his actions. If I say 'I know how to read,' this doesn't say anything about the private state of my mind, invisible, inaudible, and so on, but just means that if you put a book in front of me I can read it. That kind of thing. There's a whole series of potential statements that can thus be 'unpacked'—Ryle's expression—at will. Ryle reached the triumphant conclusion that there are not two parts to the person but, rather, one entity, which is—well, it's not just body. This conclusion is not quite behaviorism—which doesn't recognize any mind—but posits a machine with a plus. As always, though, various people were soon as dissatisfied with Ryle as he had been with the behaviorists, and as the behaviorists had been with Descartes' Ghost-in-the-Machine man. For my part, I've never been very clear what's supposed to be wrong with 'The Concept of Mind,' except that I myself do believe that there is a ghost in the machine and I do not see how you can get on without one. I realize that this attitude is disreputable. I mean *absolutely* disreputable, not just unprofessional, for *today* my belief would be considered full of logical lacunae."

Because I wanted John to make a connection between Ryle and Strawson before I lost "The Concept" in the philosophical fog in my mind, I didn't pause to commiserate with him but pressed on. "How does Strawson improve on Ryle?" I asked.

"Strawson is very good in this, because he tries to preserve something from Descartes, on the one hand, and behaviorism revised by Ryle, on the other," John said. "He says that you can't understand the meaning of the word 'thinking' unless you can understand both its mental and its physical aspects. Take pain, for example. Descartes would have said that pain was only a mental occurrence; the behaviorists, with modifications from Ryle, said that pain was mere physical behavior—hopping up and down and going 'Ow!' or something like that. But Strawson says that you can't understand the word 'pain' unless you understand both its aspects: (1) the hopping around and (2) the feeling of pain; and that since *both* other people and I hop around when we are in pain, and since *both* also feel it, pain is checkable, is, in a way, objective. Thus, by including both these aspects in the concept of 'persons' (which in turn includes oneself and other people), he is able to add further pluses to the old machine. Strawson's on to something new, but all the philosophers here are niggling at one or two logical flaws in his chapter on persons, because most of them still tend to cling to behaviorism. There's one chap who carries behaviorism to such an extreme that he says that even to dream is merely to acquire a disposition to tell stories in the morning."

John rose to go. "I must get to the Bodleian before it closes," he said.

"One or two minutes more, John," I begged, and he accepted another half pint.

John told me a few things about Ryle. He came from a family of clerical dignitaries, and this probably explained his anticlericalism. He was educated in a "marginal public school" and at Queen's College, Oxford. He read both Greats and P.P.E., with enormous success, and managed at the same time to be on the rowing crew. The Senior

Common Room atmosphere—any Common Room would do—fitted him like a glove. He essentially liked drinking beer with his fellowmen. He pretended to dislike intellectual matters and publicized his distaste for reading, but he had been known to reveal encyclopedic knowledge of Fielding and Jane Austen. He loved gardening, and he also loved going to philosophical conventions, where his charm overwhelmed everyone. Young philosophers swarmed round him and he was too kind to them. He was a perfect Victorian gentleman; he would have been a sitting duck for Matthew Arnold's criticism of Philistinism, just as he actually was for Gellner's attack on idle philosophy. "Once, Ryle saw Isaiah Berlin coming from a performance of Bach's B-Minor Mass in the Sheldonian Theatre," John said. "Berlin was totally absorbed by the moving experience he had just undergone. Ryle shouted to him across Broad Street, 'Isaiah, have you been listening to some tunes again?'"

John put down his mug and stood up. "I really must go," he said. "I hope you won't assume from my hasty picture of Ryle that I don't like him. Actually, he's a very lovable man, and a highly intelligent one. I simply don't share his distrust of imagination. You know, Hume devoted very little space in all his works to the imagination. He said that it was only a peculiar faculty of mind that could combine primary experiences, enabling one to picture centaurs and mermaids. Well, Ryle has very much the same conception. His own images are mundane, like so many gateposts, firm in the ground." John waved and departed.

My next call was at Professor Ayer's rooms, in New College. He was sitting at his desk, writing, and after he had risen to greet me, he said, rather grandly, "Would you terribly mind waiting a bit? I'm just writing the last paragraph of my address." His professorship at Oxford was recent, and he still had to deliver his public inaugural lecture. I sat down across from the philosopher at work. His whole appearance was very striking. He was a rather small man, with a fine, triangular face and a slightly hooked nose. His curly hair, turning silver gray, was beautifully brushed; he seemed to have just come out of a barbershop, and had a sort of glamorous sheen that I had not theretofore met up with among the philosophers. He was smoking not a pipe but a cigarette, in a long holder. And now, instead of writing, he was leaning back in his chair and impatiently twisting his hands. He looked rather self-consciously thoughtful. Then he leaned forward and started writing rapidly, and a few moments later he laid down his pen. "There!" he exclaimed. "I have written my last sentence." Talking in a somewhat birdlike voice, he explained that his lecture surveyed postwar philosophy in England and interpreted the philosophical handwriting on the wall. If one thought of philosophers as idealists and realists, the idealists were out—had been since the demise of Josiah Royce (1916) and F. H. Bradley (1924). The army of philosophers thus lacked a soft, or idealist, wing, though it did have marginal people like Hare, Foot, and Anscombe. Its tough wing was made up of Wittgenstein, Wisdom, Austin, Ryle, Strawson, and Ayer himself, with his logical positivism. "But then," Ayer chirped, "it's very unprofessional to talk about philosophers as tough or tender, dry or wet. The whole idea is quite absurd, quite absurd." He would leave all that out of his final draft, he said.

We had a quick drink and then walked out of his beautiful college and up Catte Street and down the High to the Mitre Hotel for some dinner. On the way, I told Ayer which philosophers I had met. "A very good selection it is, too," he said. "Hampshire is the only other one I wouldn't miss if I were you." Hampshire had left Oxford to take Ayer's former chair at London University. "Why don't you catch the train with me to London this evening?" Ayer suggested. "I honestly think more Oxford philosophers will simply mix you up."

I said I would think about it over dinner.

We were soon dining, and during the meal I learned something about Ayer. Like the great Berlin, he was born of foreign parentage—his mother was Dutch, his father French-Swiss—and the father, like Berlin's, had been a timber merchant. "Though Isaiah's father was a successful timber merchant, mine wasn't," he added, playing with a silver watch chain and smiling. Ayer had been a scholar at Eton. He had come up to Christ Church in 1929; most of his Oxford contemporaries were rather undistinguished and had been forgotten. "It wasn't like the late thirties, which were really the vintage years of undergraduates," Ayer explained. "Oxford owes many of its great philosophers to the prewar harvest. Some of my friends, post-university acquisitions, are Left Wing playwrights and novelists—I mean people like John Osborne, Kingsley Amis, and John Wain. I just like their society and their way of living, and perhaps this explains why I find London much more exciting than Oxford—also, incidentally, why people sometimes connect me with the so-called Left Wing Establishment. As for my interests, I rather like rereading old novels. I only go through the new ones when they're written by people I know. I love being on television and I love watching it, and I do think the B.B.C. is a wonderful institution. They used to invite me at least once every six weeks to lecture or to appear on the intellectual discussion program 'The Brains Trust,' and they show those wonderful Westerns and programs like 'Panorama' and 'Tonight.' Both my stepdaughter, Gully, and I enjoy them very much. I actually don't think my television discussions interfere with my philosophy, because if I consistently worked a four-hour day on my subject I could produce a philosophical work every six months. Though I came to philosophy from Greats, as almost everyone here did—for that matter, all recent English philosophers except Russell, Wittgenstein, and Strawson were first Greek and Latin scholars—language qua language has never been a great passion of mine. This makes me temperamentally closer to Russell than to anybody else, and probably rather a freak at Oxford."

By the end of dinner, I had decided to catch the train with Ayer. He had a first-class return ticket, so I joined him, and we had a big carriage to ourselves. He pulled Amis's "Take a Girl Like You" out of his briefcase and laid it beside him, and then he put his legs up on the seat opposite and asked me, with a little smile, if I had any burning philosophical puzzles.

I said I really felt I was steaming away from the subject, but perhaps he could separate Wittgenstein and Austin for me, since they had now got linked in my mind like Siamese twins.

"Wittgenstein was interested in fundamental philosophical problems, Austin in language for its own sake," Ayer said. "Yet Austin, despite Gellner, was not a linguist, in any ordinary sense of the word; he was not interested in etymology or in the growth of language. He applied himself only to the function of words." He agreed that there was some truth in the view that philosophy for Austin was an impersonal investigation but for Wittgenstein was intensely personal. Indeed, Wittgenstein thought of himself as a living philosophical problem. "I think that before you finish your researches, you ought to read Norman Malcolm's memoir of Wittgenstein," Ayer said. "The book is in a sense a piece of destructive hagiography; the genre is hardly a model for anyone—in any case, it's not well written—but it does incidentally reveal a few things about the saint of postwar philosophy." Ayer also said that Wittgenstein often made friends not because of their intellectual gifts but because of their moral qualities, so that some of the stories passed around about him were a little fuzzy. Until the middle thirties little was known about Wittgenstein's ideas outside Cambridge, for to give his teaching continuity he preferred the same band of disciples year after year. And although some of his students' lecture notes were authorized and circulated, his ideas of the thirties were available only to the elect until the posthumous publication of his "Blue and Brown Books." Wittgenstein's pupils were very remarkable for their intelligence and sometimes for their reproduction of the Master's mannerisms. His eccentricity was contagious, and few people came in contact with him without acquiring a touch of his habits, which fitted him, as a genius, but did not always suit others, who were just great intellectuals. His most conspicuously distinguished pupil was Wisdom, but the closest to him was Miss Anscombe, whose brilliant translations of his German works would have been enough in themselves to earn her a place in the English pantheon of philosophers. Wittgenstein had a pathological fear that his ideas would be perverted by anyone who did not understand them fully. Although Ayer had never been a pupil of Wittgenstein's, he had pieced together a statement of Wittgenstein's current ideas and published it in *Polemic* in the forties. This had enraged the Cambridge philosopher, and for a while he showed a snarling hostility. "He had that side to his character also," Ayer said.

Ayer picked up "Take a Girl Like You" and started leafing through it. "I don't really think it's as good as 'Lucky Jim,'" he said. "In its way, that was a first-rate work." The train was jerkily jogging its way through the night. A look out the window was drowsy-making, but Ayer seemed very fresh.

I racked my sleepy brain for some more questions, and finally asked him whether there was one particular quality that all philosophers shared.

He was thoughtful for a moment and then said, "Vanity. Yes, vanity is the *sine qua non* of philosophers. In the sciences, you see, there are established criteria of truth and falsehood. In philosophy, except where questions of formal logic are involved, there are none, and so the practitioners are extremely reluctant to admit error. To come back to Austin, no one would deny the incisive quality of his mind, and yet when Strawson defeated him in an argument about Truth, it never seemed to have once crossed Austin's mind that he was the vanquished. To take another example, Russell attacks Strawson as though he were just another Oxford philosopher, without reading him carefully. But perhaps at his age Russell has a right to make up his mind about a book without reading it." Some of the philosophers were vain not only about their thoughts but about their personal influence, Ayer added. Wittgenstein dominated his classes, and, of course, Austin was an absolute dictator at his Saturday mornings.

"Is there anything like those groups now?" I asked.

"Well, I've just organized one," Ayer said. "We meet Thursday evenings, but I hope we do things in a more relaxed way than either Austin or Wittgenstein did." His Thursday meetings were very informal, he explained. There was no preordained leader, but to make the discussion effective only a handful of philosophers were allowed to join in. Disputation took place after dinner over whiskey or beer, and it centered on one subject, chosen for the term. The topic for the next term was "Time." " 'Truth' may be going out," Ayer said, "but 'Time' is coming back into the philosophical purview."

"What is the spread of Oxford philosophy?" I asked. "Is it practiced far and wide?"

"There are some exceptions, but I should say that you find at Oxford a fair representation of the kinds of philosophy that are studied in England, for the simple reason that Oxford staffs other universities with philosophers," Ayer said. "The real spread of Austin's linguistic philosophy is in the Dominions and the United States. For this, Ryle must take some of the responsibility. He likes Dominion and American students, and some people feel that he admits too many of them to Oxford for postgraduate work. Most students arrive already intoxicated with the idea of linguistic philosophy, but they soon find the scene much more diversified than they had expected. Not all of them profit by the discovery. So, many return to their countries to practice Austin's methods wholesale. The first-rate people in America, like W. V. Quine, at Harvard, and Ernest Nagel, at

Columbia, and Nelson Goodman, at Pennsylvania, don't give a curse for Oxford philosophy, but I should imagine there are more second-rate people doing linguistic analysis in America than in England and the Dominions put together."

We pulled into the Paddington station and, taking separate taxis, closed the philosophers' shop for the night.

I spent that night at John's. He was in bed when I arrived, and he had left for the British Museum library when I woke up, so I didn't get a chance to talk to him until the middle of the afternoon, when he returned from the Museum to make himself a sardine sandwich.

"What's on your philosophical agenda?" he asked, between bites.

"I'm having a drink with Hampshire," I said.

"You'll like him very much," John said. "He's still the idol of all the young Fellows of All Souls, where he spent many years before coming to London." He added that Hampshire was a great figure, who was not only still admired by All Souls men but looked up to by the whole of Oxford. This I could easily believe, because I remembered how highly he had been regarded in my own undergraduate days. He had also been passionate about Socialism in a youthful kind of way, which had made the undergraduate societies court him as an after-dinner speaker. Intelligent Oxford—at least, since the thirties—was Left Wing, and he had been a patron saint of the politically conscious university. His beliefs were reasoned, and he was emotionally committed to his ideas—a rare thing for an Oxford philosopher—and because his convictions were a matter of the heart as well as of the head, he had the rare ability to electrify clubs and societies. He might share his politics with Ayer, but Ayer had only recently returned to Oxford; besides, Ayer's Socialism was perhaps a little remote.

I asked John what he recalled about Hampshire.

"Well," he said, "as you probably know, he was a star pupil at his school—Repton—and was very much under the influence of one of its masters. Hampshire inherited his liberal principles from his mentor. Sometime in the early thirties, he came up to Balliol, where he fortified his Leftist views with wider reading. The last year of the war found him in the Foreign Office, and they didn't know what to make of him, because he used to start discussions by saying, 'The first thing to do is to find out if our foreign policy is Socialistic.' Hampshire claimed he started doing philosophy because he liked to argue, but in fact he avoided philosophical arguments."

Leaving John, I taxied to University College (this time, of London University), and found Professor Hampshire standing on the steps of the building where he had his office. His hands were clasped rather boyishly behind his back, and his curly blond hair was flying in the wind. "Hello!" he called. "I've just locked myself out of the office." He looked at me expectantly, as though I might have brought him the key. Taking hold of the handle of the door, he shook it vigorously and waited in vain for it to spring open. "I like the Oxford system of not locking doors," he said. "This sort of thing would never have happened to me there. There isn't a pub for some stretch." Nevertheless, we started in search of one. We came upon a Lyons Corner House, and ducked in for some tea, because Hampshire was thirsty. Sitting down, he surveyed the motley tea drinkers in the room and said, "This is what I like about London. You always feel close to the people." But the clatter and noise of Hampshire's people were so deafening that we were soon driven out.

We finally spotted a pub. When we had settled down in it, I asked him about his latest book, "Thought and Action."

"I'm not very good at summing up my own arguments," he said. "But my view of philosophy couldn't be further from Austin's. Like the ancient philosophers, I feel our function is really to advance opinions, and I think philosophy should include the study of politics, aesthetics . . . In fact, I think it should be an all-embracing subject. I also think English philosophers ought to take cognizance of Continental thought. I feel uncomfortable talking about philosophy. I don't really like to talk about things when I'm writing about them, and since I write philosophy, I try to avoid it in conversation as much as possible." But he went on to say he hoped that his new book had put him in the middle of the cultural stream of Europe. He said that, like Miss Murdoch, he was very much interested in Existentialism and literature, and, indeed, was now mostly working on aesthetics.

He and Ayer shared many friends, but his closest friend was Isaiah Berlin. He had just spent two weeks with him in Italy. "Isaiah, rather indirectly," he said, "does illustrate one great aspect of Oxford philosophy—the boon of just talking. As you know, he learned most of his philosophy at the feet of Austin. They were both at All Souls at the same time, in the thirties, and they used to sit around in the Common Room and talk philosophy day and night. During the war, once, Isaiah found himself in a plane, without Austin, and some mysterious thing happened that made him decide to give up philosophy." Hampshire thought that Berlin now regretted giving up philosophy, mainly because he missed the intellectual stimulation of talking. He had no one to talk with about his subject—the history of ideas. There were only one or two great historians of ideas, and they were not at Oxford, so Berlin was forced to work in solitude. Since his great conversational gifts could not be exercised in the service of his work, he relied on an occasional American postgraduate student who was studying ideas to bring him out of the isolation ward of his subject. The reason Berlin could not be counted as an Oxford philosopher was simple. He worked not at pure but at political philosophy. Where a pure philosopher might begin by asking the meaning of the word "liberty," Berlin opened one of his lectures by saying, "There are two sorts of notions of the word 'liberty'—negative and positive—in the history of thought. Kant, Fichte, Hegel believed . . ."

Hampshire rose to get another drink and was pounced upon by an African youth of about sixteen who had heard him speak in a public lecture hall. "Sir, do you mind if I join you?" he asked, edging his way over to our table.

"If you really want to," Hampshire said, sounding a little discouraged. He bought the boy a double whiskey and placed it before him.

The boy only sniffed at it, while discomfiting Hampshire with repeated compliments. "I heard, sir," he said, "you're a man of great vision, really very great vision, and you believe in equality—independence for Algerians and Maltese."

Hampshire asked him about his interests, and the boy said that he'd always wanted to be an engineer, but that since hearing Hampshire he had wondered whether he ought not to be a philosopher. "I'm torn in my conscience," he remarked, with a sigh.

Hampshire counselled him to be an engineer. "In that way, you can do more for your country," he said.

After a while, the boy left, but the philosophical calm—if it could be called that—of our conversation had been shattered. Hampshire moved his hands restlessly, and, after some nervous false starts, began reviewing the gallery of Oxford philosophers. His words were reeled off in the rapid fashion of All Souls conversation, and the philosophical lights whizzed past. "On occasion, Wittgenstein would say, 'Wittgenstein, Wittgenstein, Wittgenstein'—the 'W' Anglicized into a soft sound, instead of the Teutonic 'V'—'you are talking nonsense,' and he would smite his brow. He was the only person permitted—and no doubt the only person qualified—to utter that particular proposition. . . . Among other things, Austin was the chairman of the financial committee of the Oxford University Press—the biggest university press in the world. He occupied the post with an enveloping halo, and his terrifying efficiency raised him above all past and future chairmen. . . . Elizabeth Anscombe, in some ways, is like Wittgenstein— she even has his mannerisms. Her classes, like the Master's, are brooding séances. She wrote a series of letters to the *Listener* in which she opposed awarding former President Truman an honorary degree, because of his responsibility for dropping the atom bomb. She made an extraordinary speech at the concilium, saying, 'If you honor Truman now, what Neros, what Genghis Khans, what Hitlers, what Stalins will you honor next?' . . . Hare is a little puritanical in his views. . . . Miss Murdoch is elusive. . . . Warnock talks slowly—a thin sheath over his sharp mind for those who've only met him once. . . . Strawson, very exciting. Though sometimes he may build a spiral staircase for his thought out of hairsplitting distinctions. . . . Ayer, like Russell, well known as a philosopher, brilliant performer on television, who, among all his other achievements, can simplify. . . . Gellner's charge that these philosophers have things in common will not bear examination. Sociology can be bad history. It sometimes classifies its subjects of study indiscriminately. Gellner may be a victim of his own art. Good with the Berbers."

After saying goodbye to Hampshire, I returned to John's rooms and took from the shelf "Ludwig Wittgenstein: A Memoir," by Norman Malcolm, with a prefatory biographical sketch by Professor Georg Henrik von Wright, of the University of Helsinki. Because each meeting with a philosopher had made me more curious about Wittgenstein, I set myself the task of finding out more about him.

Ludwig Josef Johann Wittgenstein was born in 1889. His parents were Saxon, but at the time of his birth they were living in Vienna.

His paternal grandfather was a convert from Judaism to Protestantism; his mother, however, was a Catholic, and the child was baptized in her faith. His father was an engineer, whose remarkable intelligence and will power had raised him to a leading position in the steel-and-iron industry of the Austro-Hungarian Empire. Ludwig was one of eight children. Both of his parents were extremely musical, and their home was a center of artistic activity. He received his early education at home, learning mathematics and the clarinet, and acquiring a burning boyhood wish to become a conductor. At fourteen, he was sent to a school in Linz, and after three years there he was ready for the engineering course at the Technische Hochschule in Berlin. He completed his Berlin course in two years and went to England, where he registered at the University of Manchester as a research student. His first step on the path of philosophy was the reading of Bertrand Russell's "Principles of Mathematics," published in 1903, to which he turned when he wished to plumb the foundations of mathematics. After Russell, he read Gottlob Frege, the German mathematician, thus coming face to face with the two most brilliant exponents of the "new" logic. He sought out Frege in Jena, only to be directed by him to go back to England and study with Russell. By 1912, he was housed in Trinity College, Cambridge, whose walls also enclosed Bertrand Russell, G. E. Moore, and John Maynard Keynes. Young Wittgenstein was immediately befriended by them, and he found himself part of the golden years of Cambridge. He was there for eighteen months, and, in addition to his other work, did some psychological experiments in rhythm and music. Even though he was on intimate terms with the leading minds of England, he did not take to the relaxed atmosphere of Cambridge life. In the autumn of 1913, he visited Norway, and he returned there later that same year in a sort of intellectual huff, to live in seclusion near Skjolden; he soon became fluent in Norwegian. His father had died in 1912, and his stay at Manchester and Cambridge had simply driven him deeper into a depression whose history was as long as his life. "It is probably true that he lived on the border of mental illness," Professor von Wright says at the opening of his sketch. "A fear of being driven across it followed him throughout his life." The outbreak of the First World War found him a volunteer in the Austrian Army, and he eventually fought on both the eastern and southern fronts. For Wittgenstein, war was a time of personal crisis and of the birth of great ideas. At one moment he was calmed by Leo Tolstoy's ethical writings—which led him to the warm light of the Synoptic Gospels—and at the next he was excited by his own revolutionary views.

Wittgenstein's earthquake hit the philosophers of the twentieth century as hard as David Hume's cyclone—which swept away cause and effect from the human experience—had hit their eighteenth-century predecessors. The new philosophical shudder started at the Austrian front. One day in the middle of the war, while Wittgenstein was reading a newspaper in a trench, he was arrested by a sketch of a possible sequence of events in a car accident. As he studied it, he became aware that the diagram of the accident stood for a possible pattern of occurrences in reality; there was a correspondence between the parts of the drawing and certain things in the world. He noticed a similar correspondence between the parts of a sentence and elements of the world, and he developed the analogy, coming to regard a proposition as a kind of picture. The structure of a proposition—that is, the way in which the parts of a statement were combined—depicted a possible combination of elements in reality. Thus he hit upon the central idea of his "Tractatus": Language was the picture of the world. The "Tractatus" and the Wittgenstein revolution in philosophy were under way.

When Wittgenstein was captured by the Italians, in 1918, he had the manuscript of his first great philosophical work in his rucksack, and he was able to bring it through the war intact. He thought his masterpiece had solved all philosophical problems, and when the work was published (first in Germany, in 1921, and then in England, the following year), some leading minds agreed, with him, that philosophy had come to the end of its road. Wittgenstein, on the other hand, was at the beginning of his. Both his livelihood and his reputation were assured. He had inherited a large fortune from his father, his genius was proclaimed to the world, and he was free to live in leisure and intellectual preëminence. But such safe ways were not those of Ludwig Wittgenstein. In the first year after the war, he renounced his fortune, became indifferent to the success of the "Tractatus," and enrolled in a teachers' college in Vienna. When he had completed his education course, he taught in schools in Lower Austria for six years, wandering from one remote village to another. Being a schoolmaster enabled him to lead a life of simplicity and seclusion, but Wittgenstein was not at peace with himself or the world. He gave up the profession and for a time became a gardener, working mostly at monasteries, and, as he had done in the past, considered joining a religious order. Once more, however, the monastic life did not seem to be the answer. Terminating his restless wanderings, he returned to Vienna, and spent two solid years designing and constructing a mansion for one of his sisters. A modern building of concrete, steel, and glass, it provided an outlet for his particular architectural genius, and, according to Professor von Wright, "its beauty is of the same simple and static kind that belongs to the sentences of the 'Tractatus.'" But architecture could not contain Wittgenstein's soaring genius, and he spent some time sculpturing at a friend's studio. Again according to Professor von Wright, his sculpture of an elf has a perfection of symmetry that recalls the Greeks. Wittgenstein's period of withdrawal from philosophy was now nearing an end. In Vienna, he heard a philosophical lecture and decided that perhaps philosophy did have a little way to go, so he allowed his old friend Keynes to raise some money for his return to Cambridge. He arrived at his college in 1929, and presented his "Tractatus" as a dissertation for a Doctorate of Philosophy—a degree that was a negligible accolade to a philosopher with a worldwide reputation. A year later, at the age of forty-one, he was elected a Fellow of Trinity College, Cambridge.

As suddenly as a sketch of a car accident had inspired the ideas in "Tractatus," so a gesture of an Italian friend destroyed them. The gesture that divided Wittgenstein I from Wittgenstein II was made sometime in the year 1933. "Wittgenstein and P. Sraffa, a lecturer in economics at Cambridge, argued together a great deal over the ideas of the 'Tractatus,'" Professor Malcolm records. "One day (they were riding, I think, on a train), when Wittgenstein was insisting that a proposition and that which it describes must have the same 'logical form,' the same 'logical multiplicity,' Sraffa made a gesture, familiar to Neapolitans as meaning something like disgust or contempt, of brushing the underneath of his chin with an outward sweep of the fingertips of one hand. And he asked: 'What is the logical form of that?' Sraffa's example produced in Wittgenstein the feeling that there was an absurdity in the insistence that a proposition and what it describes must have the same 'form.' This broke the hold on him of the conception that a proposition must literally be a 'picture' of the reality it describes." It was many years before Wittgenstein II worked out his new ideas, but the old views, which at one time had finished philosophy forever, were discarded in the train.

Wittgenstein II, though he spent thirteen years at Cambridge, did not surround himself with any of the atmosphere of an English college. The stark simplicity of his way of living would have put any undergraduate to shame. His two rooms in Whewell's Court were like barracks; he did not have a single book, painting, photograph, or reading lamp. He sat on a wooden chair and did his writing at a card table. These two objects, with two canvas chairs, a fireproof safe for his manuscripts, and a few empty flowerpots, constituted the total furnishings of the room that served him as both study and classroom. His other concession to life was a cot, in the second room.

His classes were held late in the afternoon, and his pupils arrived carrying chairs from the landing. They always found the philosopher standing in the middle of the room, by his wooden chair. He was slender, of medium height, and simply dressed, habitually wearing a flannel shirt, flannel trousers, a leather jacket, and no tie. Unlike the other Fellows, he did not have any notes or set procedure for his lectures; he just sat on his wooden chair and, according to Malcolm, "carried on a visible struggle with his thoughts." His lectures were simply a continuation of his other waking hours; as always, he thought about problems and tried to find new solutions. The principal difference between his lonely hours and the lecture time was the difference between a monologue and a dialogue. He would direct questions to the members of the class and let himself be drawn into discussions, but whenever he sensed that he was standing on the edge of a difficult problem or a new thought, his hand would silence his interlocutor with a peremptory motion. If he reached an impasse or felt confused, he would say, "I'm just too stupid today," or "You have a dreadful teacher," or "I'm a fool." He worried about the possibility that his teaching might stop the growth of independent minds, and he was also besieged by a fear that he would not be able to last the period, but somehow he always managed to go on.

The years of the Second World War found Wittgenstein working as an orderly, first at Guy's Hospital, in London, and then in an infirmary at Newcastle-upon-Tyne. Toward the close of the war, he returned to Cambridge to take up the Chair of Philosophy. When Malcolm returned there to study with him, in 1946, he found Wittgenstein trying, with strenuous work, to dam the depression that always threatened to flood him. Wittgenstein was composing his "Philosophical Investigations" (which he kept on revising for the rest of his life). "One day," Malcolm recounts, "when Wittgenstein was passing a field where a football game was in progress, the thought first struck him that in language we play *games* with *words*. A central idea of his philosophy [in "Investigations"], the notion of a 'language game,' apparently had its genesis in this incident." At this time, most of his day was spent in teaching, talking, and writing the "Investigations." His only relief from the constant motion of his thoughts was an occasional film or an American detective magazine. But this was no opiate, and he ultimately felt compelled to tender his resignation to the Vice-Chancellor of the university. Late in 1947, when the decision was taken, he wrote to Malcolm, "1 shall cease to be professor on Dec. 31st at 12 P.M." He did. Now began the loneliest period of his never convivial life. He first moved to a guesthouse a couple of hours' bus ride from Dublin, where he lived friendless and in a state of nervous instability. He tired easily, and his work on "Investigations" went slowly and painfully. He wrote to Malcolm that he did not miss conversation but wished for "someone to smile at occasionally." After five months at the guesthouse, he migrated to the west coast of Ireland, where he became a legend among the primitive fishermen for his power to tame birds. But there was no rest for him. He went to Vienna, visited Cambridge, returned to Dublin, rushed again to Vienna, where a sister was now dangerously ill, proceeded from there to America to see the Malcolms, and was forced back to England and Cambridge by an undiagnosed illness. He was eventually found to have cancer. His father had been destroyed by this disease, and his sister was even then dying of it. He left for Austria and his family, but some months later he returned to England—this time to Oxford, which he quickly came to dislike. He called it "the influenza area" and "a philosophical desert." After spending some time at Miss Anscombe's house in Oxford, he visited Norway, only to return to Cambridge and live with his doctor. Never a happy man, he became convinced during the last two years of his life that he had lost his philosophical talent; he was also haunted by the suicides of three of his brothers. He died in April, 1951.

I read the last paragraph of Malcolm's memoir: "When I think of his profound pessimism, the intensity of his mental and moral suffering, the relentless way in which he drove his intellect, his need for love together with the harshness that repelled love, I am inclined to believe that his life was fiercely unhappy. Yet at the end he himself exclaimed that it had been 'wonderful!' To me this seems a mysterious and strangely moving utterance."

When John returned, he found me in a sombre mood.

"Yes," he said. "Wittgenstein was a tortured genius. He could have been a first-class conductor, mathematician, architect, or sculptor, but he chose to be a philosopher." He started leafing through "A Memoir," and read aloud: " 'A person caught in a philosophical confusion is like a man in a room who wants to get out but doesn't know how. He tries the window but it is too high. He tries the chimney but it is too narrow. And if he would only *turn around,* he would see that the door has been open all the time!' "

To both of us, this particular passage seemed to stand as an epitaph for Ludwig Wittgenstein.

Next morning, I rolled out of my makeshift bed and, with the help of my jottings, started writing furiously the conclusions of my researches. To my great surprise, complicated sentences streamed out of my typewriter and I discovered that I had a philosophical voice keyed somehow to the right pitch.

"Modern philosophy," I wrote, "has had two great pushes, one from Russell and one from Wittgenstein, and we're now waiting for another one. Like all philosophies, its claim to be heard rests on two assumptions: first, that what it says is true and lucid; second, that these particular truths are more satisfying than any alternative answers to the inquiring and reflective mind. Naturally, not all reflective minds will be better satisfied at Oxford than, say, in Paris, Moscow, New Delhi, or New York, but some clearly are. Oxford philosophers do not claim to be sages. In few cases, indeed, would the claim be credited if it should be made. By their own admission, they are not wiser than other men. They often assert that their researches do not lead to wisdom but only relieve certain feelings of puzzlement (which you are bound to have if you ask their questions). Once they have found answers to their questions, they go on living just as before, and, unlike their French contemporaries, many remain *dégagé;* they lead dons' comfortable lives in north Oxford (though, even so, a few manage to be evangelists, Socialists, or great eccentrics). This has led Gellner to ask what the point of their activities can be, since they seem to cure only a disease they have induced in themselves and, in many cases, in their students. Why should one pay philosophers, he asks, if philosophy really, as Wittgenstein said, 'leaves the world as it is'? Gellner's is a mistaken objection. Certainly many philosophers are unadventurous, prosaic, and boring, but there are also Strawsons and Ayers and plenty of others who are not. Whatever they may do in their private lives, it cannot correctly be said that in their work they 'leave the world as it is.' If one man begins to see more clearly how the *rest* of the world is, then the world is not as it was. One man sees more truth than was seen in the past; the more widely this truth is disseminated, the more the world is changed. Indeed, once one considers this, Gellner's criticism seems absurd. For philosophy has never changed the world except by bringing to consciousness in the minds that engage in it certain truths that they did not know (or did not know clearly) before. Oxford philosophers are fond of quoting a remark of Wittgenstein's to the effect that there need be nothing in common among all the members of a class of things called by the same name. If we must generalize about the Oxford philosophers and their subject, their philosophy is essentially agnostic, not in respect to the question of God's existence but in relation to many of the great problems whose definitive solution has in the past been taken as the aim of philosophy: questions like whether life is meaningful, whether history has a purpose, whether human nature is good—in fact, all the questions that have to be asked when a man reflectively considers the question 'How should I live?' It is true that most Oxford philosophers are not agnostic in religion; on the contrary, several are Catholic or Protestant communicants. But they regard these matters as being outside their philosophy. As men, they decide to answer these questions in one way; as philosophers, they teach and develop techniques that are neutral in respect to the different answers to them.

"Oxford philosophers tend to talk chiefly to each other—and, in cases like Wittgenstein's, to themselves. These practitioners are highly technical (even if they claim they make a 'technique of being non-technical'). There are exceptions: Ayer is one; another is Hampshire, who on some subjects—especially literary subjects, as opposed to philosophical ones—succeeds in being illuminating to the simple. Still, most of the philosophers go on thinking that technical philosophy is a good thing, necessary in order to keep the subject from 'popularization,' which they interpret as oversimplification or quackery. The pity is that their insistence on professionalism means that 'ordinary men' are left not without any philosophy at all but with old, dead, or quack varieties of it. Oxford philosophy, by comparison with the past, is non-systematic. Where traditional practitioners thought it right to deal with questions like 'What is Truth?' Oxford philosophers are liable to say, following the later Wittgenstein, 'Look at all the different ways the word "true" is used in ordinary speech.' (They refuse to look into the uses of words in extraordinary speech, like poetry, because English philosophy has been dominated since Hume by a prosaic contempt for the imagination.) When you have considered all the ways 'true' is used in ordinary speech, they say, you have understood the concept of 'Truth.' If there is a further question lingering at the back of your mind ('But all the same, what *is* Truth?'), this is the result of a mistake—a hangover from reading earlier philosophers. This approach—philosophy as the study of language rather than as the means of answering the big questions about life and the universe—which is basically that of the later Wittgenstein, has given Oxford philosophy a tendency to formlessness. Until recently, the body of philosophical thought has existed mainly in a vast number of small articles minutely considering a few uses of some single concept. Only the aesthetic sense of some of its practitioners—Wittgenstein I, Ayer, Hampshire, Strawson, and a few others—has kept it from overwhelming diffuseness.

"Now there is a change coming. The Oxford school is breaking up; all the signs are that there isn't going to be an orthodoxy much longer—that things are going to get eccentric again. Austin is no more, and at the moment Ryle is not producing. Strawson is going in for talking about metaphysics in the old vein, and there is every indication that the Wittgenstein wave is petering out rather rapidly. In the ten years since Ryle tried to solve the mind-body problem by a vast number of small chapters on different psychological concepts in 'The Concept of Mind,' Oxford philosophy has begun to develop its own system builders. Probably the strict discipline of the late Austin helped induce guilt about the looseness and untidiness that these uncoördinated researches—each one precise and tidy—were creating in the subject as a whole. Two recent books, Hampshire's 'Thought and Action' and Strawson's 'Individuals,' offer quite systematic approaches to some of the most puzzling traditional problems in philosophy: the value of freedom of thought and the relation of intelligence to morality, in the first; the problem of sense data and the mind-body puzzle, in the second. The new systematic quality comes from a recent insight: that while linguistic philosophy is the study of language, certain wider truths *can* be deduced from the conditions that must be presupposed if there is to be language at all—or language of the kind we have. On propositions deduced from the statement of such conditions, necessary truths (like the relation between the mind and the body) can be built systematically. The non-systematic decades may have been an aberration—partly, no doubt, owing to the tendency of philosophers to imitate Wittgenstein II and his stylistic lapses from the poetic and architectural sensibility he displayed in the 'Tractatus.' As Shakespeare said of the pedants in 'Love's Labour's Lost,' 'They have been at a great feast of languages, and stolen the scraps. O! they have lived long on the alms-basket of words.' But then, as the proverb, more than two thousand years old, has it, 'Those that study particular sciences and neglect philosophy'—however defined and however studied—'are like Penelope's wooers, who made love to the waiting-women.' "

These sentences were no sooner out of my typewriter than they seemed to have been written by a stranger. Reading them over, I couldn't shake loose the feeling that they were one more walker on that common street where on a morning stroll I'd first met Lord Russell.

Originally appeared, under the heading "Onward and Upward with the Arts," as "A Battle Against the Bewitchment of Our Intelligence" in The New Yorker, *December 9, 1961. Reprinted in "Fly and the Fly-Bottle," Atlantic-Little, Brown, Boston, and Weidenfeld & Nicolson, London, 1963.*

TWO

The Train Had Just Arrived
at Malgudi Station

When I was visiting my home, in New Delhi, a while back, I considered making a journey to the state of Mysore, a thousand miles to the south, to see R. K. Narayan, the writer, but my pilgrimage got lost in my empty pockets. I wanted to meet Narayan not because he had written eleven novels and produced two volumes of short stories, not because he was acclaimed the best novelist in India (fiction-writing is a fledgling art in my country), not even because he had the reputation of being something of a saint (there are too many poseurs in Hindustan), but for an almost obsessive personal reason. I was drawn to Narayan because his books, though they were written in English, a language foreign to most of his countrymen and also to most of his characters, had the ring of true India in them. He had succeeded where his peers had failed, and this without relying on Anglicized Indians or British caricatures to people his novels. My fascination with his art was personal, for, as I had written him, "like you, I find myself, but only now and again, writing as an Indian for an audience thousands of miles away, spectators with moods and habits so different from our own that it is not easy to be more than a tourist guide to them." For me, the magic of his unpretentious, almost unliterary novels was his astonishing marriage of opposite points of the compass. My wish to know him was fulfilled in New York, when I picked up my telephone one summer afternoon and heard a soft voice from the other end: "Um! This is Narayan. 'If the mountain will not come to Mohammed, Mohammed will go to the mountain.' You know, we are living practically next door to one another. I am just a couple of blocks away from you. Um! Can I come over?"

Within a few minutes, Narayan was at my apartment, on East Fifty-eighth Street. A neither too stout nor too lean figure, he strolled in rather boyishly. One shoulder appeared to be lower than the other, and his lilting walk recalled the end of the Bharat Natyam, an Indian classical dance in which the performer finishes by returning to the place where he took his first step, his shoulders gracefully preceding his legs in a swaying motion. Narayan dropped into my best armchair and, with a smile revealing a great many polished teeth, said, "I feel at home. Um! Do you?" I had to laugh.

Narayan, who was fifty-five, had a sharp face, with full lips, a slightly hooked nose, and a very impressive forehead, capped with thinning gray hair. The most noticeable thing about his face, however, was his eyes, impish and mischievous, peering out from behind thick, black-rimmed glasses. His body was loosely, carelessly clothed in non-descript gray trousers, a tweed jacket, and a white shirt, which was oddly finished off with an improvised tie pin, a piece of red thread wound around one shirt button. If it were not that he had the wheat-colored complexion of a Brahman, he might pass unnoticed in India as an anonymous member of the roving multitude; only a constant expression of innocence and a certain elusiveness about him saved him from seeming bland.

I asked him if he would like a cigarette. He flashed his teeth in a quick smile and said, "Once upon a time I used to smoke, and then one day it struck me how ridiculous it was for a grown-up man to have fire between his teeth—now puffing, now inhaling. Once this thought had lodged in my mind, I couldn't light a cigarette. It seemed so silly that I broke into a laugh at the thought of it, which was actually a tickle." He flashed his teeth again. "New York is the absolute yend in the summer," he said. "I should come here wonly in the winter. What is this—Consolidated Edison digging the ground, jets overhead, soot in the air, trucks running people down, no place to walk, and no children in the streets? It's hotter than the inside of an engine. I shall leave very soon. Oh, Lard, all one can do in this city is barricade oneself in an air-conditioned room. It is the absolute yend." As Narayan talked on, I discovered that he spoke a certain sort of Indian English; he made some of his "o"s into "a"s, and prefixed "y" and "w," respectively, to words beginning with "e" and "o." It gave his English a soft, balmy tone.

"You know, it's a beautiful season in my Mysore now," he continued. "The monsoon is just breaking, and the winter breeze is yeverywhere." Narayan went on to explain that Mysore, the capital of the onetime princely state of Mysore, is about twenty-five hundred feet above sea level. The Cauvery, one of the biggest rivers in India, coils around the capital, so one cannot travel eight or ten miles away from the city in any direction without coming upon it. Mysore has probably not changed in at least a thousand years, and the landscape of the place has not yet been manicured by industrial implements; the countryside encircles Mysore with a dense and snug forest. The only inroad the twentieth century has made in this town is in the installation of underground drainage, water tanks, and electric power. Mysore nestles at the foot of a hill a thousand feet tall, which has a temple on its crest. Both hill and temple are named after the goddess Chamundi, the patron deity of the two hundred and fifty thousand inhabitants of Mysore. Narayan then told me that when the demon Mahisha, taking the form of a buffalo, threatened the world with destruction—he had the ability to produce demon buffaloes as numerous as the drops of his blood—the goddess Chamundi came charging on a lion with swords and lances. She managed to kill the fiend, and her lion licked up all his blood before it could multiply itself into countless likenesses of him. A millennium ago, King Raya Chamundi, who took the name of the savior, carved out a thousand steps in the side of the hill for the convenience of her votaries. As a youth, Narayan often ran up the steps, taking thirty or forty minutes to reach the temple. "Comparatively recently, they also built a five- or six-mile road leading up to the temple," Narayan said proudly. "The way is well lighted, and at night the home of Chamundi gleams like a lighthouse."

I asked Narayan whether he would like some tea.

"A little later," he said, taking out of his pocket a small Kodak film box. "I carry my lifeblood in this." He shook the box and then took out an areca, or betel nut, which he sucked happily, like a child relishing a sweet. "You know, I find that my pen moves only when I have a betel nut in my mouth," he said. "Without one, I can neither think nor write."

I asked him if he had always lived in Mysore.

"No, no, we are not Kannadiga, yindigenous to Mysore," he said. "We are Tamilians, from the province of Madras. And our family's ascent from a village to Madras, the capital city, took many generations. I have no sense of history, but I know that my initial 'R' stands for Rasipuram, the village which must have housed my ancestors." Neither he nor his characters are villagers, he said; rather, they are *hommes de ville*. Narayan has no illusions about noble rustics. As far as he is concerned, villagers' lives are monotonous and sedentary, and there is no story waiting in a village, the birthplace of a good novel being a halfway house between a static village and an anonymous industrial city. "By the time I came into the family, my kinsmen were happily urbanized," Narayan said. "In fact, soon after my arrival, my father, Krishnaswami Iyer—'K' in my name—followed many of his classfellows from Madras University to idyllic Mysore, where there were greater job opportunities. My mother, Gnanambal, who was very weak and was about to have another child, took my brothers and sisters to Mysore, but since I was very small she left me behind in Madras with my grandmother, whom I called Ammani—that is, Madam. I soon established myself as her favorite, and was still living there long after my mother was well."

Narayan's first novel, "Swami and Friends," published in 1935, when he was twenty-nine, grew out of his urchin days at Ammani's. Until this book was written, his surname was Narayanswami, but the publishers, not wanting the novel to be confused with an autobiography, persuaded Narayanswami to drop the "swami" ("religious leader") from his name. The plain "Narayan" has always served as both his first and his last name, since, according to custom, he could not be called by the appellation of his father or of a village. He was the only child in the house, and Ammani, instead of disciplining him, gorged him with sweetmeats and, when he was especially good, with betel nuts. Kunjappa ("Little Fellow"), as she called him, grew up into a wild, idle lad who, in preference to studying his lessons in arithmetic and English grammar, swung like a monkey in a tree from one rafter of Ammani's tall, spreading house to another. "The house was built around an enormous Indian-style courtyard," Narayan told me. "Its doors were thick teakwood slabs four feet wide and six or seven feet high, covered with studs and ornaments, and flanking the doors were matching smooth pillars crowned with little brass figures of monkeys, elephants, eagles, and pigeons. I would climb up the columns, jump from door to door, raise myself to another tier by the balustrade, and wander from one empty room to another. Ammani could never find me." Kunjappa did put in fairly regular appearances at the Christian Mission School, where he learned to love the Hindu gods simply because the chaplain extolled the Christian God and made fun of what Narayan called "His Indian brothers and sisters." The chaplain ridiculed Ganesha for having an elephant's head, Hanuman for having a monkey's body, and Krishna for habitually stealing butter and chasing girls. "What sort of gods are these?" the chaplain would say. And when Kunjappa once boldly asked the chaplain "Why was Christ crucified if He was so much better?" the missionary slapped the blasphemous boy and sent him spinning out of the room. "I was thinking the other day why it is that I can't write a novel without Krishna, Ganesha, Hanuman, astrologers, pundits, temples, and *devadasis,* or temple prostitutes," Narayan said. "Do you suppose I have been trying to settle my score with the old boy? Um! In any case, that has turned out to be my India."

Kunjappa's father, who was the headmaster of the government school in Mysore, finally got news of the boy's idleness, and sent for him. He took his son by the ear and gave him a tour of his own extensive library. Kunjappa was not impressed. At his new school and then at Mysore University, Narayanswami sat daydreaming, looking out of the window at trees and passersby, listening to nothing, reading practically nothing; the only book that made an impression on his vegetating mind was Rabindranath Tagore's romantic tract against academic education. He failed his intermediate and baccalaureate examinations several times, finally managing to receive his Bachelor of Arts degree at twenty-four—a shameful age for an Indian. His elder brother Srinivas had received his at eighteen, and many Madrasi boys were Bachelors of Arts at fifteen or sixteen. (Narayan's long college career provided material for his second novel, "Bachelor of Arts," whose publication, in 1937, marked the beginning of his reputation as an author in England.)

I asked Narayan again whether he would like some tea.

"If it isn't too much bother," he said.

I invited him to walk with me to a nearby shop for some pastry.

He was disappointed that we were not going to do our errand by subway. "You know," he said, wiping his forehead with his sleeve, "I like travelling underground, because the people there remind me of the crowds in our bazaars. Except that the subterranean travellers are much more intense and purposeful—they are always going to some definite job in a rush."

In the pastry shop, Narayan quickly made friends with the sales-lady, who was Swedish, and he accepted an impulsive invitation she extended to him for dinner the following week. Aside to me, he said, "Yevery day I like to meet a new person." His innocent face lighted up at the sight of pineapple pastry, and he carried it back to the apart-ment himself.

When I had put some water on to boil, he asked me if I had read his story "A Breach of Promise," and I told him I had. "That was almost my first tale," he said. "It is very truthful—autobiographical, you know. It concerns a student, myself, who fails a lot of examinations." The story is set in Chamundi Temple. There is an Indian superstition that a perfect work of art invites the wrath of the gods. To placate the deities, the ancient Indian sculptors chopped off a toe or a finger of a statue. Similarly, the beauty of the perfect temple is carefully marred by two monstrous gargoyles that squat on its tower. They have enor-mous rolling tongues, flashing eyes, and ugly noses. The hero of "A Breach of Promise," resolving to take his life, scales the hill and then the temple tower, and straddles a gargoyle's tongue, which is as large as a platform. "In reaching the tongue of death, he has somehow skinned his elbow, and just when he has poised himself for the big jump, the sight of blood on his arm frightens the boy, and he shuffles back into the room of the tower," Narayan explained. "I like to con-clude my stories with such things when I can. I don't remember if, after one of my exam failures, I got as far as the gargoyle's tongue, but I do remember scribbling my name in charcoal on the wall of the tower room, for posterity. I never had any intention of committing suicide, so the whole thing was farcical. That's the way life is in our temples and our houses."

The water reached its boiling point in a snoring whistle, and Narayan jumped. When I explained the simple mechanism of the kettle, he said, "Oh, Lard, what is this modernity, all these gadgets and such?"

I poured him out some tea and sliced the pastry for him. He drank the tea in long, noisy sips and ate with two fingers. He has small, feminine hands, and as he lifted his cup, his little finger flew out. (His hand looked more natural than its genteel counterparts in Kensington spinsterdom.) He wore two rings, on the last two fingers of his left hand; one had a sapphire inset, and the other was a plain gold band. I asked him about them.

"This sapphire one is an heirloom, a hundred years old," he said. "I received it on my wedding day. My father-in-law, Nagswara Iyer, who, incidentally, was also a headmaster, gave it to me, and he got it from his father-in-law. The gold band I received from my wife at her deathbed. Her name was Rajam." As he spoke her name, tears came into his eyes.

I poured him another cup of tea, and for some minutes he remained silent.

It seemed to me after a while that he wanted to talk about his wife. "How did you meet her, Narayan?" I asked.

He cleared his throat, took a bite of pastry, munched it, and said, smiling his prompt smile, "I escarted my elder sister Janaki from Mysore to nearby Coimbatore, where her husband was a practicing advocate. While I was standing at the carner of the equivalent of a big-city mall there, I saw a girl about eighteen. She was tall and slim and had classical features; her face had the finish and perfection of sculpture. She walked past me as in a dance. I kept looking for a gargoyle or some such imperfection, but there was none. It was spring and I was twenty-eight. I suppose that had something to do with my falling completely and instantly in love with her. But when I myself, instead of my parents, approached her mother and father, they were outraged at my picking my own wife, the unconventionality of my love. But they asked me what was going to be my profession, what means I had for supporting a wife. I said simply, 'I write.' In those days, no one could own up to writing stories in India. It was the most penniless thing one could do. After some pressure from my family, Rajam's parents did consult their astrologer, who immediately declared that my horoscope showed that I would be either a polygamist or a widower. I forced the issue. I found another astrologer, who went into ecstasies at the sight of rupees. He was an accomplished debater and defeated the other pundit, and Rajam's parents, realizing that I was from a good and large family, and that, whatever happened to me, she would always be taken care of, gave in to the marriage."

Rajam and Narayan were a happy couple. Like a good Indian wife, she did not show public affection for Narayanswami, and her attention was distributed equally among his mother, his father, and his three younger brothers—Balram, Ramachandar, and Laxman—who were still at college. (Laxman is now one of the better-known cartoonists in India.) He also had two sisters, Janaki and Alamelu, and two older brothers, Srinivas and Pattabhi, but the sisters had married and were settled in homes of their own, and the older brothers had moved away (one to take a job in a fertilizer plant, the other to take a government position), so Rajam was spared the need to spread her affection further. Narayanswami spent most of his time sitting and talking with his family, and after the birth of his daughter, Hema, he spent hours every day watching her in her cot or on her mat. Now and again, he stole a couple of hours to do a little writing in an upstairs room, but even then he called out for his wife every half hour or so to bring him Hema and some coffee. Rajam could not read English, the only language in which Narayan found he could write. Nevertheless, she took a keen interest in his hundreds of rejection slips and, later, in the reviews of his books—"Swami and Friends," "Bachelor of Arts," and, in 1939, his third novel, "The Dark Room," which dealt with a Hindu wife who submits passively to a positive or inconsiderate (depending on which side of the Suez one lives on) husband.

"But the prophecy of her family astrologer turned out to be right," Narayan said sadly. "My father-in-law, who was quite well-to-do, wanted to settle a house on Rajam, and one day he came up from Coimbatore and we went around searching for a place. We looked through a number of remodelled houses, and late that afternoon we happened upon one that seemed suitable. It had the solidity of an wold house and the bright cleanness of a new one. While my father-in-law and I were canvassing the land, Rajam went into the bathroom, an outhouse, to wash. She did not rejoin us. I got worried and walked back to the bathroom. Rajam was pounding away at the shut door, screaming, 'Someone open it! Someone open it!' I gave the door one or two hard kicks and Rajam fell out in my arms. She was convulsed with sobs, and her face was a feverish red. She cried out that it was the dirtiest place she had ever been in. She said a fly had settled on her lips. I took her home, but she wouldn't yeat anything. She kept washing herself, time and time again. By the evening, she had a temperature, and she remained in bed with typhoid for twenty days. It was 1939, and no one had heard of chloramphenicol. Rajam died. A fly had killed an almost five-year-old marriage."

Narayan said that he considered following her onto the funeral pyre, but there was Hema, the very likeness of Rajam. For the next few years, Narayan battled with the fact of death. He periodically left Mysore for Madras, where he met a lawyer who claimed to communicate with the dead through so-called automatic writing. The lawyer transcribed messages from Rajam.

"He was no hoax," Narayan said. "For one thing, he wrote three or four thousand words in a half hour, and no man can compose so much so quickly. For another, Rajam, through the automatic writing, gave proofs of her yexistence by such precise instructions as 'Give the brooch lying in the tortoise-shell box on the third shelf of my mother's cupboard to such-and-such a beggar woman.' When she entered the room to dictate, the air current changed perceptibly. I could breathe her presence. Since that time, I have lost all distinction between life and death."

After a moment's silence, he continued. "But the therapy did not really yend until I published my fourth novel, 'The English Teacher,' in 1945. It was all about my life with Rajam." The concluding chapters of the book were concerned with the psychic experiments, and the English critics lashed out at them. "Of course," Narayan said, "the reviewers did not realize that the whole story was autobiographical—that I myself had been a witness to the experiments. But what's the use?" He sighed. "You don't believe it, yeither."

I asked Narayan to stay for dinner. He said, "Thank you very much. Thank you very much. But no. I'm a vegetarian and am completely South Indian in my eating habits. When I eat out in this country, I mostly go hungry." He said he would dine with me some other day, when I had mastered his dietary ways.

I walked Narayan home. We strolled half a block out of our way to wave goodbye to the saleslady in the pastry shop. "Isn't it lucky that I eat yeggs?" he said, smiling with his eyes and teeth. "Wotherwise, I would never have gone there and made friends with the Swedish lady." At the corner of Third Avenue and Fifty-eighth Street, a new building was going up. Narayan took one look at the Consolidated Edison workers who were digging up the street, and put both his hands up to his ears. He didn't take them down until we had turned east on Fifty-seventh Street. "Oh, Lard, this is equally noisy," he said, glaring at the two-way traffic.

To take his mind off the noise and America, I said, "Narayan, why is it that your books don't show a trace of Western influence?" I told him I had also been struck by the fact that he hardly ever touched on politics, of either British or free India. Except for a Mr. Brown and an American journalist in "The Guide," published in 1958, I could recall no foreigners in his books, I said, and his Indians had the logic and idiom, and the ambitions, not of the scientific West but of the almost agrarian East.

"To be a good writer anywhere, you must have roots—both in religion and in family," Narayan replied thoughtfully. "I have these things. I am rooted to the right triangle of Madras, Mysore, and Coimbatore, none of them much more than a couple of hundred miles distant from the others." For the first forty-nine years of his life, he had stayed within the boundaries of the triangle, he said as, taking advantage of a green light, we dashed across Second Avenue, and he had passed most of his life in the communism of the joint-family life, where everything was owned in common and no one asked questions about income.

"But must one have such ties?" I asked. "What about the expatriate Steins and Hemingways, and all those Irish writers who have worked successfully away from their homeland?"

"I have not read many of them, but I am sure they have nothing to say to me," Narayan said emphatically. They could have had no religion, no values, no feelings, he went on. His greatest test of a good author was his "readability." Tolstoy, Joyce, and Faulkner were all "bores." He had read a hundred pages of "War and Peace" and could not understand why E. M. Forster considered Tolstoy a happy god who could play with the entire world. Shakespeare was readable and fun only in paperbacks, where there were no footnotes and things like that. There were no Indian novelists to speak of. Indian writers were either too "Westernized" or too "deliberate." "I can't like any writing that's deliberate. If an author is deliberate, then I can't read him—he's not readable," Narayan concluded.

We paused at the Fifty-seventh Street approach to the Queensboro Bridge. There was an unbroken stream of rush-hour cars. "This is the worst intersection in New York," Narayan said. "Why can't they put more policemen here? This crossing paralyzes me. My two favorite avenues are on the West Side, around Twenty-third Street. I like the Ninth Avenue, which is like Madras, and the Tenth, because it reminds me of Bombay. Why do you suppose that is?"

I said I didn't know, since there could be no architectural resemblance; perhaps it was because of the children and the slums. "But then you should like Hemingway," I said, picking up our conversation about good writers. "Isn't he immensely readable?"

Narayan broke into a wheezing laugh. "You must allow me my contradictions. I contradict myself all the time."

"Do you find Hemingway deliberate?"

"From the little I have read, I shouldn't think so." We waded across the bridge approach. "I don't read much, because I don't want to be influenced. I suppose my wonly love is Graham Greene. I've read most of his things, because he's my champion and my best English friend." I knew that it was thanks to Greene's support that Narayan was first published. "Novels may bore me, but never people. To me, all individuals are like characters in my own stories, with whom one has to live for many pages of writing, even if they stop being interesting after a while."

We reached the apartment house that Narayan was living in, on East Fifty-seventh Street. He invited me into his vestibule, which was a little larger than a telephone booth. "You may have gathered that I'm not an academic sort," he said, his words rebounding from the walls. "In fact, I don't like graduate students writing theses on me. They always try to read meaning into my books, trace a theme, relate this character to that, make a connection between hero and hero. I wish they would leave me and my books alone. And now I must go and prepare my dinner upstairs, which for me here is not a family ritual but a lonely meal." Breaking into his smile (very much like Rosie, the heroine of "The Guide," whose smile he had called an "open sesame" to her future), he added, "For twenty-seven years, except for short periods when I was away, I ate three meals a day from the same silver platter, which I'd received at my marriage. The platter was too heavy to carry across to America." He said it would embarrass him to have company while he cooked and ate his vegetarian meal, so I made arrangements to visit him the next evening.

As I walked back to my flat after three or four hours with Narayan, I couldn't help marvelling at him. He seemed to carry his home, his cosmos, on his back, as did the ageless swamis.

I dropped in on Narayan after dinner on the following day. He was so inept with mechanical devices that he kept his finger firmly on the buzzer unlocking the front door until he saw me step out of the lift on his floor.

"Woh, you've arrived," he said, his eyes twinkling. He showed me into his one-room apartment, which he was borrowing from Harvey Breit, the former assistant editor of the New York *Times Book Review,* who used it for a retreat from a larger apartment, on Park Avenue. For America, the room seemed bare; there was a painting by William Walton (given to Breit by Hemingway), a framed article of Breit's ("The Haunting Drama of Dylan Thomas") from the magazine section of the New York *Times,* and a small collection of books. The floor was covered with a neutral bluish-green carpet, and for furniture there were a couple of canvas chairs, a studio couch, and a small table, which was loaded like a mule with the results of Narayan's day's shopping—Uncle Ben's rice, Aunt Jemima's pancake mix, a variety of Indian herbs and spices, and jars of pickled onions and mangoes. Narayan rapturously explained that during his morning walk he had found a most splendid international food shop at Twenty-eighth Street and Third Avenue. "They carry all the Indian things except quality betel nuts," he said. "I made some good friends there, with Indians who come there regularly for supplies. Incidentally, once I meet a person I always like to keep in touch. I've spent most of my days in my room telephoning all my friends and acquaintances in this city. I write everyone's name and telephone number in my diary as soon as I get to know him. I have all sorts of friends. There are the Breits, who give me hospitality in America, and Santha and Faubion Bowers, who love me for myself, and Donald Keene, professor of Japanese at Columbia, who visited me in Mysore." There were John and Jane Gunther, who, he said, liked his novels; Greta Garbo, who took him to be a specimen of the mystic East; Cal Whipple, editor of *Life*'s International Edition, who thought him a good reporter on India; Marshall Best, the editorial vice-president of the Viking Press, who was interested in him as an author on his list; Helen Strauss, the literary agent with the William Morris Agency, who regarded him as a valuable client; Allene Talmey, of *Vogue*, who "memorized" his books; Lyle Blair, of the Michigan State University Press, who first published him in America and didn't want Narayan to be "commercialized." Then, he had scores and scores of acquaintances (most of whom had not read his books) in the New York Indian colony, including people in government service, in commerce, and in the universities. "Like true reality, I am many things to many men," he said. "Shall we sit down?"

I leaned back in one of the canvas chairs; he perched on the other. Narayan was barefoot. He proudly held up his pair of shoes for my inspection. "I got these at Saxone, in England, five years ago. The shoes have been resoled only once." He put the worn shoes down affectionately and offered me a betel nut. I took one and began to chew it, whereupon he admonished me to suck it slowly. Narayan was dressed in an ill-fitting brown suit he had picked up that morning for forty-three dollars at a clothing store on lower Seventh Avenue.

"I have written the first page of my new novel today, while waiting in the shop for my suit to be altered," he said. The story had begun to form in his head when one of his friends, a lawyer, was handling a lawsuit that a wasteful son had brought against his indulgent father, a prosperous sweetmeat dealer, to get more money from him. In the new novel, Narayan's merchant was to be similarly taxed in both pocket and endurance by his debauched son, until he decided to abandon his boy and do penance for the sins of his ancestors and progeny by building a temple. But in the path of godly service, too, he was to run into difficulties. He would be swindled by corrupt contractors and prehensile bricklayers. "Such are the ways of the world and of my novels," Narayan said, chuckling. "You might say my sweetmeat dealer is defeated in his purpose by the scratch of silver rupees on the elbows of anyone and yeveryone. The actual sweetmeat dealer may build a temple yet." Narayan laughed. The strange thing was, he said, that actual people, without ever setting eyes on his books, did fall in line with their plots. There was the remarkable instance of Margayya, the central character of "The Financial Expert," published in 1952. In the first pages of the book, he was almost the exact double of a real Margayya. Narayan had observed this kindly financial wizard at work in the shade of a banyan tree, which he used as an office in lending small sums of money to various illiterate peasants, who squatted in a semicircle around him. They preferred his personal, if antiquated, style of lending money—always for a small fee—to the cold formalism of the Central Coöperative Land Mortgage Bank, around the corner. Margayya becomes a fictional character when the bank officials, feeling their jobs and system threatened by his methods, try to drive him out of business, and when his son, Balu, in a tantrum, throws his father's only account book into a drain. A deity answers Margayya's prayers for assistance by making him the publisher and salesman of a pornographic book, "Bed Life, or, The Science of Marital Happiness"—or, as Margayya euphemistically retitles it for publication, "Domestic Harmony." "The choice of a smutty profession for Margayya was an extraordinary premonition on my part," Narayan now told me gleefully. "I saw him recently. He was hawking books of popular film tunes, which are the only best-sellers we have in India. Hidden under the leaflets were two-anna obscene books." And this, Narayan said, was by no means the only time that life had imitated his art.

I asked Narayan if he was ever oppressed by a sense of diminishing literary powers or powers of prophecy.

"Woh, no," he said. "I really have more stories than I can write in a lifetime, and probably in the next *janma*"—incarnation—"I will be not an author but a publisher." He smiled, and then suddenly stood up. "It's too noisy here!" he exclaimed. He shut the window, but the room faced Fifty-seventh Street and nothing could seal out the roar of the traffic. He returned to his canvas seat, discouraged. "How nice it would be to live in Malgudi," he said.

Malgudi is the domain of Narayan's imagination. There is no such town in any directory, almanac, or atlas of the subcontinent. There is a Lalgudi in Madras province, but Narayan says that the similarity of the two names is a coincidence. As the setting of his dozen books, Malgudi corresponds to Faulkner's Yoknapatawpha County. The resemblance, however, is remote, because Malgudi is an infinitely simple place, and because its landmarks—the Albert Mission College, the Regal Haircutting Saloon, the railway station, the temple, the bazaars, the lead statue of Sir Frederick Lawley, the Central Coöperative Land Mortgage Bank, the office of the *Banner* (a newspaper), the huts of the Harijans (children of God) in which Gandhi stayed, Market Road, Kabir Lane, the Taj Hotel, the banyan-tree office, the river steps, Mempi Hill—all, from book to book, chaotically change position. Compared to Faulkner's spiritual home, Malgudi is quiet, dusty, and uneventful, lacking political and social problems, sexual outrages, and hundreds of other things. The dominant force in Malgudi is ineluctable fate, playing one ironic trick after another on the simple inhabitants, who rise and fall, a little blandly, as fortune dictates. But the bland cosmos of Malgudi is blessed with grace, because its people are innocent and comic—copies of Narayan, with his dazzling smile fixed on their faces.

"You know," Narayan told me, "I remember waking up with the name Malgudi on Vijayadasami, the day on which the initiation of learning is celebrated." It was in September, 1930, he said, that the name of the town had been vouchsafed him by the divine patrons of knowledge. "Malgudi was an yearth-shaking discovery for me, because I had no mind for facts and things like that, which would be necessary in writing about Lalgudi or any real place. I first pictured not my town but just the railway station, which was a small platform with a banyan tree, a stationmaster, and two trains a day, one coming and one going. On Vijayadasami, I sat down and wrote the first sentence about my town: 'The train had just arrived at Malgudi station.' But it was some years before I could write the opening words of 'Swami and Friends': 'It was Monday morning.' The sentence about the train got revised." Since that Vijayadasami, the town boundaries had expanded to take in streets, people, industries. "Many academicians are hard at work trying to find where, exactly, Malgudi might be situated," Narayan said, all his teeth shining in a smile. "My books are full of contradictory leads. Once, a researcher wrote to ask me how long it took to go from Malgudi to Madras by train. I wrote back that the train journey from Mysore to Madras was fourteen hours but that it took Margayya more than twice as long to get from Malgudi to Madras. I never heard from that gentleman again."

I said I thought one could cover the entire perimeter of his right triangle in a couple of days.

He smiled happily, and offered me a betel nut. "Don't feel guilty at sharing this elixir with me," he said, and he went on to explain that he had taken precautions against running short of betel nuts on this visit to America, which was his third. After his first visit, when he was without them for six months, he had made arrangements with his mother to buy some from his favorite shop in Mysore and send them to him by air. His main problem was to convince the American customs officers that he was not getting a consignment of dope.

I put one in my mouth and sucked it, as he had instructed me to do. He was very much pleased, and offered me coffee, which I accepted.

"I think of myself as the globe's best coffee taster," Narayan explained through the kitchen door. "I can't tell wine from beer; all alcohol seems poison to me. But I know the vineyards of coffee beans in southern India well. I can distinguish them by a sip." He turned on a tap. "You know," he continued, "I read somewhere the other day that the cause of cancer is frozen meat. Is it true?"

"Some causes of cancer, at least, come and go," I said. "There is a flurry of controversy about lipsticks one month, waxed milk containers the next, and—"

"Oh, really? Still, it comforts me to be a vegetarian." After fumbling with a box of matches for some time, he finally had the stove lighted. But he remained in the kitchen to watch the kettle. "You know, I wish I had an apartment like this in Mysore—clean, neat, and compact," he said. "As it is, I have an enormous house, which I built six or seven years ago." He told me that his house, which was on the edge of the city and was surrounded by wilderness, occupied half of a three-quarter-acre plot. He was thinking of building a replica of Breit's one-room apartment on the other half and moving into it, for the house, which had five bedrooms, four bathrooms, a big drawing room and dining room, and servants' quarters—modern ones—in the basement, remained empty for half the year, when he was travelling or was visiting his daughter, Hema, now married and living in

Coimbatore. He could not understand why, but ever since he made his first journey to America (in response to repeated invitations from Chadbourne Gilpatric, of the Rockefeller Foundation), in 1955, and gave Hema in marriage a year later, he had been restless.

The water boiled, and, after much clattering and shuffling, Narayan brought two coffee cups to the table. He held his cup in a gingerly manner and drank the coffee slowly. "I originally built my house in the hope of getting all my family to move there," he said. "But my mother wouldn't hear of it, because she was frightened of the woods around me and also did not really like the thought of giving up her old way of living." So, Narayan went on, he had never taken the trouble to furnish the place. He had just carried in a few chairs, a table, and a bed, and given one of the rooms a semblance of life. He spent as little time in the room as possible, because he missed his family, even though he visited them daily. (They lived only fifteen minutes away.) He used his one habitable room as a sort of retreat for writing. "It's quite nice," he said. "I can see the countryside around me for more than ten miles."

Narayan told me about his Mysore day. It begins with a three- or four-hour stroll. He considers his morning walk his office hours, because he stops and talks to people, many of whom chat with him freely about their doings or their troubles, or give him advice about renting his house (empty houses bring bad luck) or about making profits on his books, which they cannot read. Only a few ask him for practical help, probably because they know him to be a mere writer; most demand his ear and his sympathy. If, on his promenade, Narayan sees three or four men in a huddle, he observes their ways closely. In his many years of living in Mysore, he has made friends among artisans, businessmen, lawyers, teachers—the men and women of his novels. After lunch, he may do an hour or two of writing—his limit for a day's serious work. He composes fast, and two thousand words in a couple of hours is not an unusual achievement for him. "I am an inattentive, quick writer who has little sense of style," he said candidly. Once he has written the first few pages of a novel, he seldom retouches a sentence, believing that writing is "a dovetailing process," by which he means that a novel well begun writes itself. After his writing, he meditates, and his barren room is especially suited to that. He begins his exercises by reading a little bit of the *puranas,* or Sanskrit sacred poems, after which he repeatedly recites to himself the Gayatri Mantra, a prayer to the light that illuminates the sun to illuminate all minds. After he has had a short rest, the late afternoon finds him at his family's house; he dines, then makes the rounds of his intimate friends, and goes home to bed.

"I've been talking to you like Railway Raju," Narayan said, referring to the tourist-guide saint who is the hero of "The Guide." "I sometimes feel like him; it is difficult not to, especially when I'm telling about Mysore, which I know better than any other place." As he finished his coffee, he added that some family incidents and his own character had given him the conception of Raju (successively a tramp; a guide to the historical sights of Malgudi; the savior, seducer, and manager of Rosie; an unfortunate jailbird; and an unwilling rainmaker and saint), and that Rosie (a wavering Hindu wife and a great classical dancer) and her husband, Marco (who prefers ancient pictures of dancers to the beauty and genius of his wife), had a similar genesis.

It was very late, and over Fifty-seventh Street hung a sort of Malgudi hush, shattered only now and again by the clap of a passing truck. Narayan yawned a little, and we stood up. "Have some more betel nuts," he said as he fitted one of them into each side of his mouth. He tilted his film box over my hand and shook out two more, like a man throwing dice who is confident that luck will not let him down. "Someone was telling me the other day that in this country all good writers have to be unhappy to write well," he said. "Why is that? I find I write best when I have no burden on my mind, when I am absolutely at peace with myself. That's why for many years after Rajam died I couldn't write anything."

At the door, we embraced each other in the Indian way, and he started ringing the door buzzer again to call the lift up. I took him into the hallway and showed him the right button. "All this gadgetry confounds me," he said as the automatic door closed.

A couple of days later, Narayan dropped in on me. First, we sucked a couple of betel nuts together, and then we dined; an Indian friend had cooked a vegetarian meal for us and left it in the oven. Narayan ate his rice, vegetable curry, and yoghurt in silence; from time to time he rested his fork on the plate, as though he were about to tell me something, only to resume eating. He seemed depressed. After we had finished dinner, he said slowly, "I'm troubled about the dramatization of 'The Guide,' but I really don't know where to begin."

Not wanting to press him, I merely served him some coffee, which he did not drink.

"Oh, Lard," he said after a while. "I feel a little bit like Raju, whose wonderful career and affair with Rosie, in 'The Guide,' came to an yend because of a small forgery, a little technicality. How nature imitates art!" He smiled. "I sometimes find myself preferring the Indian literary life to the American."

"What does the Indian literary life have to do with Raju?" I asked.

"Nothing, nothing," Narayan said. "There is no such thing as the Indian literary life." He smiled again, dazzlingly. There were vernacular writers and poets, he explained, but there was no methodical criticism in the provincial languages, since the Indians were not as rigorous as English and American critics in separating the wheat from the chaff when it came to Indian writers working in English. This meant that the men of letters writing in underdeveloped languages had neither fame nor audience and probably no critical tradition (in the Western sense), and so, possibly, had no compulsion to improve themselves—or, indeed, to write at all. As for Indian literature in English—which had never been more than a trickle—it was on its way out with the raj language itself. Narayan said that for him the only thrill that the Indian literary life—if it could be called that—had to offer was an occasional letter from a magazine editor whom he had never met that went something like this: "My dear Narayan, I have taken a great deal of pride and interest in your long and astounding career and feel a personal investment in all your manifold and multifarious achievements, which bring a great deal of credit to our great country, and, indeed, to me personally, since I've always thought of you as part of my family. We are going to press with a special children's supplement. Undoubtedly you would not wish to be absent from its table of contents, and undoubtedly we would not wish you to be. Of course, we will not be able to pay you as much as your greatly deserving genius warrants, but we hope the postal order of fifty rupees that will follow the receipt of your submission will be taken as a token of our abiding faith and pride in your works and person. With warmest regards. Yours affectionately . . ." "And then," Narayan said, "years after the 'submission'—never acknowledged—when no postal arder has reached me, if I drop a line to the editor about the promised sum, he will immediately spread the word that 'Narayan is mercenary.' What a strange and wonderful country we come from!"

I remarked that Narayan was to the Indian literary landscape what Daniel Defoe was to the English, and then asked how a writer survived in that strange and wonderful country.

The answer was that he did not, unless he had a private income, an indulgent family, or some sort of job. Narayan's father, a learned headmaster, whose heroes were Thomas Carlyle and Walter Pater, tried to force his son into earning a living by pushing him first in one direction and then in another, but Narayan's first experience as a teacher soured him on that profession for life. He was paralyzed with fear at the sight of the burly boys, was tongue-tied during lessons, and was insolent to his permissive headmaster, who merely asked him to stay with the class, even when he had nothing to say, for a full period, rather than dismiss it after a few minutes. Narayan also balked at joining the civil service, because he was sure he hadn't the patience, the presence, or the discipline—the triple *sine qua non* of officialdom. An attempt he made to become a sub-editor was foiled because, as it happened, the chief requirement for the position, in India, was a mastery of shorthand. Finally, Narayan resolved to "sell" himself no more, to do nothing—simply to write novels that neither Carlyle nor Pater nor his father would have been caught reading, and live off the joint-family system. Happily, his father loved him very much and was glad to have the do-nothing son at home. He died, however, without reading the manuscript of "Swami and Friends," which Narayan had never had the courage to show him. "But I remember that my father was very pleased at the sight of my book cover, which arrived just before his death," Narayan told me. "He also smiled whenever I showed him a small check or postal arder for a short story or an article." Narayan used to write tales for the *Hindu,* and occasionally did small news stories on sanitation, the law courts, scandals, and so on for *Justice,* a now defunct anti-Brahman newspaper. "Mr. Sampath" (a novel that appeared in the United States as "The Printer of Malgudi"), which he wrote and published in 1949, was a success, and he adapted it for a popular Indian film called "Mr. Sampath," with the actor Motilal and the actress Padmini. "I never sold myself into a job," Narayan said, "but people were buying me yeverywhere." Narayan got so tired of dealing with profiteers who passed as Indian publishers that at one point he started printing his own books. When he left me that evening, he was happily sucking betel nuts.

The next day, Narayan and I had both been asked to dinner by the Indian writer Santha Rama Rau, who is married to the American writer Faubion Bowers. When I arrived at the Bowers apartment, a walkup on East Ninety-fifth Street, I found Narayan there already. He was standing—looking like a little boy—between a low canvas chair and the tall Miss Rama Rau. She has an Indian complexion but was in European dress—stockings and a cotton frock. "Darling, how lovely to see you!" Miss Rama Rau said, taking my hand. "Isn't it jolly for three Indian writers to be able to have dinner together? I'm glad we were able to fit it in. I'm leaving for Hollywood in a day or two. Faubion and my son, Jai, have already started. Let's all sit down. You, darling," she said warmly, nodding at me, "come and sit beside me." Narayan perched on the canvas chair. Miss Rama Rau and I settled on a divan.

Miss Rama Rau asked Narayan what he had been doing lately, and he said he had met a demonstrative Indian donkey in the Central Park Zoo during his walk that morning. Narayan went on to tell us that the animal was just an ordinary *dhobi*'s donkey, who, with his brethren, roamed the Indian streets by the million. But in America, apparently, he was a great success; nobody who saw him could doubt that the zoo-goers fed his vanity—an attribute never associated with donkeys in India. The donkey, however, had paid a price for his American importance; he had to live behind bars day and night. In Narayan's opinion, he was not happy. His incarceration frustrated him, and all day long, whenever he was not braying for his admiring audience, he flipped the lock of his cage with his tongue. In India, donkeys had an equally hard row to hoe. They were not treated mercifully. After carrying a big load all day, they were not fed but were put to pasture on the streets, where they ate not grass but discarded newspapers. So the choice for a donkey was poverty, a long day's work, and unhappiness in India or riches, self-expression, and unhappiness in America. If he were a horse, a camel, or an elephant, his alternatives would not be so limited. But in the reincarnation cycle prizes are more often reserved for those who fulfill their nature than for those who overreach themselves; a donkey is rewarded with a higher rebirth for being a mere donkey, not for competing with a peacock. "I think I'll write a little fable about him for *Harper's,*" Narayan said, smiling. "Do you think they will take it?"

We smiled back, and then I asked Miss Rama Rau if she was going on a Hollywood holiday.

"No, no," she said. "I'm going there to write the next treatment of that mad Indian picture of mine. When I was in Madras with Narayan the last time, I received this exciting telegram from David O. Selznick to write the Jesus Christ–Mary Magdalene story for his wife, Jennifer Jones, to be set in India. Why India? You may well ask. One of those Hollywood coincidences, you know. Miss Jones—he always calls her Miss Jones—goes to India and loses her heart to it; meanwhile, David is approached to do the Christ-Magdalene picture, but refuses, because there are too many Christian films already. Then he has one of those fantastic, spooky inspirations: Why not shoot Christ and Magdalene in India, put the Christian story in a Hindu setting? And bingo! The idea takes wing and catches me in Madras. I read the telegram again and again, and wire back something to the effect that a religious picture in India is a giddy, jolly idea. Mad, but exciting stuff, don't you think?"

Narayan nodded benignly. I must have looked a little skeptical.

"Yes, darling," she said, fixing me with her gaze. "I thought the same. But, after all, wasn't Gandhi like Christ? Who else in two thousand years has caught the spirit of the Saviour so well? My story line is based on a disciple of the old boy's—naturally, a celibate. He thinks he knows everything about life until a lowdown American girl—in the film, Miss Jones—comes along, seduces him, and begins his education from scratch. I haven't worked out the details of this yet. But I think the whole thing is giddy. The idea is historical, universal. Here is the Saviour, Christ; here is Mahatma Gandhi; and here is the woman who ate the apple. I can be as pompous as the next woman."

Miss Rama Rau chatted on rapidly about the check that popped out of the mailbox every week, about the fairy-tale château on Sunset Boulevard awaiting her arrival in Hollywood, and about pending visits there of Garbo and the Gunthers. "Narayan, why don't you join the Hollywood party?" she asked.

Narayan said nothing.

"How about your usual tonic water, Narayan?" she went on. "There is no lime in the house. Will a little lemon do just as well?"

"That will be quite nice," Narayan said.

She turned to me, and I said I would take a little whiskey-and-soda.

Miss Rama Rau went into the kitchen. She returned and handed us our drinks. "Here, my darlings. Indians are inveterate talkers. We can't stop talking, talking, talking—a mile a minute. One of the reasons I left my Sixty-third Street apartment was that there was a dog who barked all day. His mistress used to wash him every few minutes and give him birthday parties, with paper napkins that had 'Happy Birthday, Doggie' written on them. She'd invite her neighbors to the parties. She used to call me Mrs. Bow-wow-wowers. I don't like animals. That's one sense in which I'm not Indian. Come on, foremost novelist, tell us a little bit about *you.*"

Narayan laughed, flashing all his teeth. "You know," he said tentatively, "part of me is always somewhere else—in the paragraph I may write tomorrow, the character who has to be dovetailed into my novel—and then I am forever focussing my eyes on those vague, floating ideas that keep on buzzing in my head."

"Come on, foremost novelist," Miss Rama Rau said, "tell us the happiest and the saddest moments in your life. I asked my eight-year-old boy the same question the other day, and I was so touched to hear him say, in his American accent, that the happiest time was when I took him, for a short while, to India, and that the saddest was when he left India and my sister."

There was a silence, and then Narayan said matter-of-factly, "I suppose the saddest moment in my life was the passing of my wife."

We ate a simple vegetarian meal. After dinner, Narayan washed his hands and then strolled into the bedroom-nursery, where he squatted and played with Miss Rama Rau's son's turtle. Narayan said that the philosophy of vegetarianism was based on a reverence for life—from turtles to human beings. "But I can qualify that a little," he added, smiling. "A reverence for a certain sort of moving life. You might say we are not supposed to yeat anything that moves horizontally. Happily, plants move vertically, skyward, and eggs drop from the chicken like rain from heaven." When we said good night to Miss Rama Rau, it was getting late, but she was still effervescent.

Downstairs, a taxi stopped for us, and we whizzed down Lexington Avenue to Fifty-seventh Street, where I went up with Narayan to his apartment for a quick after-dinner betel nut. When we were settled in our canvas chairs, I asked him to tell me about the dramatization of "The Guide," by Harvey Breit and his wife, Patricia Rinehart.

"It is a good play of its kind, but I now wish I weren't connected with it," he said. "I worry about it so much that I go to sleep at one and wake up at one-forty-five." Narayan rubbed his eyes like a child heavy with sleep. "Actually, there is one thing I haven't told you," he continued. "You see, I probably prefer 'The Guide' to be a quiet, serious production, with an Indian cast; in any case, I never cared about big names, and all that, but when Harvey told me about the money I could make on Broadway, I rather rashly promised my daughter and son-in-law and Minni—my little granddaughter—a trip to America if my play was successful."

At that moment, Narayan did look like a grandfather—benign and benevolent and slightly resigned—but whenever he smiled, he was again like a little boy from a pastoral hillside. Until 1955, when he visited England and America, the train that arrived at Malgudi station from the twentieth century had brought in only water tanks and electric power. Since then, the train to Malgudi had carried in, among other things, the dramatization of "The Guide."

I asked Narayan how he was getting on with his new book.

"I've been a little disturbed lately, so I haven't progressed very far," he said. "Instead of serious writing, I have been trying to do little pieces for *Vogue*, on such things as boredom and contentment and 'Are We Civilized?' " He had no theories about these assigned subjects, he added, but he thought some ideas might come to him somehow. "Will you have a betel nut?" he asked, handing me one. "Actually, I have been doing more reading than writing recently, and I have just stumbled upon a very good case for my sort of writing. You know, one or two critics are always attacking me for not having a style." From under a pile of groceries on the table he pulled a faded blue volume. It was edited by Forster and was called "Original Letters from India, 1779–1815." In his soft English, Narayan read some bits from Forster's introduction to Mrs. Eliza Fay's letters: " 'On one of her voyages a pair of globes accompanied her, but geography could never have been her strong point, for she thought the Alps were only one mountain thick, and the Malabar Hills the third highest range in the world. . . . Archdeacon Firminger observes with concern that "she frequently arranges her words in such an order that she is bound to get into trouble with her relative pronouns." She does. . . . And her mouth: how she does relish her food! She is constantly registering through her senses, and recording the results with . . . [an] untrained mind. The outcome is most successful, and it is strange that her letters are not better known in this country. . . . Style is always being monopolized by the orderly-minded; they will not admit that slap-dash people have equal literary rights, provided they write slap-dash. If Mrs. Fay got her relative pronouns correct she would be a worse writer, for they can never have been correct in her mind, she can never have spoken quite properly even when calling at Government House or learning sweet little Miss Rogers the use of the globes. She wrote as well as she could, she wrote nothing that she herself was not.' " After pausing a moment, Narayan said, "I say, how beautifully Forster writes, doesn't he!"

When I left him, he was perched before his table, which was crowded with nuts, herbs, rice, flour, tomatoes, and onions.

Originally appeared, under the heading "Profiles," as "The Train Had Just Arrived at Malgudi Station" in The New Yorker, *September 15, 1962. Reprinted in "John Is Easy to Please," Farrar, Straus & Giroux, New York, and Secker & Warburg, London, 1971.*

THREE

Pastor Bonhoeffer

Next to the late Dietrich Bonhoeffer, the Right Reverend John Robinson, Suffragan Bishop of Woolwich, relied most heavily for his book "Honest to God" on Rudolf Bultmann, who was, and is, one of the two preëminent living Protestant theologians on the Continent, the other being his main adversary, Karl Barth—who has written twelve brilliant volumes of theology, in his "Church Dogmatics," about the impossibility both of writing theology and of speculating at all about the divine nature, so far separated, Barth argued, was man from God. (Once, Emil Brunner, of Zurich, was thought to be in the same class, but his star has been in eclipse now for many years.) Some months ago, I wrote to both of them, in the hope that I might be able to talk with them, though I knew that Barth was touching eighty, while Bultmann had passed it, and that neither one of them was in very good health. Both wrote to say that they would be glad to see me. I went first to Basel, where Barth lives and used to teach, at the University of Basel.

Barth's house, a modest three-story structure, was on Bruderholzallee, in the southeast of Basel. The door was answered by an anxious-looking elderly lady with white hair, who was wearing a blue wool dress. This was Mrs. Barth. *"Guten Tag,"* Mrs. Barth said. "My husband can't talk very long. He's just come back from the hospital, where he has been for three months." She conducted me to the stairs, then paused indecisively at the foot, and took me into a small living room overlooking a withered, wintry garden. She said, "My son-in-law is a landscape architect. He helped design this garden. In summer, this garden will be very nice; there will be flowers. When my husband gets stronger, we will have seminars in the restaurant across the street. His students come there, to discuss and write. That's where he wrote some of the 'Dogmatics.' We rent a room from the restaurant." Hesitating a bit longer, she told me how Barth spent a day when he was teaching and in good health. From her account, he appeared to have led a monk's life. He used to get up a little before seven o'clock; he thought aloud to himself from seven to seven-thirty; from seven-thirty to seven-forty-five he listened to Mozart, his favorite composer, about whom he had written a book; he read and wrote from seven-forty-five until lunch, which, if he was too preoccupied, he missed; at three-forty-five, having worked until the last minute—most of the time on a lecture that later became a chunk of the next volume of the "Dogmatics," the book growing with each such addition, volume by volume, year after year—he left the house for his four-fifteen lecture at the university; and he worked again after the lecture from five-thirty to one or two at night (relying, by day and evening, on the help of his long-time, devoted secretary, Fräulein Charlotte von Kirschbaum, who had studied with him), finishing off with some detective stories, which, with Mozart, gave him his only relaxation. Occasionally, he liked a good bottle of wine or a plate of snails (which he had eaten for the first time five years before). Otherwise, his needs were simple.

Mrs. Barth then led me back to the stairs, which were covered with a worn red carpet. On the wall alongside them were prints of famous philosophers and theologians, ascending from Kant to Schleiermacher to Nietzsche to Neander to Richard Rothe to Blumhardt to Wilhelm Herrmann to Harnack. At the top of the stairs was a rather wasted figure with a strong, pugnacious peasant's face. He had on black-and-white striped trousers and a green wool shirt open at the neck, and he was wearing glasses and smoking a short pipe. This was Barth himself, the pupil of Harnack. Having greeted me warmly, he led the way into a very small and austere room—his study. In the center of the room was a round table, spread with a plain beige cloth. All around were worn gray books, in English, French, German, Latin, Greek, and Hebrew. One shelf, at eye level, held volumes upon volumes of his own works. On another shelf, next to the ceiling, were books written about him. One could just make out a few of the titles: "Karl Barth," "Catholicism and Barthianism," "Portrait of Karl Barth." The two of us sat down at the table.

"I wish you had come five years ago," Barth said. "You would have found another fellow. He would have been quick, but I've just come out of the hospital, and I'm lucky to have any memory at all."

I said that I was grateful for the opportunity to shake his hand, and I went on to say that in the rounds I had been making among the theologians I had discovered two Barths: one the radical Barth, who in 1918 had published the revolutionary book "The Epistle to the Romans," which was still constantly read and referred to, and the other the conservative Barth, who was known for the "Church Dogmatics," to which he had devoted himself since the late twenties. How did the two manage to get on together?

He laughed, but only for a moment; it seemed a strain. With an effort, he said, "Yes, the commentary on Romans is a radical work, written in my youth. Then I became more tranquil, peaceful, universal-minded, and I wrote the 'Dogmatics.' Most people like the commentary, because it is radical, but the 'Dogmatics' is my more important work—if it is not so much read, it is because people don't take the trouble to read twelve volumes. The commentary is one-sided, but the 'Dogmatics' is many-sided."

I remarked that the late Pope John had compared him and his "Dogmatics" to Aquinas and the "Summa Theologica."

"I didn't know that," Barth said, looking away. He continued, "Dogmatic theology repeats the big yes that God gave the world. God loves the world in which we have to live. We have to say yes to the world. The presupposition of the 'Dogmatics' is that the Gospel is the word of God. Most theologians—most notably Bultmann—begin nowadays with the morals, the ethics of religion, or with man, but the presupposition of all dogmatic theology is that one has to begin with God."

"The God of the New Testament seems very different from that of the Old," I remarked hesitantly.

"The Old Testament is the story of the people of Israel, and this story is a prefiguration of Christ," he said. "Christ is the final revelation. Among the Gospels there are differences, contradictions, but the similarities are far greater, and they have to be kept in mind. The Gospel writers were the witnesses to the word of God."

Barth looked tired, and I felt I should take my leave.

As I got up, he rose and put a hand on my shoulder. "My eldest son, Markus, is in America," he said. "He teaches New Testament theology in the Pittsburgh Theological Seminary. Perhaps you will meet him someday."

Some people see Bultmann as a sort of Atlas, supporting with his doctrine of demythologization the world of radical theology (though Bultmann can easily pass as a theologian in a classical sense, too; it is thought that a work like "Das Evangelium des Johannes" has such exegetical and critical value that it will be read long into the future, regardless of the fate of any one of Bultmann's philosophical ideas). Indeed, it is said that the German Evangelical Church would like to try Bultmann for heresy if a prosecutor could be found who was his match in theology. About the doctrine of demythologization Bultmann has written:

> The question inevitably arises: Is it possible that Jesus's preaching of the Kingdom of God still has any importance for modern men and the preaching of the New Testament as a whole is still important for modern men? . . . We must ask whether the eschatological preaching and the mythological sayings as a whole contain a still deeper meaning which is concealed under the cover of mythology. If that is so, let us abandon the mythological conceptions precisely because we want to retain their deeper meaning. This method of interpretation of the New Testament which tries to recover the deeper meaning behind the mythological conceptions I call "demythologizing"—an unsatisfactory word, to be sure. Its aim is not to eliminate the mythological statements but to interpret them. It is a method of hermeneutics. . . . According to mythological thinking, God has His domicile in heaven. What is the meaning of this statement? The meaning is quite clear. In a crude manner, it expresses the idea that God is beyond the world, that He is transcendent. The thinking which is not yet capable of

forming the abstract idea of transcendence expresses its intention
in the category of space; the transcendent God is imagined as
being at an immense spatial distance, far above the world: for
above this world is the world of the stars, of the light which en-
lightens and makes glad the life of men. When mythological
thinking forms the conception of hell, it expresses the idea of the
transcendence of evil as the tremendous power which again and
again afflicts mankind. The location of hell and of men whom hell
has seized is below the earth in darkness, because darkness is tremendous and terrible to men. These mythological conceptions of
heaven and hell are no longer acceptable for modern men, since
for scientific thinking to speak of "above" and "below" in the universe has lost all meaning, but the idea of the transcendence of
God and of evil is still significant. . . . The eschatological preaching of Jesus was retained and continued by the early Christian
community in its mythological form. But very soon the process of
demythologizing began, partially with Paul, and radically with
John. The decisive step was taken when Paul declared that the
turning point from the Old World to the New was not a matter of
the future but did take place in the coming of Jesus Christ. . . . An
objection often heard against the attempt to demythologize is that
it takes the modern world-view as the criterion of the interpretation of the Scripture and the Christian message and that Scripture
and Christian message are not allowed to say anything that is in
contradiction with the modern world-view. It is, of course, true
that demythologizing takes the modern world-view as a criterion.
To demythologize is to reject not Scripture or the Christian message as a whole, but the world-view of Scripture, which is the
world-view of a past epoch, which all too often is retained in
Christian dogmatics and in the preaching of the Church. . . . For
the world-view of the Scripture is mythological and is therefore
unacceptable to modern man, whose thinking has been shaped by
science and is therefore no longer mythological. . . . Now it is the
Word of God which calls man into genuine freedom, into free
obedience, and the task of demythologizing has no other purpose
but to make clear the call of the Word of God. It will interpret the
Scripture, asking for the deeper meaning of mythological conceptions and freeing the Word of God from a bygone world-view.

But the more Bultmann has tried to give this doctrine an intellectual basis, the more he has discouraged many Christians with what they consider his essential irrationalism. In conversation with me, Ian Ramsey, a sympathetic critic, said, "Insofar as Bultmann is saying, Don't think the Gospels are just picture books, exact records of, for instance, what Christ did; they are about something much more telling than this, about a mighty peculiar kind of thing, which might be called 'authentic existence,' or what he calls 'the deeper meaning'— so far he's all right. I think he's also very right when he says that the kind of situation the Gospel is trying to portray is one of metaphysical—theological—significance but nevertheless one in which we are personally very involved. I think he's weak, or inadequate, at any rate, insofar as he tends to minimize the historical elements in the Bible—by taking refuge behind Heidegger, he almost cuts himself off from any possibility of arguing reasonably about this authentic existence. You see, I think that we have to pay more attention than he does to the historical elements and have to establish much better than he does what are more and what are less reliable ways of talking about this authentic existence. But in drawing people away from a mere kind of historicism, I think he is first-rate. And in suggesting that you don't understand the Bible or the New Testament unless there is some kind of personal commitment here—all this is first-rate. But I think he tends to be a bit, in the broad sense of the word, irrational. To despise the historicity arguments, as it were, and to think that whatever can be found out by historical criticism makes no difference—to think of this as of no account, so to say—I think this is irrational."

Appropriately, Bultmann's house, in Marburg, in Germany, proved to be on a hill, on Calvinstrasse. Mrs. Bultmann, a matronly lady dressed in gray, greeted me at the door, took my coat, and at once accompanied me into her husband's study.

"Will you have a pipe?" Bultmann said, taking a few steps toward me, which revealed a pronounced limp.

"Many thanks, I don't smoke," I replied.

Bultmann looked me up and down. He had a prudent eye, and the succinct, detached manner of someone who doesn't suffer fools gladly. He was dressed, rather carelessly, in a gray pinstriped suit and a very wide gray tie. After a few moments, he sat down by a round table that was almost a duplicate of Barth's. Mrs. Bultmann took a chair near him, and so did I.

"It's not a very nice day out," Bultmann said, in a voice that was thin and querulous. "I feel the changes of the weather in my head. It's not the wetness or the winter that I mind but the continual changes of the weather from day to day. But I am over eighty now."

I asked him whether he and Mrs. Bultmann had thought of living in a warmer, more stable climate.

"My husband loves this house," Mrs. Bultmann said. "He would not be happy anywhere else. He gets fresh air here. He walks out on the terrace."

"I can't walk very much now," Bultmann said. "From my childhood, I have had trouble with my left leg."

"My husband recently celebrated his eightieth birthday," Mrs. Bultmann said. "We told all our friends that we didn't want any celebration, but we had lots of telegrams and cards and long letters and short letters. The dean of the theology faculty of the University of Marburg, the rector of the university, and the Minister of Culture from Wiesbaden all came, and stayed for two hours. Two of our daughters made music for us. Our third daughter, who lectures on library science at Syracuse University, in America, arrived late and didn't have time to practice with her sisters."

"For my eightieth birthday my students gave me a third *Festschrift*," Bultmann said. "I've been spending all my time since then writing to each of the contributors."

To lead up to the subject of demythologizing, I asked Bultmann if he had any common ground with Barth.

"We both started out being opposed to liberal theology and its argument that men were religious by nature," he said. "Both Barth and I thought that this made religion too subjective. For us, God was an objective occurrence in the world. After that, we parted company. I don't read much Barth now. He's too orthodox—he believes in the literal word. I think philosophy and theology should be combined, but he doesn't. He doesn't like me, or Paul Tillich, for bringing in philosophy—he likes Brunner even less—but he and I still have very amusing exchanges." (Before coming to Marburg, I had spent a little time with Brunner in Zurich. Between playing Bach's Prelude in B

Minor on the piano and playing Bach's Prelude in C Major, he had told me that though Barth and he were nearly of the same age— Brunner was almost seventy-six—and of the same nationality, lived only sixty miles apart, and had both started out as dialectical theologians, they had rarely met. Explaining that such conduct was by no means an oddity in the scholarly world, Brunner had gone on to quote a sort of theological justification that Barth had offered a B.B.C. interviewer who had asked about the chilly relationship existing between the two Swiss theologians: " 'In His good creation, God saw fit to create such diverse creatures as an elephant and a whale. Each has his own function and purpose. But they are so different that they cannot communicate with each other or even fight with each other. As a result, they also cannot conclude a peace pact with each other. Why God chose to place such diverse creatures in the same universe no one knows. For the answer to this question we must wait until the eschaton. Only then will it become clear as to why God created the elephant and the whale.' " In 1960, however, a common friend had managed to arrange a meeting between the whale and the elephant, and they had got on famously, posing with Mrs. Brunner and Mrs. Barth for several photographs.)

"Yes," Mrs. Bultmann said. "When Barth was bringing out the booklet 'Rudolf Bultmann—An Attempt to Understand Him,' he sent a copy of it to my husband with a letter opening 'O Angel, forgive me'—a line borrowed from the last scene of 'Figaro.' "

"What are the limits of demythologizing?" I asked. "I know that students of Barth have said it can be the death of religion if it is carried too far."

"There are no limits," Bultmann said. "I think we should take it as far as it can go."

"After the Second World War, I worked in a hospital in Marburg," Mrs. Bultmann put in. "Ministers used to preach to the wounded and disabled soldiers about sin, and so on, and it didn't mean anything to them. Professor Bultmann's and Professor Tillich's religion did mean something. Every Sunday, even now, I read aloud to Professor Bultmann a sermon of Tillich's."

"In any case, all I want to say about demythologizing I have said in my books," Bultmann said. "I now have only one task left. I must finish writing my commentary on the Epistles of John. After this task is finished, my work is done."

"Last year was the first time he missed going to the reunion of his pupils," Mrs. Bultmann said. "He wasn't well enough. But I came back and told him everything that had happened—the debates and the controversies." The reunion that Bultmann had missed for the first time was of his own "school"—all the people who had studied with him—which, I had discovered earlier by talking to a Bultmann-ian, numbered in the hundreds and met annually in a sort of academic convention. The coherence of the school could be judged by the fact that within that large school was a smaller school made up of the members of The Graeca, or "circle"—students who over the years had studied with Bultmann and had met with him once a week to read aloud classical literature over some wine.

Soon afterward, again in deference to an elderly man's health, I left Bultmann.

The late Dietrich Bonhoeffer has probably affected more Christian theologians and, through them, more Christians of every sort than any other one theologian of our time. Indeed, Bonhoeffer was at the center of the labyrinth disclosed by "Honest to God," all paths eventually leading to him. An observer has said of him, "Bonhoeffer has been sweeping through the theological world like a fire. You have only to look at the footnotes of the books on theology published in the last decade to know this is true." And, surprisingly, the fire was kindled by the small, fragmentary volume called "Letters and Papers from Prison," which was edited posthumously by Bonhoeffer's closest friend, Pastor Eberhard Bethge, who also arranged for its publication. The book is a collection of miscellaneous jottings, poems, miniature sermons, essays, and letters to his family and his friend Pastor Bethge, many of these being routine and only a few meditative—all written over a period of two years or so, beginning after he was arrested by the Nazis in April, 1943, as a suspected member of the Resistance and going up almost to the time of his death, in the concentration camp of Flossenburg, in April, 1945. Quite apart from the literary and chronological limitations that are inherent in any such collection, many of the printed letters dwell on the prisoner's daily needs, his regrets over his plight, and the wavering prospects for his release. Moreover, the editor has seen fit to omit a majority of the letters for family and other reasons, and Bonhoeffer, even though his letters were smuggled out, could not be unmindful of the prison censors. The result is that one shares Bonhoeffer's uneasy feeling that he is writing with someone reading over his shoulder. But at other times, because the letters were intended to be private, the reader feels a different embarrassment—as though he himself were an intruder. In addition, such theological reflections as Bonhoeffer was able to set down (they take up no more than fifty pages) bear the marks of intellectual isolation and of the abnormal conditions in Nazi Germany during the Second World War—circumstances that have to be taken into account in evaluating Bonhoeffer's ideas. Finally, the theological letters, instead of presenting his own views, record, as a rule, his objections to certain theologies and established religious practices, so there are only tantalizing hints of his constructive thinking. It is nothing less than extraordinary, then, that his book, with so many limitations, should have influenced a whole generation of theologians. The books of Robinson and Paul van Buren, among others, would, by their authors' own testimony, have been inconceivable without the "Letters and Papers from Prison." David L. Edwards, managing director of the Student Christian Movement Press (London), the publisher of "Honest to God," sees an even closer connection between Bonhoeffer and his successors. During my conversation with him, he compared Robinson and Bonhoeffer: "The life Robinson led was very much like that of Bonhoeffer. Both had to come to terms with secularism, one in the Resistance, one in Southwark. Bonhoeffer, like John Robinson, came from a very well-connected background. He saw nothing but intellectuals and Christians till he decided to join the Resistance. Again, like Robinson's experience with the Southwark parishioners, Bonhoeffer found that many non-believing soldiers and conspirators he was with had better values than the Christians with whom he had been brought up." However pervasive Bonhoeffer's influence, he has nevertheless had his critics, particularly among the theological elders, like Tillich, who said, "Everyone is always quoting 'Letters and Papers from Prison.' Bonhoeffer's martyrdom has given him authority—martyrdom always gives psychological authority—but in fact he didn't live long enough for us to know what he thought." Bonhoeffer was thirty-nine when he died.

To penetrate the aura of martyrdom, I decided to seek out one or two of the men who had known Bonhoeffer. Two who had known him well, it appeared, were Pastor Bethge, who had met him in 1935, and another pastor, Wolf-Dieter Zimmermann, who had met him a few years earlier, and had recently brought out "Begegnungen mit Dietrich Bonhoeffer—Ein Almanach," a collection of reminiscences about the theologian by members of his family and by friends who had known him since childhood. I met Pastor Zimmermann first—in his two-story house, on Wichernstrasse, in a good residential area of West Berlin. Pastor Zimmermann, a rather smooth-looking man in gray flannels, who spoke English with a sprinkling of Americanisms, made both of us comfortable in very modern chairs in his living room, and had time to tell me only that he was a religious editor for radio and television, with a two-hour radio slot to fill each week, before a lady in a red-and-blue plaid skirt and a blue sweater entered with a sprightly step, carrying a tea tray on which were not only a teapot and its accessories but a bowl of soup. This was Mrs. Zimmermann. I stood up as she entered. She put down the tray, touched me on the arm, and said, "We German women aren't used to men standing up," and left.

"If you don't mind, I'll eat my dinner now," Pastor Zimmermann said, taking some pills with the soup. "Some people smoke: I have to take pills."

I had found Zimmermann's collection of reminiscences somewhat opaque, and now I asked him if he, as an editor, was satisfied with the picture of Bonhoeffer that emerged from it.

"When I came to collect the material for that book, I discovered that it was very difficult to get information about Bonhoeffer," Pastor Zimmermann said. "Several professors whom I asked to write about him replied that they remembered him only vaguely. The three groups who did remember him, and contributed to the collection, were his family, his pupils, and his personal friends. But his pupils never numbered more than a hundred and fifty all told, and only half of them were what one might call close to him, and half of *these* died in the war. His personal friends all remembered certain observations he made, or little things about him, that didn't suffice to make a picture. Strangely, I myself can remember him dressed only in light colors, though I know he must have had at least one dark suit for church purposes."

I asked him how he had first met Bonhoeffer.

"Well, it was in 1932, when I began attending his lectures on the Nature of the Church, at the University of Berlin," he said. "I remember that his lectures were very theoretical. At that time, he was a *Privatdozent* in theology, and, with his kind of career behind him, it was clear that if things went along normally, he would soon be a professor. He told me he would like all of us, his students, to meet with him once a week and discuss some of the theoretical problems he was lecturing on. At the time, he was living in his parents' house in Grunewald—a prosperous and rather exclusive area, where many professors lived—and Bonhoeffer didn't want us to meet there. He didn't want to have a boss-and-student relationship, he wanted a more normal relationship, and he asked me if the group might meet in my room. I was living near the Alexanderplatz, a working-class neighborhood, and we met there. That was the situation in which I knew him, and I find that my life has been interpenetrated by his."

"What were your impressions of him at the time?" I asked.

"I don't remember him as a terribly good theologian, in the sense that he was good at theory," Pastor Zimmermann said. "Yet, as theologians go, he was a more normal person than most. He was a bit arrogant, a bit intellectual, a bit isolated and lonely, a bit narcissistic. He was the narcissistic type. He looked in his own mirror."

I asked the Pastor what he meant by that, and instead of replying he said, "You see, he did everything early. He received the Licentiate of Theology when he was twenty-one. He was quick at picking up things. He had never done any high jumping, for instance, but when, in his student days, they had a competition for high jumping at the university, he simply went out on the field and jumped higher than anyone else. He was able to do many things this way. He loved playing tennis, and he was very good at table tennis, too. He played the piano, sometimes in the morning and then after lunch and then after dinner and then at two o'clock in the morning. As a child, he went about learning things as a grownup would. He had discipline. He would set an hour a day aside to go and play tennis, say, and then he would come back and read and reread books. He read all the time. One day, Bonhoeffer and I and a friend of mine were camping in the woods two hours north of here—I say a friend of *mine* because Bonhoeffer never really made friends. Well, he did make friends with Pastor Bethge, but Bethge, a very quiet, shy man, was a good sounding board for Bonhoeffer. Anyway, the three of us were sitting on a little hill by a brook at sunset, and my friend said to Bonhoeffer, who was reading a book on Christology, 'Bonhoeffer, look, there is such a lovely sunset.' Bonhoeffer looked up for barely a second. A thrilled expression came over his face, but he immediately went back to reading. That was typical of him. He had seen the sunset and had been thrilled by it, and now could go back to Christology."

I asked what he thought was the extent of Bonhoeffer's influence in Germany now.

"As it happens, in West Germany today his influence is fragmentary," Pastor Zimmermann said. "There are a lot of youth hostels named 'Bonhoeffer,' and the German Evangelical Church accepts certain elements of his theology, but no one in West Germany accepts him completely. Curiously, his influence is considerable in the Communist countries. In East Germany, the C.D.U.—the Christian Democratic Union—has taken Bonhoeffer over. So has the Prague Peace Movement. They find Bonhoeffer's religionless Christianity perfect for them."

I had to catch my breath. I had come across some pat speculation in newspapers that Communism, as it finally moved into the twentieth century, was discarding some of its nineteenth-century baggage, like the dogma of scientific materialism, just as capitalism had abandoned some of its inherited doctrines, such as rugged individualism; in different ways, it was thought, both were putting aside antiquated ideologies, and from opposite sides both were developing the same sort of welfare state. It was, in fact, argued that in this convergence lay the hope for a reunified Germany, which might one day become a bridge between the East and the West. Even in the context of such speculation, however, the adoption of a Christian martyr by a Communist country seemed bizarre, and now I said as much to Pastor Zimmermann.

"You know, in our scholarly tradition in Germany we divide theoretical thinking from practical action," he said. "This goes so far that a professor isn't supposed to do anything practical. I mean, things have changed a bit since the war, but before that we used to have people who would just sit somewhere and think. Kant was such a thinker— you know, he spent all his time sitting and thinking in Königsberg, that one little town. He never left the town—wrote all his books there. Similarly, for centuries after the Reformation the churches of the German states were separated from real life. They were governed by the states. In all that time, the only alternative to the state ethics was pietism. In 1919, when the Kirchenbund, a very loose federation of the independent provincial churches, established in 1871, finally got a little authority, and there could be such a thing as a church social ethic that was different from the social ethic of the state, this independence created a lot of problems, because the Church had had no experience in ruling itself. Bonhoeffer's book 'Act and Being' was concerned with this problem: What is a Christian ethic in everyday life? This problem became all the more important when the Church capitulated to the state once again, under Nazism, at which time the dream of the National Church was finally realized. The German Evangelical Church was established only in 1945, but it still does not enjoy much authority, as the provincial churches go on maintaining quite a lot of their independence."

Pastor Zimmermann concluded, "You know, Bonhoeffer told me dozens of times, beginning as early as 1933, that he wanted to die at the age of thirty-nine. He did die at the age of thirty-nine. When I asked him why he wanted to die early, he said that life should be going up and up and up, that he didn't want to grow old, lose some of his powers, become senile, lose some of his intelligence, lose a certain physical facility. He didn't want to go down."

Bonhoeffer had been dead just twenty years. He had left behind him a fairly substantial record, in the letters and papers he wrote, and in such of his books as "Sanctorum Communio," "Act and Being," "Life Together," and "The Cost of Discipleship," yet the outline of his life had already begun to lose sharp definition. (Even the translations of his books fail to do him justice. The English one of "Letters and Papers" abounds in errors, such as "piano" for "*Klavichord,*" and "sensitive gums" for "*empfindlichen Gaumen.*") Pastor Zimmermann, for example, considered Bonhoeffer to have predicted his death at the age of thirty-nine, whereas a number of theologians I had talked with who had also known Bonhoeffer gave different versions, one saying that Bonhoeffer had always hoped to live to be fifty, another declaring he had never given a thought to death, and Roger Manvell and Heinrich Fraenkel, in their book "The Men Who Tried to Kill Hitler," wrote, "Even as early as 1933 he [Bonhoeffer] had told his friend Pastor Zimmermann that he wanted, after a full life, to die young at the age of thirty-eight. This was his age when the Nazis assassinated him in 1945." It brought one up short, especially since Terence Prittie, in another book on the Resistance, "Germans Against Hitler," had also written that Bonhoeffer "was under thirty-eight when he was murdered." Actually, both discrepancies could best be explained as printing errors, since all the accounts recorded Bonhoeffer's dates accurately as February, 1906, to April, 1945. And, in any event, if Bonhoeffer had expected to die at an early age, why should the "Letters and Papers," chronicling his last two years, have centered, as they did, on aspirations for the future? Some letters showed him considering the coming years with hope, as he awaited the emergence of a better Germany. Some revealed his thoughts on what the role of the Church should be in a defeated Germany. Other papers were in fact notes or outlines for books he expected to write one day.

Even allowing for the fact that a martyr by the manner of his death brings idolaters to life (and in the past it has sometimes taken centuries to see through to the martyr as he was), it was still jarring to come up against such conflicts of testimony. Then I recalled one of Bonhoeffer's letters, written a few months before his death: "I remember talking to a young French pastor at A. thirteen years ago. We were discussing what our real purpose was in life. He said he would like to become a saint. I think it is quite likely he did become one. At the time I was very much impressed, though I disagreed with him, and said I should prefer to have faith, or words to that effect." The portentousness of the remark—and, one could almost say, the prescience of it—unsettled me further. I felt I was just beginning to see the deeper meaning of the ungainly word "demythologize." I began to wonder if, without quite being aware of it, I might not have been put in touch with the authentic Bonhoeffer by something that Paul Lehmann, a professor of theology at Union Theological Seminary, had once told me. He had been Bonhoeffer's best American friend—he insisted that

Bonhoeffer had a great capacity for friendship—and he had seen him for the last time on Bonhoeffer's second, and last, visit to America, in 1939. Lehmann had said to me, "Dietrich had come from a country where only the best was encouraged, only the best could get on. This was very evident in him. He once said to me that somebody who was as bad at tennis as I was had no business occupying the court. This was characteristic of him, and very Germanic. He was very good at tennis." But then Lehmann, too, had turned reverent: "You see, Dietrich was rather like a Greek god. His blond hair was the only physical thing that told you he was German. He had perfect proportions; he was a very handsome man. In 1949, I met Pastor Bethge for the first time. I took to him in exactly the same way I had taken to Bonhoeffer. It was as though Pastor Bethge and I had known each other from the very start, and, in a sense, we had, for we were both close friends of Dietrich's. Our immediately taking to one another like that was the kind of spiritual community that Bonhoeffer had written about in 'Sanctorum Communio.'"

It was Pastor Bethge who, through the "Letters and Papers," was responsible for first bringing Bonhoeffer to public notice, and he had since established himself as the principal authority on Bonhoeffer. He was married to one of Bonhoeffer's nieces, and had access to all the family letters and papers. From 1945 on, he had devoted himself to studying the life and work of his friend, and now he was engaged in collecting and editing his papers, and in writing his biography. Bonhoeffer, over the last ten years of his life, when he was struggling toward his fateful decision to commit himself to the Resistance, made Bethge his confidant and, over his last two years, when, as a prisoner, he was denied a "father confessor," gratefully allowed Bethge, through correspondence, to take on that office as well. (Though the identity of the recipient of some of the most important letters in "Letters and Papers" was originally withheld, it was revealed, as soon as the book became well known, that they were addressed to the editor himself.)

Recently, when, after immersing myself in Bonhoeffer literature, I spent some time with Pastor Bethge in Germany, and, in the hope of unwinding the tangled skein of Bonhoeffer's life, I asked Pastor Bethge to "interpret" Bonhoeffer (in the special Bultmannian sense, as it were) for me and explain the contradictions in the theologian's life, Pastor Bethge told me that Bonhoeffer's life could be understood in terms of the Bonhoeffer family. The traits of his character, his decision to take up the study of theology, even his martyrdom—all had their sources in the family, in some cases as far back as four generations. (Most of the Bonhoeffer family were involved in the Resistance, and a brother and two brothers-in-law were imprisoned with Dietrich.)

His father, Karl Bonhoeffer, was descended from a Dutch clan that settled in Württemberg, Germany, in 1513. Originally goldsmiths, in time they had become a leading family of lawyers, ministers, and doctors in the Freie Reichsstadt. The family seal shows a lion with a bundle of beans in its paw on a blue ground, the word "Bonhoeffer" meaning "beanfield." Karl had grown up in Swabia, a predominantly agricultural or forested region that contains the Black Forest, and is associated with the names of such literary and philosophical figures as Schelling, Schiller, Hegel, and now Bultmann. As a child, Karl was regularly required by his father to walk the twenty-five miles from the family home, in Tübingen, to Stuttgart, where his grandmother lived. Karl's father was himself so fond of walking that, for short journeys, he thought trains too slow; it was said that in the spring he would go for walks in the Schwäbische Alb carrying bags of radish seeds that he would sow along the way, returning in autumn for the harvest. Karl took after his father, and, as a man, used to go for long walks, gathering mushrooms. Sometimes he would take Dietrich with him, and instruct his son in how to distinguish the edible varieties from the poisonous ones. The mushrooms would be brought home, dried, and served at the table. Dietrich grew up to be a great walker and a mushroom collector. Karl, after an exacting university career, had become a well-known physician, an authority on neurology and psychiatry. (There was an indirect mention of him in Ernest Jones' biography of Freud.) Because of the background of the father, the Bonhoeffer household was solidly grounded in science. Karl's working day was fairly leisurely. He would go to the local clinic, in Breslau, where he had made his home and where the family lived until Dietrich was six, at nine-thirty and return home at two. He might see two or three patients in the afternoon, but that was all. Like an Englishman, he always had the air, however busy he might be, of someone with unlimited time at his disposal. He was a man of few words, however, and always talked to the point. If the children spoke up too vociferously at the dinner table, Karl brushed their remarks aside with a few well-chosen words that left them in no doubt that what they had said was nonsense. Later on, his letters to imprisoned members of his family were simple and controlled. He was incapable of grandiose words or grandiose sentiments.

Dietrich's mother was the former Paula von Hase, the daughter of Klara von Hase, née Countess Kalckreuth. Paula's father had been a chaplain to the Emperor, and her grandfather a nineteenth-century church historian of some distinction. She had blond hair and blue eyes, whereas her husband had black hair and brown eyes, and she was a contrast to him in practically every other way as well. Dietrich's looks, his feeling for music, and his exuberant spirits are said to have come from her. She had a keen interest in other people and a way of coming up with quick solutions to their problems. She was spirited, and she had an engaging manner. She was, as a rule, controlled, and when, during the First World War, Walter, her second son, who was a patriot and something of a poet, was dying in France of wounds received in battle, her sense of duty to Germany restrained her from rushing to his bedside, as her instincts prompted her to do. After Walter's death, however, she bitterly regretted this restraint, for she felt she might have nursed her son back to health, and as a consequence she was ill for half a year. It was the family custom to write down the significant events in the life of the family at the end of each year, but for ten years after Walter's death there were no entries. During the Second World War, when two of her other sons, Dietrich and Klaus, and also her two sons-in-law, Hans von Dohnanyi and Rüdiger Schleicher, had been imprisoned under suspicion of plotting against Hitler, she thrust herself upon the City Commandant of Berlin, Paul von Hase, who was her cousin, and, demanding that he intervene, succeeded in having the conditions of their imprisonment made less rigorous. All during their imprisonment, she poured her heart out to them in high-flown letters, but after they died, she tried hard not to give way as she had after Walter died. She had always been musical (Saturday evenings in the Bonhoeffer household were set aside for music) and had a special weakness for Schumann lieder. She had often sung, with Dietrich accompanying her on the piano. Later, when he was in Finkenwalde Seminary, he kept up the family tradition by organizing a quintet, of which he was the pianist. No matter how inadequate the other players were, it is said, he was able to lead them into giving a respectable performance.

Dietrich grew up in Berlin, to which the family moved from Breslau. In Berlin, the Bonhoeffers lived on Wangenheimstrasse, in the Grunewald district, in a large house appointed with heavy oak furniture and heavy velvet draperies. The walls were hung with paintings, among them pleasant landscapes by Dietrich's great-grandfather Stanislaus Graf Kalckreuth and portraits by his great-uncle Leopold Graf Kalckreuth, of which some hang today in an art gallery in Hamburg. There were five servants, including a governess, who spoke French with the children, and a personal maid for Mrs. Bonhoeffer. The district, like the house, was upper bourgeois, with an academic flavor (Harnack and Max Planck lived there), and the Bonhoeffers themselves were members of the cultivated upper middle class. Altogether, there were eight Bonhoeffer children—Karl Friedrich, Walter, Klaus, Ursula, Christine, Dietrich and his twin sister, Sabine, and Suzanne, in that order. Every one of Dietrich's brothers and sisters had an important place in his life.

Karl Friedrich grew up to be a biochemist. He had studied with Max Planck and was on friendly terms with Einstein. He undertook research on heavy water, but in the thirties he left it for the study of the interaction between leaves and the air. Karl Friedrich had been in the First World War, with Walter, and because of that he enjoyed a certain prestige in the Bonhoeffer household. It was due to his influence that Dietrich, to assert himself and have a domain of his own, first turned to theology—something out of favor among the Bonhoeffers, and even ridiculed. The Bonhoeffers were not a churchgoing family, and all the family baptisms, weddings, and funerals were performed in the house by an uncle, who was a pastor, and, even so, was the victim of a certain amount of derision, as was another uncle, whose interest in the family genealogy had led him to claim that the Bonhoeffers were descendants—very remote ones—of Luther.

Walter, who aspired to be a biologist or a zoologist, modelled his poems after Hölderlin, who, in his turn, had been influenced by Schiller. Walter was a bit of a stoic. The hours before his death found him composing a letter about how he had anesthetized the pain of his

wounds by thinking about his comrades-in-arms. Owing to his influence, Dietrich was a nationalist in the twenties, though in the thirties
his detestation of Nazism made him turn pacifist for a time.

Klaus was the adventurer in the family. He was fond of travelling,
and had once gone to Spain, where he became an enthusiast of bull-
fighting, bought a painting by the then unknown Picasso (or he later
came to think that it was by Picasso), and enjoyed the society of
aristocrats; in fact, he made a hobby of studying the aristocracies of
other countries. Klaus was responsible, along with Ursula and Christine and their husbands, for Dietrich's becoming involved in the Resistance. Christine, the cleverest of the Bonhoeffer girls, as the wife of
Hans von Dohnanyi (Hans' father, Ernst, was the well-known pianist
and composer, and Hans' son, Christoph, is now a conductor of the
West German Radio Orchestra in Cologne), was the Bonhoeffer
woman closest to the plot, and it was her great sorrow that she had not
been born a man.

Next in line were the twins, Dietrich and Sabine, he taking after
their mother in appearance, she after their father. Sabine, too, had her
part in the conspiracy of the family. She had married a Jew—Gerhard
Leibholz, the youngest professor of political economy in Berlin (he is
now a judge of the West German Supreme Court)—and when the
Bonhoeffers learned that Hitler was about to decree that all Jews must
have their passports stamped "J" (for men) or "S" (for women), they
got Sabine and her husband across the French border, from which
the couple made their way to England. Not only did the Leibholzes,
who passed the war in Oxford, dramatize the Jewish predicament for
Dietrich but Gerhard Leibholz wrote speeches for George K. A. Bell,
the Bishop of Chichester, who became a British spokesman for the
plotters.

Suzanne, who married a church historian named Walter Dress, also
played a role in the plot, but a very minor one—she infrequently
smuggled messages to and from her imprisoned brothers. During the
war, she was busy with the bringing up of two small children.

In the eyes of the Bonhoeffer parents, Dietrich was neither the cleverest of their children (Karl Friedrich was regarded as that) nor the
most daring or heroic (Walter had died at the front). In fact, after the
war they found it very interesting that Dietrich, because of Bethge,
should have become the best-known member of the family. Even as

children, the dominant figures in the household had been the three elder brothers, in contrast to whom Dietrich was classed, with Sabine and Suzanne, as one of "the little ones." The elder brothers were all aggressively agnostic and intellectual, and were all interested in science. They contributed to the secular atmosphere of the household, and at Christmas, more often than not, the boys' presents were books on science. From the very beginning, Dietrich exchanged his books for Suzanne's, which were likely to be more reflective and literary.

Although Dr. and Mrs. Bonhoeffer were not inclined to force their children in any direction, they did once present Dietrich to Leonid Kreutzer, the distinguished pianist, then a professor at the State Academy of Music, in Berlin, to find out how gifted the boy was in music and whether he should think about becoming a pianist. Dietrich, however, took his future into his own hands. As a matter of course, all boys studied Latin, Greek, and French in the *Gymnasium,* and in the last two years of school they added a fourth language, of their choice, which was most often English, but Dietrich returned from school one day and informed his mother that as his fourth language he had chosen Hebrew. The decision meant only one thing—that Dietrich was going to be a theologian—and he had reached it all alone. An average student, he made his *Abitur* in 1923 and proceeded to the University of Tübingen, as his brothers had before him. He studied there for a year, attending lectures in theology, as well as in philosophy and epistemology. After a summer in Italy and North Africa, he moved to the University of Berlin, where he studied first with the aging Harnack, and then, in turn, with Karl Holl and Reinhold Seeberg, both of them leaders of the Lutheran renaissance. He received the Licentiate of Theology in 1927, at the age of twenty-one, having studied for it under Seeberg's direction. Bonhoeffer had settled on Seeberg because Seeberg seemed to him the weakest professor and therefore the one who would allow him the greatest independence. Bonhoeffer's thesis, entitled "Sanctorum Communio: A Dogmatic Investigation of the Sociology of the Church" and written, oddly, in the incompatible traditions of Barth and Troeltsch, was concerned with the Church in its dual role as a heavenly institution and an earthly power. (Barth, who during the lifetime of Bonhoeffer was cool to his work, called this dissertation in 1955 "far more instructive and stimulating and illuminating and genuinely edifying reading today than many of the more famous works which have since been written on the problem of the Church.") In 1927, Bonhoeffer took the first of two theological examinations that were required of anyone wishing to become a pastor, and went as a curate to Barcelona, which had a German colony estimated at six thousand. The Protestant congregation, however, numbered no more than three hundred, of whom fewer than fifty were regular churchgoers. There he read the writings of the late Albert Schweitzer and began questioning the kind of future that Christianity could have in Europe. He also read a good deal about Buddhism in an effort to discover in that religion an alternative to the Christian solution to the problem of power and, more specifically, to the Lutheran solution to the problem: that the exercise of power was sinful but men had to exercise it in the name of responsibility. His wish to find an alternative to the Christian solution rose out of his dissatisfaction with the hierarchy of the established church and its system of privileges, though at the time he took it for granted that organized religion was necessary. He apparently made a great impression on the children in his congregation by telling them Bible stories as though they might be fairy tales.

After a year in Spain, Bonhoeffer returned to Berlin, where he worked on and finished his *Habilitationsschrift*—a dissertation required for admission to a theological faculty in Germany. Published as "Act and Being: Transcendental Philosophy and Ontology in Systematic Theology," it dealt with the problem of God's continuity and contingency in the world, and ended what Bethge came to regard as the first of Bonhoeffer's three theological phases. This phase, which began with "Sanctorum Communio," was a mixture of Barth's "Word of God," or "revelation," theology—dominant in the twenties—with Troeltsch's sociological approach. Of Bonhoeffer's thought in this period Bethge has written, "We usually think of concreteness in terms of the application after the explanation of the text. But this separation into two additional activities in order to grasp the revelation is precisely what Bonhoeffer was fighting. . . . Concreteness is to be understood not as an addition or second activity but as a genuine attribute of revelation itself. . . . There is no God, Bonhoeffer emphasizes, other than the incarnated one known to us and meeting and claiming us in the 'Christ existing as the community of men,' the Church."

The middle period was a sort of bridge between the relatively peaceful existence of an academic theologian and the perilous life of a conspirator. It was a restive period, in which an intellectual was transformed into a practical churchman, and in which Bonhoeffer was forced by circumstances to take positions that in retrospect seemed to have made his role in the Resistance inevitable. In 1930, Bonhoeffer was awarded a fellowship to Union Theological Seminary in New York, and came to the United States for a year. He was not excited by the American theologians he encountered. On the contrary, he found them inadequately informed about the theology of revelation, and, though he himself was now moving away from it, he started defending it, in order to introduce American theologians to Barth. He found nearly all the sermons in America vacuous, probably because sermons in Germany, though dull, always had intellectual substance, and the American tradition of inspirational preaching was wholly unfamiliar to him. He made friends with Lehmann and also with the pacifist Jean Lasserre. (With Lasserre he drove to Mexico during the summer holidays.) He was drawn to Negro churches, and spent Sundays in Harlem, where he acquired a taste for Negro spirituals. At the end of his year in America, he thought of going home by way of India, in order to deepen his understanding, this time, of Gandhiism and Hinduism, but he did not want to go alone and could not find anyone to make the journey with him, so he went home the way he had come, except that he spent some time in Bonn with Barth, and attended a World Alliance Conference in Cambridge, before settling down in Berlin. There, after ordination, he taught courses in systematic theology at the University of Berlin, served as a student-chaplain—preaching regularly—at the Technical Academy in Berlin-Charlottenburg, conducted a confirmation class in Wedding, founded a settlement house there, and became a secretary of the Youth Commission of the World Alliance for International Friendship Through the Churches and of the Universal Christian Council for Life and Work. He was a *Privatdozent* at the University of Berlin (a step toward an eventual professorship), and was still living in the genteel bourgeois ambience he had known as a boy, but he was gradually beginning to be caught up in practical work for the Church. In Berlin, as in Barcelona, he made an impression on the children. He read opera librettos with his confirmation candidates, and took them to hear performances. Most of the boys died at the front or in concentration camps, but a number of letters they wrote to Bonhoeffer survive and testify that his influence on them lasted as long as they lived.

What was now happening in Germany was so momentous that no one could stand aloof, least of all a Christian interested in pastoral work. In July, 1933, church elections were held all over Germany, and as a result of Hitler's intervention Nazis took over more than seventy per cent of the positions on the ecclesiastical governing bodies—a prelude to the "Brown Synod," so named because the majority of the delegates attended wearing the brown shirts of the S.A. This General Synod of the Prussian Provincial Church (Preussische Landeskirche), which was by far the largest provincial church, was assembled that September in Berlin, and it introduced into the Church constitution the Aryan clause, already operative in the state. Since there were only something like twenty pastors with Jewish blood out of a total of twenty thousand, and since they alone were affected, most pastors, taking the view that the action of the Brown Synod made little actual difference, were prepared to prove their Aryan heritage. Bonhoeffer was so deeply disappointed by the reactions of his superiors in the university and in the Church that he decided to leave them both and become pastor of two small, independent German-speaking congregations in London. Over the protests of his colleagues, but with the encouragement of his parents, who wanted him out of Nazi Germany, he broke with his country and his past, choosing the simple life of a pastor and practical involvement in the Church in preference to the comfortable academic career for which his family background and his years of study had prepared him. He went to England in October, 1933, accompanied by a pastor named Franz Hildebrandt, who is half Jewish. Hildebrandt, at that time Bonhoeffer's best friend, had to leave Germany, because of his Jewish blood. Pastor Hildebrandt took up in London some of the clerical duties of Bonhoeffer, who, in turn, shared with him both his house and his salary.

In England, Bonhoeffer formed a friendship with George Bell, the Bishop of Chichester, and he also met C. F. Andrews, the biographer of Gandhi, and Marilyn Slade, the Englishwoman who had taken the Indian name Mirabehn and had become a follower of Gandhi. The influence of Andrews and Mirabehn led Bonhoeffer to toy once more with the idea of going to India, particularly since he now thought that Gandhi's ideas about nonviolence might be used to resist Hitler in

Germany. In the meantime, in Germany, the Brown Synod had pro-
voked the beginnings of organized resistance within the Church by a
group originally two thousand strong called the Pastors' Emergency
League, which by the end of that year had tripled its clerical strength.
Then, in May and October, 1934, this group had convened synods
of its own, in Barmen and Dahlen, which solemnly declared the
Deutsche Christen, or Nazi church government, to be heretical, and
set up an emergency church government—the Brethren Councils of
the Confessing Church. (In subsequent years, as Hitler consolidated
his hold on Germany, the group all but disappeared.) In April, 1935,
Bonhoeffer accepted a call from the Confessing Church to come back
to Germany and head a seminary, and he became the guiding spirit
of a small, newly founded seminary for Confessing Church ordinants
in Finkenwalde, in Pomerania. It was here that he first met Pastor
Bethge.

In Finkenwalde, Bonhoeffer established a community within a
community—the Bruderhaus, or Brethren House, a sort of island of
withdrawal from the world, which later became quite well known
through his little book "Life Together." The tradition of monastic life
was not associated with Protestantism. Indeed, ever since Luther's day
any kind of monastic order was assumed by Germans to be Roman.
Yet Bonhoeffer now tried to revive monastic life in Finkenwalde.
While the members of the order did not take vows of poverty, chastity,
and obedience, and were free to marry and leave the community at
any time, they did try to live simply and own everything in common,
the day being planned around prayer, the singing of hymns, and other
devotional exercises. The inspiration for this life evidently emanated
almost completely from Bonhoeffer himself. Pastor Bethge remembers that Bonhoeffer introduced a period of meditation as part of the
daily routine, and that when he went away for a time the period of
meditation was quickly abandoned. On his return, the members con-
fessed to him that they didn't know what to meditate about. He
instructed them: "Run after your thoughts, get them back, concentrate." But the natural exuberance of Bonhoeffer would often break
up the routine that he himself had brought into existence. Sometimes
for days it would be replaced by hiking or tennis or practicing chamber music together. In the evenings, the members might play bridge
or quiz games. Characteristically, Bonhoeffer never laid down any

rules. He made up procedures as he went along and revised them as practice required. Intellectual matters were not stressed, and he led the community in prayer in a childlike way that its members found touching. As part of the loose-knit routine, he introduced the custom of confession, and he made Pastor Bethge his confessor. He confided to Pastor Bethge that he distrusted theory in theology, that religion sometimes seemed to him "a big lie," that he felt himself guilty of doubt, pride, ambition, and intellectual arrogance. And a book he wrote during this period, "The Cost of Discipleship," which offers perhaps the best and most coherent statement of his views, shows him to be turning more and more to the person of Christ as the paradigm for all men—mapping out, in the words of Karl Barth, "a program in which we try to shape our lives by the example of the life of Jesus as sketched in the Gospels and the commandments which He gave to His own people and to all men generally." In Barth's estimation, the book was easily the best one ever written on the subject. About the first and the more original part of the book, he added, again in a posthumous salute in 1955, "The matter is handled with such depth and precision that I am almost tempted simply to reproduce them [the opening sections] in an extended quotation. For I cannot hope to say anything better on the subject than what is said here by a man who, having written on discipleship, was ready to achieve it in his own life, and did in his own way achieve it even to the point of death."

In 1937, the Nazis launched a campaign against the Confessing Church. They arrested hundreds of its pastors, sought to limit the effectiveness of others by forbidding them to travel, and, in September, dissolved Finkenwalde by force, though they let Bonhoeffer go free. The two years that followed were uncertain and confused for Bonhoeffer, but they were the gestation period of what was probably the most important decision of his life—to become a political conspirator against Hitler in the name of Christianity. As it happened, most of the people who took a leading part in the plot were Christians and intellectuals. Manvell and Fraenkel explained, "In its various forms, the heart of the German Resistance drew its strength from the Christian faith. . . . Though many thousands of men and women shared in the resistance movement as a whole, those who finally took action as principals in July, 1944, found the courage and resources to do so because of the reserves of the human spirit on which they knew they could draw in the event of catastrophe, torture, and violent death." Yet in Bonhoeffer's case the decision was apparently taken more on the basis of accidental and personal factors than as a result of careful deliberation either on the consequences of his participation or on any justification for it to be found in Christian doctrine. In 1940 he met Colonel Hans Oster, second in command of the *Abwehr,* or Military Intelligence Department. The *Abwehr* was headed by Admiral Wilhelm Canaris, who, though he was considered one of Hitler's right-hand men, was willing to avert his eyes from some of the treasonous activities that were going on in his department. Later, Oster was to take Bonhoeffer on as a secret agent and so put him beyond the reach of the Gestapo, and give him the opportunity—denied to all Germans, let alone the persecuted pastors of the Confessing Church—to travel in Europe and evade military service.

In March, 1939, Bonhoeffer went to London to visit his former congregations, and he also called on Reinhold Niebuhr, who happened to be teaching in Scotland at the time, and asked for help in getting to America for a year. Niebuhr immediately made plans for Bonhoeffer to teach at Union Theological Seminary that summer, and wrote to Lehmann about ways of arranging a longer stay for Bonhoeffer: "My concern is in regard to Bonhoeffer. He . . . is anxious to come to America to evade for the time being a call to the colors. . . . I am wondering whether you would be willing to constitute a committee with me, call me the chairman and yourself the secretary, and send out a mimeographed letter offering Bonhoeffer's services to colleges and universities. . . . You could have him give you topics and a description of his activities in behalf of the confessional synod. . . . Don't write him too much, but if you are willing to do this just tell him that you will get in touch with him as soon as he arrives at Union to work out plans which I have suggested. There will be some difficulty in getting him out, and if he fails he will land in prison. He has done a great work for the Church."

Lehmann could not have been more coöperative, and the suggested mimeographed letter was sent out in June, 1939, over his signature. It was an excellent introduction to Bonhoeffer at that time:

A committee, of which Dr. Reinhold Niebuhr, Professor of Applied Christianity at the Union Theological Seminary, New York, is the chairman, is venturing to bring to your attention the Reverend

Dietrich Bonhoeffer, Licentiate in Theology. Reverend Mr. Bonhoeffer is one of the ablest of the younger theologians and one of the most courageous of the younger pastors who have undertaken the task of the faithful exposition and perpetuation of the Christian faith in the present critical time in Germany. He comes from a distinguished line of forebears both in the pulpit and in the university. . . . Among the more notable of Mr. Bonhoeffer's contributions to theological learning are three brilliant and profound volumes on "The Communion of Saints," "Act and Being," and one published only recently under the title "Life Together." During the academic year, 1930–1931, Mr. Bonhoeffer was a fellow in theology at Union Theological Seminary and after his return to Germany he began a promising theological career as *Privatdozent* in the theological faculty at Berlin. Political circumstances have interrupted these hopes. After a pastorate in the German Church in London, Mr. Bonhoeffer returned to his country and assumed the difficult responsibility of teaching the future ministers of the Confessional Church. Some time ago, his little seminary was closed by the government and he has been continuing his work since then in a private capacity in the parsonages of Pomerania. . . . If your institution has a lecture foundation or lecture series on a variety of problems, will you give favorable consideration to an invitation to Mr. Bonhoeffer to appear? He is in full command of the English language and prepared to discuss in a reliable and challenging manner problems of theology, philosophy, and the contemporary situation of Christianity in Germany. The committee is venturing to suggest an honorarium of not less than twenty-five dollars and, wherever possible, of fifty dollars. I hope very urgently that we may have some word from you at the earliest possible moment. . . . Your active coöperation in this venture will be a real expression of the spirit of ecumenical Christianity.

In the meantime, Bonhoeffer had reached America and had already begun to agonize over whether he should have come at all. He had thought that in the United States he would be able to make friends for the beleaguered Confessing Church as well as to find sanctuary from German military service, but one of the jobs that were found for him in America involved work with German refugees, and he was tormented with the fear that his association with these exiles would bar his return to Germany. He wrote to one of his American benefactors:

> Before I left Germany, I had long talks with my brethren from the Brethren Council and pledged myself to return to Germany after about a year's time to take up the training work in the Confessing Church again. . . . From the point of view of the Confessing Church, my trip to America was meant to be an ecumenical link between our isolated Church in Germany and our friends over here. . . . All of us, of course, were well aware of the fact that it means running a risk for a Confessional pastor to go to America with the intention to go back to Germany, and we all agreed that I should take that risk and pay the price for it, if necessary, if it is of a true value to the Church of Christ there and here. But, of course, I must not for the sake of loyalty to the Confessing Church accept a post which on principle would make my return to Germany impossible. Now, my question is whether that would not be the case with any post that is officially concerned with refugee work? As a matter of fact, I am afraid, it would be so. Now, if that is true, what can we do about it? . . . Finally, let me add a very personal remark. My best friend in Germany, a young Confessional pastor, who has been working with me for many years [this was Pastor Bethge], will be in the same conflict with regard to military service, etc., at the latest by next spring, possibly in the fall of this year. I feel it would be an utmost disloyalty to leave him alone in Germany when the conflict comes up for him. I should either have to go back to stand by him and to act with him or to get him out and to share my living with him, whatever it be, though I do not know if he would be willing to leave Germany.

Bonhoeffer was on the verge of making his critical decision. Only a week after his arrival in America, he decided to call off his visit, cancel all the arrangements made for him, and rush back to Germany while he was still able to do so. He wrote that night in the Prophets Chamber at Union, "Quite obviously, one was disappointed, even cross. For me it means more than I can realize at present." And later he wrote to Niebuhr, "I have had the time to think and to pray about my situation and that of my nation and to have God's will for me clarified. I have come to the conclusion that I have made a mistake in coming to America. I must live through this difficult period of our national history with the Christian people of Germany. I will have no right to participate in the reconstruction of Christian life in Germany after the war if I do not share the trials of this time with my people. . . . Christians in Germany will face the terrible alternative of either willing the defeat of their nation in order that Christian civilization may survive, or willing the victory of their nation and thereby destroying our civilization. I know which of these alternatives I must choose; but I cannot make that choice in security."

The unease that Bonhoeffer felt throughout the American episode was betrayed in his style, which was so repetitious and overfull that not only did his touch sometimes appear lacking in grace and tact but he left the impression that he himself was not convinced by the reasons he gave for having come to America in the first place and for then having abruptly chosen to return. It happened that during Bonhoeffer's stay at Union, Lehmann was teaching in Illinois, so that the two men had to explain everything to each other by letters, and in informing Lehmann of his decision Bonhoeffer wrote:

Thank you so much for your good letter, which is so full of friendship and hope for the future. I find it very hard to tell you that I have decided in the meantime to return to Germany in a few weeks. The invitation I got to come to America was based on the misunderstanding that I would stay here for good. I was supposed to supervise the social welfare of the Christian refugees, which meant that I could never go back to Germany. Now all necessary decisions have been made and I have informed the Church about it, and I shall return in July or August. I regret it for various reasons; on the other hand, I am very glad to give a helping hand over there. I am drawn toward my fighting brothers; I am sure you will understand me. And now I have a very urgent request to make: In your very kind letters to the colleges you mentioned my work in Pomerania. If such a letter gets into the hands of the German authorities, the whole of my job would be finished. Will you understand me if I ask you kindly and at the same time urgently, to write to the same people that I have returned in the meantime and the whole thing did not come off and perhaps also (which would be important to me) that this whole undertaking was based on a misunderstanding. I hope that they are reliable enough not to circulate the letters any further. . . . I am sorry for all the trouble I have given you. Please see to it that people just think that the whole matter is finished. And please do not mention in your letter Pomerania again, and also not that the matter should not get into the hands of the German authorities. Just say simply that "the matter regarding Mr. D. B. was in the meantime settled as he has returned to Germany due to some misunderstanding." That would suit me best and would also be more helpful for my work, which is so urgent just now. If you say any more, somebody might be unnecessarily interested. And please do it right away. Please do not think that I regret having come here. I am very glad to have seen it all and I have learnt a lot. My greatest worry is that I have not seen you and your wife. And now farewell, my dear Paul. May God take care of you and your wife and give you strength and joy for your work and also keep up our friendship as it always has been.

Back in Germany, Bonhoeffer resumed his teaching of Confessing Church ordinants, but in 1940 his work was again dissolved and he became a wandering preacher in the northern provinces. One afternoon while he and Bethge were in Memel, in Prussia, on an evangelical tour, they were seated in a crowded café when they heard on the radio the blast of trumpets that always preceded an important news announcement. This time, it was the fall of France. According to ritual, the broadcast concluded with the singing of the Horst Wessel Song. The customers in the café jumped up jubilantly, raised their right arms, and joined in the singing. Bethge hung back, but then saw that Bonhoeffer not only was on his feet but had his arm up and was singing. Bonhoeffer managed to whisper to Bethge. "Are you mad?" Bethge followed his example, and afterward Bonhoeffer explained, "We mustn't sacrifice ourselves in protest against such ridiculous things. We have to sacrifice ourselves for something far graver." Pastor Bethge knew that whatever hesitation Bonhoeffer might have had about living a life of deception in the name of Christianity had vanished, and that he was now launched on his treasonous career. (Later, it would be called the third and last phase of his life.) By now, Bonhoeffer had come to believe that his service to God could not be divorced from his political beliefs and actions. He knew that if he was captured he would have to lie and deceive and become a part of what he called "the great masquerade of evil"; he believed that under the circumstances this was his duty as a Christian. For a cleric, he held unconventional moral opinions, personal as well as political. He believed that men should live well—should eat, drink, and love well. (Twice, he seems to have considered marriage; the second time—in 1942—he was actually engaged to a nineteen-year-old girl, Maria von Wedemeyer, against the wishes of his mother, who disapproved, at first, because of the pair's difference in age.) In a chapter of a projected book on ethics he wrote:

> Love that is really lived does not withdraw from reality to dwell in noble souls secluded from the world. It suffers the reality of the world in all its harshness. The world exhausts its fury against the body of Christ, and the Church must be willing to risk its existence for the sake of the world.

That he had a chance to put this theory into practice was due to the fact that he was still able to escape military duty, though when his pastoral activities were completely suspended in 1940 he was required to report regularly to the police. He would have been conscripted if he had not been taken, as noted earlier, under the protection of the *Abwehr*. Oster's group, which included Hans von Dohnanyi, was known to Britain as the center of the resistance to Hitler, because it supplied the governments of enemy and neutral countries with accurate information regarding Germany's impending invasions of Norway, Denmark, Holland, and Belgium. However, when the fall of these countries brought Churchill to power, the new Prime Minister had immediately proclaimed unconditional surrender as the policy of his government, which, by putting all Germans, whether pro- or anti-Hitler, on an equal footing, had deprived the resisters of any hope that a government made up of Germans who had succeeded in overthrowing Hitler could negotiate an honorable peace. Since Oster's group, early in its existence, had claimed Bonhoeffer for the *Abwehr* and had made him nominally one of its secret agents, partly to put his knowledge of Britain and his connections there to use on behalf of the Resistance, the resisters looked to him, among others, to obtain from the Churchill government some sort of modification of the policy of unconditional surrender. Now he made his cause one with theirs, and this was to have a remarkable effect on this theological outlook.

Bonhoeffer's active participation in the Resistance culminated when he carried out a secret mission at the end of May, 1942, travelling to Sweden, where he met in the little town of Sigtuna a secret agent from Britain, his old, trusted friend the Bishop of Chichester. Bonhoeffer told the Bishop about the size of the Resistance and its need for British support, yet in a sense he undermined his own mission, because he was filled with doubt about whether Britain should, in fact, grant special treatment to any Germans who had managed to liquidate Hitler. For some time, he had been praying for the defeat of Germany, and he had already declared at an ecumenical meeting in Geneva, in 1941, "Only in defeat can we atone for the terrible crimes we have committed against Europe and the world." He now said to the Bishop, almost in Old Testament accents, "There must be punishment by God. We do not want to escape repentance. . . . Christians do not want to escape repentance, or chaos, if it is God's will to bring it upon us. We must take this judgment as Christians." In any event, the Bishop's subsequent entreaties, at home, to support the Resistance fell on deaf ears. He was told merely that the pastors were being "used . . . without their knowledge." But even if England had given the assurances asked, it is debatable whether they would have so stiffened the resolution of the resisters that they might have actually brought about the assassination of Hitler, for Bonhoeffer, who urged assassination, stood in the minority; most Christians could not find any sanction in their religion for such a violent act. Even after 1943, when the Resistance passed into the hands of young staff officers who had the resources to bring about a coup d'état, no coup could be arranged, for the plotters were frustrated not simply by Hitler's uncanny luck but by their own quarrels and ineptitude and by a poor grasp of the political realities.

The S.D., which handled foreign and domestic security for the S.S., had never liked the independence of the *Abwehr*. It eventually got one of the *Abwehr* agents to talk, and as a result, in April, 1943, Bonhoeffer was arrested, though the Gestapo was unable to come up with any charge against him more serious than evasion of military duty. For the next eighteen months, Bonhoeffer was in the military section of Tegel Prison, near Berlin, where he occupied himself in fabricating a defense, by attending meaningless preliminary hearings, by waiting for a trial that never took place, and in writing letters. These centered on two parallel themes—one suggested by his cry, in a poem, "Lord Jesus Christ / Thou wast poor / and in misery, / a captive and forsaken as I am," the other embodied in his oblique remark "Talk of a heroic defeat is not heroic, because it means failure to face the future." (Commentators have seen in this remark a warning both to the members of the Resistance and to the German survivors of the two world wars.) That he was able to write at all was due to the special privileges he enjoyed as a prisoner, which were granted him within a few days of his arrival at Tegel, when it became known that General von Hase, the City Commandant of Berlin, was his mother's cousin. His mother or father or Ursula (who now lived next door to them in Marienburger Allee) or Maria von Wedemeyer was permitted each week to leave for him clean clothes, papers, and books, the books being also message-carriers, since, according to a system worked out in advance between the family and Bonhoeffer, words on alternate pages had been marked. Soon Bonhoeffer turned his cell into a small study, and how he adapted himself to his new surroundings is shown in several letters he wrote to his parents in the period that closed with his first Christmas in prison. On August 3rd, he wrote:

> I eat and drink very little, and sit quietly at my desk, and in this way manage to work without hindrance. From time to time I refresh both body and soul with your wonderful things.

On August 17th:

> Above all, please don't worry over me unduly. . . . Prison life seems to give one a certain detachment from the alarums and excitements of the day.

On August 31st:

> I . . . have got quite a lot of writing done. . . . It is quite interesting to watch this gradual process of self-adaptation. I was given a knife and fork to eat with a week ago—a new concession—and they seemed almost unnecessary, it had become so natural to spread bread, etc., with a spoon.

And on December 17th:

> For a Christian there is nothing peculiarly difficult about Christmas in a prison cell. I daresay it will have more meaning and will be observed with greater sincerity here in this prison than

in places where all that survives of the feast is its name. That misery, suffering, poverty, loneliness, helplessness, and guilt look very different to the eyes of God from the way they look to man, that God should come down to the very place which men usually abhor, that Christ was born in a stable because there was no room for him in the inn—these are things which a prisoner can understand better than anyone else.

During this period, German defeats on the Western Front and the appearance among the resisters of a remarkable officer, Colonel Claus von Stauffenberg, who had lost in the war the use of his left eye, his right hand and forearm, and two fingers of his left hand, made it seem likely that the resisters would be able to assassinate Hitler at last. Indeed, Stauffenberg, on July 20, 1944, went as far as to smuggle a bomb in his briefcase into Hitler's isolated headquarters—the Wolf's Lair, as it was called, nine miles from Rastenburg, set deep in the forest, and surrounded by minefields, barbed wire, electrified fencing, and many security checkpoints—when he went to a staff officers' meeting with Hitler, where Stauffenberg was expected to report on the state of certain divisions in the Reserve Army. He managed to get some privacy to start the time fuse of the bomb, to carry the well-filled briefcase into the conference room—a wooden structure built aboveground and reinforced with concrete—to take his place at Hitler's table, and to slip the briefcase under that table, even arranging it to face Hitler, and then to leave the conference room on the pretext of a telephone call and watch the explosion from a distance of a hundred yards. The cataclysm convinced him that Hitler was dead, so Stauffenberg confidently helped to put into operation the mechanism worked out by the resisters for wresting power from the Nazis. Hitler, however, though injured, lived, apparently owing to the mere circumstance that an officer in the conference room, in order to get closer to the table, had moved the briefcase slightly so that it faced away from Hitler. He now visited revenge on the plotters. He ordered an exhaustive Gestapo investigation, which, as one of its minor results, turned up some secret papers directly implicating Hans von Dohnanyi, Rüdiger Schleicher, and Klaus and Dietrich Bonhoeffer. All four would have been executed immediately if it were not that Hitler had just come to realize the extent of the conspiracy and wanted further intelligence. As it was, the Gestapo let them live on—they were carted from one prison or camp to another for six wearing months—just on the chance that they should prove of some value to the investigation. In October, Dietrich Bonhoeffer was transferred from Tegel to a prison in Gestapo Headquarters, on Prinz Albrechtstrasse, in Berlin, and in February, during the intensive bombing of Berlin, he was taken to Buchenwald, where he apparently made a great impression on Captain S. Payne Best, an agent of the British Secret Service who was interned there as a special prisoner of war and who lived to write, "Bonhoeffer . . . was all humility and sweetness; he always seemed to me to diffuse an atmosphere of happiness, of joy in every smallest event in life, and of deep gratitude for the mere fact that he was alive. There was something doglike in the look of fidelity in his eyes and his gladness if you showed that you liked him. He was one of the very few men that I have ever met to whom his God was real and ever close to him."

It is part of the charm of Bonhoeffer's letters, which go up almost to his transfer to Buchenwald, that he reveals himself to be absolutely human. One finds him by turns complacent ("I can't help feeling that everything has taken its natural course; it has all been inevitable, straightforward, directed by a higher Providence"), nostalgic ("I recall those quiet summer evenings in Friedrichsbrunn, then all the different parishes I have worked in, and then all our family occasions, weddings, christenings, and confirmations"), introspective ("I wonder if we have become too rational. When you have deliberately suppressed every desire for so long, it burns you up inside, or else you get so bottled up that one day there is a terrific explosion"), stoical to the point of harshness ("I told him in no uncertain terms what I thought of people who can be very hard on others and make grand speeches about living dangerously, etc., etc., and then crumple up themselves under the slightest test of endurance. . . . I don't believe I find it easy to despise anyone in real trouble, and I have made that perfectly clear, which no doubt made his hair stand on end; but I can only regard that as contemptible"), despondent ("I should tell you how my grim experiences often follow me into the night, and the only way I can shake them off is by reciting one hymn after another, and that when I wake up it is generally with a sigh, rather than a hymn of praise"), impractical ("The clergy should live solely on the free-will offerings of their congregations"), contradictory ("It's true that the importance of illusion in human life is not to be underestimated, but for the Christian it is essential to have a hope which is based on solid foundations"), serene ("I am going through another spell of finding it difficult to read the Bible. I never know quite what to make of it. I don't feel guilty at all about it, and I know it won't be long before I return to it again with renewed zest"), and, occasionally, prudish, snobbish, tasteless, and polemical as well ("When God was driven out of the world, and from the public side of human life, an attempt was made to retain Him at least in the sphere of the 'personal,' the 'inner life,' the private life. And since every man still has a private sphere, it was thought that he was most vulnerable at this point. The secrets known by a man's valet, that is, to put it crudely, the area of his intimate life—from prayer to his sexual life—have become the hunting ground of modern psychotherapists. In this way they resemble, though quite involuntarily, the dirtiest gutter journalists. Think of the newspapers which specialize in bringing to light the most intimate details about prominent people. They practice social, financial, and political blackmail on their victims: the psychotherapists practice religious blackmail. Forgive me, but I cannot say less about them. From the sociological point of view, this is a revolution from below, a revolt of inferiority. Just as the vulgar mentality is never satisfied until it has seen some highly placed personage in his bathing attire, or in other compromising situations, so it is here. There is a kind of malicious satisfaction in knowing that everyone has his weaknesses and nakednesses. In my contacts with the outcasts of society, its pariahs, I have often noticed how mistrust is the dominant motive in their judgments of other people. Every act of a person of high repute, be it never so altruistic, is suspected from the outset. Incidentally, I find such outcasts in all ranks of society. In a flower garden they grub around for the dung on which the flowers grow. The less responsible a man's life, the more easily he falls a victim to this attitude. This irresponsibility and absence of bonds has its counterpart among the clergy in what I should call the 'priestly' snuffing around in the sins of men in order to catch them out. . . . It is the same kind of thing you find in the novels of the last fifty years, which think they have only depicted their characters properly when they have described them in bed, or in films where it is thought necessary to include undressing scenes"). In the last letter included in the book, there is a poignant sentence that might be said to epitomize Bonhoeffer, fated prisoner that he was: "Could I please have some toothpaste and a few coffee beans?"

In the last days of the war, with the American forces moving rapidly across Germany, Bonhoeffer was transferred again and again. The hellish journey started on Tuesday, April 3rd, when Bonhoeffer and fifteen other Buchenwald inmates, including Payne Best, were crowded in a prison van powered by a wood generator, and headed for Weiden, the village nearest Flossenburg. The front part of the van was packed with billets of wood, while the prisoners, with all their luggage, were squeezed into the small back section of the van so tightly that their legs were pushed up against the baggage and their arms pinned to their sides. The van, filled with exhaust fumes, could move only fifteen miles an hour, and had to be stopped every hour in order to refire the generator and clean the flues, and still the engine had to be raced fifteen minutes more before they could set out again. The journey was long and the prisoners had nothing to eat or drink. Bonhoeffer, a smoker, had saved up his scanty ration of tobacco, which he now shared, touching his companions with his generosity and goodness. They reached Weiden on Wednesday, but the Flossenburg camp was too full to receive them; three were admitted the next day, and the rest were again on the road in the van, proceeding southward in search of accommodations. The thirteen inmates spent Thursday night in the Regensburg state prison, five to a cell, but the next day they were sent on again, only to have the van break down on the road and to spend a cold, stormy night among the bomb craters. Saturday, a replacement for the van arrived, a bus with plate-glass windows and upholstered seats and guards with tommy guns. The entire day was spent trying to get the prisoners across the Danube and behind the crumbling German frontier. At last, a pontoon was found which had escaped bombing, and that night they slept in the local schoolhouse of the Bavarian village of Schönberg. The next day was Sunday, April 8th, and Payne Best recounts, "Pastor Bonhoeffer held a little service and spoke to us in a manner which reached the hearts of all, finding just the right words to express the spirit of our imprisonment and the thoughts and resolutions which it had brought. He had hardly finished his last prayer when the door opened and two evil-looking men in civilian clothes came in and said: 'Prisoner Bonhoeffer. Get ready to come with us.' Those words 'come with us'—for all prisoners they had come to mean one thing only—the scaffold. We bade him goodbye—he drew me aside—'This is the end,' he said. 'For me the beginning of life,' and then he gave me a message to give, if I could, to the Bishop of Chichester."

Bonhoeffer was once more on the road. He was driven back to Flossenburg, through the narrow stretch of territory still under German control, and reached the concentration camp that night. The next morning, the camp doctor saw him praying in his cell, and later his Bible and a volume of Goethe in which his name was inscribed were found in the guardroom, among the small belongings of the dead, by the liberating armies, who took possession of Flossenburg within a few days.

The exact circumstances of his death—the manner of his execution, and whether he died at the hands of capricious officers acting on their own or by official order of the Nazi government—remain in doubt. But this uncertainty is important only to those skeptics who would resort to a technicality to deny Bonhoeffer even political martyrdom. Niebuhr wrote soon after Bonhoeffer's death, "The story of Bonhoeffer . . . belongs to the modern Acts of the Apostles. . . . It is safe to say that his life and death will become one of the sources of grace for the new church in a new Germany."

Bonhoeffer's afterlife on this earth begins in what has come to be called the theology of liberation, which was conceived in prison and expounded in the form of letters to Pastor Bethge. Because he was a theologian of distinction who had been alternately Barthian and Bultmannian, there had been those who thought he might be able to effect a sort of synthesis of the thought of the two adversaries: of, on the one hand, accepting the really inaccessible word of God as revealed in the Bible, and, on the other, treating that word existentially—that is, discounting everything in the Bible as mythological except insofar as it speaks to us in the accents of our own time. It was thought that such a conjunction, if it were achieved by him, might give theology a lease on life valid for our century. Since Bonhoeffer's death, the number of theologians who think he might have been able to combine the two schools has increased, and not only have his letters on Barth and Bultmann—which, in a sense, are the core of the theological letters—been scoured for clues to what direction he might have taken if he had been allowed to live but his criticisms of the two men, registered there, are still constantly debated in the theological world. In fact, it is impossible to understand Bonhoeffer's influence without looking at them closely. In one important letter he contends that Barth is still a child of nineteenth-century theology, and Bultmann, at best, perhaps a very reluctant child of the twentieth. He writes to Pastor Bethge:

> I expect you remember Bultmann's paper on the demythologizing of the New Testament? My view of it today would be not that he went too far, as most people seem to think, but that he did not go far enough. It is not only the mythological conceptions, such as the miracles, the ascension, and the like (which are not in principle separable from the conceptions of God, faith, and so on) that are problematic, but the "religious" conceptions themselves. You cannot, as Bultmann imagines, separate God and miracles, but you do have to be able to interpret and proclaim *both* of them in a "nonreligious" sense. . . . What do I mean by "interpret in a religious sense"? In my view, that means to speak on the one hand metaphysically, and on the other individualistically. Neither of these is relevant to the Bible message or to the man of today. . . . Barth was the first theologian to begin the criticism of religion—and that remains his really great merit—but he set in its place the positivist doctrine of revelation, which says in effect, "Take it or leave it": Virgin Birth, Trinity or anything else, everything which is an equally significant and necessary part of the whole, which latter has to be swallowed as a whole or not at all. That is not in accordance with the Bible. There are degrees of perception and degrees of significance, i.e., a secret discipline must be reestablished whereby the *mysteries* of the Christian faith are preserved from profanation. The positivist doctrine of revelation makes it too easy for itself, setting up, as in the ultimate analysis it does, a law of faith, and mutilating what is, by the incarnation of Christ, a gift for us. The place of religion is taken by the Church—that is, in itself, as the Bible teaches it should be—but the world is made to depend upon itself and left to its own devices, and that is all wrong.

In another letter he returns to his criticisms of Barth and Bultmann, this time setting them in a much wider historical context and subsuming them under his own ideas. There is hardly a passage in recent theological literature that has received more attention than this one, and the letter deserves to be reproduced almost in its entirety:

> I will try to define my position from the historical angle.
>
> The movement beginning about the thirteenth century . . . toward the autonomy of man (under which head I place the discovery of the laws by which the world lives and manages in science, social and political affairs, art, ethics and religion) has in our time reached a certain completion. Man has learned to cope with all questions of importance without recourse to God as a working hypothesis. In questions concerning science, art, and even ethics, this has become an understood thing which one scarcely dares to tilt at any more. But for the last hundred years or so it has been increasingly true of religious questions also: it is becoming evident that everything gets along without "God," and just as well as before. As in the scientific field, so in human affairs generally, what we call "God" is being more and more edged out of life, losing more and more ground.
>
> Catholic and Protestant historians are agreed that it is in this development that the great defection from God, from Christ, is to be discerned, and the more they bring in and make use of God and Christ in opposition to this trend, the more the trend itself considers itself to be anti-Christian. The world which has attained to a realization of itself and of the laws which govern its existence is so sure of itself that we become frightened. False starts and failures do not make the world deviate from the path and development it is following; they are accepted with fortitude and detachment as part of the bargain, and even an event like the present war is no exception. Christian apologetic has taken the most varying forms of opposition to this self-assurance. Efforts are made to prove to a world thus come of age that it cannot live without the tutelage of "God." Even though there has been surrender on all secular problems, there still remain the so-called ultimate questions—death, guilt—on which only "God" can furnish an answer, and which are the reasons why God and the Church and the pastor are needed. Thus we live, to some extent, by these ultimate questions of humanity. But what if one day they no longer exist as such, if they too can be answered without "God"? We have of

course the secularized offshoots of Christian theology, the existentialist philosophers and the psychotherapists, who demonstrate to secure, contented, happy mankind that it is really unhappy and desperate, and merely unwilling to realize that it is in severe straits it knows nothing at all about, from which only they can rescue it. Wherever there is health, strength, security, simplicity, they spy luscious fruit to gnaw at or to lay their pernicious eggs in. They make it their object first of all to drive men to inward despair, and then it is all theirs. That is secularized methodism. And whom does it touch? A small number of intellectuals, of degenerates, of people who regard themselves as the most important thing in the world and hence like looking after themselves. The ordinary man who spends his everyday life at work, and with his family, and of course with all kinds of hobbies and other interests too, is not affected. He has neither time nor inclination for thinking about his intellectual despair and regarding his modest share of happiness as a trial, a trouble, or a disaster.

The attack by Christian apologetic upon the adulthood of the world I consider to be in the first place pointless, in the second ignoble, and in the third un-Christian. Pointless, because it looks to me like an attempt to put a grown-up man back into adolescence, i.e., to make him dependent on things on which he is not in fact dependent any more, thrusting him back into the midst of problems which are in fact not problems for him any more. Ignoble, because this amounts to an effort to exploit the weakness of man for purposes alien to him and not freely subscribed to by him. Un-Christian, because for Christ Himself is being substituted one particular stage in the religiousness of man, i.e., a human law. Of this more later.

But first a word or two on the historical situation. The question is, Christ and the newly matured world. It was the weak point of liberal theology that it allowed the world the right to assign Christ His place in that world: in the dispute between Christ and the world it accepted the comparatively clement peace dictated by the world. It was its strong point that it did not seek to put back the clock, and genuinely accepted the battle (Troeltsch), even though this came to an end with its overthrow.

Overthrow resulted in capitulation and an attempt at a completely fresh start based on consideration of the Bible and Reformation fundamentals of the faith. . . . Tillich set out to interpret the evolution of the world itself—against its will—in a religious sense, to give it its whole shape through religion. That was very courageous of him, but the world unseated him and went on by itself: he, too, sought to understand the world better than it understood itself, but it felt entirely *mis*understood, and rejected the imputation. (Of course the world does need to be understood better than it understands itself, but not "religiously," as the religious socialists desired.) Barth was the first to realize the mistake that all these efforts (which were all unintentionally sailing in the channel of liberal theology) were making in having as their objective the clearing of a space for religion in the world or against the world.

He called the God of Jesus Christ into the lists against religion, "*pneuma* against *sarx.*" That was and is his greatest service (the second edition of his "Epistle to the Romans," in spite of all its neo-Kantian shavings). Through his later "Dogmatics," he enabled the Church to effect this distinction in principle all along the line. It was not that he subsequently, as is often claimed, failed in ethics, for his ethical observations—so far as he has made any—are just as significant as his dogmatic ones; it was that he gave no concrete guidance, either in dogmatics or in ethics, on the nonreligious interpretation of theological concepts. There lies his limitation, and because of it his theology of revelation becomes positivist, a "positivism of revelation," as I put it. . . .

Bultmann would seem to have felt Barth's limitations in some way, but he misconstrues them in the light of liberal theology, and hence goes off into the typical liberal reduction process (the "mythological" elements of Christianity are dropped, and Christianity is reduced to its "essence"). I am of the view that the full content, including the mythological concepts, must be maintained. The New Testament is not a mythological garbing of the universal truth; this mythology (resurrection and so on) is the thing itself—but the concepts must be interpreted in such a way as not to make religion a pre-condition of faith (cf. circumcision in St. Paul). Not until that is achieved will, in my opinion, liberal theology be overcome (and even Barth is still dominated by it, though negatively), and, at the same time, the question it raises be genuinely taken up and answered. . . .

The world's coming of age is, then, no longer an occasion for polemics and apologetics, but it is really better understood than it understands itself, namely on the basis of the Gospel, and in the light of Christ.

The form of Christianity suited to this world-come-of-age is, to use Bonhoeffer's phrase, "religionless Christianity"—an idea so paradoxically expressed that some people find it hopelessly elusive. Indeed, the key fragment in which Bonhoeffer discusses this answer shows him to be only on the verge of formulating the concept himself, and somewhat fearful of its implications. He writes to Pastor Bethge:

You would be surprised and perhaps disturbed if you knew how my ideas on theology are taking shape. This is where I miss you most of all, for there is no one else who could help me so much to clarify my own mind. The thing that keeps coming back to me is, what *is* Christianity, and indeed what *is* Christ, for us today? The time when men could be told everything by means of words, whether theological or simply pious, is over, and so is the time of inwardness and conscience, which is to say the time of religion as such. We are proceeding toward a time of no religion at all: men as they are now simply cannot be religious any more. Even those who honestly describe themselves as "religious" do not in the least act up to it, and so when they say "religious" they evidently mean something quite different. Our whole nineteen-hundred-year-old Christian preaching and theology rests upon the "religious premise" of man. What we call Christianity has always been a pattern— perhaps a true pattern—of religion. But if one day it becomes apparent that this *a priori* "premise" simply does not exist but was an historical and temporary form of human self-expression, i.e., if we reach the stage of being radically without religion—and I think this is more or less the case already, else how is it, for instance, that this war, unlike any of those before it, is not calling forth any "religious" reaction?—what does that mean for "Christianity"?

It means that the linchpin is removed from the whole structure of our Christianity to date, and the only people left for us to light on in the way of "religion" are a few "last survivals of the age of chivalry," or else one or two who are intellectually dishonest. Would they be the chosen few? Is it on this dubious group and none other that we are to pounce, in fervor, pique, or indignation, in order to sell them the goods we have to offer? Are we to fall upon one or two unhappy people in their weakest moment and force upon them a sort of religious coercion?

If we do not want to do this, if we had finally to put down the western pattern of Christianity as a mere preliminary stage to doing without religion altogether, what situation would result for us, for the Church? How can Christ become the Lord even of those with no religion? If religion is no more than the garment of Christianity—and even that garment has had very different aspects at different periods—then what is a religionless Christianity? Barth, who is the only one to have started on this line of thought, has still not proceeded to its logical conclusion, but has arrived at a positivism of revelation which has nevertheless remained essentially a restoration. For the religionless working man, or indeed, man generally, nothing that makes any real difference is gained by that. The questions needing answers would surely be: What is the significance of a Church (church, parish, preaching, Christian life) in a religionless world? How do we speak of God without religion, i.e., without the temporally influenced presuppositions of metaphysics, inwardness, and so on? How do we speak (but perhaps we are no longer capable of speaking on such things as we used to) in secular fashion of God? In what way are we in a religionless and secular sense Christians, in what way are we the *Ekklesia*, "those who are called forth," not conceiving of ourselves religiously as specially favored, but as wholly belonging to the world? Then Christ is no longer an object of religion, but something quite different indeed and in truth the Lord of the world. Yet what does that signify? What is the place of worship and prayer in an entire absence of religion? Does the secret discipline, or, as the case may be, the distinction (which you have met with me before) between penultimate and ultimate, at this point acquire fresh importance? . . .

I find after all I can carry on writing. The Pauline question whether circumcision is a condition of justification is today, I consider, the question whether religion is a condition of salvation. Freedom from circumcision is at the same time freedom from religion. I often ask myself why a Christian instinct frequently draws me more to the religionless than to the religious, by which I mean not with any intention of evangelizing them, but rather, I might almost say, in "brotherhood." While I often shrink with religious people from speaking of God by name—because that Name somehow seems to me here not to ring true, and I strike myself as rather dishonest (it is especially bad when others start talking in religious jargon: then I dry up completely and I feel somehow oppressed and ill at ease)—with people who have no religion I am able on occasion to speak of God quite openly and, as it were, naturally. Religious people speak of God when human perception is (often just from laziness) at an end, or human resources fail: it is really always the *Deus ex machina* they call to their aid, either for the so-called solving of insoluble problems or as support in human failure—always, that is to say, in helping out human weakness or on the borders of human existence. Of necessity, that can only go on until men can, by their own strength, push those borders a little further, so that God becomes superfluous as a *Deus ex machina*. I have come to be doubtful even about talking of "borders of human existence." Are even death today, since men are scarcely afraid of it any more, and sin, which they scarcely understand any more, still genuine borderlines? It always seems to me that in talking thus we are only seeking frantically to make room for God. I should like to speak of God not on the borders of life but at its center, not in weakness but in strength, not, therefore, in man's suffering and death but in his life and prosperity. On the borders it seems to me better to hold our peace and leave the problem unsolved. Belief in the resurrection is not the solution of the problem of death. The "beyond" of God is not the beyond of our perceptive faculties. The transcendence of theory based on perception has nothing to do with the transcendence of God. God is the "beyond" in the midst of our life. The Church stands not where human powers give out, on the borders, but in the center of the village. That is the way it is in the Old Testament, and in this sense we still read the New Testament far too little on the basis of the Old. The outward aspect of this religionless Christianity, the form it takes, is something to which I am giving much thought, and I shall be writing to you about it again soon. It may be that on us in particular, midway between East and West, there will fall an important responsibility.

In short, he defines one paradoxical idea by another—"religionless Christianity" by "the beyond in our midst." It is somewhat confusing, but one has to remember the circumstances in which Bonhoeffer was writing. In any event, one is held by the voice, as when he grapples with this general theme farther on: "I find it's very slow going trying to work out a non-religious interpretation of Biblical terminology, and it's a far bigger job than I can imagine at the moment." He continues, almost in an intellectual shorthand:

On the historical side I should say there is *one* great develop-ment which leads to the idea of the autonomy of the world. In theology it is first discernible in Lord Herbert of Cherbury, with his assertion that reason is the sufficient instrument of religious knowledge. In ethics it first appears in Montaigne and Bodin with their substitution of moral principles for the ten commandments. In politics, Machiavelli, who emancipates politics from the tu-telage of morality, and founds the doctrine of "reasons of state." Later, and very differently, though like Machiavelli tending to-ward the autonomy of human society, comes Grotius, with his in-ternational law as the law of nature, a law which would still be valid, *etsi Deus non daretur*. The process is completed in philoso-phy. On the one hand we have the deism of Descartes, who holds that the world is a mechanism which runs on its own without any intervention of God. On the other hand there is the pantheism of Spinoza, with its identification of God with nature. In the last re-sort Kant is a deist, Fichte and Hegel pantheists. All along the line there is a growing tendency to assert the autonomy of man and the world.

In natural science the process seems to start with Nicolas of Cusa and Giordano Bruno with their "heretical" doctrine of the infinity of space. The classical cosmos was finite, like the created world of the Middle Ages. An infinite universe, however it be conceived, is self-subsisting *etsi Deus non daretur*. It is true that modern physics is not so sure as it was about the infinity of the universe, but it has not returned to the earlier conceptions of its finitude.

There is no longer any need for God as a working hypothesis, whether in morals, politics, or science. Nor is there any need for such a God in religion or philosophy (Feuerbach). In the name of intellectual honesty these working hypotheses should be dropped or dispensed with as far as possible. A scientist or physician who seeks to provide edification is a hybrid.

At this point nervous souls start asking what room there is left for God now. And being ignorant of the answer they write off the whole development which has brought them to this pass. As I said in an earlier letter, various emergency exits have been devised to deal with this situation. To them must be added the *salto mortale* back to the Middle Ages, the fundamental principle of which, however, is heteronomy in the form of clericalism. [In other words, bowing to ecclesiastical authority.] But that is a counsel of despair, which can be purchased only at the cost of intellectual sincerity. It reminds one of the song:

It's a long way back to the land of childhood
But if only I knew the way!

There isn't any such way, at any rate not at the cost of deliberately abandoning our intellectual sincerity. The only way is that of Matthew 18:3, i.e., through repentance, through *ultimate* honesty. And the only way to be honest is to recognize that we have to live in the world *etsi Deus non daretur*. And this is just what we do see— before God! So our coming of age forces us to a true recognition of our situation *vis à vis* God. God is teaching us that we must live as men who can get along very well without Him. The God who is with us is the God who forsakes us (Mark 15:34). The God who makes us live in this world without using Him as a working hypothesis is the God before whom we are ever standing. Before God and with Him we live without God. God allows Himself to be edged out of the world and on to the cross. God is weak and powerless in the world, and that is exactly the way, the only way, in which He can be with us and help us. Matthew 8:17 makes it crystal clear that it is not by His omnipotence that Christ helps us but by His weakness and suffering.

This is the decisive difference between Christianity and all religions. Man's religiosity makes him look in his distress to the power of God in the world; he uses God as a *Deus ex machina*. The Bible, however, directs him to the powerlessness and suffering of God: only a suffering God can help. To this extent we may say that the process we have described by which the world came of age was an abandonment of a false conception of God, and a clearing of the decks for the God of the Bible, who conquers power and space in the world by His weakness. This must be the starting point for our "wordly" interpretation.

Two days later, multiplying the paradoxes, he writes:

Man is challenged to participate in the sufferings of God at the hands of a godless world.

He must therefore plunge himself into the life of a godless world, without attempting to gloss over its ungodliness with a veneer of religion or trying to transfigure it. He must live a "worldly" life and so participate in the suffering of God. He *may* live a worldly life as one emancipated from all false religions and obligations. To be a Christian does not mean to be religious in a particular way, to cultivate some particular form of asceticism (as a sinner, a penitent or a saint) but to be a man. It is not some religious act which makes a Christian what he is but participation in the suffering of God in the life of the world.

This is *metanoia*. It is not in the first instance bothering about one's own needs, problems, sins, and fears, but allowing oneself to be caught up in the way of Christ, into the Messianic event, and thus fulfilling Isaiah 53. . . . This being caught up into the Messianic suffering of God in Jesus Christ takes a variety of forms in the New Testament. It appears in the call to discipleship, in Jesus' table fellowship with sinners, [and] in conversions in the narrower sense of the word. . . . All that is common between them is their participation in the suffering of God in Christ. That is their faith. There is nothing of religious asceticism here. The religious act is always something partial, faith is always something whole, an act involving the whole life. Jesus does not call men to a new religion, but to life. What is the nature of that life, that participation in the powerlessness of God in the world? More about that next time, I hope.

Just one more point for today. When we speak of God in a non-religious way, we must not gloss over the ungodliness of the world, but expose it in a new light. Now that it has come of age, the world is more godless, and perhaps it is for that very reason nearer to God than ever before.

And three days later still:

During the last year or so I have come to appreciate the "world-liness" of Christianity as never before. The Christian is not a *homo religiosus,* but a man, pure and simple, just as Jesus was a man, compared with John the Baptist anyhow. I don't mean the shallow this-worldliness of the enlightened, of the busy, the comfortable or the lascivious. It's something much more profound than that, something in which the knowledge of death and resurrection is ever present. . . . Later I discovered and am still discovering up to this very moment that it is only by living completely in this world that one learns to believe. One must abandon every attempt to make something of oneself, whether it be a saint, a converted sin-ner, a churchman (the priestly type, so-called!), a righteous man or an unrighteous one, a sick man or a healthy one. This is what I mean by worldliness—taking life in one's stride, with all its duties and problems, its successes and failures, its experiences and help-lessness. It is in such a life that we throw ourselves utterly in the arms of God and participate in his sufferings in the world and watch with Christ in Gethsemane. That is faith, that is *metanoia,* and that is what makes a man and a Christian (cf. Jeremiah 45).

When he leaves paradoxes behind, it is only to turn to metaphors, it seems. The results, however, are more convincing, since the imag-ery, being emotional, tends to add a personal quality to his views, making one think that the problems themselves, however great the efforts to solve them, were intractable. One feels as he trips over a paradox that the stumbling block may be the very subject that the paradox is trying to resolve. One particular passage comes to mind:

There is always a danger of intense love destroying what I might call the "polyphony" of life. What I mean is that God requires that we should love him eternally with our whole hearts, yet not so as to compromise or diminish our earthly affections but as a kind of *cantus firmus* to which the other melodies of life provide the counterpoint. Earthly affection is one of these contrapuntal themes, a theme which enjoys an autonomy of its own. Even the Bible can find room for the Song of Songs, and one could hardly have a more passionate and sensual love than is there portrayed (see 7:6). It is a good thing that that book is included in the Bible as a protest against those who believe that Christianity stands for the restraint of passion (is there any example of such restraint anywhere in the Old Testament?). Where the ground bass is firm and clear, there is nothing to stop the counterpoint from being developed to the utmost of its limits. Both ground bass and counterpoint are "without confusion and yet distinct," in the words of the Chalcedonian formula, like Christ in His divine and human natures. Perhaps the importance of polyphony in music lies in the fact that it is a musical reflection of this Christological truth, and that it is therefore an essential element in the Christian life.

But it would be unfair to leave the impression that precision always plays, one is tempted to say, second fiddle to metaphor or paradox. In a letter concerning the doctrine of salvation, he writes:

To resume our reflections on the Old Testament. Unlike the other Oriental religions the faith of the Old Testament is not a religion of salvation. Christianity, it is true, has always been regarded as a religion of salvation. But isn't this a cardinal error, which divorces Christ from the Old Testament and interprets him in the light of the myths of salvation? Of course it could be urged that under Egyptian and, later, Babylonian influence, the idea of salvation became just as prominent in the Old Testament—e.g., Deutero-Isaiah. The answer is, the Old Testament speaks of *historical* redemption, i.e., redemption on this side of death, whereas the myths of salvation are concerned to offer men deliverance from death. Israel is redeemed out of Egypt in order to live before God on earth. The salvation myths deny history in the interests of an eternity after death. Sheol and Hades are no metaphysical theories but images which imply that the past, while it still exists, has only a shadowy existence in the present. It is said that the distinctive feature of Christianity is its proclamation of the resurrection, hope, and that this means the establishment of a genuine religion of salvation, in the sense of release from this world. The emphasis falls upon the far side of the boundary drawn by death. But this seems to me to be just the mistake and the danger. Salvation means salvation from cares and need, from fears and longing, from sin and death into a better world beyond the grave. But is this really the distinctive feature of Christianity as proclaimed in the Gospels and St. Paul? I am sure it is not. The difference between the Christian hope of resurrection and a mythological hope is that the Christian hope sends a man back to his life on earth in a wholly new way which is even more sharply defined than it is in the Old Testament.

The Christian, unlike the devotees of the salvation myths, does not need a last refuge in the eternal from earthly tasks and difficulties. But like Christ himself ("My God, my God, why hast thou forsaken me?") he must drink the earthly cup to the lees, and only in his doing that is the crucified and risen Lord with him, and he crucified and risen with Christ. This world must not be prematurely written off. In this the Old and New Testaments are at one. Myths of salvation arise from human experiences of the boundary situation. Christ takes hold of a man in the center of his life.

Wherever one pauses over a paradox, a metaphor, or a concrete example in the theological letters, one is faced with conclusions so unmistakably this-worldly in their implications that in the end it sometimes becomes difficult to remember that what is under discussion is Christianity.

It was to find out how Bonhoeffer was regarded in Germany twenty years after his death that I paid my visit to Pastor Bethge, who turned out to live in Rengsdorf, a village so small that it had to be identified as near another town, Neuwied. One fine winter morning, I arrived by train in Koblenz, where I found Pastor Bethge waiting on the station platform. A fifty-five-year-old man, six feet one inch tall, with an open and extraordinarily friendly face and graying black hair, he was dressed in a pastor's black suit under a black overcoat, and he was carrying a gray hat in one hand and a blue airline bag under the other arm. Even so, he insisted on carrying my luggage. As we walked through the station, he began telling me about his wife.

"My wife, Renate, is going to pick us up," Pastor Bethge said. "She is driving back from Bonn, where she attends the university. She is studying psychology there." As though to forestall any questions, he went on, "She was unable to complete her education, because of the war. She wouldn't go to the university before the children had grown up, because she wanted to be a good mother. This is typical Bonhoeffer, *ja?* That a mother should give herself completely to her children. She is a daughter of Rüdiger Schleicher and Ursula. Renate had seen the Bonhoeffer widows. They felt lost after their husbands died. That's why Renate wanted to do psychology, to be something in her own right, *ja?*"

By now we were standing on the pavement outside the station. An Opel Rekord drew up, and out jumped a young-looking woman with blond hair and blue eyes. She shook my hand energetically. We all got in, Mrs. Bethge behind the wheel again.

"I hope you are comfortable," Pastor Bethge said.

"We bought this car second-hand last year to go to Berlin for the twentieth anniversary of the July plot," Mrs. Bethge said.

"Until then we had never tried to interest our children in the Resistance movement," Pastor Bethge said. "But in Berlin our children met the children of men who had died in the German Resistance. They got so interested that later two of them went to France on their own to a meeting of the families of members of the French and German Resistance."

I asked how many children they had.

"Three," Mrs. Bethge said. "On the way home, we will pass through Neuwied. Our two daughters go to school there. Gabriele, who is nineteen, is going to make an *Abitur* this week. Sabine is the younger one—she is eighteen."

"Sabine is named after Dietrich's twin sister," Pastor Bethge said. "We named our son, who is twenty-one now, after Dietrich. He was our son's godfather, and the baptism sermon in the 'Letters and

Papers' was for him. Dietrich is at Christ Church, Oxford. Before that, he was in Westminster. He was admitted to the school with the help of the Bishop of Chichester."

In due course, we reached Rengsdorf bei Neuwied, an ancient village deep in clean snow; it seemed that the plow was used only on the main roads. Above, there was an extraordinarily bright and warm sun.

I remarked on how peaceful things were.

"In Germany, every pastor should go into retreat periodically for one or two weeks and take a refresher course in some theological subject," Pastor Bethge said. "Rengsdorf is a place of retreat, and next week we are having a conference on the New Testament here. I teach the pastors studying in Rengsdorf. This means I have to read all the books on religious matters that come out, and this I cannot do, because of the work I am doing on Dietrich's biography."

"Rengsdorf has a population of only about two thousand," Mrs. Bethge said. "But it has been rather lively lately, because the burgomaster has got the government to recognize it officially as a resort. People can come here now on social security."

Pastor Bethge pointed out the remains of an old wall, to our left, and remarked, "That's a Roman wall. Now we are leaving civilization." Indeed, there were now woods all around us.

Presently, we pulled up in front of a small house and got out. Inside, the house was snug and friendly; there were low ceilings and plenty of heat.

We had lunch right away. At the dining table, Mrs. Bethge talked with spirit about the Bonhoeffer family. "The Bonhoeffers see more of each other than many families do," she said, "and are very much alike."

"Michael, Suzanne's son, however, is in London," Pastor Bethge said. "He has now taken up composing. He telephoned the other day and asked for a copy of one of Dietrich's poems, which he wanted to set to music. The piece was commissioned for a Dietrich Bonhoeffer anniversary celebration in London, which is to be attended by the Archbishop of Canterbury and Bishop Robinson. The celebration will take place in St. Mary le Bow Church."

Mrs. Bethge, who was serving soup, said to me, "Your soup spoon is from the Bonhoeffer house. The family was so large that each of us children got one or two things."

Two blond, blue-eyed girls, both dressed in yellow sweaters and yellow skirts, joined us. They were Gabriele and Sabine.

"How is the sewing of your very pink dress?" Pastor Bethge asked Sabine, and he explained to me that this was her first venture in dressmaking.

"It's not a *very* pink dress, Papa," Sabine said shyly but firmly.

"Gabriele plays the violin," Pastor Bethge told me proudly. "Neuwied is a very small town, but it has three orchestras, and Gabriele has played in all three of them."

"Her playing has been reviewed in the Neuwied newspaper," Mrs. Bethge added with a smile.

"It's a terribly bad paper," Gabriele said with an intellectual air. "Besides, the reviewer was my violin teacher at school."

At a word from Mrs. Bethge, the two girls swiftly removed the soup plates and brought in platters of English cheeses and German liver sausages, a large bowl of pea salad, and a basket filled with black bread. We all served ourselves. There was some discussion about whether Gabriele would be called to sit for an oral examination the following day. Everyone except Gabriele felt she had done so well in her studies that she would be exempt from that part of the *Abitur*.

"I don't like the thought of an oral examination at all," Gabriele said. "They can ask you anything they want."

"The oral part of the pastoral examination was all that got me through," Pastor Bethge said.

"But you like talking," Gabriele said.

"When we first came back to Rengsdorf, we were very much worried about the education of our girls," Mrs. Bethge said. "I called the headmaster of the school in Neuwied and told him that our girls had spent many years in English public schools and had done well there, but that they were not very good in German. I said I thought they would be able to pick up German in about half a year. The headmaster said, 'I think two years.' You see, in England, if you have deficiencies, they try to help you overcome them, but in Germany it's not like that."

"England is far more democratic," Pastor Bethge put in. "And the teachers there always stress a student's good qualities. In Germany, the teachers notice your bad points."

"The headmaster did finally agree to see the two girls," Mrs. Bethge resumed. "And then, when I told him that my father and my uncles had died in concentration camps, he immediately consented to take Gabriele and Sabine."

"He's the best history teacher I've ever had, Mama," Sabine said. "When he tells about Nazism, he gets so angry that he stamps his foot."

"The headmaster talks too much about Nazism," Mrs. Bethge continued. "Because you know how children are—whatever their elders say, they tend to resent it. I don't understand the Germans today. When I first came here, I had difficulty finding a cleaning woman, and I called on a neighbor to ask if she knew of anyone. Before I left, she said to me, 'If my father had lived through the war, he would have been hanged at Nuremberg.' Imagine that—boasting to me about her Nazi father! I told her that my father and my uncles had died in the Resistance. She didn't even know there had been a German Resistance, and asked me to lend her some of my books on it. She returned the books within a week."

"I'm sure she didn't read them, Mama," Gabriele said.

"Oh, I don't know—one ought to be charitable," Mrs. Bethge said, and continued, "And when we were in London, a German who had been in a concentration camp came up to me and said, 'Renate, I wish I had been as clever as your Uncle Dietrich and got myself killed in the camp. Then I would have hostels and churches named after me today.'"

"As though he had got himself killed! How awful, Mama!" Gabriele said.

"But we also have a friend who was in a concentration camp," said Pastor Bethge. "In a sermon I gave once I mentioned the word 'Pharisee,' and he did not like my Christian devaluation of this group of Jewish leaders. He thought it sounded anti-Semitic."

The girls cleared the table quickly and brought in a very fluffy mousse.

"This mousse is just the kind of thing a Bonhoeffer *would* come up with," Pastor Bethge said, with anticipation. "Something fantastically complicated when there is a guest in the house."

Pastor and Mrs. Bethge now started talking about how troubled they were by what was going on in Germany just then. Erhard's government was asking for special powers in case the East Germans or

the Russians should take it into their heads to violate the West German borders, as though, if that happened, West Germany could not
rely on the protection of the French, the English, the Americans—the
whole free world. To the Bethges, Erhard's emergency powers were
reminiscent of Hitler's. They said that the former Defense Minister
Franz Josef Strauss had ridden roughshod over police and journalists,
and that some of the younger generation, forgetting Hitler's part in
the war and the persecution of the Jews, now talked of his achievements—full employment and the building of the *Autobahnen.*

The girls had disappeared again, and now the dining room suddenly vibrated with a hum. Pastor Bethge and Mrs. Bethge stood up.
"That's the dishwasher—my present to Renate when she decided to
start going to the university," Pastor Bethge said. "Let's go into the
living room."

In the living room were a grand piano, a clavichord, and some
pieces of Biedermeier furniture. "I can't drink port," Pastor Bethge
said, making himself comfortable in a chair next to Mrs. Bethge. "It's
very sad, but I'm a little asthmatic, and wine exacerbates the condition. I do, however, smoke a cigar, and if you'll allow me, I'll light
one." He lit a large cigar, and continued, with a long, contented sigh,
"Do you remember a letter from prison in which Dietrich says he
imagines us sitting together as we used to, smoking, occasionally
strumming a tune on the clavichord, and discussing the day's events?
This was the clavichord he was talking about. We bought it together."

Going over to the clavichord, Pastor Bethge played a few notes on
it. It was painfully out of tune. "We don't use it much," he said. "In
England, some time back, I was pastor of the same German church in
London that Dietrich served. We had a very damp Victorian house,
and when we brought the piano back to this house from there, it
sounded horrible. It took a year to get acclimated." He talked of how
difficult it was in any case to tune an instrument well, and said that
one had to master the old organ builders' technique of tuning strings
(or pipes) in pairs, one a little flatter than the other, for maximum
resonance.

"We all have musical evenings here, but this room isn't very good
for music," Gabriele said, bringing in coffee. "The ceilings are too
low. Once, when my brother Dietrich was here, he put a loudspeaker
under the clavichord, so it wouldn't be drowned out by his cello."

"Dietrich is a very keen cellist," Mrs. Bethge said. "He plays in several orchestras at Oxford."

After coffee, Pastor Bethge took me into his study. (From upstairs came the sound of Gabriele confidently practicing the violin.) Around the walls were the books that I had come to associate with German theologians—the collected works of Nietzsche and of Kant, of Troeltsch, of Emil Brunner, of Karl Barth—and, surprisingly, Cervantes and Balzac were also there. Bultmann was not.

"These were Dietrich's books," said Pastor Bethge.

"No Bultmann?" I asked.

"In Dietrich's academic period, Bultmann wasn't of so much interest, *ja?*" Pastor Bethge replied. "Later, Dietrich owned a Bultmann, but during his imprisonment it was destroyed in the house of his fiancée, in the Neumark, east of Berlin. He left his books to me in his will." The pastor turned to his desk, which was covered with untidy stacks of papers. From the top of one stack he handed me a copy of the will, which was in the form of a letter, and was dated November 23, 1943. It read, in part:

> DEAR EBERHARD: After yesterday's air raid I think it is good to let you know what testamentary dispositions I have made in the event of my death. . . . You will, so I hope, read this with your own peculiar lack of sentimentality. . . . You will get my whole library, including all the untheological things, and the grand piano, the car, the motorcycle, the money in the postal-savings account, one of the icons, the doctor-books, the Rembrandt Bible . . . the carpet in the house of Heinz Lang, the Chinese carpet. . . . All you need of my clothes you will get anyhow.

I asked Pastor Bethge how he and Bonhoeffer had happened to become such close friends.

"I met Dietrich in 1935, in Finkenwalde," Pastor Bethge said. "He somehow got interested in me. Perhaps he saw there was something in me that wasn't developed but that he could develop. I spent holidays with him. We couldn't have been more different. He came from a very good family. I was the son of a simple country parson, and my father had died at an early age. In Germany, you know, becoming a pastor is something that lower-middle-class people do. The son of a worker might become a pastor in order to take a step up; his eldest son might also become a pastor, and in the third or fourth generation, if the family had saved enough money, one of the grandsons might go to a university and become a doctor or a professor. Dietrich was the son of a well-known doctor. His becoming a pastor was a step down. If it hadn't been for the war, I wonder how I would have married into the Bonhoeffer family. Even so, I was told later that there was quite a lot of discussion between Renate's parents over whether I could be permitted to marry her. Dietrich and I were different in so many ways. Having been brought up in a simple country parson's home, I believed that sleeping pills were bad, *ja?* But Dietrich always carried all kinds of powders and compounds in his shaving bag. He never thought that taking pills was somehow unhealthy. I suppose he got into the habit of taking medicine from his mother. She was a doctor's wife, and she had great confidence in medicine. When I was ill, Dietrich would dose me with the authority of a doctor. He himself took sleeping pills freely, but I still get a hangover from a sleeping pill. Recently, Gabriele and her brother went to Greece, and when they came back Gabriele told me that her brother had handed out pills to everybody."

Pastor Bethge laughed, and went on, "When I first met Dietrich at Finkenwalde, I had no self-confidence. Dietrich, for his part, sometimes felt he had taken advantage of me. He knew I was a weaker person than he. He once wrote from prison asking me to forgive him for the mental violence he might have done me. From the time I met Dietrich, demands were made on me for which I had no preparation, *ja?*"

I asked him what he meant.

"I am now writing a biography of Dietrich, in two volumes," he said. "But I feel that I haven't the education or the experience to do it. I am not an academic type of theologian—I have no doctorate—and this biography is the first full-length piece of writing I have ever tried to do. I know so little about writing that I wrote my first draft on both sides of the paper, so when I came to do my second draft, I couldn't cut it up. Well, all the material I have on Dietrich will be in the biography. It won't be a book that anybody will be able to read, but from it some future person will be able to write the real biography."

Pastor Bethge laughed. It was a free, boisterous, English kind of laugh, different from any other laugh I had heard in Germany. He went on, "Goethe, you know, had his secretary, J. P. Eckermann. Every decent German has the 'Conversations with Goethe,' by Eckermann, on his shelf. It is not read very much now, but Eckermann did put down all the golden words of Goethe—what he said when he was cleaning his teeth in the morning, what he said over breakfast, what he said just before he went to sleep. Well, I could never be an Eckermann, but Dietrich, late in his life, did begin to make jokes about my writing his biography. He would say, 'One day perhaps you will write my biography, and so you should know this.' But I didn't take any notes on Dietrich's golden words when he was alive."

I asked Pastor Bethge what had actually got him started on the biography.

"When Dietrich died, he left an unfinished book of ethics, which I regarded as his last will and testament," he said. "I finished it, and after that I came across all these papers of Dietrich's in my desk. His parents had kept practically everything he wrote them, and they had given everything to me. The surviving members of his family have since given me most of his letters to them. I am now missing the letters he wrote to the two girls he was in love with, and I may be missing many things more."

Pastor Bethge showed me some of the papers on his desk. There were the originals of a number of Bonhoeffer's prison letters; they were written very small, as if to make the most of a sheet of paper. Many of them were in pencil, but a few were in ink. There were some soiled pieces of paper scribbled on both sides with notes for his defense. Almost all the papers lying on Pastor Bethge's desk were dog-eared and discolored by age or damp. Some of them were held together with tape, and others were so mutilated that they had had to be placed between celluloid covers. Moreover, many of the sheets were marked up, crossed out, underlined, or otherwise annotated in another, almost illegible hand. It was Bethge's. The effect was that of a palimpsest.

"I'm afraid the damp got into these papers," Pastor Bethge said. "When I was in the Army, I used to send all the letters I received from Dietrich to my mother and Renate, who would bury them in the garden; we didn't want Himmler's Gestapo to find them. Paul Lehmann visited me once and asked me what I was doing with the letters. That was when I first realized that I might have something valuable. Later, I collected a third of them for the 'Letters and Papers from Prison.' But when I was putting the 'Letters and Papers from Prison' together, I marked them up for the secretary, *ja?* I should have had them copied first, but I didn't realize what a great treasure I had. The 'Letters and Papers from Prison' came out in a very small edition, but Gerhard Ebeling, in Switzerland, and Helmut Thielicke, in Hamburg, gave it good reviews. Professor Ronald Gregor Smith, who was then the director of the Student Christian Movement Press, and who had always been interested in Bonhoeffer, immediately decided to publish the 'Letters and Papers from Prison' in England. I was surprised by its success. I began getting invitations to speak on Dietrich."

I asked Pastor Bethge how the biography was going.

"It gets longer and longer," he said. "The first few pages are going to be a sort of verbal portrait of him."

I asked what it would be like.

"It will go something like this," he said. "Dietrich was a tall man, but he looked a little too heavy for his legs. His head was big, so although his shoulders were broad, they didn't seem so. He had a broad forehead, which made his nose seem shorter than it actually was. His lips were full, and always gave the impression that he was savoring good food. His appearance of heaviness was misleading. He was actually very athletic. In fact, his physical movements were nervous and quick, and he talked like a machine gun. You heard Renate talk. She talks exactly like Dietrich, and she has his laugh. As a person, he was very restless, *ja?* He worked with great concentration—what takes me twenty-four hours he could do in three. For this reason, he had time to do many different things."

Because the books on the Resistance were obscure about the size of Bonhoeffer's role in the conspiracy, I asked Pastor Bethge about it.

"In 1940, Dietrich only knew about the plot, *ja?*" Pastor Bethge said. "Of course, after the July attempt in 1944, any knowledge of a conspiracy was enough to get you hanged. Actually, Dietrich was only connected with the *Abwehr,* and that was just one place out of many all over Germany where resisters were making plans. He never considered murdering Hitler himself, nor did anyone ever suggest that he should, because in the last analysis everything depended on technique, and Dietrich didn't know how to hold a gun. He didn't have a uniform, and no one who wasn't in uniform was allowed near Hitler.

In fact, there was no practical way that Dietrich himself could have assassinated Hitler, *ja?* The matter did come up once, hypothetically, and he told me that he would murder Hitler if he could."

I then broached a question that detractors of Bonhoeffer in the Church sometimes asked—whether he was Christian, in any traditional sense.

"For Dietrich, the main thing about Christ was that He was defenseless," Pastor Bethge said. "Dietrich's favorite quotation from the Bible was 'My God, my God, why hast Thou forsaken me?' On the Cross, Christ did not have even the protection of God. This was the ultimate defenselessness."

"But did this insight and the ideas contained in 'Letters and Papers' amount to a new theology?" I asked.

"It depends on who it is you are talking to," Pastor Bethge replied. "Karl Barth still won't allow his students to write a doctorate on Dietrich's last period, because it's 'fragmentary,' he says—although he himself, in a sense, opened the door to the Death of God movement when he made Christ the unique and final revelation, and ruled out any metaphysical speculation about God. The Church in Germany still feels very uncomfortable at any mention of Dietrich's name, *ja?* They wish that Bonhoeffer hadn't dirtied his hands with politics."

With amusement, Pastor Bethge gave me a few examples of this unease. When the pastor and people of Flossenburg put up a plaque to commemorate Bonhoeffer, the late Lutheran Bishop of Munich, Hans Meiser, refused to have anything to do with the dedication, on the ground that Bonhoeffer was a political casualty, not a Christian martyr. Then again, in Hanover, the Church government, under its president, Bishop Hanns Lilje, had refused to let a church be named after Bonhoeffer, on the ground that it had to wait a hundred years before declaring anyone a martyr. Pastor Bethge then said he would like to quote a sentence or two from a message commemorating the martyrs which was sent out by the Church administration on the first anniversary of the July plot. Putting on his glasses, he rummaged through the papers on his desk, found the message, and read it, pausing to laugh and repeat phrases that seemed to disavow Bonhoeffer's martyrdom—though he was not mentioned in the message by name—because of his political role and his advocacy of the assassination: " 'Our eyes are set on . . . martyrs in the full'—full!—'sense

of the word. . . . We would like to name one, Vicar Paul Schneider'—
he didn't engage in politics and so he was the kind of martyr the
Church can understand—'and there are other'—other!—'ones who
tried to get a different government for our people before the last German town was ruined. . . . The Church of Jesus can never justify an
attempt on a human life no matter what the purpose was'—justify!"

Putting down the paper, Pastor Bethge went on, "Even a sculptor
who was doing a bust of Bonhoeffer for a school doesn't understand
how Bonhoeffer could have done the things he did. The sculptor
asked, 'How is it possible that Bonhoeffer, who was a theologian,
could take part in an attempt on a human life?' "

Pastor Bethge then handed me what he said was the choicest example of all. It consisted of a letter from the minister of the town of
Bielefeld and a reply from Dietrich Bonhoeffer's father:

Bielfeld, 1/4/1948

DEAR MRS. BONHOEFFER,

On behalf of the Conference of Communal Ministers of Bielefeld,
I take the liberty of addressing the following request to you. The
local council has decided, as per motion of the Social Democratic
parliamentary group, to name one of the streets "Bonhoeffer
Street" after your late husband, as part of the change of name of a
goodly number of streets. A number of people were selected who
had been victims of National Socialism, including two ministers,
our brother Schneider-Dickenschied and your husband. We, the
ministers of our town, are seriously concerned about both names,
because we would not like to see our brethren in office, who were
killed because of their faith, equated with "political" martyrs.
Since we have no say in government decisions, as the town parliament is ruled by a Socialist majority, we ask you—if you agree with
us—to write to the chief mayor of our town (Ludebeck, Social
Democrat), voicing your objection to the naming of a street after
your husband, and to deny permission.

Very sincerely yours,
HAMMERSCHMIDT, Minister

Karl Bonhoeffer replied:

2/11/1948

Dear Reverend,

Only yesterday did I receive your kind letter of 1/4. There is a misunderstanding, inasmuch as my son was not married. Therefore I have to answer your letter.

My son Dietrich would not have cared about having a street named after him. On the other hand, I am convinced that it would not be his desire to dissociate himself from the political victims killed, as he had been with them in prison and in concentration camps for years. Therefore, I would rather not protest against the decision of the town council, particularly since the choice of the two ministers seems to indicate that the parliament made its selection without consideration of political position.

With respectful regards, I remain,

Very sincerely yours,
Karl Bonhoeffer, Privy Councillor

"Of course, in those days Socialist more or less meant agnostic and atheist, too," Bethge observed.

I asked him how, in fact, Bonhoeffer would have justified his conduct, and if it was true that in Hitler's time the only Christian martyrdom was political martyrdom.

"An Italian professor once asked Dietrich himself a similar question," Pastor Bethge said. "Dietrich said that if he were walking down the Kurfürstendamm, in Berlin, or Oxford Street, in London, and he saw a madman driving a car, he wouldn't just stand there on the pavement. He wouldn't say to himself, 'I am a pastor. I'll just wait to bury the dead afterward.' His responsibility as a human being would come before any Christian commandment; in fact, killing the madman might become his duty as a Christian."

"But, in any event, do the Protestants have a tradition of martyrs?" I asked.

"Martyrs went out during the Reformation, with the Calendar of Saints and other Catholic practices, it's true," Pastor Bethge said. "The German Evangelical Church doesn't believe in making much of certain individuals, putting them between God and man. But, for my part, I like the Anglicans. They have a tradition of great lives, and in every church you go to, there's a little grave commemorating someone. There is going to be no special recognition by the Church in Germany even of the twentieth anniversary of Dietrich's death. But I've been invited to the Dietrich Bonhoeffer anniversary celebration in London, for which Michael is composing that piece. Both Robinson and I are to speak, and our speeches will be broadcast all over Europe."

And, finally, I asked which Pastor Bethge considered more important—Bonhoeffer's life or his theology.

"Ah, that is a very interesting point," he said. "I think the two were closely connected, but I, since I am not an academic type of theologian, would say his life."

I spent the night in one of Rengsdorf's two inns, and the next day I returned to the Bethge house to learn the results of Gabriele's examination and to say goodbye. I found Pastor Bethge in his study. He was on the telephone, saying excitedly, "*Ach so. . . . Ach so. . . . Ach so. . . . Ach so.*" When he hung up, he told me, "That was the headmaster's wife. Everyone in the class had to sit for the orals except her daughter and Gabriele. They were excused because they had done so well on their written papers." With his free laugh, he added, "We gave Gabriele a sleeping pill last night. It was wasted."

There was a fumbling at the study door. Pastor Bethge opened it, and in came Mrs. Bethge, carrying a large silver tray with coffee and tea, a collection of wine and spirits, soda water, cocktail glasses, a shaker, and an ice bucket. Sabine came in behind her. "Ah," Pastor Bethge said, standing back. "When a guest comes, everything belongs to him. Renate will break up any conversation just to be hospitable."

"It's nothing," Mrs. Bethge said, and she slid the tray firmly onto the desk, scattering the precious papers.

Pastor Bethge told them the good news about Gabriele, which they received with great enthusiasm. He explained to me, "Now Gabriele can go to the University of Bonn and study medicine. Bonn has a very good clinic, because, thanks to the presence of Adenauer and other important people, some of the best doctors have been assembled in the capital. After speaking at Dietrich Bonhoeffer House in Bonn last December, I talked to some people there about taking Gabriele in, and they agreed to. That's very good, because it will enable her to live close to the clinic."

I accepted a glass of sherry from Pastor Bethge. Mrs. Bethge settled herself in a chair and poured out three cups of tea.

"Papa, is this Uncle Dietrich's school report?" Sabine asked, picking up a piece of paper from the desk. "He got only a couple of 'Very Good's. The rest of his marks were average or below average. My report is better than his."

"Perhaps it was just a bad year," Pastor Bethge said.

There were footsteps in the hall, and Gabriele came in, looking very formal in a long-sleeved black dress. She was roundly embraced and then was presented with opera glasses and a china cup. She took all the fuss quite casually.

"The cup is so that she can begin a hope chest," Pastor Bethge explained to me, beaming.

"Papa, do you know what?" Gabriele said. "The burgomaster's daughter, who was doing history, was given a passage from Dietrich Bonhoeffer on civil courage to comment upon." (The passage, I learned later, was from an essay in "Letters and Papers" which he had sent to a few of his friends as a Christmas present in 1942, and which contained sentences like "The last ten years have produced a rich harvest of bravery and self-sacrifice, but hardly any civil courage, even among ourselves. . . . In the course of a long history we Germans have had to learn the necessity and the power of obedience. . . . Who can deny that in obedience, duty, and calling we Germans have again and again excelled in bravery and self-sacrifice? But the German has preserved his freedom—what nation has talked so passionately of freedom as we have, from Luther to the idealists?—by seeking deliverance from his own will through service to the community. . . . Inevitably, he was convicted of a fundamental failure: he could not see that in certain circumstances free and responsible action might have to take precedence over duty and calling. . . . Civil courage . . . can only grow out of the free responsibility of free men. Only now are we Germans beginning to discover the meaning of free responsibility. It depends upon a God who demands bold action as the free response of faith, and who promises forgiveness and consolation to the man who becomes a sinner in the process.")

Mrs. Bethge, Sabine, and Gabriele left us in order to prepare a small luncheon party to celebrate Gabriele's success. Three of her school friends were going to join her, they explained, and although a bakery was supplying the cake, there was quite a lot of cooking to be done.

"Now I would like to ask you a question," Pastor Bethge said when the others had gone. "I don't know how to finish my biography of Dietrich. I have three documents with which I can close it. One is a letter from Dietrich's father to a colleague in Boston; it was the first letter he could get out of Germany after the war. Another is a letter that Dietrich's eldest brother, Karl Friedrich, wrote to his children while he was sitting in his bombed laboratory in Leipzig. He didn't know what had happened to his brothers and brothers-in-law, and he didn't know what would happen to him, so he wrote a letter to his children, in order that they might know all he could tell them." Pastor Bethge broke off, and remained silent for a moment. He resumed, "Then, there is a letter that Hans von Dohnanyi sent to his wife after she had brought him some diphtheria germs, so that he could infect himself and stop the questioning. Karl Bonhoeffer and Karl Friedrich have since died, too."

I read over the three documents. The Dohnanyi letter, dated March 8, 1945, read, in part:

> You can hardly imagine how my heart was beating yesterday when I noticed the red-lidded cup emerging from the suitcase. . . . The misery around me is so great that I would throw away that little bit of life, if it were not for all of *you*. . . . I am quite sure I would lie down with the feeling that this is salvation not only for me but for many others, too, whose cause is connected with mine. . . . I took the diphtheria swab into my mouth right away and chewed it thoroughly. . . . I *must* get out of here and manage to get into a hospital, *so that I cannot be examined any further!* [His italics.]

The second one, a letter from Karl Bonhoeffer to Dr. Jossmann, in Boston, read, in part:

10/8/45

DEAR COLLEAGUE:

I was most delighted to receive your regards through your neighbor and to learn that you are doing all right over there and that you are engaged in an interesting activity. I understand that you were told about the sad events we experienced—we lost two sons (Dietrich, the theologian, and Klaus, Chief Syndikus of the Lufthansa) and two sons-in-law (. . . Schleicher and Dohnanyi) through the Gestapo. You can imagine that we old folks were quite hit by these happenings. All those years people were under the terrible pressure of worrying over those arrested, and over those not yet arrested but in danger. Since we all agreed about the necessity of acting and since my sons were fully aware of what they faced in case the plot did not succeed, and had settled their accounts with life, we are sad, but at the same time proud of their straight line of action. We have beautiful souvenirs from the two sons from prison—from Dietrich poems and from Klaus letters of farewell to us and to his children, that stir us and their friends very much.

Finally, there was the letter from Karl Friedrich Bonhoeffer to his children in Friedrichsbrunn, in the Harz Mountains, a portion of which read:

FOR MY CHILDREN

I would like to tell you about my parents' home, about your grandfather and your grandmother, whom you know so little, about my sisters and brothers, with whom I was brought up, about their lives and their destinies, about Berlin, the big busy town in which I met your mother. I would like to tell you about all this. Why? Because my thoughts are there, there in the ruins, and from where no news penetrates to us; it is there that I visited your Uncle Klaus in prison three months ago; he was sentenced to death. The prisons of Berlin! I know about them, but how different they are to me now! . . . I have accompanied Aunt Ursel and

Christel, Aunt Emmi and Maria, who went there daily to take
some little things. Often they went in vain and were laughed at by
the officers; occasionally, however, they met a kind porter, who
was human and who forwarded a word of greeting, who accepted
something outside the established hours, or who delivered food to
the prisoners despite orders to the contrary. Yes, to take food to
the prisoners! It was not very easy during the recent years, and especially Aunt Ursel gave more than her share. She lost weight until
she looked like a skeleton. . . . The last time I was in Berlin was at
the end of March. I had to go back there shortly before Grandfather's seventy-seventh birthday. Uncle Klaus and Rüdiger were
still alive; Uncle Hans sent a message through a doctor, which was
not completely hopeless; and from Uncle Dietrich there was not
a word—he had been sent somewhere by the S.S. It was on
April 8th, shortly before I came to see you in Friedrichsbrunn, that
I telephoned the last time with the grandparents. At that time
nothing had changed. It is more than two months now. What else
happened before the conquest of Berlin by the Russians? A man
who came from there told me that four thousand political prisoners had been murdered. And what may have happened during
the conquest and afterward? Are all still alive? I wonder whether
the grandparents stood up to these difficult days? Both of them
had very few reserves. Grandmother suffered very often from fits
which were due to too much work, not enough food, and worry.
They do not have help in their house. Uncle Dietrich had talked
to somebody on April 5th—it was near Passau. From there he had
been taken into the concentration camp at Flossenburg, near
Weiden. Why has he not been back? If I have to sit every evening
alone in my room, without Mother and you, without being able to
write to the Berliners [the Bonhoeffer parents and sisters] or to a
friend, without a visit from somebody—it is so empty here and all
my friends are dispersed—I cannot always "work." My thoughts
are with Mother and all of you. . . . And when I don't think of you
and am thinking of the grandparents and your aunts and uncles, I
cannot forget what has happened to them. Therefore I thought I
would write down what I wanted you to know about them so that
you can understand how it all happened. It . . .

In reply to Pastor Bethge's question about how to end his book, I said that I thought the letter of Karl Friedrich Bonhoeffer would serve his purpose.

As I took leave of Pastor Bethge—and, by extension, of the New Theologian—it struck me as appropriate that, Pastor Bethge having first made Bonhoeffer's acquaintance in Finkenwalde, I should later have made Pastor Bethge's acquaintance in another retreat, the ancient village of Rengsdorf bei Neuwied. It seemed to me marvellously appropriate, too, that the account of Bonhoeffer's remarkable life should conclude with a father speaking of his sons and one of those sons instructing *his* children and, thereby, the children of his children about one family's sufferings—and glories—and its minuscule but inspiring role in a specific sequence of what is called history. My own particular quest had, in a sense, ended in a political thicket—the bloodiest one in the forest. Yet, I felt, all that the New Theologian considered distinctive in the contemporary spirit, and his calling now, could be found in the Hebraic tradition of the Psalmist, in the pagan traditions of the Sophists and Stoics, and in such modern movements as the humanism of the Renaissance and the rationalism and deism of the Enlightenment. Not unique to our time was the treacherous Christian (thirty pieces of silver was enough to seduce Judas Iscariot) or the doubting Christian (Christ's own disciple Thomas comes immediately to mind) or the denying Christian (there is Peter's thrice-repeated rejection). Nor was unique to our time the Christian with eccentric views (the Protestants, once heretics in the eyes of the Catholics, were now "separated brethren," and the instruments of the Inquisition and the documents of excommunication and heresy hunts were already museum exhibits) nor the Christian who was a doctrinal maverick (central doctrines like that of the Trinity have been a matter of controversy from the time of their teaching)nor the worldly Christian (the life of Cardinal Wolsey, not to mention the doings of some of the popes in lustier times, will testify to that) nor the Christian distrusting reason even as he reasoned (Aquinas in the end had no more use for his "Summa" than Barth now has, in a way, for his "Dogmatics") nor the Christian without a vocabulary for God (the mystical experience in Christianity is as old as the religion). Even the "New Pentecost," whether it was Protestants or Catholics who awaited it, might, when it came, only start up old confusions. Perhaps the New Theologian was retreating before the rush of disaffection all around him. But then some lines of Matthew Arnold, written in 1867, came back to me:

> The Sea of Faith
> Was once, too, at the full, and round earth's shore
> Lay like the folds of a bright girdle furled.

In that time for which Arnold longed, I reflected, how easy must have been the dialogue between the men who talked about God and the men who looked to those men for knowledge of God! But even when Arnold was writing, only the "melancholy, long, withdrawing roar" of the sea could be heard:

> . . . retreating, to the breath
> Of the night wind, down the vast edges drear
> And naked shingles of the world.

How much vaster and drearier had those strands since become; instead of dialogue, there were now only indistinct cries from the edges of the ungirdled world as the New Theologian set himself the old task of equating faith and theology with reason and secularism, and doing so without any sacrifice on either side—a task, in its way, no less tantalizing than squaring the circle. But it was a testimony to the continuing power of the message, I realized, that there should be modern Acts of the Apostles, and that these should have the power to illuminate what Arnold, long before the Somme and Auschwitz, called "a darkling plain . . . where ignorant armies clash by night," and that shores far bleaker than those of Arnold's poem should be heralded as the world-come-of-age. Perhaps the New Theologian might find courage by remembering how the Psalmist of the Old Testament at times gave himself over to doubt and despair ("Out of the depths have I cried unto thee, O Lord") and yet praised God no less devoutly. How ancient was the problem of the urge to praise God!

I thought of the Magi setting out on their search to find and praise the King, the God incarnate. Yeats wrote about them in 1913 in a voice that was more truly distinctive of the contemporary spirit, celebrating, as it did, the connection between the idea of the divine and human suffering (between God and that blood-drenched forest).

Yeats looked up into the unfathomable blue of the sky and imagined that he saw there the stiff figures in procession, the Wise Men on their never-ending quest. The Magi of the poet's dramatic monologue, with their abstract expectations, stood frozen, pale, and unsatisfied:

> And all their eyes still fixed, hoping to find once more,
> Being by Calvary's turbulence unsatisfied,
> The controllable mystery on the bestial floor.

Originally appeared, under the heading "Profiles," as "The New Theologian—Pastor Bonhoeffer" in The New Yorker, *November 27, 1965. Reprinted in "The New Theologian," Harper & Row, New York, and Weidenfeld & Nicolson, London, 1966.*

FOUR

City of Dreadful Night

On the Banks of the Hooghly

The Calcutta Metropolitan District bears such a large responsibility for India's industrial effort and is such a mixture of ethnic communities and ethnic traditions that it has been seen as a perfect reflection of India as a whole and as a test case to determine whether India (or any other underdeveloped country) can ever succeed in building a modern, industrialized nation. Though Calcutta proper, or, technically, the Calcutta Corporation, as the largest single center in the Calcutta Metropolitan District is called, is today the official capital only of the state of West Bengal, it actually serves as the commercial and cultural capital of all of east and northeast India—an area that has a hundred and fifty million inhabitants, or a little less than a third of India's total population. (Calcutta is also, in a similar sense, the capital of Sikkim, Bhutan, and Nepal.) India's two greatest exports, tea and jute, which are grown in West Bengal and Assam, are processed in the Calcutta Metropolitan District and shipped out of the Port of Calcutta. Most of the equipment and the supplies for the steel and engineering industries in West Bengal, Bihar, and Orissa also pass through the Port of Calcutta. These three states are known for their rich deposits of iron and coal, for their concentration of heavy engineering and locomotive works, and, above all, for their production of most of India's steel. (All her ironworks except the Bhilai steel plant are in this region.) The Calcutta Metropolitan District handles—according to the latest available set of government statistics, for 1963 and 1964— forty-two per cent of India's exports and twenty-five per cent of her imports, clears thirty per cent of all bank transactions in India, contributes thirty per cent of the national revenue from income tax, and manufactures about fifteen per cent of all the goods produced in the country. Calcutta—and, by extension, the Calcutta Metropolitan District—is India's single dominant city and port.

The Calcutta Metropolitan District lies on the Hooghly, a river in the Gangetic delta of West Bengal. The Hooghly is actually an eastern channel of the Ganga, which is known by different local names in different regions, and this channel, being the only one navigable from the sea, has always been the most important commercially. About ninety miles inland from the head of the Bay of Bengal, the Hooghly, which generally runs from north to south, loops in a semicircular bend toward the west, creating a bulge of land on the eastern bank. This bulge marks the uppermost point of the river which is navigable by oceangoing ships, and it was around this point that the European traders—Portuguese, Dutch, French, and British, in that order—who sailed up the river in the sixteenth and seventeenth centuries founded their settlements. The British settlement, which was established on the bulge in 1690, by Job Charnock, of the East India Company, and was called Calcutta, grew into the capital of British India—a position it held from 1774 until 1911, when, in the reign of George V, the British built New Delhi, deeper in the interior, so that their capital might be equidistant from the three great imperial cities of Karachi, Bombay, and Calcutta. Today, the Calcutta Metropolitan District—a recent official designation for Calcutta and numerous surrounding clusters of urban communities and strings of rural villages, each with its own more or less autonomous local government—sprawls over both banks of the river and extends from the town of Budge-Budge, ten miles below the bulge, to the new township of Kalyani, forty miles above the bulge. The Calcutta Metropolitan District, where about seven and a half million people live in an area of four hundred and ninety square miles, has a population—and in a few cases an area—

greater than that of any one of about eighty countries in Africa, Asia, the Americas, and Europe, among them the Congo, Ghana, Tunisia, Israel, Jordan, Lebanon, Syria, Bolivia, Chile, Cuba, the Dominican Republic, Guatemala, Denmark, Finland, Ireland, Norway, and Switzerland. Half the population of the Calcutta Metropolitan District lives in Calcutta. Across the river from Calcutta is the second-largest urban community, the Howrah Corporation. Chandernagor, the original French settlement on the Hooghly, which is now in the process of being formally incorporated, will be the third-largest urban community. And there are thirty-one smaller independent municipalities. The majority of them date from the nineteenth century, and almost all of them came into existence with the growth of the jute industry—which was then, as it is now, the main industry in the area—its mills being established by British businessmen all along the Hooghly to take advantage of water power and water transport. Each new mill brought with it factory workers, who settled nearby in a sort of unplanned shantytown, supported and governed by the British millowners to the extent that these owners provided a modicum of municipal services. As the population and area of the original city of Calcutta expanded, this series of temporary settlements became permanent industrial slums. The mills, which, for the most part, are still in operation, and are still owned by British industrialists, are surrounded both by thick walls and by barbed wire and are protected by watch-and-ward staffs, and they are as spacious, clean, and orderly as the communities outside them are congested, insanitary, and chaotic. In addition to these thirty-one small municipalities—almost none of them have areas of more than six square miles, and some of them have areas of less than two square miles—there are thirty-two still smaller semi-municipalities and no fewer than four hundred and fifty villages. Calcutta, where the port facilities, the major river crossing, the financial markets, the fashionable residences and shops, the clubs, the official buildings and monuments, and the main university buildings are situated, is alone a city in any modern sense. Except for Calcutta and Howrah, not one of the urban or rural communities has more than six thousand ratepayers, and the rates in all of them—with the same two exceptions—are so low that the local governments have no funds for providing such services as running water, sanitation, public housing, health centers, and education, for maintaining streets and roads, or, indeed, even for adequately assessing and collecting rates. (In 1963 and 1964, the tax receipts of Howrah came to only fourteen rupees per person, and the receipts of all the other communities fell far below that, many villages collecting less than one rupee per person.) Except for Calcutta and Howrah, not one of the urban or rural communities has any borrowing capacity, any means of undertaking new projects, or any chance at all of coping with the demands of either a growing population or a changing technology. Even in Calcutta, which is responsible for most of the industrial income, funds are not always allocated to essential municipal services, because these are considered non-productive investments. Owing to the Calcutta Metropolitan District's importance to West Bengal and to India as a whole, there are hundreds of state and federal government departments and agencies and many private organizations that are all devoted to directing local affairs, and many of them have overlapping, and conflicting, jurisdictions; for instance, there are at least fifty bodies concerned with traffic and transportation. All attempts to merge the proliferating local governments have so far been frustrated by rivalries and pressure groups.

In the past, the Hooghly was the chief distributary of the Ganga, emptying into the Bay of Bengal at the westernmost point of the delta, and in the early period of Calcutta's growth it was a deep, open river, offering ideal access from the Bay of Bengal to the inland trade. Any of the oceangoing ships of the time, however deep their draft, could sail in and out of the Port of Calcutta easily at any season, for though the flow of the Ganga changed as the year advanced, diminishing in the summer months (April through June) and swelling in the monsoon months (July through September), the current of the Hooghly was so strong and constant that it swept any silt out to sea or washed it up on the riverbanks. Over the past two hundred years, however, the main flow of the Ganga has gradually shifted, and the Ganga's chief distributary has become the Padma River, which runs through East Pakistan and empties into the Bay of Bengal at the easternmost point of the delta. At the confluence of the Ganga and the Hooghly—or, rather, the Ganga and the Bhagirathi, for this is what the upper reaches of the Hooghly are called—a large sandbar has now formed, so that except during the monsoon season, when the

Ganga rises over the sandbar and feeds the Hooghly, what scant water the Hooghly receives is from local drainage, and, because of the weakened current, as much as a million cubic feet of silt a year now accumulates in the riverbed. This accumulation is steadily decreasing the depth of the river, its channel being clogged by an unending series of shoals and sandbars, so that costly dredging is required to keep it open and navigable. Even when some silt is washed downstream, bore tides (these occur when the seawater trapped in the Hooghly's broad estuary is released at high tide into the channel of the river) carry it back up. At one time, the Hooghly was free of bores in the monsoon and winter months, and even in the spring months high tides came only as far as Calcutta, and whatever damage they did to the channel was offset by the strong flow of the Ganga. But now, because of the heavy deposits of silt, the Hooghly is in such a condition of deterioration that even during the monsoon, when the current is at its strongest, it does little more than check the bores ten miles below the Port. In fact, the river is so shallow and constricted that the bores, which now come almost all year round, keep gathering more momentum, rising higher over the banks, and reaching farther up the river; at present, during the powerful spring tides the bores crest as high as six feet in the area of the Port and race up as far as eighty miles north of it. Even if the river could somehow be released from the cycle of weak current, silt, bores, more silt, and weaker current, the life of the Port would still be in jeopardy, because of the sharp bends in the river. In recent years, the technology of shipbuilding and the economics of trade have led to the construction of tankers that often weigh forty thousand tons and sometimes weigh well over a hundred thousand; other heavy-cargo carriers often weigh twenty-five thousand tons. Such ships are built long and have a draft of over thirty feet. But for most of the year ships weighing more than ten thousand tons or with a draft of more than twenty-six feet cannot risk negotiating the bends to call at Calcutta. Even during the high spring tides, most big modern ships must make their voyage in stages, sometimes discharging part of their cargo at Haldia, a subsidiary port thirty-five miles downstream from Calcutta. As for the Port of Calcutta itself, not only is it far from the open sea but its wharfing and docking facilities, which date from the nineteenth century and are concentrated in the central business area of Calcutta, are crowded, old-fashioned, and generally inadequate. Since the height of the bores and the strength of the flow in the river vary not just from season to season but from day to day, daily calculations have to be made to determine the size of the ships that can enter the port. (Heavy bore tides decrease the berthing and holding capacity by as much as twenty-five per cent.) The Calcutta Port Commissioners recently estimated that the average turn-around time for a ship calling at Calcutta was more than seventeen days—the longest and most expensive turn-around time at any major port.

The silting up of the Hooghly also threatens to choke off the supply of fresh water for much of the population along its banks. Apart from a number of large and small tube wells, the only source of fresh water for the Calcutta Metropolitan District is the Hooghly, the principal waterworks being situated at Palta, seventeen miles north of Calcutta. These waterworks were built in 1865 to provide filtered water for six hundred thousand or, at the most, a million people. At the same time, subsidiary waterworks were built to supply standpipes in the streets with unfiltered water for fighting fires, for cleaning the streets, and for washing carriages. These waterworks distribute water only to Calcutta; the other municipalities and semi-municipalities—except for Kalyani—have no municipal waterworks and only very limited access to filtered water through the tube wells, and the villages have no filtered water at all. Even in Calcutta, the amount of filtered water is so limited and its distribution so haphazard that nearly half the population now routinely uses unfiltered water from the standpipes for bathing and drinking, and in this water cholera vibrio is often found. Moreover, the equipment and the mains of the Palta waterworks are so old and worn that even the filtered water is not always free from adulteration, and the mains carrying the unfiltered water are often blocked by silt. As the current in the Hooghly has continued to slacken, an undercurrent of salt water from the sea has moved farther and farther upstream, and in the summer, when this undercurrent is strongest, the salt content of the river near Palta is often ten times what is generally considered fit for human consumption. So far, engineers have managed to keep on supplying the ration of filtered water to Calcutta by pumping and storing water at Palta during the hours of each day when the salt content is lowest. But the salinity of the river is increasing so rapidly that within a few years the waterworks at Palta may be unusable for weeks or months at a time. Even moving the waterworks many miles upstream would be no more than a temporary solution. Throughout the Calcutta Metropolitan District, a full-scale water famine is an ever-present threat.

In the entire Gangetic delta, which is flat (it is uninterrupted by a single hill), the only good land is along the margins of the Hooghly. This land, which was formed over the centuries by silt deposits washed up onto the banks when the river was deep and the current strong, is nowhere more than thirty feet above sea level or more than two miles wide, for it slopes sharply away into salt lakes, brackish streams, and malarial marshes. And even these stretches of good land are subject to the ravages of an unhealthful climate; the delta is simmering hot for eight months of the year, the temperature regularly rising as high as 117°F., and it is deluged with rain for much of the remaining four months, when fifty out of a total of sixty-four inches of annual rainfall comes down in concentrated monsoon showers. Although the delta is crisscrossed by many small rivers and streams, it has always had bad drainage, and now the rivers and streams, too, are silting up and losing what little drainage capacity they once possessed. During the monsoon, when even the comparatively high ground is flooded for weeks at a time, the standing water paralyzes land transportation—and seeps into the foundations and walls of buildings—and has to be removed artificially by methods that are extremely slow and costly. Most of the Calcutta Metropolitan District is without municipally organized sewerage systems, without piped drains or sewers, and even without privately owned means of sewage disposal, like septic tanks. Most people have only the use of primitive communal latrines—low, cramped, open brick sheds with platforms above earthenware bowls on dirt floors—of which some two hundred thousand are scattered throughout the Calcutta Metropolitan District. Only Calcutta has a functioning municipal sewage-disposal system, but even in Calcutta the latrines are cleaned only erratically, and then are emptied manually into trailers, which carry the waste matter to disposal pits outside the city limits. Moreover, only about half of Calcutta's area is sewered; in the rest, sludge and ordure are carried in a maze of open gutters that run along the surface of the streets, lanes, and alleyways, and often alongside the worn water pipes, with the result that seepage is not uncommon. Stoppages and backups are so frequent that, especially during the monsoon, the contents of the gutters freely overflow into the streets. Poor drainage and poor sewerage aggravate the unhealthy conditions of life in the Calcutta Metropolitan District, where malaria, cholera, and practically all other gastrointestinal diseases are rampant, as are smallpox and tuberculosis. Although in recent years malaria has been controlled somewhat by the constant saturation of lowlands and stagnant waters with DDT, and cholera by comprehensive inoculations, the Calcutta Metropolitan District has not been able to rid itself of either scourge. Malaria afflicts a large percentage of the population, and cholera, which is often fatal, is endemic in the entire delta, reaching its peak in the summer months of every year. The sanitation conditions, made hopeless by the water shortage and the water pollution, expose the Calcutta Metropolitan District to a permanent siege of mosquitoes, flies, and vermin—all breeding disease, carrying disease, and spreading disease.

Despite disease and an occasional but devastating famine, like that of 1943, the population of the Calcutta Metropolitan District has been growing relentlessly. The population trebled between the census of 1921 and the census of 1961, and it is expected that by 1986 the current population will nearly double. A part of this increase represents migrations from other regions of India. Indeed, thirty-nine per cent of the present population is drawn from all parts of India: merchants and financiers from Gujarat and Rajasthan; bureaucrats and office workers from Andhra Pradesh, Madras, Mysore, and Kerala; skilled laborers and entrepreneurs from the Punjab; unskilled laborers and factory workers from Bihar and Uttar Pradesh; sweepers and tanners from Orissa. The migrations began early in this century, when, because of the general increase in population throughout India and the consequent pressure on arable land, farmers were forced to leave their villages and seek work in one of the handful of urban centers. In the Calcutta area, these displaced farmers, who were often unable to bring their families with them, settled into barrackslike quarters in the *bustis* (imperfectly translated as "slums"), six or eight to a room, and resigned themselves to living under any conditions, provided they could find work, save something to send home to their families, and perhaps visit them occasionally. They generally found uncertain, temporary employment as dock coolies, rickshaw-wallahs, latrine sweepers, office peons, night watchmen, or fruit and vegetable hawkers, and they tended to live in the city as outsiders, forming enclaves, in which they kept very much to themselves, spoke only their own regional languages, followed their own religious, sectarian, or caste practices, and found jobs for new arrivals from their home villages in the trades in which they themselves had settled. Most of the minority communities entrenched themselves in the industrial areas of Calcutta and Howrah, and here they live now, as they did in the past, in little villagelike *bustis,* a restless, uprooted population. (Owing to the presence of these workers, the ratio of men to women in the Calcutta Metropolitan District today is three to two.) In recent years, moreover, there has been another migration, of a different kind—an influx of destitute refugees from Pakistan. There was a lull in the exchange of refugees for some years, but they have been coming to India in increasing numbers ever since the religious disturbances in Kashmir over the theft of Mohammed's hair and the second Indo-Pakistan war. At least four million refugees from Pakistan have settled in West Bengal, where they now constitute ten per cent of the state's population, and of these at least a million have settled in the Calcutta Metropolitan District. More are still coming, in search of assistance from relatives or the government. (About a quarter of a million refugees, it has been estimated, could be resettled in regions like the hills and forests of Orissa, but the government has not been able to undertake the expensive work of clearing and developing such land.) Some of the refugees have been absorbed into the labor market; others barely subsist on what they can earn from such occupations as weaving rugs, knitting sweaters, and forging bangles. They have set up makeshift colonies wherever they could find uninhabited ground—even in the swampland, though their reed-and-mud huts are regularly swept away by the monsoon rains.

Although parts of New York and parts of Tokyo have a population density comparable to that of parts of the Calcutta Metropolitan District, it, unlike the two other metropolises, has few buildings more than three stories high, and most of its people are housed in one- or two-story structures. Few of the houses are *pukka* structures, made of brick and cement. Rather, most are *kutcha* structures, made of bamboo, mud, or unbaked bricks. Except for the palatial quarters of the rich, most houses, *pukka* or *kutcha,* have no inside plumbing, and the *pukka* structures are often in disrepair. Many of these structures were originally intended only as temporary shelters for migrant workers, but they now house big families. Even so, a large number of people must sleep in and around dockyards, in factories, in offices, in shops, on construction sites, in railway stations, in hallways, and on stairways of buildings. More than half the Calcutta Metropolitan District is taken up by streams or by marshland that is unreclaimable for reasons of cost or technology; the demands on the remaining land are so intense that several hundred thousand people sleep out on the pavements and tens of thousands of people now live, as a matter of course, on low, undrained, disease-infested land bordering the salt marshes. All available public or private land is occupied by colonies of squatters. There is no place—not even the border of Calcutta's refuse dump—that is left unoccupied.

Unlike other metropolises that have grown up on the banks of rivers—such as London and Paris—the Calcutta Metropolitan District has been unable to spread out radially. Its suburbs have been forced to develop farther and farther away from the metropolitan center, crowding the margins of good land along the Hooghly. Yet every day huge numbers of people must somehow commute from these distant suburbs—many of which have no paved streets, and no room for much more than pedestrian traffic—to their jobs in Calcutta and Howrah. Even today, partly because of topography, there are only two main highways serving the Calcutta Metropolitan District—the Grand Trunk Road, on the west side of the river, and the Barrackpore Trunk Road, on the east side. Except for two major rail lines, which also run roughly parallel to the river, interurban transport is practically nonexistent, and the few public buses and trams are slow and overburdened. The two roads must therefore carry, in addition to commercial and industrial traffic, hundreds of thousands of commuting pedestrians, so at almost any time of day they are crowded with trucks, cars, bullock carts, rickshaws, bicycles, pedestrians, and pack animals. Of the two, the Grand Trunk Road, which connects the Calcutta Metropolitan District with the coal fields and steel mills of the industrial region, is by far the more important. But in the area of the Calcutta Metropolitan District even this road is narrow and in bad condition, and it passes through very congested parts of the metropolis. Until the end of the nineteenth century, Calcutta's position on the east bank of the Hooghly, separated from the land to the west, was not a serious disadvantage, for the city's raison d'être was shipping. But when land transport was developed, in the late nineteenth and early twentieth centuries, its major facilities, like the Howrah Railway Station, were necessarily built on the west side of the river, while the water-transport facilities, like the Port, remained on the east side. There is only one bridge across the Hooghly in the Calcutta-Howrah area—the Howrah Bridge. This is Calcutta's single point of access to the rest of the country. "Indian economists ponder: What is the point of struggling to industrialize the country, of building steel mills, if one cannot adequately transport supplies, labor, and finished products?" Paul Grimes once wrote in an article on Calcutta in the New York *Times*. "What is the point of growing tea and jute, the biggest earners of foreign exchange, if one may be unable to get them to world markets? Without foreign exchange, how can the country buy generators for power plants, petroleum for trucking, tractors for farmland, aircraft for defense?"

The partition of India dislocated the entire economy of West Bengal, and particularly that of the Calcutta Metropolitan District, parts of which are only thirty miles from the Pakistani border. Not only was West Bengal deprived of important markets in East Bengal but its industry and agriculture were also severely handicapped. Before Partition, for instance, West Bengal depended heavily on East Bengal for rice, and from eighty to ninety per cent of the jute processed in the Calcutta Metropolitan District also came from East Bengal. When that supply of jute dried up, at least a million acres of land in West Bengal had to be diverted from the cultivation of rice—which is still West Bengal's biggest crop—to the cultivation of jute. The jute industry, however, has still not entirely recovered. In 1963 and 1964, industry in the Calcutta Metropolitan District absorbed, at most, a million workers—two hundred and thirty thousand in the jute industry, four hundred and thirty thousand in other organized industries, like heavy engineering, and three hundred thousand in "cottage industries," defined as any industries employing fewer than ten workers each and relying on electric power, or employing as many as twenty workers each but not relying on electric power. Work conditions in most of the factories are as grim as those in nineteenth-century London, and work conditions in cottage industries, which are spread throughout the *bustis,* are still worse. In the Calcutta Metropolitan District, there is chronic unemployment and chronic underemployment in all industries, in all occupations, and at all income levels. There are at least four hundred thousand adult males with no employment, and no one seems to know how they manage to stay alive. Female workers have two main occupations—domestic service and prostitution.

In recent years, the Calcutta Metropolitan District has made so little progress in extending education that a lower percentage of children attend school in its urban communities than in some of the rural areas in the state; at the time of the 1961 census, nearly half of the population over five years of age in the Calcutta Metropolitan District was illiterate and nearly half of the persons who could read and write were only semi-literate. The majority of the schools in the Calcutta Metropolitan District are run not by the government but by private charitable organizations, and, whether private or public, most of the school buildings are dismal, cramped rented or requisitioned tenements, with no facilities for playing, eating, or washing. To achieve the national aim of giving free compulsory education to all children between the ages of six and fourteen by 1986, Calcutta alone must provide at least a million three hundred thousand additional school places by that time, and at least a hundred new primary schools and a thousand new teachers every year, even if every school is used for double shifts and the city does not try to lower the high student-teacher ratio that exists now. In secondary education, the problems are equally formidable. Furthermore, the Calcutta Metropolitan District is the country's most important intellectual center, educating about thirteen per cent of all the students enrolled in colleges and universities in India, but its university, which is the largest in the world—in 1966 it had an enrollment of a hundred and thirty-five thousand regular students, along with sixty-five thousand students taking external degrees—has been in turmoil for many years, its academic life disintegrating rapidly under the pressure of its numbers.

To describe conditions even in Calcutta alone, observers have resorted to epithets like "slum of the world" and "city of death," and have strained for analogies to convey their impressions, as in this passage from the *Times* article by Grimes, which superimposes Calcutta's problems on New York:

New York is the only major port in the United States except for San Francisco (like Bombay) far to the west. There is no Boston, no Norfolk, no St. Lawrence Seaway to Chicago. The industrial complexes of Pittsburgh, Detroit, and Birmingham are all concentrated near Albany. The only highway from there to New York is the Albany Post Road. The Hudson River is so full of silt that fewer and fewer freighters can reach the West Street docks each year. . . . The municipal water supply is growing dangerously salty and unsafe to drink or use in industry. . . . Block-long lines of desperate seekers of menial jobs wait outside employment agencies. In the shadow of the Waldorf-Astoria is a shanty town where thousands of persons live in the worst imaginable squalor. Times Square swarms with beggars, many of them blind, deformed, or leprous.

When a people's will to protest against intolerable conditions—and this will is considered by some political thinkers to be as important for economic development as for political change—finds expression in the Calcutta Metropolitan District, it is likely to take the form of explosive demonstrations and pointless acts of public violence, which then suddenly subside without bringing about any improvement. Although the Calcutta Metropolitan District has a very low rate of reported crime compared to any Western metropolis—many *busti* areas have no record of crime at all—public demonstrations and outbursts, some of them culminating in looting, arson, and killing, have become commonplace in recent years. Hardly a month goes by without a major strike over working conditions, a *hartal* over government policy, or a riot over some minor grievance. Recently, in Calcutta, eighty tramcars were burned in a month-long riot over a token raise in tram fares, even though the new schedule had pegged the fares to the distances travelled so equitably that some passengers would actually be paying less than before; in March, 1966, during a general strike in West Bengal that was accompanied by riots, thirty-nine people died and the estimated loss from the work stoppage and the destruction of public and private property was put at sixty-five million rupees, or more than half the total revenue receipts—one hundred and ten million rupees—budgeted by Calcutta for the fiscal year 1965–66. For many years, the Calcutta Metropolitan District's most outspoken political representatives, some of whom belong to left-wing parties, have been elected not from the poorer constituencies, which often return conservative or Congress candidates, but from the richer ones; yet even the constituents with some money and education, who feel that things can be changed, and are aware that they can choose from a variety of political ideologies and candidates, seem to ignore local issues, like water supply, housing, and education, and mobilize and demonstrate only over big national questions, like the Indian government's legislation on language or religion, or over international questions, like British policy in Rhodesia or the deployment of the United States Seventh Fleet. The explanation most commonly advanced for the general inertia in local matters is that the widespread poverty induces such passivity and resignation that any condition, however seemingly intolerable, is endured. It is said that even when the poor are aroused to an act of protest they are not capable of sustaining it, and that in the inertia of its population the Calcutta Metropolitan District is like any other poverty-stricken community where conditions for revolution exist without the will to revolution. Bengali intellectuals, however, maintain that the demonstrations and acts of public violence have so far served as a safety valve for pent-up emotions but that they have only postponed the revolution that will one day topple the established order. These intellectuals point out that Calcutta is currently a center of Communist activity in India, the ideologies here spanning the spectrum from conventional Marxism to the latest variety of Maoism. (In Calcutta, the Communists publish, by one count, a daily journal, three weeklies, and twelve monthlies, and occupy positions of power on other journals, in government, and in student, peasant, and labor organizations.) Some of these intellectuals are fond of repeating Lenin's dictum "The road to world revolution leads through Peking, Shanghai, and Calcutta."

Come Again If You Leave the City

Plane descending to Calcutta. View from air: Flat, wet land. Coconut palms. Dark, muddy Hooghly. Mills strung along the river like beads. Factories. Hovels. Touch down at Dum-Dum Airport. Hot enough to fire bricks. New airport road. More hovels. Stench. Taste of grime in the mouth. Maelstrom of traffic. Roar of humanity.

The Grand, best hotel in Calcutta, on fashionable Chowringhi Road. Best neighborhood. Offices, shops, hotels, museum. Sign in the room cautions against drinking tap water.

Alongside Chowringhi, the famous Maidan—Indian Hyde Park. Two miles long, a mile wide. Green. Cosmopolitan. Girls in frocks and boys in knickers playing hopscotch, babies in prams, young men with books of Bengali verse. Europeans, athletes at gymnastics, masseurs giving rubdowns on the grass, *sadhus*. Monuments to soldiers and viceroys. Tall column to Sir David Ochterlony, a soldier in India for fifty years. At one side of Maidan, Victoria Memorial, white marble edifice with dome, surrounded by lakes and well-maintained gardens. Notices forbidding games or running in the gardens. At other side of Maidan, vast outline of Fort William, then river. British Calcutta called "village of palaces," and around Maidan are grand residences, grand government buildings. Façades, mock-Gothic and colonial, now crumbling. Streets—Wellesley, Cornwallis, Amherst, Curzon. Clubs—Turf Club, Swimming Club, Calcutta Club. Two race courses, two golf courses within city limits of Calcutta.

Head offices of the *Statesman*. Edited by an Englishman, A. E. Charlton. His telephone keeps ringing. "Yes, it's raining," he says into telephone. "Yes. . . . What? . . . Your ants were very right. Congratulate the ants." Then, to me: "That was my right-hand man here. He told me this morning that it would rain, because he had seen a heap of ants coming out of their hole, and he rang me up to tell me the ants were right."

Howrah Bridge. People taking the evening air. Dramatic bore tide. Jetties bobbing, small boats hurrying to middle of river.

Indian heirs. Harrison Road now Mahatma Gandhi Road, Lansdowne now Sarat Bose Road, Wellesley now Rafi Ahmed Kidwai Road. Old and new names used interchangeably. Even residents have two surnames, Anglicized and Bengalicized—Chatterji and Chattopadhya, Bannerji and Bandhopadhya, Mukherji and Mukhopadhya. New residential areas—Alipore, Ballygunge, Tollygunge. Restaurants—the Peiping, the Blue Fox, the Bar-B-Q, the Kwality, Fish and sweetmeats. Cinemas. Indian sahibs in raw-silk bush shirts, Indian memsahibs in saris with wide, rich borders. Women in tribal dress, complete with anklets and nose rings. Bearded Sikhs in pajamas and *kurtas*. Bengali gentlemen in *dhotis*—umbrellas in their hands. Snatches of conversation in, seemingly, every Indian tongue.

Bengalis talkative, ebullient, charming people. Call themselves "the French of the East." Everywhere, emanation of Tagore, who, they say, started "India's intellectual renaissance." Shelves of books by Tagore, about Tagore, dedicated to Tagore. Everyone constantly invoking the Bengali contemporaries and successors of Tagore—the philosopher Sri Aurobindo, the novelist Sarat Chandra Chatterji, the mystic Ramakrishna, the social reformer Ram Mohan Roy, the revolutionary Subhas Chandra Bose, and the "Nightingale of India," Sarojini Naidu. Also, the musician Ali Akbar Khan, the dancer Uday Shankar, the painter Jamini Roy, and the film director Satyajit Ray.

Dinner at the residence of a rich Bengali. Walled compound with cast-iron balustrades, beds of flowers, rococo fountain, marble nudes. House with several inner courtyards, halls, chandeliers, mirrors.

Unpainted buildings with rash of signs advertising businesses on all floors. On sidewalks and streets, bamboo-and-burlap lean-tos, prostrate bodies with bundles, sacred bulls chewing on husks of coconut. Smells—dung, urine, sweat, incense, jasmine. Women scooping up and patting cow dung, and other women cooking on fires of cowdung chips. Heat at 117°. Children washing in runnels.

Roadside stalls. Signboards: "Four Annas Shave, Eight Annas Headcut, Ten Annas Singeing Ladies' Heads." "Loafer's Delight Restaurant. Mutton Cutlis Our Specialty. Eat Them, Enjoy Them, Repeat Them." *Pan*-wallahs folding individual scented betel leaves stuffed with lime, catechu, betelnuts. Icemen. Sherbet-wallahs—cool blends of fruit juices, served in gaudy glasses. Fortune-tellers and astrologers. More hawkers and venders, with coconut meat and coconut milk, coir intoxicants and arrack, lotus flowers. Other aromas: freshly ground pomegranate seed, coriander seed, cumin seed, mustard seed; mint, ginger, cardamom, turmeric, cinnamon, cloves, bay leaf; *ghi,* chilies, peppers, chutneys. Narrow, cobbled streets, and more stalls, more kiosks, more bazaars. A bookseller and publisher, a goldsmith, a butcher shop with goats being driven in through the door. Everywhere: *"Baksheesh! . . . Baksheesh! . . . Baksheesh!"*

Visit to a *busti* with M. S. Guha Mustaffi, assistant engineer, Calcutta Corporation. Huddles of red tile roofs crowding both sides of a paved street. Streets packed with milling, barefoot people and inquisitive, half-naked children, old cows, and stray dogs. *Pukka* houses, but moldy and decaying. Maze of spidery alleys, gullies, and footpaths leading away from the street. Ordure, rotting garbage, and mud underfoot. Overhead, wet clothes, a jumble of colors. A narrow vacant lot jammed with milch cows—the infamous *khatal,* or cattle pen. Now an agglutination of wattle-and-daub *kutcha* huts and houses, all with common walls. Near them, a tube well and, beside it, gutters and a latrine. More huts. Miserable stalls of venders. A water tap and an endless line of women waiting with buckets. "The *bustis* are on private land," Guha Mustaffi is saying, "but the Corporation tries to provide tube wells and water pumps whenever funds permit." Duck through low, narrow doorway into courtyard. Open, smoke-filled, unpaved, muddy, used communally for washing clothes and utensils and for bathing. Clustered around courtyard, a few windowless cubicles. Families of a bus-driver, a fruit seller, a taxi-driver, a tailor live in them. Go into a cubicle. Cement floor. Above, roof tiles. A single hemp *charpoy.* A few shelves holding a few utensils—iron griddle, rolling pin, pan and pot, mortar and pestle. Wife of Yusuf Mohammed, fruit seller, small and full of smiles, dressed in cotton sari printed with flowers. Brood of children. "It is very hot here in the day," she says. "Only in the evening a little breeze comes. But it is Allah's will." "Do you get enough to eat?" Mustaffi asks. "He makes only three rupees a day, and our rent is sixteen rupees a month," she says. In the doorway, a man. "You lie. The rent is only twelve rupees a month," he says. Altercation. Mustaffi explains that the system is for the actual landlord to rent a house to one tenant, who sublets rooms to subtenants. The man in the doorway, Isaac, is the tenant landlord of the subtenants. Isaac complains. Collects sixty rupees monthly from subtenants, but Corporation taxes and landlord—Addy, of Addy Estates—take more than twenty rupees. Leave nothing to live on. Visit Moti Jheel ("pearl lake") Busti. Gets name from actual stagnant pond. Other *bustis,* with roofs of tile, tin, or jute sacking. Shatubabu Lane Busti, Bibi Baghan Busti, Tangra Busti, 90 and 110 Linton Street Busti, Bedford Lane Busti, Collin Street Busti, Elliot Road Busti. Southeast limits of Calcutta, and Dhapa, the city's huge refuse dump. Dhapa: open trailers piled high with refuse are pulling up and unloading on great rubbish heaps. All around, bleak, desolate encampments. A slaughterhouse. A butchered cow wheeled by. Human figures, mostly women, scavenging in the heaps. Beyond, marshland.

Look through Calcutta *Hand Book* for tourists. Come upon an appeal—in disconcerting English—some of which reads like an official apologia, some like a personal letter. Appeal opens, "Calcutta has been variously described as the city of nightmare, the city of processions, the city of filth and squalor, etc., etc.," but continues with an optimism as charming as it is pathetic:

But here live some 30 lakhs of people in about 30 sq. miles. Here you will find the multi-storied skyscrapers proudly raising their high heads to the still beyond sky, having a broad base of slum area built of mud and tiled houses. You will find here miles and miles of underground sewer through which a man can even walk erect, carrying filth and dirt to the outskirts of the city, and you will also find vast areas with service latrine where nightsoil has yet got to be removed in Buckets by human agencies. Vast Concrete and Asphalted streets bordered on both sides by huge buildings will greet you on your entry to the city from the east or north whereas your entry from the west or south may possibly sicken you with sights of poor living conditions of the large number of refugees, sailors or seamen who throng the areas. . . .

You want a stroll? Go right along the Ganges [Hooghly] by Strand Road right up to the Dock areas. You feel tired in your unaccustomed long-distance walk? Just sit along the Bank of the Ganges and as our Commissioner says, throw pebbles into the water. The "Tup-Tip" sound will possibly sooth your nerves. . . .

You want a ride on the boat. In the rainy season, you are told
you can have your ride on the very streets of Calcutta. . . .

Do you feel depressed for all our commissions and omissions?
Why not see the night life of Calcutta and the West Bengal Government's Tourist Bureau is at your service to oblige you. . . .

Still not satisfied? Then you better go to either of the Coffee
Houses. Here you will find budding politicians or scholars calmly
but passionately discussing the evils of the World and you will find
your problem solved in no time. . . . But if you . . . crave for majestic
isolated travel—hail one of our Rickshaws—still drawn by your fellow brother who will run for Your Majesty at the risk of their lives
and neither your pity nor your wrath will help them if you just do
not like to avail yourself of their services. . . . The Chowringhee and
Central Avenue Dalhousie area will cater to your needs, if you can
pay for it. . . . A large number of Restaurants of the Park Street will
be at your service with dinner, dance and whatnot. . . .

Yes—Yes—We know. You find Garbages heaped in streets. Taxi-
wallas evading your calls, water supply not adequate, hazards of
using a public conveyance, etc., etc.

But let us have our say. Our per capita income is Rs. 19·58 [19
rupees and 58 pices] and not Rs. 53·43 as in Bombay or elsewhere. . . . We have to look after a vast number of refugees who
are yet to find their way towards a means of livelihood. You ask,
why cannot we increase the per capita income if Bombay can do
so? Well, well—why do we grow Jute to earn foreign exchange for
India when we can grow paddy to feed our people? Why do we
pay most of Income Tax, which is distributed to other provinces to
meet their needs? Many such questions can be asked, but who is
going to answer them?

The truncated Bengal is now Calcutta. Here come people from
all other provinces, form their own communities, live in peace
with Bengalees, earn for their families, and send their earnings to
their native provinces. We cannot tax them. . . . You live with us
and probably prefer to share our comparatively cheap living, and
we prefer to live moderately so that we may yet exist as Bengalees.
Cities other than Calcutta are cosmopolitan, but Calcutta still remains a city of Bengalees. . . .

Don't tell us about our failings and shortcomings. We know it all and we are being reminded of it daily. If you find anything good, tell others. Live with us in peace and come again if you leave the city. You are welcome.

This morning, I go, by prearrangement, to Rakhal Das Addy Road and to the offices of Sanat Kumar Addy, a landlord whose holdings include *busti* properties—the Shatubabu Lane Busti and 90 and 110 Linton Street Busti among them—and also houses in other parts of Calcutta and an entire bazaar. Rakhal Das Addy Road is some distance from Chowringhi, in a poorish neighborhood. This road, like most roads in Calcutta, is narrow, but, unlike most, it is relatively quiet. The offices, a couple of rooms that occupy the ground floor of a two-story structure, are indistinguishable from those of any other traditional Indian business establishment. There is one long main room with shelves and steel cupboards along the walls, all crammed with ledgers done up in jute sacking. In the back of the room is a platform about a foot high covered with a clean white cotton cloth, on which, barefoot, a half-dozen bespectacled *babus* wearing white *kurtas* and *dhotis* sit crosslegged, poring over more ledgers. In the front of the room is a long table, around which the *seths,* or rich men, of the business, also in *kurtas* and *dhotis,* sit in chairs, conferring. A brand-new pack of cigarettes and a brand-new box of matches, which are set out on a little white tin plate in the center of the table, are the only touches of modernity in the musty office. As is the custom in such establishments, no general introductions are made, but a chair is brought up and placed for me beside Addy, who is an elderly man with a weasel-like face and a circumspect air. Behind rimless glasses, his eyes are friendly, and when he smiles he reveals a few chipped teeth.

I ask Addy how he got into the real-estate business.

"The business was started by my grandfather," he says. "The house I live in was built by my grandfather. I live there with my relatives—we all live in the same house as a joint family, and they are co-owners of the Calcutta properties. The house has seventeen or eighteen rooms. We once had a rice business, but the government has taken away our rice fields, and now our Calcutta properties are our only source of income."

I ask him if he inspects his properties in the *bustis.*

"We are handicapped," he says. "In practice, we have no status as landlords in the *bustis*. We are only *de-facto* landlords, with no power to act. Since 1937, the courts have administered our *busti* properties through a receiver. It's up to the courts to make any improvements, and even the courts can't do anything unless the tenant pays a reasonable amount of rent."

Very milky tea is now served in teacups, with a couple of biscuits on each saucer, and over the tea I learn that the receiver, Niha Ranjan Ghosh, is at the table, and that the other men around it are partners and associates of Addy.

"As a receiver, I am responsible for administration and maintenance of the property and for distribution of income to the co-owners of the property," Ghosh tells me. "We receivers are compensated by the court, but my compensation amounts to only a few thousand rupees a year. But I also have my law practice."

I ask Addy about the extent of his holdings in the *bustis*.

"We own altogether sixteen or seventeen *busti* houses and we have from three hundred to three hundred and fifty tenants," he says.

I ask him how much rent he collects from the *busti* houses.

He becomes noticeably wary. "It varies," he says. "Supposing a single family has had the lease of the same *busti* house for three or four generations—then the family may pay only eight annas per month per *kutta,* which is seven hundred and twenty square feet. The highest amount we can get per *kutta* is sixteen rupees a month. In Linton Street, I have sixty *kuttas,* and I am getting from a hundred and thirty to a hundred and forty rupees per month from them as rent, yet I hear that the land in the neighborhood of Linton Street is selling very high—from twenty to twenty-four thousand rupees per *kutta.* Then, too, the tenants who rent *busti* houses from us may sublet rooms in the houses as long as they continue to live in the houses, and we can't evict them. We must go to the court. Landlords who don't have the money to fight in the court for six, seven, or eight years can't even litigate, and so they sell their holdings for nothing, because who wants to buy property where the rents are token, where the tenants can't be disturbed, and where the *busti* houses can't be torn down? I have spent thousands and thousands of rupees litigating. I spend all my time litigating. Nothing ever comes of it, but at least it kills time."

As I am leaving, he says, "Every *busti* landlord in Calcutta would stand to multiply his income many hundredfold if all the *busti* houses were razed tomorrow. We don't want to own *bustis* any more than anyone wants to live in them. We would all like to help the poor *busti*-dweller."

From Rakhal Das Addy Road, I go to an appointment with B. Malik, the Vice-Chancellor of Calcutta University. Malik is a pleasant, thoughtful man, who looks younger than his age, which is seventy-one.

"I am at least trying to do something about the administration of the university before I leave the place," he tells me. "Let me give you an example of the kind of mess it is in. There is a very learned Sanskrit lecturer here, Bhatabi Ram Shastri. He was offered a better appointment at another university, and a proposal was made to keep him here by upgrading his post. The proposal went from one committee to another, and after two years it reached the senate, which represents faculty members, deans, and graduates. The senate agreed to upgrade him. But then someone in the senate spoke up and said that since Bhatabi Ram Shastri had been waiting for two years, the upgrading of his post should be retroactive. Someone else said that in that case Bhatabi Ram Shastri should give up his two years' salary retroactively. The post had not been advertised publicly. If it had been, Shastri might have lost out to another applicant, in which case he would not have been receiving any salary at all from the university for the last two years. Wonderful, to upgrade a man's post for his benefit, and in the process to take away his salary! I had emergency powers to make the appointment, and I immediately used them to make his upgrading retroactive. Someone else in the senate now spoke up and said, 'Sir, you took over as Vice-Chancellor a few months after his appointment came up for upgrading. Therefore, how can you retroactively upgrade him?' Our senate is full of wayside lawyers. With the help of the Ford Foundation, which has taken a special interest in Calcutta, we are now trying to streamline the administration."

I ask him what other steps are being taken to improve conditions in the university.

"We scarcely know where to begin," he says. "We are a very poor university—for seventy-five per cent of our financing we are dependent on student fees. The colleges are spread out all over the city, and there is almost no social contact between students and teachers. We don't have many residential facilities, and we don't know where or how most of our teachers and students live. We don't know what happens to the students after classes, and we don't inquire. One consequence of this is that they get involved in every major riot in the city. The university is bedevilled with strikes, and examinations and degrees are continually being put off."

Afterward, I have a drink with Samar Sen, the editor of a new intellectual English-language weekly called *Now,* and some of his friends, at his house. Every ashtray is full, and the atmosphere is a little feverish. The talk always returns to *Now,* and the best-known Bengali man of letters writing in English, Nirad Chaudhuri, and his *Now* articles, of which the following passage is fairly typical:

> . . . If I were a sphinx of granite with only the brains of man and bent on intellectual laughter, I should today burst into such a peal of guffaw as with their reverberating ha-ha would crack the vast dome of the firmament. But I am a bundle of nerves and flesh, and I suffer. I am swept off my feet at intervals by uncontrollable gusts of rage at what I see. I feel like picking up a cat-o'-nine-tails and laying about among our politicians, or want to seize a machinegun to mow down the mob or, better still, a flamethrower to cauterize the earth of a suppurating vileness. I feel like going abroad to preach a crusade like Peter the Hermit, although my efforts might turn out to be only as laughable as Don Quixote's, and the result as pitiful as the Children's Crusade. But in actual fact I can only gnash my teeth, and tear my hair.

It's the Crying Baby That Gets Picked Up

In the days I spend going around Calcutta, I constantly ask myself, "Can anyone be held accountable? Can things be changed? Where is help to come from?" I seek out political figures, government officers, some Ford Foundation planners recently arrived to attack the problems of the Calcutta Metropolitan District. Most of these men work out of the buildings in and around Chowringhi or in nearby Dalhousie Square. Some of these buildings lie so close to the Port that they seem to be right on the docks. From the inside, some of them have the feeling of old ships retired from Her Majesty's service, as if long ago they had sailed up the dark, alien river and been abandoned there by their masters.

The Central Municipal Office Building is a huge four-story structure, built in 1872. It now serves as headquarters for the municipal government of Calcutta. The Mayor, P. K. Roy Chowdhury, who governs Calcutta with the assistance of a councillor from each of its hundred wards, receives me in a large, formal-looking hall lined with impressive official portraits. At one end is an enormous conference table, and at the other are several capacious black leather sofas. The Mayor, a gentle-looking elderly Bengali, is ensconced on one of the sofas. He is dressed entirely in white, and, besides the *kurta* and the floor-length, flowing *dhoti* and the open leather sandals that Indian politicians invariably seem to wear, he has a white shawl around his shoulders. A number of Bengalis, also in *kurtas, dhotis,* and sandals, are sitting around him on the other sofas, chatting and laughing, drinking tea, and eating sweetmeats and savories. The Mayor introduces them as councillors. They all seem to be named Chatterji or Bannerji or Mukherji—the Bengali equivalents of Smith and Jones and Brown.

"I myself entered politics as a councillor, but I'm a doctor by profession," the Mayor tells me. "I became a councillor not for political reasons but for medical reasons. I wanted to do something about the health problem in the Calcutta Corporation. As a councillor, I was chairman of the Standing Health and Busti Improvement Committee for six years. I got a lot of satisfaction from doing work for t.b. control, hospital improvement, and so on."

I ask the Mayor what, specifically, is being done about the numerous problems of Calcutta.

"We have several organizations that are concurrently seeking to improve conditions in Calcutta and all its suburbs. For example, we have the Calcutta Metropolitan Planning Organization, which is getting experts and money from the Ford Foundation. It is doing the planning for the whole of the Calcutta Metropolitan District. Its work has been expedited by the West Bengal government, and I hope its plans will be carried out one day. The Calcutta Improvement Trust, which was formed in 1911, and which gets almost five per cent of the Corporation's revenue, does things like taking a plot of land from us, developing it, and returning it to our jurisdiction. The Founders' Municipal Association does good work, too. But we have not made much progress, because every problem requires money. We have twenty-five thousand municipal employees, such as clerks, police, and sweepers, and fifty per cent of the income of the Corporation goes to pay them."

I ask him what is being done about the problem of the water supply, for instance.

"We have two water mains—one sixty-two inches in diameter and the other seventy-two—to carry filtered water from Palta to Calcutta, a hundred and fifty big-diameter tube wells, and fifty thousand small-diameter tube wells," he says. "We have started chlorinating our unfiltered water, and have thus brought down the incidence of cholera. Now we also have a scheme to augment the supply of filtered water by sixty million gallons per day, but it will take from a year to a year and a half to carry it out."

Next, I meet the Commissioner of the Calcutta Corporation, H. C. Mukherji, who heads the municipal civil service and supervises the work of all its officers and employees. His office, which is nearby, also has formal furnishings and an informal atmosphere, with councillors and other officials coming and going, taking refreshment, and exchanging small talk.

"My field has always been engineering, valuation, planning, and administration," the Commissioner tells me. "In the beginning, I trained as a civil engineer. After that, I qualified as a chartered surveyor in England. Except for some nominal changes in day-to-day administrative procedures, I wouldn't say that I have been able to change the administration of the Corporation in ways apparent to everyone."

A burly man stops by. The Commissioner introduces him as the chief engineer of the Corporation, and explains that he is in charge of all the municipal engineering works, plans, and estimates.

"Calcutta's worst problem is that it was never planned," the chief engineer observes. "The city has grown up without anyone's ever expecting it to have any future."

A mild-mannered gray-haired man wearing spectacles now joins us. He is the health officer of the Corporation, and his duties include supervising municipal sanitation, hospitals, laboratories, and cremation grounds, and seeing to vaccinations and inoculations. "Diseases go in cycles," he says. "In the last two years, we have been very lucky. The diseases have been on a very small scale. But this is the epidemic year in the cycle, and the epidemic might break out at any time."

"Calcutta is a bundle of problems," the Commissioner says. "I once took a couple of Ford Foundation experts from the Calcutta Metropolitan Planning Organization around the city, and I told them, 'Gentlemen, I am waiting to see how bold you are. If it were up to me, I would crash down a good part of Calcutta.'"

The Writers' Buildings, a block of red buildings built in 1880, take their name from the junior clerks of the East India Company, known as "writers," who once lived in them. They now serve as headquarters for the West Bengal government, and in them I talk with a number of Ministers of the Congress government of West Bengal. The Minister of Public Works of West Bengal, K. N. Das Gupta, receives me in his office, a large room with three air-conditioners stacked on top of each other in one window and all going at full speed. A half-drawn curtain divides the room into a sort of drawing room, which contains comfortable-looking chairs, and a sort of study, which contains a desk, a reclining chair with a well-worn cushioned footrest, and a bed with smooth, clean sheets.

"We are now beginning to construct special housing units for factory workers," the Minister tells me. "Recently, we advertised three hundred new two-room flats for such workers, and we received twenty-six thousand applications. A committee has begun screening the applicants."

He gets up, moves slowly across the room, adjusts the blinds, and absent-mindedly serves me coffee. "Because of the emergencies of the Chinese invasion and the Indo-Pakistan war, we got only two crores of rupees a year for housing during the Third Five-Year Plan," he says. "Now, for the period of the Fourth Five-Year Plan, we are asking for twice as much a year, most of it from the central government. But all this is just maneuvering. We have to ask for a lot to get anything at all."

The Minister for Local Self-Government for West Bengal, S. M. Fazlur Rahman (he is also Minister of Animal Husbandry, Veterinary

Services, and Fisheries), whom I meet next, is a Muslim in his fifties, dressed in Punjabi-type pajamas and a *kurta*. "I am responsible for dispensing assistance to municipal governments in West Bengal, including any notified area authority," he informs me, putting his feet up on a footrest. "A notified area authority is an officially recognized new area that aspires to the status of a municipality."

I comment on the bewildering number of municipalities already existing in Greater Calcutta.

"You must call this 'Metropolitan Calcutta,' not 'Greater Calcutta,'" he says. "The term 'Greater Calcutta' should be reserved for the day when Calcutta is a developed city. Now, about the subject you raise, perhaps it would be a good thing to have some of the municipalities consolidated one day. But in a democracy you cannot do things without taking into account the interests of everyone concerned. Much, much legislation is required before any consolidation can take place. In my three years' tenure, I have so far been able only to consolidate two municipalities into one and to link up one municipality with the Howrah Corporation."

The Chief Minister of West Bengal, P. C. Sen, to whom I pay my last visit in the Writers' Buildings, sits behind a large semicircular desk with chairs ranged in a semicircle to his right and left. He talks to me between hearing petitioners, who enter, make their requests, and depart.

I ask him how he got into politics.

"I went into Congress politics formally in 1920, when Mahatma Gandhi gave the call," he says. "Between 1914 and 1920, I was somewhat loosely connected with the revolutionary movement of West Bengal. Part of that time, I was a student at the Scottish Church College, in Calcutta."

He orders coffee and cashew nuts, and goes on to talk about various obstacles to getting things done. "Even when we do have the resources, we can't change things quickly, because we're a democracy," he says. "We had to stop work altogether on the important new road from Dum-Dum Airport to Calcutta because a group of refugees had squatted on a piece of land it had to cross. It took us a year to gain legal possession of that land. It is a matter of people trying to assert their rights."

I ask him about the increasing public violence in Calcutta.

He gives me what I have come to recognize as the Congress line. "It is caused by political agitators who have no use for the ballot box and who are interested only in seizing power," he says. "The Maoist Communists have a cadre of saboteurs all their own, and now some of them are even talking about calling in a Chinese Army of Liberation. They say that as soon as this Army of Liberation comes, all the travail and suffering of India will be over. We have had to put some of these Communists in jail because of their connection with Communist China."

At Congress Party headquarters for West Bengal, I call on Atulya Ghosh, the Congress boss who—with two other party bosses, S. K. Patil, Union Minister of Railways, and Sanjiva Reddy, Union Minister of Transport, Aviation, Shipping, and Tourism—is considered to be all-powerful at both state and national levels; the triumvirate, which dominates the Congress Party leaders, known collectively as the "Syndicate," is said to have engineered the election of Mrs. Gandhi as Prime Minister. Ghosh turns out to be a tall, heavy-set Bengali in his early sixties, with well-groomed white hair. He is dressed in *kurta, dhoti,* and sandals, and he is wearing, incongruously, a pair of large, round-rimmed dark glasses and is smoking a cigar.

I ask him about his role as "kingmaker."

"I have no official position in the government," he says, in a big, booming voice. "I am not a Minister. I am not a mayor—how can I have any power? There can't be any position of personal power in a democratic party like the Congress. One person may become popular or strong, but by himself he can do nothing. It is all teamwork. In fact, I can't understand the interest in me. The other day, somebody wrote to me from a university in England and said he was doing a thesis on me and wanted personal details. I detest all this interest in me. I've done what I could for my country. I joined Congress as an ordinary volunteer when I was fifteen, and I have spent, all told, ten or eleven years in British jails. I have given my life to the party, and have remained a bachelor, even though I came from a very good family— my mother's side was well known for its literary activities and my father's side was well known for its money—and had many matrimonial proposals."

I ask him about the threat to continued Congress rule.

"Eighty per cent of the agitation here is by refugees for whom there is nothing on the horizon," he says. "The remaining twenty per cent of the agitation is by students who have no future. They are all frustrated human beings, with no real politics to speak of."

(In subsequent elections in West Bengal, the Congress Party was all but obliterated. The state is at present ruled by the United Front, consisting of about a dozen parties, led by the Communist Party of India, Marxist.)

Utpal Dutt, a talented Bengali playwright, actor, and director, who is known for his Maoist radicalism, has just been released from Calcutta's Presidency Prison, where he was held for six months, under the Defense of India Rules, along with many other political activists who were arrested in Calcutta during the second Indo-Pakistan war. It was generally assumed that the cause of his arrest was a series of vitriolic attacks he had made on the Congress Party. He had, for instance, contributed to *Now* an article entitled "The Indian Kulturkampf," in which he struck out against the Congress Party and its "kept press" and traced what he regarded as a "resurrection of fascism" and a ruthless suppression of all intellectual dissent to the Congress Party's cynical exploitation of the border issue with China.

In October, 1962, with the Chinese invasion [he had written], a chauvinism of the most degenerate kind raised its head. . . . Vicious slogans were raised primarily by leaders of our ruling party. . . . It was always "the Dragon," "the Yellow Peril," "the Yellow Rats," "the Yellow Pirates." . . . There was certainly a keen competition to coin picturesque obscenities involving the snub nose, sallow complexion, and silken barbarism of the Chinese. . . . But the most devastating was his [the Union Home Minister's] warning to those Communists who *think* India is wrong on the border issue. To think is now dangerous business.

To meet Dutt, I go to the Minerva Theatre, a shabby old structure in an impoverished area of Calcutta, where he directs his own stage company, called the Little Theatre Group, in performances of his own plays, often acting in them himself. Vagrants are hanging around the box office. In the lobby, more vagrants are sitting on benches under posters and photographs advertising "Kallol," a historical drama by

Dutt about a naval mutiny in Bombay during the last year of the raj and about the Congress Party's compromising role in it. Upstairs is Dutt's office, a faded room with peeling walls and windows that seem never to have been washed. All over the floor are haphazard piles of papers and junk, and in the middle of the room are two wooden tables. At one table, two men are bent over stacks of coins, which they are counting aloud, over and over again. At the second table sits a dark, stocky man of medium height in a striped American T shirt. He has wavy hair and a beard and mustache, and wears glasses. This is Dutt.

I ask him how "Kallol" is being received—like everything he turns his hand to, the play is surrounded with controversy.

"Ever since we opened, more than a year ago, the Congress government of West Bengal, which is essentially a communal establishment of high-caste Hindus, has been looking for an excuse to close the play," he says. "But 'Kallol' has been such a popular success that they haven't dared to do it. The Congress Party wants to hush up its dirty toady role in the mutiny—hush up that part of history. It has seen to it that even the National Archives have only two typewritten pages with some schoolboy facts about the mutiny. We had to do research for three years to find out what really happened—how Congress betrayed the mutiny, betrayed the Indian people. The people are now realizing that there will never be enough food in the country as long as the Congress Party is in power."

I ask him what, precisely, he means.

"It is obvious that the Congress Party's power depends upon the support of the profiteers and hoarders, so the Congress Party protects them," he says. "The people haven't got anything to eat. But now they demand more than food, more than kerosene. The general strike and the riots in West Bengal last March prove this. Now the people are getting ready for a much bigger struggle. As yet, the people haven't quite realized how they should go about overthrowing this Congress government. When the people fully realize how weak the Congress government is, there will be violence. Some terrible things will have to happen before anything good can happen."

I ask him if he has a Communist revolution in mind.

"I think Communism offers a solution to India's problems," he says.

As we talk on about politics, it becomes clear that his own violence takes the form of words and art, and that in respect to specific Indian problems he is as thoroughly confounded as his chosen enemies. Yet one thing appears to set him apart, and this is that the signs of disturbance in his mind seem also to be signs of his personal torment over the problems he speaks about.

"I have had a checkered past," he tells me at one point. "My father was an agent of materialism—he was a gendarme, and the police were the backbone of the raj. Yet I was able to see through it. I had a middle-class education, but I lived in Calcutta, in the middle of these streets and *bustis*. I formed the Little Theatre Group, and we began by doing plays in English for middle-class audiences. But in recent years we have been performing in Bengali, and only in the working-class areas of this city and in poor villages. Revolutionaries are born of contradictions."

A new building on Lower Chitpur Road (the street was renamed Rabindra Sarani not long ago, but it is still called by the old name) houses the offices of the Calcutta Metropolitan Planning Organization, which since 1961 has been preparing a series of plans for the regeneration of the metropolis. The introductory volume of the series, entitled "Basic Development Plan: Calcutta Metropolitan District, 1966–1986," has just been issued. Although it is intended as a master plan for development and includes specific recommendations for immediate action, it seems to be haunted by the afflictions that paralyze the metropolis, and reads throughout more like a diagnostician's report than like a prescription for a remedy. To get a first-hand impression of what the planners think, I spend some time talking with M. G. Kutty, a Bengali, who is the director of the Calcutta Metropolitan Planning Organization; Dr. Colin Rosser, a British social anthropologist, who is the consultant on community facilities and services for the Ford Foundation group; and C. Preston Andrade, an American architect and urban planner, who is the director of planning for the Ford Foundation group.

Kutty, a tall, heavily built man in his forties with a chubby, boyish face and pomaded hair, sports a mustard-yellow bush shirt with a silky finish and lounges in a comfortable-looking chair, like an old-fashioned bureaucrat. "Perhaps you would like to start the discussion, and summarize the history of planning in Calcutta," Kutty says, turning to Rosser.

Rosser, who is short and compactly built, and is dressed in a short-sleeved shirt, a baggy pair of trousers, and sandals, is perhaps forty, and has the appearance of someone who has spent his life burrowed deep in work. "The fact that the Calcutta Metropolitan District is the world's worst area for endemic cholera attracted the attention of the World Health Organization, and in 1959 they sent a team here to find out what could be done to reduce the incidence of all gastro-enteric diseases," he says. "The team recommended preparing a master plan for water and sanitation, and the work on the plan was begun with financial help from WHO and the U.N. Special Fund. But it was realized quite early on that the problems of the metropolis required a much broader attack. The preliminary visit of our Ford Foundation people followed, and the West Bengal government set up the C.M.P.O. and charged it with the task of preparing a comprehensive development plan. That was in July, 1961, and since then the Ford Foundation has been helping the organization with a group of professional advisers. A succession of people have come and gone, and there are about twenty of us here now."

"May I interject something here by way of explanation, Colin?" Andrade asks. He is tall and lean, with sharp, clean looks, and has dark-brown eyes and light-colored hair that is turning white. "Although our experience in most cases is with Western cities, we make a cultural adaptation quickly and have developed a considerable familiarity with the problems of the metropolis of Calcutta."

I ask Rosser and Andrade how they happened to become involved in planning for the Calcutta Metropolitan District.

"I was with the Indian Army during the Second World War, and got interested in India," Rosser says. "After the war, I went to Cambridge, where I read anthropology. I came out to India again for field research. I went to Katmandu, where I got interested in urban areas, though the happy hunting ground of most anthropologists is the villages. When the Ford Foundation was looking for people who had worked in Indian cities—or, at least, were interested in Indian cities—it asked me if I would come to Calcutta, and I came, intending to stay here two months. I've stayed four years. It's very hard to disengage oneself from Calcutta."

"We all have our particular stories of involvement with the Calcutta project," Andrade says.

"Until the C.M.P.O., no one seems to have taken any interest in the city," Kutty says. "Even basic statistics and basic engineering surveys didn't exist. In other metropolises, which already have all the statistics and surveys, the preparation of such a master plan would have taken a decade. We've done it from scratch in five years."

"We weren't even able to find an epigraph for the plan, though we searched the literature," Rosser says. "Calcutta has produced so many famous men that one would have supposed it would be easy to find one good comment on the place. Not at all. Take Tagore. There isn't one good word about Calcutta in all his writings. He rejected the city, left it, and founded Shantiniketan University, in Shantiniketan, a hundred miles from Calcutta. The only comment that even came close to the kind of thing we were looking for was something Mrs. Gandhi said the other day, and she was speaking not about the problems of the Calcutta Metropolitan District but about the problems of all India. She said, 'It's the crying baby that gets picked up.' Calcutta cries from time to time—mostly in public violence."

"The problems encountered in a metropolis of Calcutta's population, complexity, and economic significance are greater than those encountered in many sizable nations," Andrade says. "The population of the Calcutta Metropolitan District is soon expected to exceed Australia's. The planning that's going on at the C.M.P.O. now is comprehensive not only in the sense that it brings together various disciplines, like hydrology, engineering, economics, and sociology—many of the physical and social sciences—but in the sense that it considers all aspects of the needs of the community, rather than each aspect as a separate entry in the ledger of credits and debits. We don't talk about the problem of providing housing in terms of building x number of housing units. The focus of our planning is not just building x number of housing units but providing a suitable infrastructure for an integrated, comprehensively designed human city. This includes environmental services—that is, shelter, water, drainage, sewerage, refuse collection, and utilities; and social services—that is, education, welfare, health, employment, and transportation. What I'm saying is that it's easy enough to recognize the problems qualitatively, but it takes a good deal of work to analyze them quantitatively."

"We have to remember to set our sights on things we have some hope of achieving," Kutty says. "Until recently, there wasn't even such a thing as the Calcutta Metropolitan District. And the Water and Sanitation Authority, formed this year by the West Bengal government, is the first body to have jurisdiction over the entire District. Our hope is that the formation of similar metropolitan authorities for education, housing, transportation, and so on, will gradually achieve a kind of de facto consolidation of municipalities. The greatest need at the moment is for a planning authority, because you can't just produce a plan and go away and leave it."

"To give you a concrete example of the kinds of problems we are up against in planning, take housing," Rosser says. "The housing emergency here requires not only the replacement of the inadequate housing of most of the present population of seven and a half million but the provision of new housing to take care of the population increase of five million expected over the next twenty years—an increase that will give us about two hundred thousand new people to house each year. If the average size of a family is five, you need roughly forty thousand new housing units a year just to cope with the population increase, and even if we could somehow build these units, that would do nothing for the people who are already here, eighty-five per cent of whom are living in housing units that do not meet the government's minimum standard of forty square feet per person. Say you wanted to do as much for the old population as for the new—you'd need at least eighty thousand new housing units a year. Now, the present annual rate of construction here is only about six thousand *pukka* housing units. To raise that figure to eighty thousand units a year, or even to forty thousand, would involve an enormous development of the construction industry, to say nothing of the development of related industries, like utilities. Even if the industries could somehow be developed, the problem of paying for the housing units would remain. Eighty thousand new housing units a year over the next twenty years would cost at least thirteen hundred crores of rupees. This is a truly astronomical figure for the budget of the entire country, let alone the budget of a single urban district. So the only thing we have been able to do in the plan is to suggest stopgap measures. Thus, we recommend building *kutcha* structures, of mud and thatch, with a life of ten or fifteen years, and perhaps building *pukka* structures later, when we have more money. The minimum cost of a *kutcha* unit is between a thousand and fifteen hundred rupees, whereas the minimum cost of a *pukka* unit is eighty-five hundred rupees."

"May I interject a comment?" Andrade says. "What we are really doing now, and what, to a very large extent, we are bound to do, is simply to build better *bustis*. The snag in the *bustis* already built is that the environmental services are either inadequate or totally nonexistent. Consequently, one of the ideas that we're working on is to see whether the sites of *bustis* can be selected in the future by planners rather than haphazardly by individual landlords, as they are now."

"The selection now is so haphazard that large areas in the center of the city of Calcutta are covered with *bustis,*" Rosser says. "This is a totally uneconomic use of the land, so in the plan we recommend measures that would relate *busti* clearance from the center of the city to the development of satellite towns, where there will be some opportunity to earn a living."

"In a society initiating a really fundamental development program, the question of priorities is a very important one," Andrade says. "For instance, how high do you rate investment in housing—which is economically unproductive even though it may be of very great human importance—compared to, say, investment in education, or even in transportation? Now, in our view, the priorities that attach to public investment in housing are very low compared to, say, resuscitating the Hooghly."

"Calcutta's worst problem is simply that it is on the wrong side of the river," Rosser says. "At one stage of the plan, we actually considered moving the river to the east of the city, but that proved impractical, so other steps are being taken to resuscitate the Hooghly. The central government is building an arrangement of dams and channels—the Farraka Barrage—a hundred and sixty miles north of here, at the junction of the Ganga and the Bhagirathi, where the sandbar has formed. This should increase the flow of Ganga water into the Hooghly. Meanwhile, the Port Commission has started a program of dredging the river above and below the Port, and 'training' the river—that is, constructing barriers to guide the main flow of the water. This should increase the depth of the channel and prevent further erosion of the banks. These measures should help to push the salinity line thirty miles down. Other recommendations of the plan are building new pumping stations on the river to supplement the water supply from Palta; building more bridges, among them one in the Calcutta-Howrah area, to relieve the congestion on the Howrah Bridge, and one north of here, between Kalyani and Bansberia, to help to develop new satellite towns in that area; building new national highways and arterial roads; and developing the port at Haldia so that it can take bulk cargoes. The plan originally called for an expenditure of a thousand crores of rupees over the next twenty years, but, unfortunately, no more than a hundred crores have been allocated for the first five years, so we've had to lower our sights."

Notes and Thoughts on Calcutta's Imperial Past

"Cities of India," by Sir George W. Forrest (1903); "The Early Annals of the English in Bengal," edited by C. R. Wilson (1895–1911); "Old Fort William in Bengal," edited by Wilson (1906); "Bengal in 1756–1757," edited by S. C. Hill (1905): the *Imperial Gazetteer of India;* and other books to hand.

1498. Vasco da Gama opens Indian Ocean to the West.

1510. Affonso de Albuquerque takes Goa for Portugal.

1530. Portuguese vessels begin frequenting the Hooghly. Ships as far as bulge of land, small native craft to Satgaon, the commercial center nearby. Gradually build trade in Bengal silk, muslin, lac, sugar, rice. Trading posts on Hooghly.

1600. Charter of East India Company by Elizabeth.

1625. Dutch sail up Hooghly.

1639. East India Company founds Madras, first important British settlement in India.

1687. James II gives East India Company right to establish civil government in Madras. Mayor, aldermen, burgesses, guildhall, schoolhouse, jail, municipal salaries.

1688. French settlement at Chandernagor, on Hooghly.

1690. Job Charnock, of East India Company, founds British settlement, later Calcutta, at riverside village, Sutanuti. Sutanuti has already supplanted Satgaon. Charnock is said to have liked to hold court and smoke a hubble-bubble under a banyan tree in Sutanuti amid mud huts of fishermen. *Imperial Gazetteer:* "Several reasons led to the selection of this place as the headquarters of British trade in

Bengal. The Hooghly River tapped the rich trade of the Ganges Valley, and Calcutta was situated at the highest point at which the river was navigable for seagoing vessels: it was protected against attack by the river on the west and by morasses on the east." Derivation of name Calcutta unknown. Perhaps from Kalikotta, a village bordering on Sutanuti, or from Kalighat ("landing place of Kali"), on the Hooghly. According to one Hindu legend, in the "age of truth" the patriarch Daksha, who was the father of Kali, the death goddess, made a sacrifice in order that he might be blessed with a son. He neglected to include Kali's husband, Shiva, in the ceremony. Kali, insulted and injured, killed herself. Shiva, grief-stricken, speared her body with a trident and carried it through creation, threatening, in madness, to destroy the world. Vishnu intervened. Saved the world by throwing a discus at the body of Kali, scattering her fragments all over the world. Wherever the fragments fell, the ground was sanctified. The most sanctified place was Kalighat, on the Hooghly, where the toes of Kali's right foot fell. (Public religious rites held for Kali every year in Calcutta.)

1696. The Nawab of Bengal, deputy of the Mogul emperor in Delhi, grants British settlers permission to build fort to protect trading interests. Called Fort William, after William of Orange.

1698. British settlers lease Sutanuti, along with Kalikotta and adjacent village, Gobindapur, from Nawab for thirteen hundred rupees a year. Expand settlement.

1707. East India Company forms the township of Calcutta, which by now has wharf, barracks, hospital, church; Bengal a separate Presidency, on par with Bombay and Madras, the company's two other Indian Presidencies.

1710. Calcutta's estimated population ten thousand.

1717. Fort William completed. East India Company leases thirty-eight more villages on banks of Hooghly.

1727. Calcutta organized into municipality, with mayor and nine aldermen, to collect ground rent and town dues for repairs of roads and drains.

1741. Fort William as altered and expanded: Large, irregular tetragon overlooking Hooghly. Brick. North side three hundred and forty feet long, south side four hundred and eighty-five feet long, east and west sides each seven hundred and ten feet long. Small, square bastions at corners, connected by curtain walls of cemented thin tile bricks—eighteen feet high, four feet thick. Inside the fort: Governor's House, magazine, military stores, dispensary, smithy, barracks, prison, warehouses, armory, laboratory, etc. All around the outside of fort, houses of officers and employees.

1750. Calcutta's estimated population two hundred thousand.

1756. Succession of new Nawab of Bengal, Siraj-ud-daula. Differences with the British. Nawab attacks and captures Fort William. Some British escape to ships on Hooghly, but others are left behind. A hundred and forty-six said to be confined on June 20th in fort's prison, the so-called Black Hole, a room about fourteen by eighteen feet, where all but twenty-three of them die of suffocation. The Black Hole tragedy chief event in Calcutta's history; at least one historian says British Indian Empire its consequence. Celebrated account of it in a letter by a survivor, J. Z. Holwell, magistrate:

> Before I conduct you into the Black Hole, it is necessary you should be acquainted with a few introductory Circumstances. The Suba [Nawab] and his troops were in possession of the fort before six in the evening. I had in all three interviews with him: the last in Durbar before seven when he repeated his assurances to me, *on the word of a soldier,* that no harm should come to us; and indeed I believe his orders were only general. That we should for the night be secured; and that what followed was the result of revenge and resentment in the breasts of the lower Jemmautdaars ["jemadars," or Indian junior officers]. . . .
>
> We were no sooner all within the barracks, than the guard advanced to the inner arches and parapet-wall; and with their muskets presented, ordered us to go into the room at the southernmost end of the barracks, commonly called the Black-Hole prison; whilst others from the Court of Guard, with clubs and drawn scymitars, pressed upon those of us next them. This stroke was so sudden, so unexpected, and the throng and the pressure so great upon us next to the door of the Black-Hole prison, there was no resisting it; but like one agitated wave impelling another, we were obliged to give way and enter; the rest followed like a torrent, few amongst us, the soldiers excepted, having the least idea of the dimensions or nature of a place we had never seen: for if we had, we

should at all events have rushed upon the guard, and been, as the lesser evil, by our own choice cut to pieces. . . .

I got possession of the window nearest the door, and took Messrs. Coles and Scot into the window with me, they being both wounded (the first I believe mortally). . . .

Figure to yourself, my friend, if possible, the situation of a hundred and forty-six wretches, exhausted by continual fatigue and action, thus crammed together in a cube of about eighteen feet, in a close sultry night, in Bengal, shut up to the eastward and southward (the only quarters from whence air could reach us) by dead walls, and by a wall and door to the north, open only to the westward by two windows, strongly barred with iron, from which we could receive scarce any the least circulation of fresh air. . . .

The moment I quitted the window, my breathing grew short and painful. . . .

I laid myself down on some of the dead behind me, on the platform; and recommending myself to heaven, had the comfort of thinking my sufferings could have no long duration. . . .

At this juncture the Suba, who had received an account of the havock death had made amongst us, sent one of his Jemmautdaars to inquire if the chief survived. They showed me to him; told him I had appearance of life remaining, and believed I might recover if the door was opened very soon. This answer being returned to the Suba, an order came immediately for our release, it being then near six in the morning. . . .

The little strength remaining amongst the most robust who survived, made it a difficult task to remove the dead piled up against the door; so that I believe it was more than twenty minutes before we obtained a passage out for one at a time. . . .

When I came out, I found myself in a high putrid fever, and not being able to stand, threw myself on the wet grass. . . .

The rest, who survived the fatal night, gained their liberty, except Mrs. Carey, who was too young and handsome. The dead bodies were promiscuously thrown into the ditch of our unfinished ravelin, and covered with the earth.

1757. British force under Clive and Admiral Watson, arriving in Bengal from Madras, defeats Siraj-ud-daula and French at Plassey, a village on the Bhagirathi. British given compensations, *zamindari* (proprietorship) over Calcutta, right to establish mint, etc. (In due course, British advance from Bengal to rest of India.) Clive begins work on New Fort William, near the original Fort William. *Imperial Gazetteer:* "Modern Calcutta dates from 1757."

1758. East India Company removes goods from Fort William, now used exclusively as military barracks. (Later, Holwell, having become Governor of Fort William, erects memorial obelisk at place where his fellow-sufferers were buried.)

1759. Thirty vessels call at Calcutta. Main exports opium, silk, muslin, indigo, saltpetre. Main import bullion.

1760. Area between Fort William's East Gate and Black Hole prison made into temporary church.

1764. Civil authority over much of Bengal conferred in perpetuity on East India Company by reigning Mogul emperor, Shah Alam. Center of East India Company's power shifts from Madras to Calcutta.

1767. Fort William, with new buildings added, made into a customhouse. Wilson's "Old Fort William in Bengal": "From this time onwards its fortunes steadily declined."

1773. New Fort William completed, at cost of two million pounds, and jungle around New Fort, cleared for military reasons, becomes Maidan. Customhouse now called Old Fort William.

1774. British Parliament invests control of East India Company's Indian possessions in Governor-General and Council of Bengal. Sets up Supreme Court in Calcutta, which now officially becomes capital of British Empire in India.

1780. British Calcutta "village of palaces." But Indian Calcutta very different. William Macintosh's "Travels in Europe, Asia, and Africa" (1782):

> It is a truth that, from the western extremity of California to the eastern coast of Japan, there is not a spot where judgement, taste, decency, and convenience are so grossly insulted as in that scattered and confused chaos of houses, huts, sheds, streets, lanes, alleys, windings, gullies, sinks, and tanks, which, jumbled into an undistinguished mass of filth and corruption, equally offensive to human sense and health, compose the capital of the English Company's Government in India. The very small portion of cleanliness

which it enjoys is owing to the familiar intercourse of hungry jackals by night, and ravenous vultures, kites, and crows by day. In like manner it is indebted to the smoke raised on public streets, in temporary huts and sheds, for any respite it enjoys from mosquitoes, the natural production of stagnated and putrid waters.

1818. Old Fort William demolished.

1819. Foundation stone of new customhouse laid.

1821. Holwell's obelisk, which has fallen into disrepair, pulled down.

1850. Calcutta's estimated population four hundred thousand.

1854. First jute mill in Bengal. Jute, woven on hand looms, in common use in Bengal villages in eighteenth century, but only in nineteenth introduced to England, where process of bleaching and dyeing is soon mastered. *Imperial Gazetteer:* "If it may be said that Bombay is built upon cotton, it is no less true that Calcutta is built on jute."

1858. East India Company transfers its functions in India to the British government.

1874. Opening of Howrah Bridge, giving Calcutta overland access to rest of India, where roads and railways in process of development.

1875. British get control of Suez Canal. More and more sea trade. More and more steamships—Peninsular & Oriental Steam Navigation, British India Steam Navigation, City, Clan, Harrison, and Anchor lines. Bengal gaining monopoly of many of India's exports— jute, coal, tea, hides, linseed, lac. Imports include textiles, metals, machinery.

1876. Calcutta Corporation constituted, with elected and appointed commissioners. Completes a drainage scheme, increases supply of filtered and unfiltered water, etc.

1882. Mr. R. R. Bayne, of East Indian Railway Company, while digging foundations for new Railway office building, discovers wall of Old Fort William.

1883. Bayne reports his discovery to Asiatic Society of Bengal, exciting interest of another Englishman, Dr. H. E. Busteed, who continues excavations.

1886. March. Visit of Lord and Lady Dufferin to Calcutta. Extract from "Our Viceregal Life in India," by Lady Dufferin:

This being our last day at Calcutta, we crammed a little sight-seeing into it. D. and I went with Dr. Busteed to look at the site of the Black Hole. This gentlemen . . . has worked away until he has discovered the exact spot where it was, besides collecting all the interesting details concerning that terrible disaster. Having found the place, which is now part of a courtyard leading to the Post Office, he has laid down a pavement the exact size of the little room called the "Black Hole," and has put up a tablet to explain this fact. Dr. Busteed gave me a little model of the place as it was, which shows that it was not a "hole" but a room. . . .

Dr. Busteed is very anxious to put up a stone to show where it [Holwell's obelisk] stood, and to place in the church a tablet with the names of the persons who died in the Black Hole, which names Holwell had been at some pains to preserve. He (Holwell) was painted by Sir Joshua Reynolds with the plan of this monument in his hand, and his descendants, who live in Canada, have the picture, and sent Dr. Busteed a photograph of it.

1886. May. Dr. Busteed writes to a Colonel Trevor:

The excavation was allowed to remain open for some short time, and attracted very numerous visitors and received much popular attention. The Government of Bengal with ready interest sympathized in the generally-felt desire that so very historical a site should be marked, and directed that what, for the present, was considered the most practicable thing under the circumstances should be done—namely, that as the roadway under which the chamber lay was essential to the Post Office traffic, the excavation should be filled in and decently paved over with granite, and that a tablet bearing this inscription should be placed on the most convenient spot near: "The stone pavement close to this marks the position and size of the prison cell in Old Fort William, known in history as the Black Hole of Calcutta."

1889. An eighteenth-century map of Calcutta and Old Fort William found in British Museum. Proves erroneous some inferences Busteed drew from his excavations and published in his work "Echoes from Old Calcutta."

1891. C. R. Wilson, with map, begins further excavations, which continue for years.

1900. Lord Curzon convenes meeting in yard of General Post Office. Considers question of another Black Hole obelisk. Assembly decides to remove massive masonry gate at one end of yard and pave with black marble the part of prison site not covered by building.

1901. Census. Calcutta's population eight hundred and forty-eight thousand. Howrah's a hundred and fifty-eight thousand. Total population of other suburbs a hundred and one thousand. Population of metropolis of Calcutta exceeded only by populations, severally, of metropolises of London, Constantinople, Paris, and Berlin. In Calcutta, fifty-seven languages—forty-one Asiatic, sixteen non-Asiatic. Greatest rate of population increase in the most crowded wards. Ratio of males to females two to one. Very high mortality rate.

1902. Lord Curzon delivers address on the occasion of unveiling marble obelisk in Calcutta to commemorate dead of Black Hole:

> I daresay that the worthy citizens of Calcutta may have been a good deal puzzled on many occasions during the past four years to see me rummaging about this neighbourhood and that of the adjoining Post Office in the afternoons, poking my nose into all sorts of obscure corners, measuring, marking, and finally ordering the erection of marble memorials and slabs. This big pillar, which I am now about to unveil, and the numerous tablets on the other side of the street, are the final outcome of these labours. But let me explain how it is that they have come about and what they mean.
>
> When I came out to India in this very month four years ago [as Viceroy of India], one of the companions of my voyage was that delightful "Echoes from Old Calcutta," by Mr. Busteed, formerly well known as an officer in the Calcutta Mint, and now living in retirement at home. There I read the full account of the tragic circumstances under which Old Fort William, which stood between the site were I am now speaking and the river, was besieged and taken by the forces of Siraj-ud-daula in 1756, and of the heroism and sufferings of the small band of survivors who were shut up for an awful summer's night in June in the tiny prison known as the Black Hole, with the shocking result that of the 146 who went in only 23 came out alive. I also read that the monument which had been erected shortly after the disaster by Mr. Holwell, one of the survivors, who wrote a detailed account of that night of horror, and who was afterwards Governor of Fort William, in order to

commemorate his fellow-sufferers who had perished in the prison, had been taken down, no one quite knows why, in or about the year 1821; and Mr. Busteed went on to lament, as I think very rightly, that whereas for sixty years after their death Calcutta had preserved the memory of these unhappy victims, ever since that time, now eighty years ago, there had been no monument, not even a slab or an inscription, to record their names and their untimely fate.

It was Mr. Busteed's writings accordingly that first called my attention to this spot and that induced me to make a careful personal study of the entire question of the site and surroundings of Old Fort William. The whole thing is now so vivid in my mind's eye that I never pass this way without the Post Office and Custom House and the modern aspect of Writers' Buildings fading out of my sight, while instead of them I see the walls and bastions of the old fort exactly behind the spot where I now stand, with its eastern gate and the unfinished ravelin in front of the gate, and the ditch in front of the ravelin into which the bodies of those who had died in the Black Hole were thrown the next morning, and over which Holwell erected his monument a few years later.

Nearly twenty years ago Mr. Roskell Bayne, of the East Indian Railway, made a number of diggings and measurements that brought to light the dimensions of the old fort, now almost entirely covered with modern buildings; and I was fortunate enough when I came here to find a worthy successor to him and coadjutor to myself in the person of Mr. C. R. Wilson, of the Indian Education Department, who had carried Mr. Bayne's inquiries a good deal further, cleared up some doubtful points, corrected some errors, and fixed with accuracy the exact site of the Black Hole and other features of the fort. All of these sites I set to work to commemorate while the knowledge was still fresh in our minds. Wherever the outer or inner line of the curtain and bastions of Old Fort William had not been built over I had them traced on the ground with brass lines let into stone—you will see some of them on the main steps of the Post Office—and I caused white marble tablets to be inserted in the walls of the adjoining buildings with inscriptions stating what was the part of the old building that originally stood there. I think that there are some dozen of these tablets in all, each of which tells its own tale.

I further turned my attention to the site of the Black Hole, which was in the premises of the Post Office, and could not be seen from the street, being shut off by a great brick and plaster gateway. I had this obstruction pulled down, and an open iron gate and railings erected in its place. I had the site of the Black Hole paved with polished black marble, and surrounded with a neat iron railing, and, finally, I placed a black marble tablet with an inscription above it, explaining the memorable and historic nature of the site that lies below. I do not know if cold-weather visitors to Calcutta, or even the residents of the city itself, have yet found out the existence of these memorials. But I venture to think that they are a permanent and valuable addition to the possessions and sights of the capital of British rule in India.

At the same time I proceeded to look into the question of the almost forgotten monument of Holwell. I found a number of illustrations and descriptions of it in the writings of the period, and though these did not in every case precisely tally with each other, yet they left no doubt whatever as to the general character of the monument, which consisted of a tall pillar or obelisk rising from an octagonal pedestal, on the two main faces of which were inscriptions written by Holwell, with the names of a number of the slain. Holwell's monument was built of brick covered over with plaster, like all the monuments of the period in the old Calcutta cemeteries; and I expect that it must have been crumbling when it was taken down . . . for I have seen a print in which it was represented with a great crack running down the side, from the top to the base, as though it had been struck by lightning. I determined to reproduce this memorial with as much fidelity as possible in white marble, to re-erect it on the same site, and to present it as my personal gift to the city of Calcutta in memory of a never-to-be-forgotten episode in her history, and in honour of the brave men whose life-blood had cemented the foundations of the British Empire in India. . . . Though Holwell's record contained less than fifty names out of the 123 who had been suffocated in the Black Hole, I have, by means of careful search into the records both here and in England, recovered not only the Christian names of the whole of these persons, but also more than twenty fresh names of those who also died in the prison. So that the new monument records the names of no fewer than sixty of the victims of that terrible night.

In the course of my studies, in which I have been ably assisted by the labours of Mr. S. C. Hill, of the Record Department, who is engaged in bringing out a separate work on the subject, I have also recovered the names of more than twenty other Europeans who, though they did not actually die in the Black Hole, yet were either killed at an earlier stage of the siege, or, having come out of the Black Hole alive, afterwards succumbed to its effects. These persons seem to me equally to deserve commemoration with those who were smothered to death in the prison, and accordingly I have entered their names on the remaining panels of this monument. We, therefore, have inscribed on this memorial the names of some eighty persons who took part in those historic events which established the British dominion in Bengal nearly a century and a half ago. They were the pioneers of a great movement, the authors of a wonderful chapter in the history of mankind; and I am proud that it has fallen to my lot to preserve their simple and humble names from oblivion, and to restore them to the grateful remembrance of their countrymen.

Gentlemen, in carrying out this scheme I have been pursuing one branch of a policy to which I have deliberately set myself in India, namely, that of preserving, in a breathless and often thoughtless age, the relics and memorials of the past. To me the past is sacred. It is often a chronicle of errors and blunders and crimes, but it also abounds in the records of virtue and heroism and valour. Anyhow, for good or evil, it is finished and written, and has become part of the history of the race, part of that which makes us what we are. Though human life is blown out as easily as the flame of a candle, yet it is something to keep alive the memory of what it has wrought and been, for the sake of those who come after; and I daresay it would solace our own despatch into the unknown, if we could feel sure that we too were likely to be remembered by our successors, and that our name was not going to vanish altogether from the earth when the last breath has fled from our lips. . . . How few of us who tread the streets of Calcutta from day to day ever turn a thought to the Calcutta past. And yet Calcutta is one great graveyard of memories. Shades of departed

Governors-General hover about the marble halls and corridors of Government House, where I do my daily work. Forgotten worthies in ancient costumes haunt the precincts of this historic square. Strange figures, in guise of peace or war, pass in and out of the vanished gateways of the vanished fort. If we think only of those whose bones are mingled with the soil underneath our feet, we have but to walk a couple of furlongs from this place to the churchyard where lies the dust of Job Charnock, of Surgeon William Hamilton, and of Admiral Watson, the founder, the extender, and the saviour of the British dominion in Bengal. A short drive of two miles will take us to the most pathetic sight in Calcutta—those dismal and decaying Park Street cemeteries where generations of by-gone Englishmen and English women, who struggled and laboured on this stage of exile for a brief span, lie unnamed, unremembered, and unknown. But if among these fore-runners of our own, if among these ancient and unconscious builders of Empire, there are any who especially deserve commemoration, surely it is the martyr band whose fate I recall and whose names I resuscitate on this site; and if there be a spot that should be dear to an Englishman in India, it is that below our feet, which was stained with the blood and which closed over the remains of the victims of that night of destiny, the 20th of June, 1756. It is with these sentiments in my heart that I have erected this monument, and that I now hand it over to the citizens of Calcutta, to be kept by them in perpetual remembrance of the past.

Nota Bene: Remember to review strange debate among Indian historians about the number of Englishmen who died in the Black Hole, and even about whether the Black Hole tragedy ever really occurred. Some say, incredibly, that the Black Hole was merely a British invention to justify the conquest of Bengal, maintaining that the story is found only in British accounts, and not in contemporary Indian Muslim sources. On this point, cf. the Bengali historian A. K. Maitreya, whose work on Siraj-ud-daula represents the classic Indian attempt to find gaps in the British evidence and so refute the British with their own sources. But new information on the Black Hole based on other than British primary sources, such as the translation, by A. Hughes (published in *Bengal Past & Present* in 1958), of a newly found contemporary Persian manuscript on Siraj-ud-daula, cuts most of the ground from under the arguments of Maitreya et al. Discuss problem S. C. Hill raises: "Why the inhabitants of Bengal were absolutely apathetic to events which handed over the government of their country to a race so different from their own." Analyze differences in attitudes of British and of Indians toward history, toward the dead.

Surprisingly, Rudyard Kipling (1865–1936), who was virtually a stranger to Calcutta, is the writer most often quoted on Calcutta; he was born in India and spent his early childhood, late teens, and early twenties in the country, but the Indian cities he knew best were Lahore, where he worked for about five years on the editorial staff of the *Civil & Military Gazette,* and Allahabad, where he worked for two years on the editorial staff of the *Gazette*'s sister publication the *Pioneer.* While in India, he travelled extensively, and his outlook, when not that of an imperialist, was that of a pragmatic Lahori with perhaps a trace of the spirituality of Allahabad. Certainly some of his stories and articles reveal him to be an up-country writer who spurned what he took to be the effeminate hybrid culture of Bengal and the pretensions of the British capital in favor of the rugged indigenous culture of the Punjab and the native wholesomeness of a provincial city. He wrote, in fact, very little about Calcutta, and what he did write was written between the ages of nineteen and twenty-three. Calcutta figures in one short story and three narrative poems, and in a series of eight short, informal articles that first appeared in the *Pioneer* in 1889 and, in 1899, were revised and collected under the general title "City of Dreadful Night" in his book "From Sea to Sea." (Calcutta also figures in a children's story.) The short story, entitled "The Dream of Duncan Parrenness," is about a dissolute young Englishman who is a junior clerk in the service of the East India Company and who has a dream in which he confronts his future and the consequences of a wasted youth. The tale, which is a kind of moral ghost story, is forced and awkward, perhaps because it tries to re-create the idiom of the Warren Hastings period, in which it is set. In any case, although the story does contain some specific references to Calcutta ("sullen, un-English stream, the Hugli," "the foul soil north of Writers' Buildings"), the setting is incidental. Similarly, two of the poems—"What Happened" and "The Ballad of Fisher's Boarding-House," which concern the anarchic diversity of the Indian people and a brawl in a harbor boarding house, respectively—could have been set in Bombay or a number of other cities. The third poem, however, "A Tale of Two Cities"—the second city is Simla, the hill station in the Punjab that served as the British summer capital—dwells on the physical squalor and loathsome conditions of life in Calcutta, deploring the accident that brought the city into being in the first place and the avarice that sustains it. The poem, which is quoted in its entirety below, has come to be thought of almost as another curse upon Calcutta, phrases from it having become, in the English language, lasting epithets for Calcutta:

> Where the sober-coloured cultivator smiles
>> On his *byles* [cattle];
> Where the cholera, the cyclone, and the crow
>> Come and go;
> Where the merchant deals in indigo and tea,
>> Hides and *ghi;*
> Where the Babu drops inflammatory hints
>> In his prints;
> Stands a City—Charnock chose it—packed away
>> Near a Bay—
> By the sewage rendered fetid, by the sewer
>> Made impure,
> By the Sunderbunds unwholesome, by the swamp
>> Moist and damp;
> And the City and the Viceroy, as we see,
>> Don't agree.
> Once, two hundred years ago, the trader came
>> Meek and tame.
> Where his timid foot first halted, there he stayed,
>> Till mere trade
> Grew to Empire, and he sent his armies forth
>> South and North.
> Till the country from Peshawur to Ceylon
>> Was his own.
>
> Thus the midday halt of Charnock—more's the pity!—
>> Grew a City.
> As the fungus sprouts chaotic from its bed,
>> So it spread—

Chance-directed, chance-erected, laid and built
    On the silt—
Palace, byre, hovel—poverty and pride—
    Side by side;
And, above the packed and pestilential town,
    Death looked down.

But the Rulers in that City by the Sea
    Turned to flee—
Fled, with each returning Springtide, from its ills
    To the Hills.
From the clammy fogs of morning, from the blaze
    Of the days,
From the sickness of the noontide, from the heat,
    Beat retreat;
For the country from Peshawur to Ceylon
    Was their own.
But the Merchant risked the perils of the Plain
    For his gain.

Now the resting-place of Charnock, 'neath the palms,
    Asks an alms,
And the burden of its lamentation is,
    Briefly, this:
"Because, for certain months, we boil and stew,
    "So should you.
"Cast the Viceroy and his Council, to perspire
    "In our fire!"
And for answer to the argument, in vain
    We explain
That an amateur Saint Lawrence cannot cry:—
    "*All* must try!"
That the Merchant risks the perils of the Plains
    For his gains.
Nor can Rulers rule a house that men grow rich in,
    From its kitchen.

Let the Babu drop inflammatory hints
    In his prints:

And mature—consistent soul—his plan for stealing
 To Darjeeling:
Let the Merchant seek, who makes his silver pile,
 England's isle;
Let the City Charnock pitched on—evil day!—
 Go Her way.
Though the argosies of Asia at Her doors
 Heap their stores,
Though Her enterprise and energy secure
 Income sure,
Though "out-station orders punctually obeyed"
 Swell Her trade—
Still, for rule, administration, and the rest,
 Simla's best!

By far the most substantial treatment of Calcutta is to be found in
"City of Dreadful Night," which was the result of Kipling's only long
visit to Calcutta. Kipling imagines the first sensations of British "back-
woodsmen and barbarians" who, like him, have lived for a long time
in the rustic, provincial atmosphere of the Empire, away from London
and civilization, and have come to think of Calcutta as the only "real"
city in India, and who travel there hoping that their heritage of civilization will be restored to them. "Let us take off our hats to Calcutta,
the many-sided, the smoky, the magnificent," he writes. "We have left
India behind us. . . . Why, this is London! This is the docks. This is
Imperial. This is worth coming across India to see!" But in the cosmopolitan Great Eastern Hotel, where nationals of all countries are to
be found, and in the splendid Maidan, whose expanse dwarfs everything except the rows of mansions of Chowringhi, and in the palaces
themselves, which were built in the old times when money was plentiful, and which, like the houses in hill stations, are graced with outside
winding service staircases, there is a reeking, ferocious, all-pervasive
stench, worse than the worst odor of Benares, Peshawar, or Bombay.
There is no escape from it, no relief except exhaustion, for it is the "Big
Calcutta Stink," or, in Kipling's abbreviation, "B.C.S." "Stop to consider for a moment," he writes, "what the cramped compounds, the
black soaked soil, the netted intricacies of the service-staircases, and
packed stables, the seethment of human life . . . and the curious

arrangement of little open drains mean, and you will call it a whited sepulchre." Thinking that any English municipal government would have solved Calcutta's most basic problem, sanitation, he blames the stench on an experiment that Calcutta was making at the time with local self-government. "In spite of that stink, they allow, even encourage, natives to look after the place!" he writes. "The damp, drainage-soaked soil is sick with the teeming life of a hundred years, and the Municipal Board list is choked with the names of natives—men of the breed born in and raised off this surfeited muckheap!"

Kipling attends a debate of the Bengal Legislative Council. The "Councillor Sahibs," as Kipling calls the Indian members, presided over by the Lieutenant-Governor of Bengal, Sir Steuart Bayley, meet in a sumptuous blue-domed octagonal chamber in a large octagonal wing of the Writers' Buildings:

> There are gilt capitals to the half pillars and an Egyptian pat-terned lotus-stencil makes the walls gay [he writes]. . . . If the work matches the first-class furniture, the ink-pots, the carpet, and the resplendent ceilings, there will be something worth seeing. But where is the criminal who is to be hanged for the stench that runs up and down Writers' Buildings staircases; for the rubbish heaps in the Chitpore Road; for the sickly savour of Chowringhi . . . for the street full of small-pox . . . and for a hundred other things?

> "This, I submit, is an artificial scheme in supersession of Na-ture's unit, the individual." The speaker is a slight, spare native in a flat hat-turban and a black alpaca frock-coat. . . . He talks and talks and talks in a level voice, rising occasionally half an octave when a point has to be driven home. . . . "So much for the princi-ple. Let us now examine how far it is supported by precedent."

> Western education is an exotic plant. . . . We brought it out from England exactly as we brought out the ink-bottles and the patterns for the chairs. We planted it and it grew—monstrous as a banian. Now we are choked by the roots of it spreading so thickly in this fat soil of Bengal. . . . Bit by bit we builded this dome, vis-ible and invisible, the crown of Writers' Buildings. . . . That tor-rent of verbiage is Ours. We taught him what was constitutional and what was unconstitutional in the days when Calcutta smelt.

Calcutta smells still, but We must listen to all that he has to say about the plurality of votes and the threshing of wind and the weaving of ropes of sand. . . .

Why do they talk and talk about owners and occupiers and burgesses in England and the growth of autonomous institutions when the city, the great city, is here crying out to be cleansed? . . .

This is the Calcutta Municipal Bill. They have been at it for several Saturdays. Last Saturday Sir Steuart Bayley pointed out that at their present rate they would be about two years in getting it through. . . .

Meantime Calcutta continues to cry out for the bucket and the broom.

Kipling continues his explorations of the city, from the banks of the Hooghly—he visits the Port Office, where efficient *babus* daily chart the channel of the Hooghly, and the Shipping Office nearby, where mercantile outcasts wait to ship out of Calcutta—to the Park Street Cemetery (that "most pathetic sight" Curzon spoke of), which contains the graves of the early English. In the course of a night, Kipling visits brothels, dance sheds, gambling houses, and opium dens, being initiated into the dark mysteries of the city as he passes from one vice-ridden, mean neighborhood to another, from the outer edge of what he regards as the inferno deeper and deeper into its center. Everywhere people are trapped and crowded together in abominable hovels resembling pigsties, and everywhere he encounters horrors that "cannot be written or hinted at" and yet are accepted as if they were the normal order of things.

Kipling borrowed the title for his Calcutta series from James Thomson's "The City of Dreadful Night":

The City of Night, but not of Sleep;
There sweet sleep is not for the weary brain;
The pitiless hours like years and ages creep,
A night seems termless hell. This dreadful strain
Of thought and consciousness which never ceases,
Or which some moments' stupor but increases,
This, worse than woe, makes wretches there insane.

An age has crept past since Kipling wrote, but although his Calcutta writings are adolescent—the irony is heavy-handed and the point of view naïvely prejudiced—they continue to be remembered, because the passing of years has only preserved and multiplied the horrors of the city.

One Life, One Chance

Tonight, I approach a large, ghostly old house in Calcutta. An elderly, bearded man wearing a Muslim skullcap is slouching at the entrance. I ask him the way to the lodgings of David McCutchion. He points vaguely toward the entrance of the house, and then shuffles away. The entrance leads into a dark and dingy hallway, where a broken-down bicycle stands next to a broken-down couch. Leading up from the hallway is a wide, unswept staircase, and I climb to the second floor. On the landing, a figure in crimson silk emerges from a doorway. The figure turns out to be a plump little girl of not more than ten, heavily made up. I ask her if she knows where McCutchion lives. She indicates that I should follow her, and silently leads me on a surrealistic walk through a series of lightless passages and into a large, untidy garret containing a narrow iron bedstead, an old cupboard, three wooden chairs, a desk, a trunk, some suitcases, and three umbrellas. To one side of the room is a typical Indian bathing area—a sloping cement floor on which stand buckets, dippers, and mugs, and a low bench. Overhead, a ceiling fan whirs sluggishly, and stretched across the room is a string from which a wet shirt is hanging. On the desk are photographs of reliefs of mythical scenes and statues of gods and goddesses from Hindu temples, and all around the room are shelves holding books on Bengal. McCutchion, who sits reading a Bengali book when I enter, is a tall, spare Englishman in his thirties. He has on big black-rimmed glasses, and is dressed like an Indian, in pajamas and a bush shirt.

McCutchion has become known in Calcutta as a Satyajit Ray film buff; in fact, in recent years he has been one of Ray's closest associates, helping him write the English subtitles for his films. After the girl in the red dress has left, I tell McCutchion of my interest in Calcutta and in Ray, who is considered the greatest film artist in Calcutta and in the country, and perhaps India's greatest living artist. "Ray loves Calcutta," McCutchion says. "All of us who live here love Calcutta, in a way. It is a nightmare of a city in terms of filth, but the people who live here make it a great city. Like all true Bengalis, Ray has a strong feeling for Bengali culture—his films draw upon every aspect of it. He is interested in everything Bengali—in Bengali literature and the Bengali language and Bengali life. When a promoter comes to him and asks him to do a film in another language—in Hindi, perhaps—he just says no. In 1964, he did a fifteen-minute segment of an hour TV show for Esso—called 'Two.' They wanted it to be in English, but he said he wouldn't do a Bengali film with English dialogue, and he did a silent film, a pantomime. He is quite critical of Bengalis who, for instance, write in English. But he's not a Bengali purist—he doesn't feel bound to use only Bengali words. In fact, he uses a great number of English words in the sound tracks of his films; he would say he uses them in the interests of authenticity. His films are notably authentic—a Bengali house in a film of his will have an oleograph over the mantelpiece. He often uses amateur actors, and will find someone to play a part who in life is like the character he plays in the film. Ray's research is very thorough. But I am always a little disappointed in his themes. A general criticism of his films, with which I agree, is that, as a rule, he does not deal with the starker aspects of Indian life. But then, as a person, he's a typical middle-class Bengali. In fact, he is striking for his ordinariness. He lives in a very simple, middle-class way. There is nothing flamboyant about him, nothing ostentatious. He knows what he wants, and he is practical in seeking it. He is completely wrapped up in his work. In some ways, he is a very lonely man. When he is not shooting, he sits in a chair in his den for seventeen or eighteen hours at a time."

I ask McCutchion how he and Ray became acquainted.

"I came to India in 1957, soon after reading modern languages at Cambridge," he says. "I first met Ray in 1960, when I was teaching English at Shantiniketan and he came there to speak to the students. He gave me his address and asked me to look him up when I was next in Calcutta. I did. At the time, he was filming 'Teen Kanya,' and I went to watch him shoot. Gradually, we got to know each other. He has introduced me to people, given me film, and in other ways been very helpful to me in my hobby, which is photographing terra-cotta art in the temples."

To meet Satyajit Ray, the director of "Pather Panchali" (Cannes Special Award), "Aparajito" (Venice Grand Prix), "Jalsaghar," "Paras Pathar," "Apur Sansar" ("Pather Panchali," "Aparajito," and "Apur Sansar" make up what is well known as the Trilogy), "Devi," "Rabindranath Tagore," "Teen Kanya," "Kanchenjunga," "Abhijan," "Mahanagar," "Charulata," and "Kapurush-O-Mahapurush," I walk along a narrow, shabby street to the house he lives in, with his wife and their only child, a son. Having passed through an unimposing entrance into an unimposing hall, and climbed a narrow and dimly lit stairway to the second floor, I reach Ray's flat. A servant lets me into a gloomy hallway, which has a couple of glass cases displaying inexpensive knickknacks, such as are often found in Indian homes. The hallway leads into a small, close, cluttered room—Ray's den. All around the walls are well-worn books, some in soft covers but most clothbound, some in Bengali but most in English. They are a jumble of titles and authors: "Persian Tales," "Myths of the Hindus and Buddhists," Pushkin, an encyclopedia (covered in brown paper but with the paper cut away to show the alphabetical contents of each volume), "The Voices of Silence," "History of India," "Cézanne," "The Dawn of Civilisation," "The Face of New York," "The Art of India," Tagore, "Classical Literary Criticism," the Upanishads, "A Passage to India," "Ancient Art of the Andes," "Great Sanskrit Plays," "Esquire Etiquette," "The Wonder That Was India." There are a couple of paintings; a piano, a tape recorder, and a gramophone; a divan piled with Indian musical instruments, spools of tape, books, magazines, typewritten sheets, and a jar of pencils; a large round table holding more books and papers; a rectangular table on which are a typewriter and a telephone; and a couple of easy chairs. Next to the rectangular table is a frayed red chair, in which Ray sits, wearing an unstarched, rumpled white *kurta*, pajamas, and leather slippers. He has a drawing board on his knees. As I enter, he puts the drawing board down and stands up to greet me. "I am working on type faces for the International Typeface Design Competition," he explains, pacing about. "I have to send my designs off to New York by the end of this week to meet the deadline. The prize is fifteen hundred dollars. If the designs are sold, I will also get royalties. I have always been interested in graphics."

Ray sits down. He is a very tall, large, rugged-looking man in his middle forties. He has thick black hair, a big nose, a wide mouth, and eyes that protrude slightly. He gives the impression of having great physical energy held perfectly under control. When he walks about, his movements are abrupt and decisive; when he is sitting, he is quite still and self-contained. His expression, unlike that of many Bengalis, is not gentle but somewhat severe and remote.

I tell Ray a little about the time I have spent in Calcutta, and mention to him that one of the things I have noticed is an intense political involvement on the part of Calcutta's artists and writers.

"Most of the interesting work in the arts here is done by left-wingers," Ray says. "I cannot think of any right-wing Bengali who has ever done anything praiseworthy. As for me, most people would probably associate me with figures who are very strongly left-wing, like Utpal Dutt. But I think politics are a mess, and, as a rule, politicians here are not men of calibre. I have not lent my name to many political causes. Recently, I did write a letter denouncing the appearance of the new National Theatre building here. I denounced the colors, the relief work, the foyer—the ugliness of the whole building. And during the general strike and riots in Bengal this March I represented the Union of Film Workers in a procession, because film people here have the reputation of not being affected by things like that, and I wanted to give the lie to this idea. I didn't stay in the procession very long, however, because I once had sunstroke and I am not supposed to be out in the sun very long."

I ask him how he feels about living in Calcutta.

"I love Calcutta," he says. "I have lived here all my life. The best of whatever is being done in the arts in India is being done here. There is great intellectual vitality here. A lot of very good Bengali writing is being done here. The Bengali theatre is very much alive here. The coffeehouses here are full of people with ideas. Only filmmaking has not attracted many intellectuals, yet from a filmmaker's point of view no city could be better, because all kinds of things happen here all the time. It is true I don't have much of a social life, but then I don't really miss it. There is no one with whom I can discuss all the things I am interested in. In fact, it is difficult for me to find time to do everything I want to do."

I ask him about some of the things he does.

"My father, Sukumar Ray, was the greatest children's writer in Bengali," he says. "I am still referred to here as 'the son of Sukumar

Ray.' My grandfather wrote for children, too, though he made his living as a printer. He had many inventions to his credit, and his printing shop produced the finest printing of his day. He started and edited a children's magazine, *Sandesh,* which is the name of a sweet-meat that Bengali children love. I have revived *Sandesh* with my aunt, Leila Mazumdar. It is a monthly, and I design a new cover for it every six months. I do several illustrations for each issue, and I do other things for it, too. Recently I made a puzzle for it, a crossword in rhyme—the first crossword of its kind devised in Bengali. I have translated a lot of Edward Lear's limericks and a great deal of Lewis Carroll into Bengali for *Sandesh.* At present, I am trying to translate my father's nonsense rhymes into English, but I am having a great deal of difficulty with this."

I ask him what film he is currently working on.

"I'm just finishing 'Nayak,' " he says. ("*Nayak*" is Bengali for "hero.") "I'm also making a film adaptation of 'Gupi Gayen Bagha Bayen,' a fantasy written by my grandfather. 'Nayak' will have its world première in Calcutta in a couple of months. I wrote the scenario for 'Nayak' myself. It's my second original scenario—'Kanchenjunga' was my first. For my films, I now write my own scenarios, make sketches for the scenes, sets, and costumes, design the credits, and compose the music. Music is a strong interest of mine. Sometimes my music is in the classical Indian vein, sometimes in the light Western vein. Actually, I got interested in Western music first and came to Indian music only later. 'Nayak,' in which most of the people wear Western clothes, calls for a slightly Western score, so I use some *ragas* with hints of jazz here and there—keeping the orchestration light. The fantasy film will have lots of music and dancing, battles and demons, and so forth. I want to shoot it in a variety of locations, some of them perhaps outside India—say, the Middle East, to create an Arabian Nights atmosphere—because I would like to take my audiences here to places not familiar to them. I want to make it in color, but I am not sure I can achieve all the camera tricks that the story demands. I have to write the lyrics and tunes for a lot of songs. My grandfather's story just says 'So-and-So sings,' and I have to give him a song to sing. I also have to work on inventing a new language, because the fantasy is about a couple of boys who visit two communities. In one community, everyone has been struck dumb, but in the other community everyone speaks an unknown language. For that language I am thinking of using Bengali played backwards. When you play Bengali backwards, all sorts of funny things happen. Laughter sounds like crying. A sad song sometimes sounds like a happy song. If you play a song backwards, you get a completely new melody—it makes sense as music, but it has nothing to do with the original. I suppose the pattern could be worked out mathematically."

I ask him when he expects to begin shooting the fantasy.

"After I've finished editing 'Nayak' and it has had its première, I plan to go first to supervise a film that some of my assistants are hoping to make. I'm going to help them with the script, the sets, the music, and the direction. Then, after I've got their film off the ground, I'll go to Darjeeling for a month to work on the script of 'Gupi Gayen Bagha Bayen.'"

I have heard that he hopes one day to film the Mahabharata, the great Hindu epic, and I ask him about it.

"I've given the idea quite a lot of thought, but I've had to drop it," he says. "I was not able to get financial backing, and when I read parts of it with a view to making a scenario, I found that I would have to deal with fourteen or fifteen main characters, and their interrelationships were too complicated for a film. It would have been a tremendous job to explain the relationships. I would still like to do a section of it one day. The film I'd most like to do now, however, is 'A Passage to India.' Of course, it would be a complete departure for me, and there are a lot of things about the novel that would present problems. When I saw the stage production of 'A Passage to India' in London, I was very much disappointed. Everything was overacted and overdone; the Indians came across as caricatures—comical and exaggerated. I think I could avoid that by using two languages in the film, so that when there are no English people present—say, when Aziz and Hamidullah are speaking together—they would speak in their own language, as they naturally would in life. I think the effect you get, even in the book, of the Indian characters' sounding comical results from the fact that they speak English."

He takes the book from a shelf, finds a page, and begins to read. "'The young man sprang up on to the verandah. He was all animation. "Hamidullah, Hamidullah! Am I late?" he cried. "Do not apologize," said his host. "You are always late." "Kindly answer my question. Am I late? Has Mahmoud Ali eaten all the food? If so I go elsewhere. Mr. Mahmoud Ali, how are you?" "Thank you, Dr. Aziz, I am dying." "Dying before your dinner? Oh, poor Mahmoud Ali!" ' " Ray laughs explosively; he is slow to smile but quick to laugh. "In Urdu, this exchange would sound natural in a way it doesn't in English," he says.

"But surely Forster wants the effect of an Indian speaking English," I say.

"Yes, but then he can explain in the book, in a way you can't in a stage production or a film, that the dialogue is intended to show the gulf between the colonial English and the Indians. Anyway, the question is academic, because Forster won't allow the book to be made into a film."

I ask him about his own life.

"I was an only child, and I have always been more or less on my own," he says. "I was two when my father died. I hardly remember my father, and my grandfather died before I was born. After my father's death, my mother and I lived with my mother's uncle here in Calcutta. He kept moving from flat to flat, and we moved with him. I attended Calcutta University, and after that I went to Shantiniketan to study fine arts. I was at Shantiniketan for three years. There I painted a little, and I also started developing a serious interest in the cinema. I read some books on the aesthetics of the cinema—on film forms, film technique, film acting. I read books by Eisenstein, by Pudovkin, and by other great directors. I did not finish my fine-arts course, however, because the Japanese started bombing Calcutta, and I left Shantiniketan the day after the bombing started, to be with my mother, who was living here—she died in 1960. A few months after that—this was in 1943—I joined D. J. Keymer, the advertising agency, as a layout man, although I'd had no training in commercial art. After I got the advertising job, my mother and I moved to a small flat in the Ballygunge section. In 1947, my friends and I started the Calcutta Film Society, the first film-appreciation club in the city. We had something like twenty or twenty-four members. Now there are two thousand. I was married in 1949. I started shooting my first film, 'Pather Panchali,' in 1952, and finished it three years later."

I ask him how he came to make "Pather Panchali."

"When I was at Keymer, I was doing book illustrations, book

covers, book design, and typography for a publisher on the side," he says. "Around 1949, the publisher asked me to do illustrations for a new edition of 'Pather Panchali,' a novel by one of the best-known Bengali writers, Bibhutibhushan Bannerji. It was first published in the early nineteen-thirties, and the author had recently died. While illustrating the book, I got the idea of turning it into a film, and I did a few rough drawings. 'Pather Panchali' is not the kind of book that most directors and producers would think of making into a film. It hasn't the dramatic structure, the single, unified episode. It has loving descriptions of rural life, of little, subtle relationships among brother, sister, parents, and an old, unwanted aunt. The old aunt dies and the daughter dies. But when I read the book I loved it, and immediately thought what a wonderful film it would make. I talked about this with Mrs. Bannerji, who knew my entire family. She had known my father and my grandfather, and knew me through the book designs I was doing. Mrs. Bannerji told me that her husband used to say, 'My books would make very good films, but no one wants them.' I showed her all the sketches for scenes I had done. There were two fat sketchbooks. She was very much impressed, and showed faith in me by giving me the film rights. When the newspapers announced that I had been given the film rights, she started receiving letters from people who said she had no business giving the film rights of a classic to someone who had never made a film. She said to me, 'Although some of these people are close friends of mine, I have full faith and trust in you. I am sure you will do something truly remarkable.' I showed her pictures of the boy and girl I was considering for the parts in the film, and she said, 'This is exactly how I imagined the children in the book looked.' Soon after this, I went to England for six months, and in that time I saw about ninety-five films. I made a point of seeking out all the films by the big names in postwar Italy, acted mainly by non-professionals, out on the streets, without any makeup. On the boat on the way back from England, I wrote a proper scenario of 'Pather Panchali,' hoping to do it on the same lines as the Italians. For a year and a half after I came back to Calcutta, I went around to producers. Nobody showed any interest in filming the story, or in me as a possible director. So I took a loan of eight thousand rupees from my insurance company and started shooting. I had a cameraman new to films, Subrata Mitra. He was twenty-one or twenty-two at the time. I had Banshi Chandra

Gupta as my art director. For my film editor I had Dulal Dutta, who had just started editing films. The three have been with me ever since. We were all in our twenties. I still had my job at the advertising agency, so we could shoot only on Sundays and holidays."

I recall reading a description Ray wrote of shooting the first scene:

> It was an episode in the screen play where the two children of the story, brother and sister, stray from their village and chance upon a field of *kaash* flowers. The two have had a quarrel, and here in this enchanted setting they are reconciled and their long journey is rewarded by their first sight of a railway train. I chose to begin with this scene because on paper it seemed both effective and simple. I considered this important, because the whole idea behind launching the production with only 8,000 rupees in the bank was to produce quickly and cheaply a reasonable length of rough cut which we hoped would establish our *bona fides*. . . .
>
> At the end of the first day's shooting we had eight shots. The children behaved naturally, which was a bit of luck, because I hadn't tested them. As for myself, I remember feeling a bit strung up in the beginning; but as work progressed my nerves relaxed and in the end I even felt a kind of elation. However, the scene was only half finished, and on the following Sunday we were back on the same location. But was it the same location? It was hard to believe it. What was on the previous occasion a sea of fluffy whiteness was now a mere expanse of uninspiring brownish grass. We knew *kaash* was a seasonal flower, but surely they were not that short-lived? A local peasant provided the explanation. The flowers, he said, were food to the cattle. The cows and buffaloes had come to graze the day before and had literally chewed up the scenery.

I remark now how much I like his description of this incident.

"Our idea was to shoot some footage and show it to the producers," he says. "We showed them twenty-five minutes of film, but they said they were not interested. I had a friend who had influence with some distributors, and the friend persuaded the distributors to give us some money. Now I filled all the parts and completed something like five reels of film, but when I showed them to the distributors, they said they were not interested in going on. For a year, there was no money and no work. I thought of shelving the whole thing. I told my unit and my actors that we were not going to go on. Then somebody had the idea of approaching the late Dr. B. C. Roy, who was Chief Minister of West Bengal at the time, and trying to get government financing for the film. My mother knew somebody who knew Dr. Roy, he was approached, and eventually the film was made with government money. The government gave us installments of money, for which we had to sign vouchers. We resumed working, and it took seven or eight months to complete the film. It was now the government's property, but the government did not know what to do with it. They thought of putting it out under the Community Development Department, and suggested that we change the ending. At the end of the film, the family decides to leave the village because it has been ruined by the storm. The government said that this did not fit in with the idea of community development, and that the family should try to rebuild its house. I said the author might object. The people in the government didn't know that the author was dead, and I got my way. Eventually, the film was put out under the Publicity Department of the Road Development Scheme. The film opened in a theatre in Calcutta, and was booked for six weeks. The first two weeks, the film didn't do so well. Then it picked up, and on the last day of the six weeks the house was full. But, beginning the next day, the theatre was booked for a south Indian film by S. S. Vasan, of Gemini Pictures. The theatre sent a telegram to Vasan asking him if they could postpone the première of his film so that they could run 'Pather Panchali' for a few weeks more. Vasan telegraphed back, 'Nothing doing.' Afterward, he came to Calcutta and saw 'Pather Panchali,' and on the next day he came to my house. I was very much moved by what he said. He said, 'Don't judge me by the films I make. I can appreciate good things when I see them. If I had only known how good "Pather Panchali" was!' "

I ask him what happened to the film after the first six weeks.

"We were able to find another theatre, and it ran for another six or seven weeks. It got excellent reviews. It ran in Bombay, Delhi, and Madras, but without subtitles. Finally, it was entered in the Cannes Film Festival, where it was championed by the film director Lindsay Anderson. In Cannes, it was shown after four other films, and many of the members of the jury did not stay for it. They were too tired. A few critics stayed. One of them—a Frenchman, André Bazin—was so impressed that he immediately arranged a second showing of the film and insisted that all the members of the jury be present. It received a special prize as the 'Best Human Document.' 'Pather Panchali' was followed by 'Aparajito,' the second part of the trilogy. When I took 'Aparajito' to the Venice Film Festival, someone asked me if I was going to make the third part. I said yes—I don't know why—and that's how 'Pather Panchali' grew into a trilogy. But I did two other films— 'Paras Pathar' and 'Jalsaghar'—before going on to make 'Apur Sansar,' the third part of the trilogy, in 1959. Then I began 'Devi,' which is a particular favorite of mine. It has a very dramatic plot—the clash between old and new. It's about early-nineteenth-century superstition—about a girl who comes to believe she is a reincarnation of Kali. A very, very grim plot, but a beautiful-looking film. 'Devi' was based on a story written by Prabhat Mukherji. The plot was a gift to Prabhat Mukherji from Tagore. Tagore had so many plots in his head that he made gifts of them to promising young writers. Incidentally, I did a documentary on Tagore for the Films Division of the government of India, for the Tagore centenary. It was only an hour long. We had to use still photographs and any amateur movies that we could get hold of. My first color film was 'Kanchenjunga.' It was all shot on location—in Darjeeling, in the shadow of Mount Kanchenjunga. The thing in my mind was to do a story unbroken in time, the action taking place in the space of a couple of hours. I decided on an upper-middle-class story, with some very Anglicized characters. I chose Darjeeling because it's a hill station very popular with upper-middle-class Bengalis, and things happen in Darjeeling that could not happen in Calcutta."

A Calcutta film critic, discussing Ray's work, has written, "The Calcutta of the burning trams, the communal riots, the refugees, the unemployment, the rising prices and the food shortage do not exist in Ray's films. The trials of the sensitive mind trying to survive the excruciating pressure of corruption, vulgarity, want, and total pointlessness find no echo in him." I ask Ray now about this criticism.

"One trouble is that I have not been able to find good stories about these subjects. I feel at home with middle-class people, but in the trilogy I dealt with poor people. Also, ever since 'Pather Panchali' I've had to select stories that I could make into films in a few months. But if I found a good story about a *busti,* say, I would make a film of it."

I ask him what he thinks of the Indian film industry, which, measured by the number of films produced per year, was long the largest film industry in the world, though Japan has overtaken it.

"You cannot take the Indian film industry seriously," he says. "The heart of the industry is in Bombay, and although it is true that some of the films made there have some good photography, some good sound recording, some good acting—even the songs, though much ridiculed, sometimes have a certain quality to them—the films always collapse when it comes to the story and direction. For a good film, you need one director who has control over everything, a single guiding hand, and in Bombay the director is nobody—everything rests with the producers and distributors."

I ask him which of all film directors he admires most.

"It is not difficult to answer *whom* I admire," he says. "It's more difficult to explain why. Besides Eisenstein and Podovkin, I admire Dreyer and Bergman very much, and Antonioni also. I got to know Jean Renoir fairly well when he was making 'The River' here in Calcutta, and I greatly admire his work—especially 'La Règle du Jeu.' I'm impressed with some of the other French directors, like Tauffaut—especially his 'Jules et Jim.' I'm also impressed by the early films of De Sica—'The Bicycle Thief' and 'Umberto D.' I admire some American directors, like John Ford—particularly for their early work. Actually, as you may have gathered, I admire individual films more than directors. My favorites are 'The Gold Rush,' 'The General,' 'Ivan the Terrible,' 'A Night at the Opera,' 'The Seven Samurai,' and 'My Darling Clementine.' Nowadays, I am very impatient with indifferent films."

The film studios of New Theatres, Ltd., in the section of Calcutta called Tollygunge, are a group of old, dilapidated low buildings spread about a spacious compound, which also has occasional clusters of trees and, lying here and there, heaps of rubbish. I am walking toward the editing department with Ray, who at present is engaged in synchronizing the sound and film tracks of "Nayak." "Bombay studios are bigger and much better equipped," Ray tells me as we go past a forlorn-looking canteen with a counter, a few tables, and a few chairs. "But I find New Theatres adequate for my needs. People coming from abroad have been amazed by the shabby look of New Theatres. But I feel we have the essentials for making good films. I think some of my films have a great deal of polish about them, even though they were shot here. There is something exciting about producing a first-class piece of work in these surroundings."

The editing department turns out to be a few rooms along a narrow veranda. The doors are ajar, and everywhere there is a great stir— people moving around, machines clattering, odd sounds. Before going into one room, Ray takes off his slippers and leaves them outside, explaining that it's a precaution to keep dust from getting on the film. The room is hung with strips of film, and three barefoot technicians are standing there waiting for Ray, who draws up a straight-backed wooden chair and stations himself in front of a table holding tape recorders and other sound apparatus and a Moviola, or film-editing machine. As he listens to sound effects and watches frames, prompting and directing the technicians all the while, he manages to tell me that "Nayak" revolves around a film star and a crisis in his life that is slowly disclosed in the course of a train ride from Calcutta to Delhi. "I wanted to make a film about a contemporary popular hero," Ray says. "I set the story on the Calcutta-Delhi Bi-Weekly Airconditioned Express, which is the latest thing in Indian trains—it's airconditioned, and besides the usual compartments it has chair cars, like the ones in American trains. On trains, you have brief encounters that reveal a lot. Of course, there are people on trains who probably just read Agatha Christie and rest and get to their destination, but then there are the others."

There is no continuous sound track yet. Ray listens to different sounds of a jet plane and discusses putting a jet's roar into the first reel as one of the sounds of Calcutta. Now frames appear in jerks and starts on the Moviola, a rickety old machine. "These are the opening frames," Ray says. "And this is Arindam Mukherji. [Moviola: Closeup of back of man's head. Mirror. Stroke of a comb. Open suitcases with clothes, whiskey bottle.] He is the *nayak*—played by Uttam Kumar, the popular film star. Arindam is thirty-six. This is his house in Calcutta. We see him shaving with an electric razor. He is not in a very good mood. It seems that his latest film may be his first flop. Also, the morning newspapers report that he was involved in a brawl in a night club. There is a hint in the newspapers that the brawl involved a woman, but only a hint. We don't know anything more than that, but we know that any scandal could damage his career, and that he tried to suppress the story. Arindam has suddenly decided to go to Delhi to receive a national prize that he has been awarded. He says, 'I don't give a damn for the prize. I just want to get away from it all for a day.' It's too late to get a reservation on a plane, so he has to take the train. Just now, he's about to leave for the railway station. The woman with whom he has been having an affair telephones him and asks if she can come to see him at the station. He puts her off."

From the sound apparatus comes the telephone voice of a woman saying, "What is the reason? Tell me, please." Ray calls out to a technician, "There should be a pause on the sound track between 'What is the reason?' and 'Tell me, please.' She must have time to realize that he isn't going to answer the question." To extend the pause by three seconds takes nearly an hour. There is more delay, because now the click of a cigarette lighter overlaps a bit of the dialogue. "For 'Devi,' I had Ali Akbar Khan play the *sarod,*" Ray says to me. "Any physicist would probably have had more sense than I had, because whenever the *sarod* sound overlapped with a consonant in the dialogue, strange things happened—sometimes 't's became 'm's. When we were mixing dialogue and music, I had to keep the volume of the *sarod* very low. Ali Akbar Khan thought I ruined his music. He hasn't spoken to me since."

New frames appear on the Moviola, and Ray resumes talking about "Nayak." "Now Arindam is at Howrah Station. [Moviola: Arindam entering train. Conductor forcibly shutting out crowds. Interior of a coupé. Old man, wrapped in a shawl, looking up disapprovingly.] Here, in the train, Arindam is first put in with this old man, who is very puritanical, the cantankerous type of reformer; he makes his hatred for drink and movies and actors known. Finally, Arindam is moved from the coupé, the best available accommodation, to a four-berth compartment. In this compartment are an industrialist, his wife, and their twelve-year-old daughter, who has a fever and is lying in an upper berth. [Moviola: Train hurtling through countryside.] Actually, the interior scenes call for two four-berth compartments, but we built only one. To distinguish the cuts back and forth, we changed things like the luggage and the seat numbers. We also changed the sound track. The train noise of Arindam's compartment is subtly different, because there is a faint rattle of glass mixed with it—like a tumbler vibrating in a rack. In trains, there are all sorts of wonderful sounds. They are almost like music. There is the sound of a platform outside, the sound in a compartment with the door shut and with the door open, the sound in the corridor. [Moviola: Arindam going into the dining car. Passengers at tables. A couple and a serious-looking girl at a corner table, drinking tea.] The girl here is Aditi. She is a journalist who writes for *Adhunika*—'Modern Woman.' She's very serious about the magazine. Arindam is pointed out to her by the couple. The wife is much excited by the glimpse of Arindam, and she suggests that Aditi go interview him for the magazine. Aditi shows no interest, because she doesn't think films are serious art, but she is eventually persuaded to talk to him. Arindam says, 'I take it you don't like films,' and she says, 'Too remote from reality. Heroes shouldn't be so godlike.' "

New frames appear on the Moviola, and Ray continues, "Arindam has returned to his compartment, and now he is having a dream. I had never done a dream before. [Moviola: Hillocks of rupees. Arindam, on a hillock, looking satisfied. Sudden darkening of the sky. Apprehension crossing his face. Skeleton arms rising from the hillocks. Arindam runs. Sinking, caught in a quicksand of rupees. Gaunt figure with outstretched hand. Arindam trying to seize the hand.] Arindam is remembering his former mentor, Shankarda, and Shankarda's warnings against leaving the stage for the commercialism of films. The sinking is to show the constant fear of 'slipping' that haunts popular stars. Arindam wakes up in a sweat. He gets out at one of the train stops and has tea in the station. He sees Aditi at the window of the dining car and holds up his cup. Aditi holds up a fork, to indicate that she's lunching. Arindam gets back on the train and sits down with her. He tells her about his dream, and she surreptitiously starts taking notes. A series of flashbacks shows that he is exposing his entire life to her. [Moviola: Image of death goddess. Excited crowds. Arindam and Shankarda lifting the image on their shoulders. Shankarda collapsing. Image falls. Arindam carrying Shankarda's body to the burning *ghat*.] At the burning *ghat,* Arindam has a crucial conversation with a friend. Arindam asks, 'Do you believe in rebirth?' The friend says, 'This is the age of Marx and Freud. No rebirth, no Providence.' Arindam says, 'I know. One life, one chance.' [Moviola: Rain, wind, cinders from the pyre.] Here is another flashback. . . ."

As it happens, I am out of Calcutta at the time of the première of "Nayak," an exuberant occasion—or so it appears from articles about it, like this one, by one of Calcutta's more influential men of letters:

"Nayak" was a fantastic blast-off. . . . A Roman arena hysteria was in evidence. . . . He [Ray] entered with a flourish. . . . Flash-bulbs popped, smiles were bared. . . . Uttam Kumar . . . entered in the semi-darkness. . . . The mob howled. Mr. Kumar looked the other way. Again the howl, this time interspersed with threatening growls. . . . Mr. Kumar rose, smiled, namaskared [bowed in greeting] with Olympian sereneness from the front row of the upper balcony. The animal below whined pleasurably, and retired with soft swishings of its tail. Mr. Ray and the entire celestial front row observed the tamed beast, sitting "Like gods together, careless of mankind." A fat, blowsy flutter of middle-aged female ran from my row down the aisle, and stood agape, clutching her ten-year-old daughter's hand, before the chief god. Mr. Kumar smiled. . . . She ran . . . back to her seat, eyes and mouth still as wide-open as monsoon manholes.

It was "Nayak" come to life. It was life satirising art satirising life.

On my return to Calcutta, I visit Ray at his flat and ask him how the film is doing.

"The reaction at the première was very good," he says. "But the première was not really a good test, because the attention of even the critics in the audience was all on Uttam Kumar. So I have gone to a number of the regular showings of the film to watch the reactions of typical audiences. In Calcutta, if they don't like a film, they shout, they boo, they walk out. So far, none of this has happened. Of course one worries about a bad reaction from the public, because if the audience doesn't like a particular film, it may not be easy to find a producer to back the next one. After all, the film is made for the public, and I always hope that my films will be liked and will be discussed. I also listen to what friends and acquaintances have to say. So far, I've had about a dozen phone calls."

I ask him about the problem of financing his films.

"In Calcutta, I have a good following, and any film of mine is certain to have a good six-week run. All my films except one have made a profit, so for the producers I am probably one of the safest film investments going. I do, however, take longer than European directors. On the average, I take forty-five shooting days spread out over three months, which is not terribly fast. 'Kanchenjunga' I shot in only twenty-five days."

The telephone rings. Ray answers it, talks for a moment, hangs up, and says, "That was a friend. He telephoned to tell me that an actor I had worked with died last night. In Calcutta, actors are always dying. The actor who played the confectioner in 'Pather Panchali' died halfway through the shooting. We found a substitute and photographed him from the back. The old woman in 'Pather Panchali' was near death when I cast her for the part—she died the other day. She had been on the stage in the twenties but had been inactive ever since. She was so excited over the chance of working again that she wouldn't even discuss the question of payment. I think the film helped keep her alive."

The Poorest of the Poor

"Although throughout India there is a general opting-out of concern about the large problems of the poor by people with any means at all," one of the Ford Foundation planners tells me, "still, all over Calcutta, in a *busti* here and a *busti* there, a ward here and a ward there, volunteers and voluntary groups are doing welfare work. We did a study of a very poor section of the city that has a population of nearly a quarter of a million, and we found there were dispensaries, family-planning clinics, hospitals, coöperatives, primary and secondary schools, reading rooms, sports clubs, all run by private welfare groups. In fact, if it weren't for this volunteer work, the city might have collapsed long ago. But each religious, ethnic, or caste group tends to concentrate exclusively on its own poor. Muslims tend to work among Muslims, Gujaratis among Gujaratis, tanners among tanners. There are, it is true, a few groups that try to cut across the divisions and work throughout the city, yet, because the problem of poverty as a whole is so vast, even they end up having their own special concerns. For instance, the Bharat Savak Samaj works among the beggars, and the Bengal Ladies' Union tries to rehabilitate prostitutes. Perhaps the most dreaded work is done by the Missionaries of Charity, who devote themselves to the lowest of the low. They devote themselves to those who are rejected by the rejected and despised by the despised. They work mostly with the lepers." A Calcutta friend, commenting on this part of the work of the Missionaries of Charity, says, "They attach special importance to their work among the lepers, perhaps because to all the rich of the world, if you really come down to it, all the poor of the world are, in a sense, lepers. The rich may give to the poor, may work among the poor, but they are really afraid to live with the poor."

The Missionaries of Charity is a Catholic congregation that was founded in 1948 by an Albanian-born nun, Mother Teresa. She is still its head, and one morning I go to meet her in the congregation's convent, which is on a narrow, unpaved lane just off Lower Circular Road. It is a small building enclosed by a high wall with an iron gate. Inside the gate is a courtyard. I am shown into a room, overlooking the courtyard, that serves as a parlor. It is furnished with a round wooden table, bearing a Bible and the *Catholic Directory of India,* and a few straight-backed wooden chairs, above which hang several framed photographs of clerical personages inscribed to the Missionaries of Charity.

Mother Teresa comes in. She is tiny and slim, but imposing. Her skin is ivory-colored, as if she had not been touched by the all-scorching Indian sun. Her face is creased with wrinkles, but she does not look elderly. Her eyes are small and gray-brown, her nose is strong, her lips are thin, and, though her smile is quick, her expression is stern and purposeful. She is wearing a plain white cotton sari with blue edging and a high-necked, long-sleeved blouse. On her, the traditional Indian dress seems transformed into a practical uniform-*cum*-nun's habit. The sari has been secured to her hair with ordinary straight pins and folded so that it looks a little like a headdress, and its free end has been fastened at her shoulder with a large safety pin, from which hangs a crucifix. "It's Christ's work we are doing here in Calcutta," she says by way of greeting.

We sit down, and I ask Mother Teresa one or two general questions about herself.

"There isn't much to tell," she says. "I was born in 1910. My father was a shopkeeper, and I had a brother and a sister. I entered a Loreto convent when I was ten, and I came to Calcutta to teach in the convent here in 1929. I have been in Calcutta ever since. I feel completely Indian now. I speak Bengali very well; my Hindi is not so good. But I would prefer it if we didn't talk about me—if you've heard about one of the Missionaries of Charity, you've heard about them all. I'd rather talk about our work, which is God's work."

I ask her how the work got started.

"I found the vocation of charity here in Calcutta within the vocation of religion," she says. "Even when I was teaching in the convent, I encouraged the senior girls in the sodality to go into the *bustis* and work among the poor, but I really began this work after the Second World War, when I saw a woman dying on the street outside Campbell Hospital. I picked her up and took her to the hospital, but she was refused admission, because she was poor. She died on the street. I knew then that I must make a home for the dying—a resting place for people going to Heaven. When God wants you to do something, He has His way of letting you know it." She goes on to tell me that in 1948 the ecclesiastical authorities gave her permission to form a congregation dedicated to relief work among "the poorest of the poor." She began the work in a couple of small rooms in a house in Moti Jheel Busti, establishing a school for orphan children in one room and a Home for the Dying in the other. Soon afterward, she received her first postulant as a Missionary of Charity, and soon after that she found different quarters for the Home for the Dying, and expanded her school for orphans into the second of the original rooms. "So, in time, the congregation and its activities grew," Mother Teresa adds, and she hands me a couple of leaflets about the work of the congregation today. One leaflet, which is about the Home for the Dying, records:

> Mother says, "They have lived like animals, we help them to die like angels." Here is the story of one poor unfortunate woman who was brought in from the sewer. She was a beggar who had, apparently overcome by hunger and fatigue, fallen into an open manhole. She lay there for five days barely alive and covered with maggots. As Mother put her to bed and began gently cleaning her, whole areas of skin came off in her hand. The woman, half-

unconscious, murmured, "Why are you doing this for me?" Mother replied, "For the love of God." This poor waif who probably never in her life had had loving hands tend her—looking at Mother, her soul in her eyes, faith in human nature restored—gave Mother a most beautiful smile and died. That is our reward—that we should make the last moments of the fellow being beautiful.

"In Calcutta, besides the Home for the Dying, we now have a children's home, sixteen schools, twenty-three Sunday schools, eight mobile clinics for lepers, seven mobile clinics for the poor in the *bustis*, a relief center for distributing food rations, and two convents for the sisters," Mother Teresa says. "Altogether, in Calcutta, we have fifty-nine centers for our work, and two hundred and eighty-five sisters, who come from all parts of India and from many other countries, too. We also have sisters doing work in twenty other Indian cities, but most of the sisters work here in Calcutta."

According to the rules of the congregation, Mother Teresa tells me, a candidate wishing to become a professed sister must display health of body and mind, the ability to acquire knowledge, common sense in abundance, and a cheerful disposition. Then, over a three-year period, she will be admitted as, in turn, an aspirant, to learn the nature of the work of charity; a postulant, to learn the rudiments of the religious life and to test her sense of vocation; and a novice, to continue the study of the religious life, to examine the vows of poverty, chastity, and obedience, and, under supervision, to work in the *bustis* among the poor. A member of the congregation must eat the same food as the poor and wear a plain white cotton sari with open sandals and a small crucifix; a dark-blue edging on the sari serves to distinguish a professed sister from a candidate. The prescribed language of the congregation is English, and the favorite ejaculation of the members is "Immaculate Heart of Mary! Cause of our joy! Pray for us!"

A bell now begins to chime in the distance, and files of nuns in white saris move across the courtyard outside. "They are going to the chapel," Mother Teresa says. "They are going to pray for one of our sisters who died this morning of rabies. She was a trained doctor, and six months ago, when she was working in one of our leper camps, a dog bit her. She didn't take the rabies injections, because the dog was just a puppy. It must have been her time to go to God." From the distance there now comes the sound of singing—of thin, high voices raised in the words of the Lord's Prayer. "I am thankful to say she died two days after the onset of the rabies. Five of us looked after her. We will all have to take injections. People who are bitten by rabid animals take about fourteen injections. We had only indirect contact with the rabies, so we will have to take only seven—it's not so bad."

Mother Teresa now prepares to visit some of the centers of the congregation. She invites me to accompany her, and asks for the ambulance, explaining that she often travels in it, so that she can remove to the Home for the Dying anyone she may see dying on the streets or in the *bustis.*

We take our places in the ambulance, beside the driver, and are immediately surrounded by a throng of beggars—sick, emaciated, lame—all with their open palms thrust forward. "Hey, *babu!*" and "Hey, *mataji!*" and "Hey, *babu!*" they cry, in a dissonant jumble of voices.

I pass out the money in my pockets.

Mother Teresa, except for crossing herself, sits impassive. As the ambulance pulls away, the beggars retreat and fall behind.

Mother Teresa tells me that her first stop will be at the Shishu Bhavan ("children's home"), which houses nearly seventy children at present and has cared for over two thousand homeless children— orphaned, abandoned, afflicted, or disabled—since it was opened, in 1955, nursing them, teaching them, finding them foster parents, and arranging marriages for them.

The ambulance stops at a crossing, and a thin, pale man comes up to the window. "Mother, I want to find work," he says.

"I don't know of any jobs," she says. "I have already told you I can't help you."

"Please, Mother . . ."

The ambulance moves away from him.

"He has five children," Mother Teresa says, after a moment. "He has t.b., and he can't do heavy manual work. People who can't do such work are the hardest to find jobs for. We are treating him at our t.b. clinic. We can do nothing more."

At the next crossing, a small boy with a sad, wasted face appears at the open window and extends his hands in appeal to her. She crosses herself, opens the door, picks him up, and takes him into the ambulance. "He needs food," she tells me, "and at the Shishu Bhavan we distribute relief rations."

The Shishu Bhavan, like the convent, has a high wall with an iron gate leading to a courtyard. But here, pressing against the gate, is a crowd of anxious-looking women, some of them old but most of them young, and all of them dressed in faded cotton saris, carrying cotton bags, and holding folded yellow cards.

Pulling the boy by the hand, Mother Teresa goes into the crowd of women, shouting, in Bengali, "Form a line! Form a line! Everyone will get her ration, but you have to form a line first."

The women do not budge, so Mother Teresa, coaxing and prodding them, lines them up herself. They begin moving into the courtyard, past a model of a grotto, and onto a veranda, where several sisters are working around a barrel of grain, a barrel of powdered milk, some large gunnysacks filled with more grain, and a stack of cartons marked "Non-Fat Dry Milk—Donated by the People of the United States of America." As the line of women moves along, one sister scoops up portions of grain with a measure and transfers them to the women's cotton bags, another sister measures portions of powdered milk into polyethylene bags and hands them out, and other sisters replenish the stores of grain and milk in the barrels from the gunnysacks and cartons, and check and punch the ration cards. A girl of about ten stares, unsmiling and without comprehension, at the face of her ration card, on which is printed:

Catholic Relief Services
NCWC
Food for Peace
A Free Gift from the People of America
Distributed by the Missionaries of Charity

Mother Teresa, after she has seen the boy from the ambulance receive his ration, strides into a little room off the veranda, where about twenty babies lie on small pallets and in basketlike wicker cribs. A plain-looking Indian nun, who wears glasses and has the cheerful manner of a primary-school teacher, is occupied in tending the babies. She is Sister Lourdes.

"Oh, Karuna, you are crying," Sister Lourdes says, bending over a baby. "You always cry whenever there are visitors and my back is turned. Oh, your diaper is wet." Sister Lourdes changes Karuna's diaper and then makes the rounds of the room, checking the diapers of the other babies.

Mother Teresa, kneeling on the floor and clapping her hands, calls, "*Shiggri, shiggri, shiggri*" ("*shiggri*" is Bengali for "quickly"), and two little boys about eighteen months old toddle up to her. "Say good morning," she says to them.

They burble.

"Oh, here is a bright fellow with a big grin," she says, picking up a third little boy, who looks about three and is dressed only in shorts. "Naughty, naughty, naughty William. He smiles the whole time, does nothing else." Turning to me, she says, "A few months ago, no one thought William would live, but now he has been adopted by the Belgian Consul. That means he has a monthly stipend of twenty-five rupees, and he'll be able to go to an English-speaking boarding school." She straightens an overturned chair and sits William down on it. "There! Now, William, you look like a sahib in your chair."

Mother Teresa goes over to a crib, lifts the arm of a baby, and admires a gold bangle on the arm, saying, almost to herself, "What a nice present from a visitor!" She moves across to another crib. "Here is a little foundling who was left in the compound of a church in Howrah," she says, chucking him under the chin. She goes from crib to crib. "This is Helen. This is Angeline. This is Josephine. This is Patricia. This is Agnes. This is another Agnes. This is Krishna." She turns to me suddenly and says, "I must talk to the sisters here about the funeral of the sister who died, but we will meet in a few minutes." She leaves, telling Sister Lourdes to take me through the rest of the Shishu Bhavan.

Sister Lourdes calls another sister to take charge of the nursery, and leads me back to the veranda, which is now occupied by children just finishing their lunch. "Besides the nice little nursery room, we have here a nice dormitory room for the young children and a nice big dormitory room for the big girls," Sister Lourdes says. "The big boys we send to a little Boys' Town that the Catholic Church runs in Gangarampur. We use this veranda for meals because we are short of space."

Moving around among the children, she shoos them all into a room crowded with beds for their afternoon rest, but the children all stretch out on the bare floor—some under the beds, some in a small open area at the far end of the room.

"They like the floor because it's cooler," Sister Lourdes says, and she conducts me into the dormitory for older girls. Some of the girls are in their teens, and others seem to be in their late twenties or early thirties. Many of them are obviously pregnant.

A girl in a printed sari, who has a round, expressionless face and paralyzed legs, drags herself across the floor. "This is Philu," Sister Lourdes says. "She has been with us for six years. She lost the use of her legs after a bad case of typhoid."

Back in the ambulance, Mother Teresa tells me that she is now going to the house in Moti Jheel Busti where she first started her work, and where she still has the original school, to take measurements for a new blackboard. "Ordinarily, we don't have special buildings for schools now," she says. "During the good season, we hold our classes under the trees, and during the monsoon we meet wherever we can find shelter."

At Moti Jheel Busti, the ambulance stops at the stagnant pond, and immediately a crowd of children collects and starts following Mother Teresa, calling "Hey, Sister!" or "Hey, Mother!" or "Hey, *mataji!*" A few grownups join the train, shouting "*Jesu pranam!*" (Bengali for "Praise be to Jesus!").

A fair-skinned man intercepts Mother Teresa. "We Anglo-Indians are scattered all over this *busti,*" he says in a stutter, wheezing and coughing. "We would all like to live together, Mother."

"Your old nonsense again," she says, and adds firmly, "Go to the sister at the mobile clinic across the way and ask her for cortisone for your asthma. Go along."

The man shuffles away, muttering to himself.

With children still following us, we go down a narrow street to a small brick building, pass through a wooden gate with a cross on it, walk across a courtyard, and enter a sad-looking old house. The school consists of two dark rooms, which have peeling walls, rows of low wooden benches, two crèches, and a few nursery pictures. As Mother Teresa is taking the measurements for the blackboard, an old man, extremely drunk and wearing only a *dhoti,* appears from somewhere, kneels down, and clutches her legs. "Please forgive me for drinking, Mother," the old man says.

"Stop drinking," Mother Teresa says, without interrupting her work.

"I can't."

"Then I can't forgive you."

Back in the ambulance, Mother Teresa tells me that we are now going to the Home for the Dying, which is near the Kali Temple. "When we wanted to move the Home for the Dying out of Moti Jheel Busti, we made a request to the Calcutta Corporation for new quarters," she says. "They gave us a *dharamshala* [a shelter for travellers] that used to serve as the overnight hostel for pilgrims to the Kali Temple, and we moved there in 1954. The *dharamshala* had two halls, and we made one of them into a dormitory for dying male street cases and the other into a dormitory for dying female street cases. Some street cases are brought to the Home for the Dying when they are nearly dead, and we can't do anything about them—many are dead within a few minutes. Some street cases are too old, too crippled, or too far gone with t.b. ever to leave the Home for the Dying, and we go on nursing them until they die. But some street cases can be helped to recover, with calcium and vitamin injections. In fact, out of eighteen thousand five hundred street cases we've admitted to the Home for the Dying so far, about ten thousand have got well enough to leave."

"Do you follow these up after they leave you?" I ask.

"We try to keep an eye on them if they are not well when they leave," she says. "Because many of them would rather live in the streets and beg than stay in the Home for the Dying, they go as soon as they can get up. But many of them come back to the Home for the Dying to die."

The Home for the Dying is a one-story yellow house off a typical Indian crossroads crowded with shops and pavement stalls. Two Indian sisters come out to greet Mother Teresa. One is short and plump, with a round face, and is dressed in the sari with blue edging. She is Sister Barbara. The other is thin, dark, and small, and is dressed in the plain white sari. She is Sister Lillian. "Our sisters always work in pairs," Mother Teresa says to me. "In emergencies, two heads and four hands are better than one head and two hands."

The entrance to the yellow house is marked by a signboard reading, "Corporation of Calcutta Nirmal Hriday Home of Dying Destitutes," and by an elaborate framed scroll headed "Holy Father's Message to Mother Teresa." Inside is a large, austere hall with an over-powering rancid smell. On each side of a long central aisle is a low platform extending the entire length of the hall. On the platforms and in the aisle are low beds, set so close together that there is very lit-tle space to move among them. They have no bedclothes, and consist of narrow metal frames with mattresses sheathed in polyethylene. Stretched out on the mattresses are men of all ages, and boys as well, some of them disfigured, all of them wrinkled and thin and motion-less, their bodies mere forms, their eyes fixed in expressionless stares.

Sister Barbara, Sister Lillian, and Mother Teresa walk through the hall, stopping at one bed or another to take a pulse or to straighten a head or a limb and place it in a more restful position. Mother Teresa moves around quickly and is methodical. Sister Barbara always has something cheerful to say, and she talks fast. Sister Lillian follows shyly, seldom speaking, but smiling continuously. None of the men in the beds, however, seem to take notice or register recognition, except for one man, who soundlessly sits up as they approach. He seems to be in his thirties, with a strong-looking body, but he has the same expres-sionless eyes. He soon falls back on the mattress.

"The Corporation ambulances bring in people who collapse on the street—street cases so hopeless that hospitals won't take them," Sister Barbara tells me. "At present, we have sixty-eight male street cases and seventy-four female street cases here. They have no known relatives, no shelter, no food. Most are cases of starvation; for the last six years things have been very bad. No one has died so far today, but you can never tell—someone may die at any moment. We try to make them as comfortable as possible. We make the beds very low, so that they can't hurt themselves if they fall out. They are so helpless."

We have reached the end of the hall, where there is a passageway, with more beds in it, holding more men. This leads into another hall, which is crowded with women, most of them almost naked. Their bodies are gaunt and their eyes wild and demented. Some of the women are sitting upright on their beds; others are lying down, crying and moaning. One woman, who is completely naked, begins to scream, and Mother Teresa rushes over and covers her with a towel.

"Once they get this sick, they have no strength even to move, yet they can scream," Mother Teresa says.

Back in the ambulance, as we are driving to one of the congregation's leper camps, at Dhapa, Mother Teresa talks about criticisms that are occasionally made of the work done by the Missionaries of Charity. It is said that their staff is medically untrained, though the major part of their work is with the sick; that their efforts are often restricted to the most extreme and dramatic cases, though they might do more to alleviate suffering if they helped care for people with more hope of living; and, in particular, that their work at the Home for the Dying does little more than prolong misery, for even when the people admitted there are nursed back to health, they are turned out to the streets to face the old problems of starvation and filth. Of these criticisms, Mother Teresa says that although the Missionaries of Charity may not have extensive medical training, their work gives relief to those who would otherwise have no relief; that although their work at the moment may be restricted, they are always trying to widen its scope; and that although their work at the Home for the Dying may be concentrated on medical attention, they do try, whenever they can, to effect rehabilitation of the street cases who get better. "We minister to all those with whom we come in contact," she says. "We turn away no one—we always try to make room for one more person in our homes and camps. For when we feed a hungry person, we feed Christ, and when we clothe a naked baby, we clothe Christ, and when we give a home to the homeless, we are giving shelter to Christ. When we know the poor, we love them, and when we love them, we serve them. There are more people here in Calcutta now who care about the poor and serve them than there were when we started. Our work would be impossible without these people. We say in the morning, 'Today we have no food for relief,' and that day someone will bring us food. It's wonderful how it comes. Just yesterday, a Brahman gentleman died. He loved mangoes, and his daughter brought us crates of beautiful mangoes, and every child in the Shishu Bhavan had a mango. Two weeks ago, a few Hindu ladies got together and cooked rice and curry, which they took to a leper camp and fed to the lepers. We need warm hearts that will love and loving hands that will work."

We reach Dhapa. Large vultures with long, thin legs glide overhead. From the refuse dump, a rough, untarred road goes alongside a slaughterhouse, where emaciated buffaloes are now being herded through a gate. A few yards beyond the slaughterhouse is a dirty river, which seems to have no flow at all. We cross the river over a small bridge, get out of the ambulance, and pick our way among puddles and stones on the slimy, uneven bank.

"The lepers have to live wherever they can," Mother Teresa says. "In the marshes, under the trees—wherever they can find a place. So far, we have not had the means to build a colony for them, but we have a mobile clinic where they can come for medicine and treatment, and at least once a week we call at different places. We began our work for the lepers because, like the dying, they couldn't get help anywhere. Everyone shrank from them."

Leprosy, which is caused by *Mycobacterium leprae,* and which takes cutaneous, tubercular, and neural forms, has such manifestations as depigmentation, lesions, ulceration, nodules, thickening of tissue, mutilation, loss of sensation, loss of sight, and impairment of speech. It disfigures the face and hands especially, and through the ages has therefore been associated with so-called "leonine" faces and "claw" hands. It is not known exactly how the disease is contracted, how it is transmitted, why only human beings seem to be susceptible to it, or whether there is any cure for it—though it can sometimes be arrested through hygiene, isolation, and medication. What is known is that the disease is fostered by malnutrition, filth, and squalor. In recent years, thanks to improved standards of sanitation, leprosy has practically disappeared from the richer countries of the West, but in poorer countries, especially in areas of Africa and Asia, it is chronic for as much as ten per cent of the population. In fact, leprosy is now associated almost exclusively with dark-skinned, poor people living in tropical climates.

I ask Mother Teresa how many lepers there are in the Calcutta area.

"No one knows," she replies. "But some say two or three hundred thousand."

Ahead is the camp. It consists of rows of huts of stone or clay built wall to wall and with low red tile roofs, like the houses in the *bustis*. Between the rows of huts are muddy lanes. Cows, dogs, and chickens are everywhere. The place swarms with flies, and overhead are the vultures. Scores of men, women, and children are out in the open—standing outside doorways, lying on *charpoys* in front of the huts, or squatting on the ground in the shade of a few trees. Most of the people are missing fingers or toes; some have lesions at the mouth and no noses.

"Everything takes shelter here," Mother Teresa says to me. "We get rid of the dogs one day, and more come the next."

"Salaam!" and "*Jesu pranam!*" the people call out to Mother Teresa as she moves around among them. She goes from hut to hut, greeting them by name and asking questions, listening, giving advice about medicine, about diet, about keeping cows tethered. "So the medicine has brought your fever down, Das," she says to a man who has lost all his fingers. "That's good. I see your children are doing well, too. That's good."

She tells me as we walk toward a hut. "One trouble with these camps is that very sick cases are mixed with not-so-sick cases, and so we rented this hut to isolate the very, very sick."

"What about all of you who work here?" I ask. "Isn't it dangerous for you?"

"Up to now, thank God, nothing," she says. "But we have to be ready."

We go into the hut, which is a few feet square. A line, on which wet cloths hang, is strung across the room. On the floor are two *charpoys* and a mattress sheathed in polyethylene, with three badly mutilated men lying on them.

The man on the mattress is sobbing. "No amount of medicine helps!" he cries out, in a heavy, constricted voice.

"The pain will go away," Mother Teresa says, bending over him and feeling his forehead. She helps a sister give him a morphine injection.

When we are outside again, she says to me, "In the early stages, the disease is not so painful, but people at his stage are in terrible pain."

When she has gone around to all the huts and has started back to the ambulance, those who can walk follow her, entreating, pleading, and crying for more medicine and more food. Mother Teresa, as she walks on, keeps talking to them, saying "Yes," and "Tomorrow," and "I will try." She crosses herself continually.

Originally appeared, under the heading "Profiles," as "City of Dreadful Night" in The New Yorker, *March 21, 1970. Reprinted in "Portrait of India," Farrar, Straus & Giroux, New York, and Weidenfeld & Nicolson, London, 1970.*

FIVE

Nonviolence: Brahmacharya and Goat's Milk

Perhaps the most celebrated passage in Mohandas Karamchand Gandhi's autobiography reads:

> The dreadful night came. . . . It was 10:30 or 11 P.M. I was giving the massage [to his father]. My uncle offered to relieve me. I was glad and went straight to the bedroom. My wife, poor thing, was fast asleep. But how could she sleep when I was there? I woke her up. In five or six minutes, however, the servant knocked at the door. I started with alarm. "Get up," he said. . . .
> "What is the matter?" . . .
> "Father is no more." . . .
> I felt deeply ashamed and miserable. I ran to my father's room. I saw that, if animal passion had not blinded me, I should have been spared the torture of separation from my father during his last moments. I should have been massaging him, and he would have died in my arms. . . .
> The shame . . . of my carnal desire even at the critical hour of my father's death . . . is a blot I have never been able to efface or forget. . . . Although my devotion to my parents knew no bounds . . . it was weighed and found unpardonably wanting

because my mind was at the same moment in the grip of lust. . . .
It took me long to get free from the shackles of lust, and I had to
pass through many ordeals before I could overcome it.

This incident occurred in 1885, when Gandhi was sixteen and had
been married for three years. His wife, Kasturbai, was in an advanced
stage of pregnancy, and Gandhi says he felt that this, quite apart from
his father's illness, should have led him to refrain from sexual intercourse. But it was not until some fifteen years later, after the birth of
his fifth child, that he began in earnest to try to restrain his sexual
needs. He did not want any more children, and he had long believed
that abstinence was the only morally defensible method of birth control. He started sleeping apart from his wife and retiring only when he
was utterly exhausted. Yet he was still not able to master his sexual
needs. Because he was growing more and more preoccupied with
what became his lifelong search for God, he resolved to take a vow of
brahmacharya, or celibacy, which among Hindu mystics and ascetics
is considered the ultimate act of self-sacrifice and personal renunciation—the surest way of avoiding all temptation and of finding God.
But five years more passed before he actually found the strength to
take the vow. By that time, he was thirty-six years old and had been
married for twenty-four years. "The elimination of carnal relationship with one's wife seemed then a strange thing," he writes. "But I
launched forth with faith in the sustaining power of God."

According to ancient Hindu scriptures, the conservation of se-
men—or "vital force," as it is called—is essential for physical, mental,
and spiritual strength, and its loss is the cause of all infirmity and
disease. Strict rules are set down to help a brahmachari keep his vow:
the brahmachari must not look at women, must not sit on the same
mat as women, must not take women as pupils, must not allow
himself any physical stimulants like milk, curds, ghi, hot baths, or
massages with oil, and must avoid not just women but also eunuchs
and animals. Gandhi, while accepting the basic teaching about "vital
force," rejected the rules, which in his opinion made the brahmachari
concentrate all his efforts on controlling his erections and seminal discharges, and so neglect the concomitant search for spiritual
strength and for God. He maintained that the brahmachari who had
developed complete self-control need never be afraid of mixing freely

with women and of taking daily baths and massages, and that the best ways to develop such self-control were by regarding every woman as a blood relative, by exercising regularly and doing physical work, by avoiding erotic literature and indecent talk, by filling the mind with good and useful ideas, and by constantly repeating the name of God. "The full and correct meaning of brahmacharya is search for the Brahman," Gandhi writes. In Hindu philosophy, Brahman is the religious principle that involves the realization of Brahma, and Brahma, in its various manifestations—Creator, Preserver, and Destroyer—is the Supreme Being, from which everything comes and to which everything, through the cycle of incarnation and reincarnation, strives to be reunited. "As the Brahman is immanent in everyone, it can be known through contemplation and the inner illumination resulting from it," Gandhi continues. "This illumination is not possible without complete control over the senses. Hence, brahmacharya means control in thought, speech and action of all senses, at all places and at all times. The man or woman who observes such perfect brahmacharya is totally free from disease and, therefore, he or she lives ever in the presence of God, is like God."

Nevertheless, Gandhi says, he found mastering his sexual needs a daily struggle, like "walking on the sword's edge." He eventually came to blame his diet for his daily struggle; like most Hindus, he believed that the palate, the source of an infant's first gratification, was the source of all pleasures. He had always been a vegetarian, and over the years he had renounced stimulants of the palate, like spices, but, as other vegetarians did, he had continued to rely on certain animal products—milk, curds, and ghi—as the staples of his diet. He now came to believe that these were responsible for his animal passion. But, try as he might, he could not give them up. Then, in 1912, he read that some Indian dairymen were in the habit of blowing hot liquid through a pipe into a cow's uterus, a process that somehow enabled them to extract the last drops of milk, and his compassion for the cow at last gave him the strength to take a vow that he would never drink milk again. But doing without milk did not bring him relief from his struggle. He continued to have sexual dreams and an occasional illness. In 1918, when he was in the city of Ahmedabad, he had a severe attack of dysentery. He writes in his autobiography about a visit from a doctor:

He said: "I cannot rebuild your body unless you take milk. If in addition you would take iron and arsenic injections, I would guarantee fully to renovate your constitution."

"You can give me the injections," I replied, "but milk is a different question; I have a vow against it." . . . Kasturbai was standing near my bed listening all the time to this conversation.

"But surely you cannot have any objection to goat's milk then," she interposed.

The doctor too took up the strain. "If you will take goat's milk, it will be enough for me," he said.

I succumbed. . . . For although I had only the milk of the cow and the she-buffalo in mind when I took the vow, by natural implication it covered the milk of all animals. . . . The memory of this action even now rankles in my breast and fills me with remorse, and I am constantly thinking how to give up goat's milk.

Although, in efforts to find a substitute, Gandhi experimented with groundnut oil, soybean oil, and coconut milk, he was not able to give up goat's milk. He continued to feel guilty about his shortcomings as a brahmachari, and blamed them on one occasion for his coming down with appendicitis and at other times for seminal discharges, one of which particularly disturbed him, because at the time he was sixty-six years old and was unwell. Gandhi finally came to believe that if he was ever to grow into a perfect brahmachari—achieve universality and union with God—he must, like some Hindu brahmachari mystics, become physically and spiritually more like a woman, or, rather, embrace in his person both male and female attributes. The nineteenth-century Hindu mystic Ramakrishna was thought to have identified himself so closely with women that he was able to "menstruate" by having periodic discharges of blood through the pores of his skin. Describing the perfect brahmachari, Gandhi writes, "Even his sexual organs will begin to look different. . . . It is said that . . . impotent [men] . . . desire erection but they fail to get it and yet have seminal discharges. . . . But the cultivated impotency of the man whose sexual desire has been burnt up and whose sexual secretions are being converted into vital force . . . is to be desired by everybody." In Gandhi's view, women were altogether nobler than men. Their interest in sex was submissive and self-sacrificing. (Gandhi assumed that women got no pleasure from sex.) Their love was selfless and motherly, stemming from the demands of childbearing and child rearing. They were more virtuous than men, because they had a greater capacity for suffering, for faith, and for renunciation—in fact, for nonviolence. They were therefore better qualified than men to teach "the art of peace to the warring world." They were the incarnation of ahimsa and the natural leaders of satyagraha.

Ahimsa—"love-force," or "nonviolent force"—involving reverence for all life, is a notion with a long religious history and has been interpreted to mean either that men and women should avoid evil by withdrawing from the world or that they should fight evil by doing good deeds in the world. For Gandhi, "ahimsa . . . is not merely a negative state of harmlessness but . . . a positive state of love, of doing good even to the evil-doer." He believed that only love, or nonviolence, would conquer evil wherever it was found—in people or in laws, in society or in government. The notion of satyagraha—"truth-force," or "soul-force"—was Gandhi's own and came to him spontaneously, he says, about a month after he took his vow of brahmacharya. According to Gandhi, a satyagrahi, or votary of satyagraha, is governed by the belief that the soul can be saved from evil in the world, and so helped along in its search for Brahma, by truth and truth alone. The satyagrahi practices ahimsa truthfully at all times and cheerfully accepts whatever suffering may result from his truthfulness. Gandhi felt that a brahmachari, being without worldly desires and attachments, was best equipped to practice ahimsa and satyagraha. For Gandhi, the vow of brahmacharya was not a form of emasculation but the greatest source of inner strength. "In India there is not only no love but hatred due to emasculation," he wrote in 1917. "There is the strongest desire to fight and kill side by side with utter helplessness. This desire must be satisfied by restoring the capacity for fighting. Then comes the choice. . . . Immediately you cease to fear, you are ready for your choice—to strike or to refrain. To refrain is proof of awakening of the soul in man; to strike is proof of body-force. The ability to strike must be present when the power of the soul is demonstrated. This does not mean that we must be bodily superior to the adversary." Yet it is hard to imagine that he didn't see some connection between nonviolence and the absence of masculinity, for why else would he have considered the submissive and self-sacrificing character of women better suited than the "brute" and selfish character of men to the practice of nonviolence?

Although truth and nonviolence were the forces governing all Gandhi's civil-disobedience campaigns against injustice, oppression, and religious strife in South Africa and India, his belief in their power was put to its most severe test in 1946 in Noakhali, a remote, swampy rural district lying in the delta formed by the Ganges and Brahmaputra rivers, in what was then Indian East Bengal and is now Bangladesh. At the time, eighteen per cent of Noakhali's population of two and a half million was Hindu and eighty-two per cent Muslim, but a small number of Hindus owned three-quarters of the land, and most Muslims were little better than serfs. In October of that year, Muslims started torturing and killing Hindus, raping and kidnapping Hindu women, looting and burning Hindu shops and dwellings, smashing temple idols, and forcing Hindus to recite the Koran and to slaughter and eat their own cows. It was one of the most savage outbreaks of the religious rioting that accompanied the partition of India and the creation of Pakistan, and it marked the first time that the religious violence had reached into a rural area. This was especially alarming to Gandhi. He had always taken pride in his knowledge of India's villages—where most Indians lived—and he now thought that if he could get the Noakhali Hindus to go back to their villages and could persuade the Muslims to accept them and love them as brothers he might have a hope of preventing and containing violence, and so prevail on India to stay united in religious toleration. Therefore, with a band of disciples and dedicated volunteers, he set out for Noakhali on a mission of peace and reconciliation, despite his age (he was then seventy-seven), and despite warnings from the Indian authorities and some of his followers that the Noakhali Muslims, always orthodox, had turned fanatic, and that he would almost certainly be assassinated—an event that would engulf the entire subcontinent in the very violence he hoped to quell. "I am prepared for any eventuality," he wrote his cousin Narandas Gandhi from Noakhali. " 'Do or Die' has to be put to the test here. 'Do' here means Hindus and Mussulmans should learn to live together in peace and amity. Otherwise, I should die in the attempt."

Charu Chowdhury, a Bengali Hindu brahmachari, who made most of the arrangements for Gandhi's tour through Noakhali and was at his side during much of it, is, like most of Gandhi's disciples, old now.

More than a quarter century after Gandhi's pilgrimage, he still lives not far from Noakhali—in Dacca, the capital of Bangladesh. He makes his home in the Ramakrishna Mission, which is the principal Hindu cultural and educational institution in the predominantly Muslim country. The mission is situated in a sort of compound off a narrow, crowded lane lined with dingy shops. In the compound are rows of low white barrackslike buildings, each with open doors on two sides; an evil-smelling, stagnant pond; a few banana trees; and a large white temple, inside which a man is just visible in the late-afternoon light, sitting in the Hindu lotus position and lost in meditation in front of an altar.

When I arrive at the mission, it's four o'clock in the afternoon. I am shown into a small room in one of the white buildings. The room has white walls, a gray concrete floor, and a single window with brown wooden shutters over it, and it is crammed with objects. There are two beds, a wooden cupboard with wire-mesh doors, two wooden straight chairs, a green wicker armchair, a table covered with a green cloth, a large, shallow wicker basket, a burlap bag, and a gray water jug. Clothes hang on a line over the two beds, and on shelves behind one of the beds are some dusty bedrolls, old suitcases, old biscuit tins, and bags of food. Piles of books and papers are everywhere. There is no fan, and the air is thick with large, heavy-bodied, vicious mosquitoes.

Two men—who prove to be fully dressed—peep out from under the covers on the beds. One of them greets me warmly, bids me sit down, gets up, and goes out with the water jug. He soon returns, and gives the jug to the other man, who now goes out with it, and the first man draws a chair up to the table and sits down. He has a square face with heavy jowls, a bulbous nose, rather thin lips, discolored teeth, short, thinning dark-gray hair, and small, parched, wrinkled hands. He is dressed in a kurta and lungi (a saronglike garment) of white khadi, has a white khadi scarf around his neck, and is wearing glasses with heavy black frames. He looks to be about seventy. He is Charu Chowdhury—or Charu Babu, as he is more generally known, Babu being an honorific title in Bengali.

"When Bapu was in Noakhali, Muslims used to come and harass him at prayer meetings," Charu Babu says. (Gandhi was affectionately called Bapu, which means "father.") "They would ask him such questions as 'Why are you here in Noakhali when Muslims are dying in Bihar and in Delhi? Why don't you go there with your peace mission?' Then, one day, when Bapu had been in Noakhali for about four months, he actually received a message from the government of Bihar saying, 'You come to Bihar at once and talk peace here.' I went with him as far as Calcutta and put him on a train for Bihar. As I bowed goodbye, he said, 'What are you going to do?' I said, 'You are not taking me to Bihar. What more have I got to do?' He said, 'You go back to Noakhali and carry on my work until I come back.' He never came back—he was shot in Delhi. But I stayed on in Noakhali, through all the changes. First it was Pakistan. Then it was Bangladesh. But I stayed on. That's what Bapu told me to do."

I ask him about Gandhi's tour through Noakhali.

"I had been working for Bapu for many years in his Constructive Programme, for the development of khadi and village industries in Bengal, when Bapu decided to go to Noakhali. Some of my friends and I went there immediately, as an advance party, to make arrangements for him. The monsoon had just ended, and streams and canals were overflowing with water and sludge. In some places the water was knee high, in other places breast high. It was almost impossible to get around. But Bapu came. I remember Bapu walking through village after village. I remember the broken glass, brambles, and filth sometimes deliberately strewn in his path. Yet Bapu always went barefoot. He said it was part of his penance. I remember Bapu wading through water, trudging through bogs, sometimes crossing canals in boats that had to be pushed and punted through weeds. Bapu saw the Hindu refugees—thousands of men, women, and children, all crying uncontrollably. Bapu saw the streams and canals filled with human and animal bodies. Bapu saw the burned and rotting crops. Bapu saw the ashes of huts and shrines. Bapu went from village to village collecting testimony of individual sufferings and assessing the amount of food and money needed for rehabilitation. Bapu tried to strengthen the Hindus spiritually, so that they would be prepared to sacrifice even their lives in order to bring about a change of heart in their Muslim persecutors. Bapu begged the Hindus to return and rebuild their villages. He tried to get the Muslims to rediscover the goodness that was within them. He begged the Muslims to stop persecuting their Hindu brethren. He fasted for the Hindu-Muslim violence. But neither Hindus nor Muslims had any use for him or his nonviolent methods. Then, one damp, chilly morning, after Bapu had been in Noakhali less than two weeks, he gathered all of us around him in our camp in the village of Kazirkhil. Bapu had decided to leave us all and go and live in Srirampur. Srirampur was a small, ravaged village four miles away, from which almost all Hindus had fled. He said, 'All the while I have been looking for the light in Noakhali, I have been groping in the dark. I know now what I must do. It's time for yajna— for yet another kind of penitential sacrifice. Father and daughter, brother and sister, husband and wife must part company and work alone. We must all renounce each other.' We protested, and said we would all be killed if we didn't stay together. But Bapu insisted that only by being more on his own could he find his bearings and test his faith not just in truth and nonviolence but also in God. He counselled us to do the same—to go and live in riot-torn villages, too, and work for our own salvation and that of Noakhali and Mother India. We said a short prayer; we sang a hymn; we wept."

A boy servant comes in with tea, and Charu Babu strokes the boy's chin.

"Of course, Bapu wasn't completely alone in Srirampur," he continues, taking some tea. "He did have three attendants with him. But he wasn't happy there. He seemed to feel that he was not making any progress in his solitary quest, and so he decided to resume his tour of the devastated Noakhali countryside. He was old, restless, weak, and dispirited, and not able to walk much at a stretch, so we arranged for overnight stops in villages a few miles apart, to make it possible for him to go from one village to the next as his morning walk. Since all the paraphernalia he needed—the buckets, the bathtubs, the commode, the syringes, and whatnot—had to come with us, it was no easy task getting from village to village."

Charu Babu is a sociable, irrepressible man, and he holds my hand as he talks. Like other brahmacharis I have met, he seems to feel the need to touch, as if the austere practice of brahmacharya were insupportable without some form of physical communion.

"Does anyone in Noakhali remember Gandhi today?" I ask.

"No," he says. "There are no monuments to Bapu anywhere in this region, except for a Gandhi ashram in the village of Jayag, in Noakhali—and there's little enough of that. The ashram's four custodians—they were Hindus—were butchered by the Pakistanis in 1971, during the struggle for the independence of Bangladesh. I would have been butchered, too, if I hadn't been in prison at the time. I was considered Pakistan's Enemy No. 1 and spent twelve years in a Pakistani jail. But I was treated well, because I was a model prisoner and spent my time reading and tending a garden, just as Bapu would have done. I was very proud of my garden."

The other man returns, puts down the water jug, and silently begins sorting some papers. He is about forty, gaunt, with shoulder-length curly brown hair going gray and a small beard and mustache. He has heavy-lidded eyes and a wary expression, and wears a white khadi lungi, a white khadi kurta, and, around his elbow, a chain hung with tiny metal prayer drums and other charms.

"This is my friend, and he was considered Pakistan's Enemy No. 2," Charu Babu says, as though that were the man's name. "We were in jail together. He owned textile mills and was a millionaire before all his property was confiscated by the Pakistani government."

An old man with a boyish face, short white hair, large eyes, and few teeth now joins us. He carries a large umbrella and is also dressed in white khadi.

"This is Pakistan's Enemy No. 3," Charu Babu says cheerfully. "Bapu lit a little lamp here and we 'enemies' have tried to keep it burning through all the years of Pakistani persecution. Now, thank God, we have Bangladesh. The new state doesn't think of us as 'enemies'—not yet, anyway."

With Charu Babu as my guide, I travel in a jeep to the house of M. A. Abdullah, who was one of the few Muslims in Noakhali to take Gandhi's message of religious toleration to heart and, after the partition of India, to give hope to the "enemies of Pakistan" that Gandhi's pilgrimage would one day bear fruit. At the time of Gandhi's pilgrimage, Abdullah was Superintendent of Police in Noakhali, and was therefore responsible for protecting Gandhi's life. "Mr. Abdullah rose to be Deputy Inspector General of Police of all of East Pakistan," Charu Babu tells me. "He would have been named Inspector General if the Pakistani government had not suspected him of being a Hindu sympathizer. After they retired him, although he was in his fifties, he became a student, qualified as a lawyer, and devoted his energies to the betterment of the poor. He's been a bachelor all his life and as good as a brahmachari. He's really one of us."

We drive for what seems like hours down a narrow main street, which must originally have been designed for horse carts and is now one long traffic jam of buses, lorries, cars, bicycle rickshaws, and wooden wagons loaded with sacks of flour and drawn by ghostly men covered with flour from head to toe. Hundreds of tiny shops are packed together, and merchants, children, cows, mules, and goats jostle for whatever space they can get.

The jeep stops abruptly, and Charu Babu hails an impressive-looking, large-boned, wizened old man wrapped in a long blue shawl who is walking along the street. "This is Munindro Bhattachary," Charu Babu says. "He's a true Gandhian, and he's carrying on the work of Gandhi's pilgrimage all by himself. He walks at least twenty miles a day, all over Dacca, preaching nonviolence and brotherly love."

Munindro Bhattachary launches into what turns out to be a speech that Gandhi gave on satyagraha in 1920. He has a squeaky voice but is something of an orator. He recites the speech in its entirety and then, without another word, stumps off.

Abdullah lives on the ground floor of a large old yellow house off a narrow alley in the noisy, congested center of Dacca. He is lying propped on one elbow on a charpoy without any bedclothes, in the middle of a large, open, but musty room, which smells of sickness. He is sixty-seven but looks older. He is bald, with small eyes, and has an enormous growth on his forehead, and a funguslike skin disease on one foot. He wears a white undershirt and dhoti. In the room are several trunks, a dusty radio, clothes hanging on a line, a bicycle leaning against a wall, and books and yellowing papers all over, on shelves and on the floor. Through the open door, an immense and menacing black beehive can be seen hanging from a branch of a large tree in the courtyard.

"Partition was caused by hatred," Abdullah says. "Hatred was of this world. Gandhiji was of the other world. Common men could not put his ideals into practice. I never thought of myself as a Muslim, a Hindu, a Christian, or a Parsi—only as a policeman."

Abdullah's voice is indistinct and hesitant; he seems to be in pain and talks with his eyes closed. (I learned later that he was dying.)

"There is no position I can lie in comfortably," he says. "The whole of my insides shake and rattle when I breathe."

"What was it like trying to protect Gandhi in Noakhali?" I ask.

"I had a good number of policemen to help me do the job," he says. "And the government of Bengal had also assigned eighteen or twenty armed soldiers to protect him. We all moved along with Gandhiji from village to village, but Gandhiji had no use for us and moved freely in hostile crowds. Any madman could have assassinated him at any time, but we all took it for granted that no one ever would, so in a way we were all responsible ultimately for his assassination."

Abdullah probably shouldn't be talking at all, but during his reminiscing his voice becomes animated. "Noakhali is a long story, and it will take a long time to tell," he says. "Leave me your address, and I'll write to you."

At the time Gandhi decided to leave his followers and go and live in Srirampur, he wrote, "Truth and ahimsa, by which I swear and which have to my knowledge sustained me for sixty years, seem to fail. . . . To test them or, better, to test myself, I am . . . cutting myself away from those who have been with me all these years, and who have made life easy for me. . . . I do not propose to leave East Bengal till I am satisfied that mutual trust has been established between the two communities and the two have resumed the even tenor of their life in their villages. Without this there is neither Pakistan nor Hindustan—only slavery awaits India, torn asunder by mutual strife and engrossed in barbarity." Gandhi had lost his will to live, lost all hope for a united, free, and peaceful India, lost confidence in his ability ever to become a perfect instrument for the practice of satyagraha and ahimsa, and therefore of brahmacharya. He was often heard to mutter, "*Kya karun? Kya karun?* [What shall I do? What shall I do?]"

The most reliable firsthand account of Gandhi's personal crisis in Noakhali is to be found in a book entitled "My Days with Gandhi." It was written by Gandhi's Bengali interpreter, Nirmal Kumar Bose, who accompanied Gandhi even to Srirampur and lived there with him. Bose was unique among Gandhi's attendants in that he was not a longtime disciple but a left-wing intellectual who had taken a leave of absence from a teaching post at the University of Calcutta in order to accompany Gandhi to Noakhali as his interpreter. He was consequently a more detached observer than any of the other attendants. In Noakhali, Bose says, Gandhi was apt to wake up in the middle of the night shivering. He would ask the attendant sleeping next to him— usually a woman—to hold him for five or ten minutes, until the shivering stopped. "He sometimes asked women to share his bed and even the cover which he used," Bose reports, "and then tried to ascertain if even the least trace of sensual feeling had been evoked in himself or his companion." In Gandhi's view, such contacts with women were "experiments in brahmacharya," an essential part of his aspiration to become "God's eunuch," as he put it, but in Bose's view they were a form of exploitation, however unconscious, since the women being used in the experiments were in a sense being treated as inferiors. He says he noticed that each of the women around Gandhi considered herself to have a special relationship with him and was so jealous of her place in his affections, so fearful of losing it, that the slightest sign of rejection from him made her "hysterical." Bose remarks, "Whatever may be the value of the *prayog* [experiment] in Gandhiji's own case, it does leave a mark of injury on the personality of others . . . for whom sharing in Gandhiji's experiment is no spiritual necessity." When Bose confronted Gandhi with what he considered the unhealthy results of the brahmacharya experiments, Gandhi replied that the women had assured him that holding him or sleeping next to him had no ill effect on them. Gandhi maintained that his brahmacharya experiments were a crucial test of his renunciation of sex, a necessary part of his yajna for the violence of Noakhali. He charged Bose with "unwarranted assumptions" concerning his relationship with the women. Bose became so troubled about the issue that he abruptly left Gandhi's service and returned to Calcutta, but the argument continued through correspondence, which Bose reprints in his book. Gandhi wrote to him:

> I do not call that brahmacharya that means not to touch a woman. What I do today is nothing new for me. . . . I am amazed at your assumption that my experiment implied any assumption of woman's inferiority. She would be, if I looked upon her with lust with or without her consent. . . . My wife was "inferior" when she was the instrument of my lust. She ceased to be that when she lay with me naked as my sister. . . . Should there be difference if it is not my wife, as she once was, but some other sister? I do hope

you will acquit me of having any lustful designs upon women or girls who have been naked with me. A or B's hysteria [Bose omits names] had nothing to do with my experiment, I hope. They were before the experiment what they are today, if they [are] not less of it.

Bose was anything but convinced, and wrote back that, according to Freud, "we . . . are often motivated and carried away by unconscious desires in directions other than those to which we consciously subscribe." Gandhi replied that he didn't know anything about Freud or his writings, and that he had heard the name mentioned only once before, and then, too, by a professor. Gandhi said he wanted to know more about Freud, but Bose apparently never pursued the matter with him.

Bose is seventy-two years old at the time of my visit, and although he is convalescing from an operation for cancer, he is eager to see me and talk about Gandhi. The taxi taking me to his house, in the old part of Calcutta, plunges off a major thoroughfare into a gully, or narrow lane, and winds through several more gullies, past once elegant but now dilapidated private houses. We pass a dead horse lying on its side, its mouth fixed in agony, and pull up in front of a beige stucco house with louvred shutters. A hammer and sickle has been stencilled on the wall. There is a gate leading into a lovely inner courtyard filled with large tropical potted plants, and a delicate wrought-iron spiral staircase ascends from the courtyard to Bose's apartment, which has a wrought-iron balcony supported by Corinthian columns.

A young, plump, dark-skinned servant boy with a shaven head and wearing only a green lungi opens the door and shows me into Bose's study, which has French windows; the calls of hawkers rise from the street below. In the study are a table stacked with books in Bengali, a couple of armchairs, and a large writing desk, which has on it the Concise Oxford Dictionary, Fowler's "Modern English Usage," "How to Teach Yourself Assamese," an alarm clock in a cardboard box, a small bronze turtle, a pink plastic letter opener, and a pot of glue, along with polished stones used as paperweights—a Gandhian trademark—and a calendar with Gandhi's picture on it. One wall is covered with well-stocked bookshelves, and another is lined with tall metal cupboards.

Bose comes in, attended by a pretty young woman, and they sit down together at the desk. He has large, weary-looking brown eyes and yellowish pale skin. He is slender and clean-shaven, with short, wispy gray hair, a straight nose, and very fine-boned hands. He is wearing a white khadi dhoti and a short-sleeved white khadi shirt buttoned down the back. The young woman has long, curly black hair and is wearing a white sari with pastel stripes.

"This is my niece," he says, adding wryly, "She looks after her bachelor uncle in the Gandhian tradition of secretary-nurses."

"Were you Gandhi's secretary-nurse as well as his Bengali interpreter?" I ask.

"Yes, of course," he says. "As a student, I had read a lot of Tolstoy and Kropotkin and other political anarchists, and thought of myself as one of them. Then I came upon the writings of Gandhiji. I felt that he was in the same anarchist tradition but that he was also a heroic figure, like Socrates or Jesus, prepared to lay down his life for truth as he saw it. I was very excited, and started compiling an anthology of Gandhiji's economic and political writings. In 1934, a friend introduced me to him, but my interest in him remained academic until 1946, when he asked me to go with him to Noakhali and act as his Bengali interpreter. I went, although I was sure we wouldn't come out alive. In no time at all, I was doing everything for him—nursing him, massaging him, bathing him. Wherever he was, he kept rigidly to his daily routine. He was so much preoccupied with the physical details of his daily life because mastering his physical self was part of his program of mastering his spiritual self. I remember once during the morning walk we came upon a child suffering from fever lying in the sun outside a hut. Gandhiji examined the child and told the parents that he would be back with a syringe to administer a saline enema. I said to Gandhiji, 'You must let me do it. If it gets into the papers that I allowed you to administer an enema to a child when I was with you and could have done it, I would lose face wherever my name is known.' So Gandhiji wrote out for me the whole prescription—how much salt to use, how much water, what the temperature of the water should be, and so on. It is preserved with the rest of my papers, which are now in the archives of the Asiatic Society here. I printed it in 'My Days with Gandhi'—which, by the way, I published at my own expense, because after Gandhiji's death everyone wanted to suppress all further discussion of the brahmacharya experiments." (Bose says in the preface to his book that when he submitted the manuscript to the Navajivan Press, which owns the copyright to all Gandhi's writings, and which functions both as the center of the Gandhi industry and as an arbiter of what is written about Gandhi, its managing trustee wrote back, "I am of opinion that you be better advised to leave out of the book Bapu's experiments in sex or brahmacharya and reconstitute the book to say about Bapu's great work in Noakhali.")

"Have you told all you know about the brahmacharya experiments?" I ask.

"I was never able to find out very much," he says. "None of the girls would talk to me—I'm considered an apostate. Anyway, the wish to be truthful died in our country with Gandhiji. It was never very strong, even among his disciples. Since Gandhiji never had any privacy—and in the camp everyone slept in one room—there could be no question of impropriety. Once, when he had been pestering the girls about how they felt about holding him during his shivering fits, I asked him, 'What's so special about hugging an old man of seventy-seven to comfort him in the night?' He gave me the standard reply that he wanted to be so pure that he would be above arousing impure thoughts in anyone else."

"Why didn't you pursue the subject of Freud with him?" I ask.

"Gandhiji died about a year after I left Noakhali," he says. "And, anyhow, I was far from being an authority on Freud."

"Do you think Gandhi ever succeeded in becoming completely sexless? Did he ever, in your opinion, become a perfect brahmachari?"

"I don't think he succeeded in identifying completely with women—in reaching the bisexual state of, say, a Ramakrishna. If he had, I don't think he would have been so concerned about what the women who lay next to him were feeling. I do think, however, that there was something saintly, almost supernatural, about him."

Bose motions weakly to his niece, and she leaves the room, returns with a key, unlocks one of the metal cupboards, and takes down a book. It is Vincent Sheean's "Lead, Kindly Light." She opens it at a certain page and hands it to him. The passage he reads, which concerns Gandhi's assassination, strikes me as Sheean at his most sentimental, but Bose seems genuinely affected by it. Bose reads:

Inside my own head there occurred a wavelike disturbance which I can only compare to a storm at sea—wind and wave surging tremendously back and forth. . . . I recoiled upon the brick wall and leaned against it, bent almost in two. I felt the consciousness of the Mahatma leave me then. . . . The storm inside my head continued for some little time. . . . Then I was aware of two things at once, a burning and stinging in the fingers of my right hand and a similar burning and stinging in my eyes. In the eyes it was tears, although of some more acid mixture than I had known, and on my fingers I did not know for a while what it was, because I put them in my mouth (like a child) to ease the burning. . . . I looked at my fingers. On the third and fourth fingers of my right hand blisters had appeared. They were facing each other, on the sides of those fingers which touch. The blister on the third finger was rather large and was already filled with water. The blister on the fourth or little finger was smaller. They had not been there before I heard the shots.

In Noakhali, Gandhi publicly disclosed the fact that he had been taking naked girls to bed with him for years but had tried to keep the practice secret in order to avoid public controversy. He said he believed that his secrecy, which amounted to untruthfulness, had been a serious error—an impediment to his becoming a perfect brahmachari. He is even reported to have boasted that if he could just be successful in his brahmacharya experiments, just prove how potent—physically, mentally, and spiritually—he had become through seminal continence, he would be able to vanquish Muhammad Ali Jinnah himself, the father of Pakistan, through nonviolence, and foil Jinnah's plans for partition. Orthodox Hindus had always condemned Gandhi for his unorthodox brahmacharya practices, such as his long daily baths and massages, often administered by girls, and his daily walks with his hands on the shoulders of girls, saying that they set a bad example to other brahmacharis, "offended the accepted notions of decency," and were "a cloak" to hide his "sensuality." Nor had they been convinced by Gandhi's protestations that there was no privacy about his baths and massages, during which, he said, he often read or fell asleep; that he considered himself a parent to the girls who served him and walked with him; that his brahmacharya vow had nothing to do with ortho-dox laws and therefore he was free to frame his own rules as he went along, provided they did not violate his principles. His public revela-tions, in the name of truth and nonviolence, about his brahmacharya experiments shocked not only orthodox Hindus but also some of his closest disciples, who, like Bose, attacked him and parted company with him on account of them.

Gandhi, however, continued his brahmacharya experiments through what were to be the last months of his life, in Noakhali and in the suburbs of Delhi, as he tried to stem the tide of religious violence and turmoil, of retaliation and counter-retaliation spreading through the entire subcontinent. He continued to defend his brahmacharya experiments with such statements as "I have called my present ven-ture a yajna—a sacrifice, a penance. . . . How can there be that self-purification when in my mind I entertain a thing which I dare not put openly into practice?" And "My meaning of brahmacharya is this: 'One . . . who, by constant attendance upon God, has become . . . capable of lying naked with naked women, however beautiful they may be, without being in any manner whatsoever sexually excited.'" And "When the *gopis* [milkmaids] were stripped of their clothes by Krishna, the legend says, they showed no sign of embarrassment or sex-consciousness but stood before the Lord in rapt devotion." And "The whole world may forsake me but I dare not leave what I hold is the truth for me. It may be a delusion and a snare. If so, I must realize it myself."

Whatever the spiritual source of Gandhi's brahmacharya experi-ments, Bose, for one, maintains in his book that their psychological source was "repression of the sexual instinct," prompted by a self-imposed penance for "having proved untrue to his father during the last moments of his life" and for not having nursed his father as a mother would have. Erik Erikson, in his book "Gandhi's Truth," agrees, and, in his discussion of the brahmacharya experiments, goes on to develop the theme of Gandhi's maternalism:

> The whole episode, as Bose brilliantly recognized at the time, points to a persistent importance in Gandhi's life of the theme of motherhood, both in the sense of a need to be a perfect and pure mother, and in the sense of a much less acknowledged need to be held and reassured, especially at the time of his finite loneliness. In

this last crisis the Mahatma appears to have been almost anxiously eager to know what those who had studied the "philosophy" of that doctor in Vienna might say about him, although he probably could do little with the interpretation offered by one of his friends, namely that his shivering was an orgasm-equivalent. . . .

As to the Mahatma's public private life, all we can say is that here was a man who both lived and wondered aloud, and with equal intensity and depth, about a multiformity of inclinations which other men hide and bury in strenuous consistency. At the end, great confusion can be a mark of greatness, too, especially if it results from the inescapable conflicts of existence. Gandhi . . . had wanted to purify his relationship to his father by nursing and mothering him; and he had wanted to be an immaculate mother. But when, at the end, he was defeated in his aspiration to be the founding father of a united India, he may well have needed maternal solace himself.

The women who may have given and received this "maternal solace" have, with one exception, passed into the Gandhi biographies and memoirs as no more than letters of the alphabet, and everyone, including Erikson and Bose, has assumed that the story of the experiments will never be fully told. The exception is Manu Gandhi, a distant cousin, who wrote a little memoir of her own, entitled "Bapu—My Mother," in which she tells how Gandhi tried to be both a father and a mother to her. It seems that in 1940, when she was twelve years old, her mother, who was dying, asked Kasturbai to be a mother to Manu, and Kasturbai took her in. When Kasturbai was on her deathbed, four years later, she asked Gandhi to be a mother to the girl in her place. Gandhi took Kasturbai's last wish very seriously. He came to have a motherly interest in the girl's physical development, and in the minutest details of her life. He told her how to wash her hair, how to wear her clothes, what, how much, and how often to eat. He took charge of her religious education, teaching her the Bhagavad Gita and the pronunciation of the difficult Sanskrit words. She cooked for him and served him his food. She washed his feet and massaged him. She read him the newspapers, and kept a diary in which she recorded the minutest details of *his* life. At first, she slept by his pallet, and doesn't seem to have minded when he woke her up in the middle of the night to talk. When she was about nineteen, she started sleeping in his bed, and that, she implies, happened in Noakhali. But, discreetly, that is all she does say about the brahma-charya experiments in "Bapu—My Mother."

Manu died young, in 1969, but Abha Gandhi—the wife of Gandhi's grandnephew Kanu—who was about the same age as Manu, and who many Gandhians say in private was even closer to Gandhi than Manu was, is still alive. Gandhi liked to call the two girls his "walking sticks"; toward the end of his life he was almost invariably seen walking with his hands resting on their shoulders—as he was when he was assassinated, on the terrace of Birla House, in Delhi. Abha is in Ahmedabad visiting her elder sister, Mrs. Vina Patel, who lives in one of the old houses connected to the Sabarmati Ashram. At the time I stop by the house, some women are sitting sewing on a large wooden swing on the veranda while at their feet two boys are shelling a big pile of peanuts.

One woman gets up and comes forward to greet me. She is short and plump, with black curly hair pulled back in a bun but straying loose, and has a round face with large eyes behind spectacles with black half-rims. She is wearing a white sari with a hand-stitched blue border and a white choli sparsely scattered with mirrorwork, and she has a red bangle on each wrist. She has small feet and hands, and her voice is light and sweet. She is Abha.

Sewing in hand, Abha takes me inside, to a room that has exposed rafters supporting a high tiled roof. A few of the tiles are made of opaque glass and act as small skylights. There is a divan with a muted gold-and-purple cover, the colors set off by bright-green cushions; a table spread with a sheet of plastic; and a built-in cupboard holding a large old radio, dishes, a Staffordshire dog, and other knickknacks. On the walls are pictures of various Hindu gods and goddesses and swamis, and one photograph of Gandhi spinning.

"My husband and I now manage the Kasturbai Ashram, some distance from here," she tells me in colloquial Hindi, going on with her sewing. "We started the ashram in 1956, in the summer residence of the raja of Rajkot, with the help of the Gandhi National Memorial Trust. The summer residence is one of the places where Kasturbai, or Ba, was imprisoned for her part in the satyagraha campaigns. It's one of the few memorials to her."

Abha presents me with an ingenuous leaflet about her ashram:

AT PRESENT ONE CAN SEE
the summer-resort of a Native Ruler
is changed into an
'ASHRAM'
DEDICATED TO THE CAUSE OF
RURAL UPLIFT
AND AMONGST ITS OTHER
MANY-FOLD
ACTIVITIES IT INCLUDES THIS
KASTURBA AROGYADHAM
(HEALTH CLINIC)
which endavours day and night

for

Physical, Intelectual, Educational, Economical, Social & Cultural
uplift of the Villages and especially for the Prevention and Eradi-
cation of diseases from Villages through Medico-Educational
Programme and serves the surrounding 30 Villages since 6 years
through:
• Maternal & Child Health Centre
• T. B. Clinic (With X-Ray plant)
• Indoor 8 bed Hospital
• Mobile Health Unit for villages
• General out-door patient department
• Opthalmic department.

"When Bapu was taken away from us forever, all I could think
about was dying," she says. "After he was shot in front of my eyes, I
couldn't speak for six months, but I went back to Noakhali and threw
myself into his work. One day, a child came up to me and asked me
something, and suddenly I found I could talk again. But it was some
time before I was able to talk easily. No one can give me the love Bapu
gave me. I think of him all the time."

"How did you become Gandhi's constant companion?" I ask.

"Through my father," she says. "He originally became interested in
Bapu's career through the newspapers and took up wearing khadi and
the Gandhi cap. One day, he wore his Gandhi cap to work—he was a
jailer in Calcutta—and his superior upbraided him. He resigned. That

was in 1930. We all went back to our village in Bengal to live. It was very difficult for us to make ends meet. There were eight of us children, and my father took part in Bapu's civil-disobedience campaign against the British salt laws, in 1930, and was arrested—he had to spend some time in jail. All along, my father had been corresponding with Bapu, and when Bapu came to Bengal for a conference in 1940 my father took us all to meet him. My father told Bapu that he wanted to send me to the Sevagram Ashram for my education. Bapu inspected me and agreed. I was twelve at the time. In the ashram, I noticed that Bapu always used two children as his walking sticks. I wanted to be a walking stick, but I used to lag behind, because I was shy. Bapu saw through my shyness right away and called me to his side and started using me as a walking stick. Eventually, I was doing everything for him, but if Manu or any of the other sisters were there, we divided the tasks."

I ask her how the sisters got along together.

"We took pains to keep up good relations," she says. "Also, we were good at doing different things. Manu was good at taking notes for him; I was good at cooking and washing. Bapu never wanted his clothes ironed, but I kept them washed and neatly folded. I loved taking care of him—it gave me a lot of happiness, of the kind that a mother gets from tending her child. Bapu often said, 'You are like a mother to me.' Once, I was bathing him and he asked me to hurry up. He had an appointment. He told me to hurry up three times, and I said, 'You are a renowned mahatma and yet you are so impatient, like any other common mortal. What does it matter if you're a little late?' Bapu laughed. 'I like your spirit,' he said. 'Only a mother would dare talk to her child the way you talk to me. They call me Rashtra Pita; they should call *you* Rashtra Mata.'" Rashtra Pita means "nation's father," and Rashtra Mata means "nation's mother." Gandhi used to refer to Kasturbai as Rashtra Mata. "I was so childish then. When I think of it now, I feel very bad. Bapu and I used to quarrel all the time."

"What did you quarrel about?"

"We often had clashes of will. Bapu left me behind in Noakhali to carry on his work, and I got a very bad case of dysentery. No medicine seemed to help, and Satish Chandra Das Gupta, who was looking after me, wrote to Bapu and said he was sending me to Calcutta for treatment. When I got there, I received a letter from Bapu saying that he felt responsible for my condition, because he had taken me to Noakhali, and that if I wanted to I could go to him in Delhi. I wrote back, 'The question is not what *I* want to do but what *you* want me to do.' He answered, 'All right—you win. *I* want you to come to Delhi. You are a very willful girl.' I went. How sad he was in Delhi! Noakhali had disturbed his peace of mind along with his routine. I said to him, 'I'm with you all day long and you don't so much as smile, and then in the evening Jawaharlal Nehru comes and you laugh with him the whole time.' Bapu said, 'You're such a foolish girl to be jealous of Jawaharlal. Don't you understand that I laugh and joke with him so that we won't cry?' "

I ask her about the brahmacharya experiments.

"It was common knowledge that Sushila Nayar often slept next to Bapu. He first asked me to sleep next to him when I was sixteen. I thought he just got cold at night and wanted me to sleep with him to keep him warm. So I did now and again, with my clothes on. But two years later, in Noakhali, I began sleeping next to him regularly."

"Did you still wear your clothes?"

She hesitates, and finally says, "He did ask me to take my clothes off. But, as far as I remember, I usually kept my petticoat and choli on."

"But what about him?"

"I don't remember whether he had any clothes on or not. I don't like to think about it."

"How did you feel about it?"

"It was nothing."

"Didn't your husband mind your sleeping with Gandhi?"

"He did mind, and he went to Bapu and told him that if he wanted someone to keep him warm, his—Kanu's—body was warmer than mine. He said that he had more vitality, more energy—was healthier all round."

"What did Gandhi say?"

"I think he said he wanted me as much for the brahmacharya experiments as for the warmth. He said our sleeping together was a way of testing that he was as pure in mind as he was in body, as free from lustful thoughts as he was from physical desire. There was a lot of hubbub among the men about the experiments, and Kanu and the other men met with Bapu and said, 'Bapu, you are a renowned ma-hatma. There is no need for you to test yourself in this unseemly manner. Anyway, such a test would be more appropriate for a virile young man.' Bapu heard them out but said nothing and continued with his experiments."

"What did Kanu say?"

"What could he say? I had always spent all my time looking after Bapu, and Kanu took care of himself. He was Bapu's typist and pho-tographer, and he kept himself very busy. God has given Kanu a strong constitution. He's never needed much looking after."

Dr. Sushila Nayar was Gandhi's personal physician. Although she received training in Western medicine and served for five years—between 1962 and 1967—as the country's Minister of State for Health, she is one of Gandhi's most orthodox disciples, espousing such causes as legal prohibition, and abstinence as the only morally acceptable method of birth control. She lives in a rather bleak area on the out-skirts of Delhi. She turns out to be a short, stout, round-faced woman of about sixty. She has graying black hair with reddish tints, and she is dressed in a crumpled white khadi sari with a yellow border and a white khadi choli with a faint green print. Her combined living room and dining room, where we sit and talk, is lined with glass-fronted cupboards in which miscellaneous china, dolls, statues, and books are crammed. In one corner is an old refrigerator, with a very loud motor. There is a woodcut of sandalled feet, probably Gandhi's, on one wall, and numerous photographs of Sushila all around—with Gandhi, with Nehru, with a statue of Buddha.

"I believe, as Bapu did, that if you are a brahmachari and live in harmony with the laws of nature you will not fall sick," she says. "If you do fall sick, you should first use natural, simple remedies—nature cures. A good night's sleep for high blood pressure, fasting for dysen-tery and flatulence. That's what Bapu did. If you get desperately sick, however, and the simple, natural remedies don't work, then it is all right to experiment with modern medicines. Bapu was not above taking a little quinine when he was down with malaria. But I wasn't just Bapu's doctor. I was his masseuse, his travelling companion, his secretary. If I was in Bapu's hut and he was talking to a visitor, I took down the conversation. All the secretaries there did, and afterward

Bapu picked for publication the version he considered most accurate. He once picked my version over Bose's. I was just a student at the time, and Bose fancied himself a distinguished scholar. He never forgave me and sought every opportunity to malign me after that as 'a hysterical, jealous woman who regarded Bapu as her private possession.' "

I ask her if she knows how and when the brahmacharya experiments got started.

"There was nothing special about sleeping next to Bapu. I heard from Bapu's own lips that when he first asked Manu to sleep with him, in Noakhali, they slept under the same covers with their clothes on, and that even on the first night Manu was snoring within minutes of getting into his bed. Sometime later, Bapu said to her, 'We both may be killed by the Muslims at any time. We must both put our purity to the ultimate test, so that we know that we are offering the purest of sacrifices, and we should now both start sleeping naked.' She said, 'Of course,' and I heard from Bapu's own lips that neither he nor she felt any sexual desire whatsoever. Manu wanted to serve Bapu in Noakhali because it was the worst place possible, full of mortal danger. But long before Manu came into the picture I used to sleep with him, just as I would with my mother. He might say, 'My back aches. Put some pressure on it.' So I might put some pressure on it or lie down on his back and he might just go to sleep. In the early days, there was no question of calling this a brahmacharya experiment. It was just part of the nature cure. Later on, when people started asking questions about his physical contact with women—with Manu, with Abha, with me— the idea of brahmacharya experiments was developed. Don't ask me any more about brahmacharya experiments. There's nothing more to say, unless you have a dirty mind, like Bose."

A man comes in. He has a pear-shaped head, heavy jowls, short white hair, and white stubble on his chin, and is wearing a white khadi kurta and dhoti.

"That's Lalaji," Sushila says. "He lives with me, answers my telephone, and helps around the house."

Lalaji cackles in agreement, but he doesn't say anything.

I ask Sushila why she, like many other women who spent their youth around Gandhi, has never married.

"I don't know about the others, but I was once engaged to Dattatreya Balkrishna Kalelkar's son," Sushila tells me. "He wanted to marry right away, but I wanted to wait, and first serve Bapu and the country. Then he said something very nasty. He said, 'All you Gandhiites profess these ideals about service, but you really just can't tear yourselves away from your lord and master. You all bask in his reflected glory. Well, go bask in his reflected hell.' That was the end of our engagement, and I never wanted to marry anyone else."

Lalaji cackles but again doesn't say anything.

"But then, for me Bapu was everything," Sushila goes on, ignoring Lalaji. "He was a god. I have always been drawn to the supernatural." She fingers a gold locket around her neck, and adds, "I recently became a devotee of Satya Sai Baba." Satya Sai Baba, who claims to be God incarnate, is enjoying a great vogue in India these days, especially among the well-to-do. One of his favorite miracles is to produce out of thin air twenty-two-karat-gold lockets with his picture inside, which his devotees wear as talismans.

Just how Kasturbai felt about being a brahmachari wife is not known. She left no record herself, and there is very little written about her, but Gandhi often speaks of their quarrels and periods of estrangement in the early years of their marriage. Gandhi, who was his own best prosecutor, says that in those years he could be quite brutal to her in pursuit of what he believed was virtue. In the later years of their marriage, he says, she conquered what he considered to be her willful, obstinate nature and adapted herself completely to the demands of his life and work. "What developed the self-abnegation in her to the highest level was our brahmacharya," he wrote after her death. "From 1901, Ba had no other interest in staying with me except to help me in my work. . . . As a woman and wife she considered it her duty to lose herself in me ever after."

Gandhi believed that sexual intercourse was a religious duty purely for the purpose of procreation but that service to society was a higher religious duty than procreation. He therefore advocated that his married disciples take a vow of brahmacharya as soon after they had completed their families as they could—which was what he had done—and that those who had never married and wanted to dedicate themselves totally to service to society eliminate sex and marriage altogether. Some of Gandhi's brahmachari disciples, however, met and fell in love in the course of their service and, without abjuring their vows of brahmacharya, started living together in what they called a "spiritual marriage" or "spiritual family," insisting that they were carrying out, in Gandhi's tradition, further experiments in the practice of brahmacharya—further explorations of the purity of sacrifice. From a Western point of view, such connubial arrangements may seem bizarre, but they are not uncommon among Hindus.

.J. B. and Sucheta Kripalani are perhaps the most eminent of Gandhi's disciples who entered into a brahmachari marriage. (Sucheta is also known to have participated in Gandhi's own brahmacharya experiments.) When I meet them, Kripalani is in his late eighties and Sucheta is in her late sixties. They live in a new gray concrete house near Qutab Minar, the old Muslim tower on the outskirts of New Delhi. The house is built in the boxy modern style typical of New Delhi but has cleaner, more elegant lines and is beautifully furnished in the best of Indian contemporary design, accented with carefully selected pieces of folk art—old statues, pottery, wall hangings. It could be the home of a wealthy, sophisticated young couple.

"The house belongs to the missis," Kripalani tells me quickly, as if he were merely a guest. "It was furnished this way against my wishes. I try to keep to as many of my old ashram habits as I can. I don't use a fan, but now I do allow my clothes to be washed and my food to be cooked. In the old days, I did everything myself, but now the missis pampers me." His voice is rather weak, but his manner of speaking is emphatic. Like Gandhi, he wears nothing but a simple white dhoti. His body is withered and emaciated. He has a sunken chest sprinkled with a few white hairs, and elongated breasts. His head is rather delicate, with thin, fine grayish-brown hair worn somewhat long, and he has small eyes with large pouches underneath, and a nice smile. He seems to have all his teeth. He gives an impression of frailty but is actually quite spry.

"I have a brother who is a fairly well-known artist and designer," Sucheta says. She is a plump woman with graying black hair in a short, businesslike cut, and has a round face with large eyes and a small nose. She is wearing glasses with brown frames, and a white khadi sari with a patterned blue border. "He designed all our furniture. We were able to afford good things because Kripalaniji inherited a considerable amount of money from his family and we were able to save quite a lot of the money I earned. I also managed to make some wise investments."

I ask them if they were brahmacharis before their marriage, and, if so, how they came to marry and whether they have continued to be brahmacharis throughout their marriage.

"We've always been brahmacharis," Kripalani says. "When we married, in 1936, I was in my late forties and Sucheta was in her late twenties, so she was not exactly a child bride. In fact, she had already been a professor for six years at the Hindu University at Benares."

"I haven't taught for many years now," Sucheta says. "We were both members of Parliament from 1946 on. We were originally elected on the Congress ticket, but Kripalaniji left the Congress Party in 1951 to form what became the Praja Socialist Party, which I then joined. But we have both long since retired from politics, and I'm just an administrator. I run a clinic and a school for poor girls."

Kripalani puts on thick glasses and starts reading a book, which he holds close to his face.

"We met through Bapu," Sucheta goes on. "I was one of Bapu's volunteers in Bihar after the earthquake there in 1934. So was Kripalaniji, but he had been working for Bapu for fourteen years before that. For me, it was love at first sight. I felt that Kripalaniji's gentle personality and my forceful, idealistic nature would make a good combination. When Bapu heard of it, he said, 'If you marry him, Sucheta, you will break my right arm. You must give him up. His life is dedicated to our struggle, and you wouldn't want him to be diverted from it, would you?' I said, 'Why do you think our marriage would take him away from your work? Our marriage will simply enrich your work. You will have two dedicated workers instead of one.' We had this argument again and again over several months. I was a very stubborn woman, but Bapu was a very persuasive man, and I finally gave up any idea of marrying Kripalaniji. But then Bapu insisted not only that I renounce Kripalaniji but that I marry someone else. That was too much, so Kripalaniji and I got married after all. Bapu gave his consent grudgingly but withheld his blessing."

"I get the impression from what you say that Gandhi mostly pressured you, rather than Kripalani, against the marriage," I say.

"Bapu thought that Kripalaniji was a confirmed bachelor and that I was the one goading him into marriage," she says. "He wanted all his close associates and workers to be brahmacharis, because he felt that married people could not be intensely single-minded about the Constructive Programme and the freedom struggle, about our service to society. We agreed. So even though we got married, from the very beginning we continued to be brahmacharis, as Bapu wanted us to, and lived like companions—like brother and sister."

"If you were both going to be brahmacharis, why did you want to get married at all?" I ask.

"We wanted to live together, and we knew that if we weren't married, this would cause a great scandal," she replies. "We've been relatively happy, but in some brahmachari marriages I know, the wives have really suffered. Some went half mad with frustration. But I kept busy in the freedom struggle."

Suddenly, Kripalani puts aside his book and launches into a tirade against the present-day rulers. "There's no difference between the British and their Indian successors. More than twenty-five years after independence, the poor are worse off than they were before. When Bapu talked about service to the country, better conditions for the poor, he didn't mean TVs, radios, and cars for the middle classes. He was talking about the basic requirements for physical life—two square meals a day, clean clothes, and shelter. What was the use of brahmacharya and the freedom struggle and all our going to jail?"

Raihana Tyabji, a disciple of Gandhi who is herself a famous brahmachari, has also become famous in India as a self-styled psychological consultant and spiritual healer for brahmacharis, among others. On occasion, because she had a haunting, soothing voice, she was the solo hymn singer at Gandhi's prayer meetings. By birth and upbringing she is a Sufi Muslim, and by inclination and choice a Vishnuite Hindu. In the foreword to a small book she wrote called "The Heart of a Gopi," published in 1936, she says that for three feverish days she became a *gopi*, "possessed" by the spirit of Krishna, who is the voluptuary incarnation of Vishnu, and who often appears in the guise of a cowherd playing a flute and dallying with milkmaids. She claims that during those three days she wrote the entire book, in English, in a fit of automatic writing. As the story opens, it appears that the world is at war and that the narrator, one Princess Sharmila, is Raihana herself. For her safety, she has been given in marriage to an actual cowherd, who takes her to his home in Krishna's mythical dominion, on the banks of the sacred river Jumna. There she is swept up into the romantic world of Krishna and his milkmaids. She becomes alienated from her husband as her senses are gradually awakened and excited by visions of Krishna. Krishna plays with her. He lurks behind every bush. He steals her clothes and her milk vessels. He is the air she breathes, the ground she walks on, the river she bathes in, the sari she wears. She writes:

> Near that great tree with flame-colored blossoms I stopped, my feet weighted down so that I could not lift them, my senses swimming. Then said a deep, golden voice, "Sharmila!" . . . It seemed a blue sun arose in the heavens. . . . And before my eager eyes stood a form celestial—so beautiful, so unutterably beautiful. . . . And then, before my eyes that incarnation of divine beauty began to shine with greater and with greater brilliance, until there stood before me a Form made, from head to foot, purely of dazzling blue light, like blue lightning chiselled and molded to the semblance of the human body. Whereat mine eyes closed, and my breath left me, and I sank quivering to my knees, my arms upflung before my aching eyes. "Enough, enough. Oh thou Marvellous One, Oh Thou Uttermost of beauty and of light!" I cried. "Mine eyes are dazzled, my heart broken with Thy blinding, blinding loveliness! Have pity, Lord, or I shall die, here, at Thy Feet, slain by unendurable ecstasy!"

In the end, Sharmila persuades herself—and her alarmed husband and in-laws—that love for a god need not interfere with love for a man. It is not so easy for her to persuade the reader, because she describes her mystical passion mostly in the language of earthly passion, even though she does attempt to make her outpourings seem innocent by portraying her Krishna as a ten-year-old boy.

It is hard to know what Gandhi thought of the book. He makes only one tantalizing reference to it, in a letter to Raihana's father, saying, "Please tell Raihana I began Gopi's diary." He did, however, have a special fondness for Raihana and for her singing. He once wrote, in reply to a letter in which she asked if she could stay with him at Sabarmati Ashram, "I should prize your presence even if you had not that rich melodious voice. What I prize is your goodness, which can act without speaking. It is like the fragrance of a sweet flower. It does not need any movement and yet the fragrance is all pervading and unmistakable, and it survives for a while even after the flower is withdrawn. How much longer must the fragrance of goodness last even after the body is withdrawn?"

Although Raihana has been in seclusion for many months, she has agreed to see me. She is in her seventies when I visit her, and lives in a gray concrete house near Gandhi's Cremation Ground, in New Delhi. The front yard is a tangle of weeds and bushes. On the front door is this sign:

> Ma in retirement
> No Entry
> NO APPOINTMENT

(Holy women are often known as Ma.) I walk around to the back of the house and come upon a youngish man and an old woman, both bent over inspecting a cornstalk. As soon as the old woman sees me, she makes off for the house.

I introduce myself to the man, who says, "I'm Shamsi. I came to Ma with neurotic complaints. She cured me and adopted me as her spiritual son." He has a shock of dark-brown hair, cut short and standing straight up from his head, and large eyes in a round, boyish face, and he is wearing a tan cotton kurta and white pajamas. He takes me into a stiflingly hot room, filled with Muslim and Hindu artifacts and smelling of burning incense and rotting guavas, where the old woman now reclines on a wooden bed. She gives a high, cracked laugh, jumps up, and embraces me. "I am Raihana," she says, and adds, to my surprise, "In my last incarnation, we were lovers—I danced to your violin throughout Europe. But now we meet as mother and son. Come and tell me about your researches on Bapu."

She lies back on the bed and takes snuff. She is small, potbellied, and rather forbidding. Her mouth is sunken and toothless, her nose large, and her chin pointed. Her eyes are dark and bulging, seemingly all pupil, her hair is gray and unkempt, and her skin is startlingly white—the result of the pigment deficiency known as leucoderma, which has affected her whole body. She wears a short blue sari knotted at the shoulder over a shapeless gray khadi dress.

"I could tell you things about my various incarnations that would make your flesh crawl," she says. "My leucoderma was the result of my recklessly indulging my sexual appetite in previous incarnations."

"*La ilaha illal 'lah, Muhammad Rasul Allah* ["Allah is one God, and Muhammad his greatest prophet"]," Shamsi murmurs as he kneels down, stands up, bows, squats, and prostrates himself, striking his forehead on the floor. "*La ilaha illal 'lah, Muhammad Rasul Allah.*"

"My devotional calling in this life is to treat neurotic patients of all kinds—brahmacharis who have neurotic problems and non-brahmacharis who have neurotic problems," Raihana continues. "But too many patients were coming. Their consciousnesses were assaulting my consciousness, and retarding the beating of my heart, and disturbing my stomach. Two years ago, I developed a most ferocious pain in my left leg. It was then that Lord Krishna appeared to me and said, 'Raihana, the pain in your leg is the result of your sitting cross-legged all these years late into the night listening to neurotic patients. The wind in your stomach has been denied its natural channel and has got trapped in your leg. But this is your final pain, the last payment for the sins of your past lives. You can now enter death consciousness.' I immediately went into seclusion, and I've been lying in this room ever since. All I know about life consciousness is that I eat and I sleep. I'm told, my son, that I eat chapattis and mushrooms and lentils and rice and toast and butter and cheese and porridge and sweet halvah and savory patties. But I taste nothing. I'm told, my son, that I sleep by day and am awake by night. That must be so, but I cannot tell."

At the first opportunity, I ask her about her relationship to Gandhi.

"I met Bapu at a grand dinner given by a cousin of mine, in Bombay, just after he arrived from South Africa. I was in my teens. I caught a glimpse of him in the midst of silks and brocades, frills and sparkling jewels. He was dressed in a coarse khadi dhoti and looked like a small-time tailor who'd wandered in by mistake. I lost my heart to him. He became my father, my mother, my girlfriend, my boy-friend, my daughter, my son, my teacher, my guru."

"*La ilaha illal . . .*" Shamsi intones.

"When I was getting ready to go to his ashram, he sent word that he could imagine that I was not used to squatting over a trench latrine without a proper seat, so I should be sure to bring my own pot and commode. When I got off the train at the railway station, the biggest thing I had with me was this commode, and I arrived at the ashram in a tonga with the commode prominently—I might say royally— perched on top of my luggage. It exhibited my latrine problem for everyone to see, and I became known as the lady with the commode. You can imagine how silly I felt—how chastened. Bapu had assigned Bibi Amtus Salaam to clean my pot. One morning, she didn't turn up. I waited and waited, and finally decided to do it myself. For a Tyabji to carry a pot of filth—my son, my son! Bibi Amtus Salaam saw me and came running after me. 'What are you doing? What do you think you're doing? You are a Tyabji.' She grabbed hold of the pot, and we struggled over it for a while. 'Bapu will be very angry,' she said. 'He's told us that we must do it until you become spiritually attuned to the holy task.' I let go. I really didn't like ashram living, but because of Bapu I learned to go anywhere, sleep anyplace, eat anything. Sex was another matter. Bapu wanted a standing army of brahmachari volunteers pledged to ahimsa and satyagraha. He insisted that if a brahmachari developed his consciousness far enough, sexual desire would disappear. Yet Bapu's brahmachari soldiers were mostly virgins or newlyweds, and the more they tried to restrain themselves and repress their sexual impulses and fill their consciousness with the satyagraha movement, the more oversexed and sex-conscious they became. I often told Bapu that there was a great difference between repressing libido and outgrowing it, and that the only way to outgrow it was to give free rein to it—to indulge it and satiate it. But he wouldn't listen. Because of my sexual indulgences in previous incarnations, I was, of course, as sexless as a stone. Bapu knew that, but he still worried about the extent of my brahmacharya experiments with men, even though they are in the ancient yogic tradition. He scolded me once for sleeping naked with one of my patients. The patient had lost his wife, and his sexual desire had reached such a feverish pitch that he lusted after his own daughters. I slept with him naked continually for a week, with wonderful results—he was completely cured. Later on, Bapu himself tried brahmacharya experiments with women, and he, too, had wonderful results."

"La ilaha illal 'lah, Muhammad Rasul Allah."
She closes her eyes and murmurs, "Lord Krishna is speaking to me.
What a dashing figure you were in your previous incarnation! Your
violin virtuosity would have inspired Paganini. But because you recklessly broke the hearts of us passionate, romantic girls, you are now
saddled with your present tawdry incarnation."

Living in the same house as Raihana are two other Gandhians—
Raihana's brahmachari "spiritual sister" Saroj Nanavati, and their
well-known brahmachari "spiritual father," Dattatreya Balkrishna
Kalelkar. Like many of Gandhi's disciples and brahmachari converts,
Kalelkar had had a violent past. As a student at Fergusson College, in
Poona, from 1904 to 1907, he had belonged to several clandestine
revolutionary organizations working to overthrow British rule, and he
had eventually been forced to take refuge from the British police in
the nearby princely state of Baroda, where he became headmaster of a
secondary school. The Maharaja of Baroda closed the school down in
1911 for "seditious activities." The Maharaja was eager to get back into
the good graces of the British authorities, who had viewed him with
suspicion since the Delhi Durbar earlier that year, when he refused to
walk backward, in the manner of other Indian princes, in obeisance to
George V. From Baroda, Kalelkar went to the Himalayas. He abandoned his revolutionary career and began a search for moksha, or
salvation from the bondage of finite existence. When he returned to
the plains, after reportedly walking for three years, he was taken for a
holy man. He proceeded to Santiniketan, the school founded in Bengal by Rabindranath Tagore, in order to further his studies in Hinduism. It was there that Kalelkar met Gandhi. In 1917, he became a
brahmachari and went to live for a time with Gandhi in his ashram,
becoming one of his chief disciples. He has been engaged in the
Constructive Programme for more than fifty years.

I find Kalelkar, who is now in his late eighties, lying on a cot in a
musty closed room adjacent to Raihana's, his head propped up by two
pillows. He has silvery hair hanging almost to his shoulders and
forming a prominent widow's peak on a wide, furrowed forehead. He
also has a long beard, reaching the middle of his exposed chest—for,
except for spectacles, he is wearing just a dhoti. His face is bright, and

there is a rakish air about him. Saroj, a maternal-looking woman with a beatific smile, is slowly massaging his feet.

"I met Kaka-Saheb through Sister Raihana," Saroj tells me, referring to Kalelkar. "Kaka-Saheb used to travel to Baroda on Bapu's work and always visited Sister Raihana's father. Sister Raihana and I both came from very good families and we were very close. Sister Raihana's father was a judge, and my father was in the Indian Civil Service. After Kaka-Saheb had finished talking business, Sister Raihana would catch hold of his hand, take him to her room, and sing *bhajans* [hymns] to him. The *bhajans* were about Krishna making merry with his milkmaids, and came to her spontaneously. I sometimes joined them. My father died in 1922, and I began having a recurring dream in which Kaka-Saheb came to me and said, 'Saroj, I am your father. Be with me always.' I told Sister Raihana about the dream, and she said, 'He is our father. Let us both accept him as our guru and go with him.' Sister Raihana had just lost her father, too. That's how the two of us came to live with Kaka-Saheb in his spiritual family."

Kalelkar has been listening good-humoredly, and now he says, "There's nothing unusual about such arrangements among Bapu's brahmacharis. They're quite common, in fact, though many brahmacharis also go on living with their wives. I was married and had children before I became a brahmachari. One of my sons was once engaged to Sushila Nayar. I continued to sleep with my wife until she died, some years ago. I embraced her, I kissed her, I fondled her, but I had to deny her the ultimate satisfaction of sexual intercourse. 'The greater the temptation, the greater the renunciation,' Bapu always said. I have to admit that I myself often felt torn between my duty to my wife and my duty to my vow of brahmacharya, because part of me believes that sex is an appetite, like eating, that should not be denied."

"It seems that the more a Gandhian tried to get away from sex, the more he was trapped by it," I say.

"I don't agree," he says. "Bapu used to tell a story about a European girl in South Africa—I forget her name. She was young and was living with Bapu as a member of his family. She suffered from headaches, and no medicine seemed to help. When she told this to Bapu, he said to her, 'You must be constipated. I'll give you an enema.' As he was preparing the syringe, she undressed and came up to him and embraced him. Bapu asked her, 'Do you take me to be your father or your paramour?' She blushed with shame and backed away. Bapu was not the slightest bit disturbed in body or mind, and proceeded to give her the enema. Then he made her confess her transgression to friends and family, and saw to it that they respected her for her truthfulness. The few times in his brahmachari life when he did feel sexual excitement, he felt that public confession was the only way to expiate his sense of sin. I myself completely approved of his brahmacharya experiments, although I never agreed with him that sleeping with Manu in Noakhali was the ultimate test of his purity, because Manu was like a granddaughter to him. But then he didn't really need to experiment, to test himself, because his relationships with women were, beginning to end, as pure as mother's milk."

Originally appeared, under the heading "Profiles," as part of "Mahatma Gandhi and His Apostles—The Company They Keep" in The New Yorker, *May 24, 1976. Reprinted in "Mahatma Gandhi and His Apostles," The Viking Press, New York, and André Deutsch, London, 1977.*

SIX

Naturalized Citizen No. 984-5165

One fresh autumn day, I present myself with two witnesses at the New York offices of the United States Immigration and Naturalization Service, at 20 West Broadway, to be examined under oath on a petition for naturalization which I am about to file. A rather stylish-looking young man, who introduces himself as Seth Roberts, an attorney for the Service, ushers the three of us into his room and calls on us to raise our right hands and swear to tell the whole truth and nothing but the truth. We do. Mr. Roberts asks the witnesses to wait in an outer office. "We will now go through your petition—No. 832653—so that you can confirm your written statements under oath," he says to me. "Please be as direct as possible. Remember, you are under oath."

I slip into the compliant role of one who is known only by his serial number, and give more or less the same old answers to more or less the same old questions that the men of the Service have been putting to me since I first came to America, in August of 1949. I keep my thoughts about who I am and why I want to become an American to myself.

"What is your name?" he asks, rather formally.

"Ved Parkash Mehta," I respond.

"Where do you live?"

"1010 Fifth Avenue, in New York City."

"Have you ever used any other names?"

"No."

"When and where were you born?"

"I was born on March 21, 1934, in Lahore, in British India."

"What is your marital status?"

"Single."

"What is your present occupation?"

"Writer."

"Your sex is . . ."

"Male." The ritual has its absurd side.

"When were you lawfully admitted to the United States as a permanent resident?"

"December 3, 1964."

"How long have you resided continuously in the United States?"

I embark on the complicated answer I have given in my petition—that I have lived in America almost twice as long as in the country of my birth, and the reasons—but Mr. Roberts interrupts me, telling me helpfully that all I need to say is "Ditto."

"For the past five years you have been present in the United States for an aggregate period of . . ." he intones.

"Fifty-two months."

"Do you plan to reside permanently in the United States?"

"Yes, I do."

Questions about my parents, my American employers, my other American residences, my foreign travels, my travelling companions, my willingness to fight in the American armed forces follow quickly. Then, abruptly, my examiner slows down and, with a grave air, reads out from my petition, "The law provides that you may not be regarded as qualified for naturalization under certain conditions: if you knowingly committed certain offenses or crimes, even though you may not have been arrested therefor. Have you ever, in or outside the United States, knowingly committed any crime? Just answer 'Yes' or 'No.'"

"No."

"Or been arrested, charged, indicted, convicted, fined, or imprisoned for breaking or violating any law or ordinance, including traffic regulations?"

"No, never."

"You need only answer 'Yes' or 'No.'"

Now he comes to my present and past membership in or affiliation with organizations, associations, funds, foundations, parties, clubs, societies, and similar groups in the United States and in other countries. He examines me closely about each group that I have listed, and at one point solemnly asks, "Is this Century Club, this Century Association, a subversive organization?"

Next come the clinchers.

"Are you now, or have you ever, in the United States or in any other place, been a member of, or in any other way connected or associated with, the Communist Party?"

"No."

"Have you ever knowingly aided or supported the Communist Party, directly or indirectly, through another organization, group, or person?"

"No."

"Do you now or have you ever advocated, taught, believed in, or knowingly supported or furthered the interests of Communism?"

"No."

"Have you borne any hereditary title, or have you been of any order of nobility in any foreign state?"

The question, on various applications and petitions, has always interested me, making me wonder if loyalty to a title, class, or caste could be considered as subversive as loyalty to the Communist Party. In any case, I don't have any titles. I do belong to the Kshatriya, or warrior and ruling, caste of the Hindus. But all he wants is a "Yes" or a "No," so I say "No."

"Have you ever been a patient in an institution or been treated anywhere else for a mental or nervous illness or disorder?"

It occurs to me to wonder if psychoanalysis would be considered such treatment, and I put the question to Mr. Roberts.

"No," he says, and he adds, a little flippantly, "That's just arty."

Now come a few relatively simple questions on the order of "Have you ever claimed in writing, or in any other way, to be a United States citizen?" And then he says, "The law further provides that you may not be regarded as qualified for naturalization if, at any time during the period for which you are required to prove good moral character, you believed in polygamy, or have been a polygamist. Have you?"

"No."

"If you have received income mostly from illegal gambling. Have you?"

"No."

"If you have committed adultery. Have you?"

Such questions seem to be an invasion of privacy, and yet they appear on all the applications and examinations for would-be legal aliens or immigrants or naturalized citizens. I've always wondered what people who have never been here and have no knowledge of the country make of the adultery question, for instance. Do they imagine that there are no adulterers here and Americans don't want to start anything new—or that there are already too many adulterers and they don't want any more? But then, of course, adultery is considered a crime.

"No," I reply.

"If you have profited by the immoral earnings of ladies."

"No."

"If you have knowingly, for gain, encouraged or helped an alien to enter the United States illegally. Have you?"

"No."

"If you have trafficked in or profited by the sale or use of narcotics or marijuana. Have you?"

"No."

"I'm sure you haven't been a drunkard."

I shake my head.

"Do you live alone?"

"Yes."

"Congratulations! You have passed your moral examination."

I stand up, relieved, but sit down again immediately, remembering that I still have to pass an examination in American history and the Constitution.

"What is the highest court in the land? . . . How many states are there in the United States? . . . What happens if the President dies? . . . Do you believe in the Constitution and form of government of the United States? . . . That's all. . . . Sign here. . . . And here." It is strange that this examination is so perfunctory when the moral examination was so lengthy.

Mr. Roberts ushers me out and closets himself with my witnesses— first one, then the other—to check up on me and my answers. Finally, all smiles, he conducts the three of us into the office of the supervisory attorney of the Citizenship Section, a kindly elderly man, who has a hefty file open in front of him. Mr. Roberts hands him my signed and attested papers, and the supervisory attorney adds them to the file, shuffling papers of many colors and sizes. "You have a big file," he remarks.

In an adjacent room, a woman with a Spanish accent is being put through her catechism. She seems to be on the verge of hysteria.

"Will you fight for this country?"

"I never fighting. You ask my neighbors. Never fighting."

"The question is," the attorney patiently says, "if someone attacked this country, would you take up arms to protect the country?"

"I no understand."

"You know what a bad man is?"

"Yes."

"Would you stop a bad man doing bad things to America?"

"Yes," the woman says in delight.

"You've passed," says the attorney in the adjacent room.

I have a sudden sense of déjà vu as many similar scenes from my own past rush through my mind.

The supervisory attorney is shaking my hand and saying, "Good luck in court. The judge puts on quite a show when he swears in new citizens."

I first started dreaming of leaving India and coming to the United States when I was five years old and my father sent me to an American missionary boarding school in Bombay, eight hundred and fifty miles away from our home, in Lahore. My father had studied in the West and was a doctor and a government servant. He was so fair-skinned and spoke English so fluently that our servants said he could easily pass for an Englishman. He sported a bowler hat, carried a walking stick, was an avid tennis and bridge player, and was one of the first Indians to be accepted into British clubs. I wanted to grow up to be like him. Soon after I arrived at the boarding school, my father entered into correspondence with one of the missionaries there, Mrs. G. Ross Thomas. He had learned that she would soon be returning to America, and he commissioned her to take me with her and enroll me in a good New England school. It was Mrs. Thomas who gave me my first few lessons in English, and I was soon able to write letters home in English. They were all more or less the same: "My dear Mummy and Daddy, how are you? I'm quite well and happy. Thank you. Your loving son, Vedi." Actually, I was often sick and miserable, but I didn't know how to say that in English.

Mrs. Thomas used to tell me stories about America. I got the impression that no one in America ever told a lie, or stole, or cheated, or needed to be washed. The passengers who rode American trams were so honest that they didn't even use tickets—they just dropped the fare in a piggy bank for the driver to collect when he was ready. There were no newspaper sellers there—just a big newspaper stand with a big hat in front, and people were trusted to pick up the newspaper they wanted and pay for it by dropping change in the hat. At street corners, there were electronic policemen who stopped the traffic and waved it on. They had no whistles or guns—just lights—but the drivers always obeyed. I remember I once asked Mrs. Thomas who did the dirty jobs in America, and she said there was no dirt there. That night, I dreamed that I was turned away at the gates of America because I wasn't clean enough. The Americans had found out that I liked to play in the mud. After I woke up, I began dreading that they would also find out about the tin of sweets: when the school matron was out making her rounds, I would steal into her room, climb onto her dressing table, take a big tin down from a shelf, pry open the top with her comb, and help myself to a fistful of lemon drops and sticky orange sweets. One day, after I had been at the school for a couple of years, Mrs. Thomas did not appear. The matron told me that Mrs. Thomas had left because a war had broken out in America (it was just after Pearl Harbor), and that for the time being America was not open to foreigners like me.

It was not until some seven years later, when I was fourteen or fifteen, that I finally began making serious preparations to go to America as a student. I first had to see an Indian doctor in New Delhi, to get a medical examination for a 4-E, or student, visa. He gave me a complete going over, which took several visits. He inspected my scalp, my gums, my nails, and my feet, checked me for amoebic dysentery, gave me a Wassermann test, took a chest X-ray, and immunized me against smallpox, typhoid, and cholera. He then handed me the record of all this in a folder and sent me over to the American Embassy to get my visa. As I sat waiting to see the consul in charge, I had visions of America as the one clean, rich, healthful haven in a poverty-stricken, disease-ridden world. I couldn't get over the idea that all the people in the country—even servants—would speak English, wear shoes, live in their own houses, and ride around in their own motorcars. My English had not made much progress since Mrs. Thomas left, and, according to a test I had taken some time earlier at the American Embassy, I had a vocabulary of only a few hundred words. But I found myself looking forward to the day when I would take out my first "date," talk to her in fluent English, take her to a drive-in movie theatre showing "Forever Amber," and spend the time kissing. My reverie was abruptly interrupted: I was being summoned into the consul's office. The consul started off by lecturing me. He said that I was very lucky to have been certified by a trustworthy Indian doctor as a fit applicant for America. He said that Indian doctors as a breed were known to be susceptible to string-pulling, blandishments, and bribery, and that there were plenty of opportunities for succumbing to such inducements. There were more "go-getting" Indians all the time, and they would stop at nothing to get themselves across to what the consul called "God's country." In fact, he said, if America were to throw open its doors to all comers, hundreds of millions of Indians would migrate there and settle over the land like a plague of frogs. The consul issued me a 4-E, and informed me that it was valid only for a period of twelve months, that if I intended to stay longer I would have to apply for a year's extension, and that if I happened to leave the United States at any time before my 4-E expired I would be forced to reapply for it and to take all the medical tests over again. I was so excited I wanted to touch his feet, but instead I thanked him stiffly, as I imagined that my father and his English friends would have done.

I felt no qualms about saying goodbye to India and having to make do in America from one extension of my visa to the next, for I was already accustomed to migration: a couple of years earlier, I had lost my bicycle, my Meccano sets, my books, my carpentry tools, along with my childhood, in Lahore, when it became part of the new nation of Pakistan, and my family and I, leaving our house and abandoning all our belongings and savings, had to flee for our lives. We were now living in newly independent India as members of a floating population of eight million Hindu and Sikh refugees. I felt that I would be no more a stranger in America than I was in independent India.

I spent my first three years in America as a student in a small boarding school in Little Rock, Arkansas—the only school in America that would take me, with my meagre knowledge of English. (At the start, I was still apt to confuse "chicken" with "kitchen," and say, "Please get me kitchen from the chicken.") The school, it turned out, had never had a student from another state, let alone another country. In fact, much to my surprise, it was an all-white school, and my fellow-students didn't know what to make of me; they seemed to think I was as exotic as a Kalahari Bushman. The girls I tried to persuade to be my dates politely turned me down. They viewed me with curiosity but no romantic interest. I myself felt anything but exotic—even though, every year, to get my 4-E extended, I had to reduce my American experiences to cold forms and send them off to Washington. I also had to go down to the local post office every January and reduce my life to a United States Department of Justice Alien Address Report Card, which, in compliance with a certain law—Section 265, 8 U.S.C. 1305—I would mail to the United States Immigration and Naturalization Service, Alien Address Report Processing Center, in Rockville, Maryland. My father had once told me that foreigners were liable to be stopped and required to show their passports, so I made sure that I had mine in my pocket whenever I left the school grounds. For a time, I even developed a nervous habit of tapping my pocket any time I heard footsteps behind me, expecting a policeman to call out "Halt!"

I took refuge from omnipresent authorities and policemen—and also from the elusive dates and curious students, who were as alien to me as I was to them—in the enveloping walls of the school library, where I set about struggling with Chaucer, Shakespeare, Milton, Johnson, Pope, Byron, and Joyce. I was obliged to compress into my three Arkansas high-school years twelve years of American schooling, feeling all the while like a tadpole washed ashore who had to learn quickly to become a frog—or perhaps even a prince, without ever being kissed by the storybook princess.

With my Arkansas diploma in my suitcase, I headed west to college in southern California, the promised land within the promised land— only to discover, to my dismay, that although I now had at my command a sizable English vocabulary, few people there could understand my Arkansas drawl. To clear up my pronunciation, I launched a self-improvement campaign, American style, and soon became a gung-ho Californian.

During my four years as an undergraduate in California, I made many friends. I remember that one of them used to try to tempt me to sneak across the Mexican border to Tijuana to take in a game of jai alai, but I never went, because I still feared the footsteps of the law— although I had long since come to realize that they weren't always following me. I knew that I could travel anywhere within the country, however, and began planning to go to New England to find out what a Connecticut Yankee might be like. But, as it happened, from California I proceeded to England, to continue my studies. When I arrived at London's Heathrow Airport, I was exhilarated to discover that, as a subject of the British Commonwealth, I was allowed to whiz through Customs and Immigration while "foreigners" impatiently waited in line.

In my ten years in the West—I had spent seven years in America, and I spent three more in England without being able to go home—I became more and more Indian even as I became more and more Western. I would lecture girls—I had no special difficulty getting dates now—on the fecklessness and folly of romantic love, and the wisdom and constancy of arranged marriages. India became a little island in my head, where I could go and speak Punjabi and act like a Punjabi. I would put old 78-r.p.m. records of Indian film music on the gramophone and daydream about an arranged marriage to a beautiful Punjabi girl in a rustling silk sari, the two of us sitting and eating pomegranate seeds in a hill station with fog closing in.

After England, I did return to India, in the summer of 1959, only to have my fantasies about my homeland rudely dispelled. Everywhere I went, I was assaulted by putrid odors rising from the streets, by flies relentlessly swarming around my face, by the octopuslike hands of a hundred scabrous, deformed beggars clutching at my hands and feet; I could not escape the choking dust, the still, oppressive air, and the incinerating heat of a summer in India. I found myself thinking of the cool, gracious comfort of a Southern mansion in Nashville—airconditioned from wine cellar to maids' quarters—where I had once been the guest of a college friend whose father made his money by importing Indian jute. I found myself longing for the ice-cold pitchers of freshly made mint julep waiting at poolside for the swimmers. My time in the Western world had spoiled me, and I could now hardly wait to get back. Fortunately, I had arranged to take up graduate studies in New England in the autumn, so I lost no time in getting to the American Embassy in New Delhi to pick up a visa. I submitted to another round of medical and bureaucratic scrutiny, and, at the end of it, again received a single-entry, twelve-month 4-E. It contained no record of my ever having been in America before.

Back in America, I completed my studies, and thereby outgrew my 4-E. I began earning my keep by writing, and was informed by the immigration authorities that I must apply for a change of status and obtain a new kind of visa if I wanted to stay on in the country. They suggested an H-1, which was granted to actors, opera singers, and other artists of "distinguished merit and ability" who wanted to live and work in America for a time. I applied for and eventually got my H-1, and became part of a community of legal aliens and expatriates in New York who had come from many lands and spoke many languages. They were all experts on the advantages and disadvantages of the different kinds of visas. None of them held the H-1 in very high esteem, because every time an H-1 left the country he had to satisfy American officials abroad that he was still an artist of "distinguished merit and ability" before he was allowed back in. Most of them aspired to the "green card"—the popular name for the alien-registration-receipt card, which shows its holder to be a "permanent resident," eligible to apply for naturalization after five years of residence.

After I had been an H-1 for several years, I got tired of proving to the far-flung, intercontinental network of American immigration officials that I was an artist of "distinguished merit and ability," and decided to plump for a green card. As a "permanent resident," I would be able to leave and reënter the country as I pleased and still continue to be an Indian national. I could live and work here as long as I chose without ever committing myself to becoming an American citizen. (Charlie Chaplin had done it for forty years.) But I could not vote, I could not run for political office, and I could not work for the federal government, although I could be drafted into the armed forces and was obliged, if I was called upon, to fight for the United States. Moreover, if I happened to stay away for more than a year I would risk losing my new status altogether. I decided to take the limitations along with the privileges, and put in for a green card. I was required to submit numerous documents, including yet another medical report, to swear that I had never been a Communist, never committed adultery, never trafficked in drugs or women, and so on—to answer, in fact, the same questions that the immigration authorities had been asking me on and off for years—and to produce not, this time, proof of "distinguished merit and ability" but "Evidence of Exceptional Ability in the Sciences or the Arts." I was obliged to retain counsel to help me find my way through the labyrinthine procedures; to remain in the country for a year while my petition was being reviewed; and, ultimately, to appear, with my counsel, as a petitioner at a hearing in the New York offices of the Immigration and Naturalization Service. My petition was granted, and I received my green card shortly thereafter. It was a bit like a credit card—a laminated affair bearing my photograph, my alien-registration number (A7 828 521), and a list of the conditions governing the card's use. For the next ten years, I possessed dual status as an Indian national and a permanent resident of the United States. Then, one day in September of 1974, I decided to give up my nationality and become a naturalized American.

As a first step, I was required to file another petition with the Immigration and Naturalization Service. The application form was a forbidding document. It read, in part:

1. You must send with this application the following items (1), (2), (3), and (4):
   (1) Photographs of your Face. . . .
   (2) Fingerprint Chart—A record of your fingerprints, taken on the fingerprint chart furnished you with this application. . . .
   (3) Biographic Information—Complete every item in the Biographic Information form furnished you with this application and sign your name on the line provided. . . .
   (4) U.S. Military Service—If your application is based on your military service, obtain and complete Form N-126. . . .

2. Fee. . . .
3. Alien Registration Receipt Card. . . .
4. Date of Arrival. . . .
5. Examination on Government and Literacy—Every person applying for naturalization must show that he or she has a knowledge and understanding of the history, principles, and form of government of the United States. THERE IS NO EXEMP- TION FROM THIS REQUIREMENT, and you will therefore be examined on these subjects when you appear before the examiner with your witnesses. The application details the various public school classes, correspondence courses, and prescribed text- books available for the purpose. You will also be examined on your ability to read, write, and speak simple English. . . .

My oral examination by Mr. Roberts was one of the requirements for filing this petition. I came away from that examination feeling agitated and ambivalent. By then, I had no particular reservations about renouncing my Indian nationality. My last visit home, in the summer of 1974, had left me profoundly depressed. I felt out of sympathy with the government—the main industry in the country. Its policies bore no relation to the humane ideals of independent India's founding father, Mahatma Gandhi, and were directed more and more toward serving the interests of the middle-class politicians, who had little use for the poor and even less use for civil liberties. Yet I knew I could not become a nationalist reformer, so committed to the land of my birth that I would stay and fight the system from within. I was a writer, not a politician, and, because I had by now spent the better part of my life outside India, I could not think of myself as altogether Indian. I was a member of a worldwide community of expatriates, whose thoughts, feelings, and dreams were a jumble of languages and countries. Now that the moment for becoming an American was at hand, however, I found myself wondering, as I often had before, whether I should not perhaps become an Englishman instead. After all, I had grown up under the British raj and, in a sense, like an English child: playing in my father's clubs, going to a hill station every summer, studying in an English university. But then I had also grown up at the time of India's struggle for independence: going to polit- ical rallies, hearing about the heroic deeds of Gandhi and Nehru, spurning many British ways as I grew older—even while I embraced others—and all the time trying to overcome the apish habits of the colonial mind. Could I ever really feel comfortable calling myself an Englishman? Even if I somehow managed to swim against the historical tide, would I not, as a "brown gentleman," always feel inferior to "real" Englishmen? As before, I knew the answers to these questions. I also knew that it was the momentousness of the step that made me dwell on them once more.

On the other hand, it had not been a simple matter to decide to become an American. Few of those who are born and die citizens of the same country, I reflected, ever consciously commit themselves to their own citizenship, but we who change citizenship by choice must commit ourselves voluntarily to the history and the heritage, the pride and the guilt of our adopted homeland. So, just as America, through its Immigration Service, had once again examined my personal history, I once again began conducting a private investigation of America. For instance, there was the matter of the Vietnam War. I had been against it even at the beginning, and had wondered then whether I should become an American while it was still continuing, especially since I had been born an Asian. What if America thought one day that India was going Communist? Would Americans go to fight there also? Then, there was the bomb. No Asian can forget that it was dropped only on an Asian country. And there was the issue of Richard Nixon and Watergate. Was America headed toward totalitarianism? I had reached my decision to file my citizenship papers only after President Nixon resigned. Fighting, though, was still going on in Vietnam. Later, I had taken note of the problem of the Vietnam refugees, whom some Americans were trying to send back to their homeland. I was an Asian about to become an American citizen at a time when many of my countrymen-to-be wanted to expel a group of Asians. But I found reassurance on this point in the remarks of another countryman-to-be—George Meany, the president of the A.F.L.–C.I.O. "Frankly, I think the attitude of people who say, 'Dump these refugees in the sea; send them back'—to me it's really deplorable," he said to the press. "We are a nation of immigrants. And to turn our backs on people who are fleeing from oppression, fleeing for their lives, and say to them that we are going to dump them in the sea—this to me is about as contrary to American tradition as anything that I ever heard of. . . . We [would be] denying the history, the background, the traditions of this country as a haven for the oppressed."

Since the American Revolution, the United States had indeed admitted, altogether, almost fifty million immigrants and refugees, yet the history of immigration was not as uniformly noble and honorable as Meany made out. The inscription on the Statue of Liberty reads, "Send these, the homeless, tempest-tossed to me. I lift my lamp beside the golden door." Until 1921, when a quota system was established, the golden door was open to just about all comers, with the exception of Asians, who were subjected to special restrictions. More than a million and a half poor refugees from the Irish potato famines of the eighteen-forties were among those who readily found a home here. Then, in 1924—the year the Statue of Liberty was designated a national monument—Congress passed a permanent-quota law. It was the first piece of major immigration legislation and, as amended in 1929, rigidly regulated the flow of immigrants to this country for thirty-six years. It fixed the total number of immigrants at a hundred and fifty thousand a year, and apportioned to each country a quota of two per cent of the number of that country's ex-nationals living in the United States at the time of the 1920 census. Immigrants from the countries of northwestern Europe were, in effect, granted an allotment of more than seventy per cent of this so-called national-origins quota, while those from the countries of Southern and Eastern Europe, who had been streaming across the Atlantic since the beginning of the century in ever-increasing numbers and were by then thought to threaten the predominantly Anglo-Saxon complexion of the country, were allotted proportionately low quotas. Historians usually give at least two reasons for the passage of the 1924 act: fear of political radicals, and the influence of contemporary theories of eugenics. At the time, there was much left-wing agitation in the trade unions, and part of the blame for this was placed on Poles, Italians, and Jews; Poles, Italians, and Jews also became targets of eugenicists, who called them "undesirables" and "biological degenerates," and whose ideas loomed prominently in the congressional hearings and debates on the bill. The eugenicists tried to show through laborious research that the human race was divided into superior and inferior types, and that America had been built up by the superior types, who originated in

Northern Europe, and was now being inundated by the inferior types, who originated in Southern and Eastern Europe. The eugenicists claimed that the inferior types were genetically incapable of performing "decently" in a free, democratic society, and that they or their children would end up by destroying it. One eugenicist—Dr. Harry H. Laughlin, of the Eugenics Record Office of the Carnegie Institution, of Washington—made several studies for the House of Representatives Committee on Immigration and Naturalization as its "expert eugenics agent." He testified before the committee on "the relative degeneracies of the several types in each of the nativity groups in the population of the United States," and produced an array of charts and statistics to prove that the more recent immigrants to the United States tended to have a greater incidence of insanity, feeble-mindedness, crime, delinquency, leprosy, epilepsy, tuberculosis, blindness, deafness, deformity, and dependency than their predecessors. At one point, he said:

> America is a melting pot. . . . If we succeed for many centuries as a great nation, historians should be able to look back and always find us exercising great vigor and vigilance in sorting out the immigrant material which applied for admission to the United States. We should be found admitting only sound metals, and those in such proportions as would alloy well with the earlier American elements already in the crucible, and should take great care to reject and eliminate all dross. The American bell should vibrate without discord.

Some of the more fanatical eugenicists actually suggested that the "undesirables" already in the country could be humanely got rid of with carbonic-acid gas. The amended 1924 act continued to govern United States immigration policy until 1965, when the national-origins quota system was finally abolished in favor of a two-part system—one part, for the Western Hemisphere, based on the principle of first-come-first-served, and the other, for the Eastern Hemisphere, on a principle of giving preference to the skilled and the talented. This system, however, continued to regulate the number of immigrants, allotting a hundred and twenty thousand a year to the Western Hemisphere and a hundred and seventy thousand (with a maximum of twenty thousand from a single country) to the Eastern

Hemisphere. (Since 1965, the total number of immigrants has actually been about four hundred thousand a year, because parents, spouses, and children of American citizens are permitted to immigrate freely.) All the immigrants who had been admitted since 1924, however, constituted a very much smaller proportion of the population, which numbered well over two hundred million, than immigrants did in 1900, when the population was only seventy-six million. But these more recent immigrants, because they tended to congregate in the big cities, seemed much more numerous than they actually were.

It would have been easier, I concluded, to have been born an American in the first place, but since I hadn't, I reasoned, it was easier to make a commitment to America than to most other countries I could think of. Coming from India, I could never become casual about America's open society, with its political freedoms and its economic opportunities. I felt that America, as a "young" country, was less weighed down by history, tradition, class, and caste, which block change in India and in so many other countries. Since America was also an affluent country, the distinctions of class and privilege that did exist here had less importance than they had elsewhere. And, since America was a big country, it could more easily assimilate immigrants. I happened to share some of these feelings and thoughts with an American friend who moves in psychoanalytic circles. "Rationalizations," he said. "Of course, you may consciously think that you are becoming an American citizen because Nixon resigned or because of what Meany said or because of your expectations of America, but, unconsciously, you are trying to reject part of your childhood."

Two weeks after my naturalization hearing with Mr. Roberts, I receive a letter from the Department of Justice—of which the Immigration and Naturalization Service is a part—summoning me to court, but I am to appear only if in the interval between my naturalization examination and my designated day in court I have not been absent from America; have not been married, divorced, separated, or widowed; have not joined the Communist Party; have not claimed exemption from military service or changed my willingness to bear arms for America; and have not committed crimes of any sort or acted immorally in any of a number of possible ways. Although I had a moment of alarm a few days back, when I received another communication from the Department of Justice, requiring me to be finger-printed immediately, because "fingerprints previously submitted are unsatisfactory," I decide that the latest letter is a good omen, since I know I have kept clean.

And so I duly appear at the imposing United States Courthouse in Foley Square. It is 8 A.M., and with me are two old friends who are part of my "family" here now—a young woman whose ancestors probably came over on the Mayflower, and a young playwright with an ability to bring a sense of occasion to any event. I take my place in a line of would-be citizens from all over the world—on this particular day, West Indians predominate—who are waiting patiently in the corridor outside the courtroom. I wonder about their many countries and their pasts, and what prompted them to converge here today, but there is already something American-seeming about them; they could be a crowd on the platform of a New York subway station. We are called one by one to a desk in the courtroom, where we have to sign our certificates of naturalization and surrender our precious green cards. Many people resist giving up their green cards, especially when they are told that they will have to wait a couple of weeks for their certifi-cates of naturalization to be processed and sent to them by registered mail. I, too, feel a pang of reluctance as I realize that I will be in limbo—no longer a permanent resident and not yet stamped and certified a naturalized citizen. There are about a hundred and fifty of us in line, and it is about two hours before all of us are through with the signing. Those of us who arrived first take seats in the courtroom with our friends and families; the rest have to stand. Everyone has been given a welcome kit, and we pass the time looking it over. There is an individual letter from the President, a thumbnail history of the Pledge of Allegiance and the music to which it is set, and a souvenir booklet containing the text not only of the Constitution and the Declaration of Independence but also of "Rules for Saluting the Flag," "The Star-Spangled Banner," "American's Creed," "The Mean-ing of American Citizenship," "The Duties of a Citizen," "Rights and Privileges of a Citizen," "The Five Qualities of the Good Citizen," and the song "America," along with some blank pages for "Memories of the Occasion."

Shortly, United States District Judge Inzer B. Wyatt, a heavyset elderly man in black robes, comes in and takes his place on the bench, and the hubbub in the room subsides. The court clerk, a big, Italian-looking man, perhaps a naturalized citizen himself, calls out the names of a few people who have not shown up to sign their certificates—he mispronounces even the simplest foreign names—and then says, "In the matter of Audor Baeder."

The young attorney of my naturalization examination steps up and says, "Good morning, Your Honor. My name is Seth Roberts, and I represent the Immigration and Naturalization Service. In the matter of Petition No. 822451"—apparently, the number refers to the person called Audor Baeder—"petitioner was a member of a proscribed organization while he lived in Hungary. After thorough investigation, the Immigration and Naturalization Service found him eligible for naturalization. I therefore move that his petition be granted."

"All right. This will be received, and on your statement the recommendation is accepted and the motion granted," the Judge says, in a big, deep voice.

"In the matter of Mui Lin Ho," the court clerk says.

Mr. Roberts then explains to the judge that Petition No. 825497 failed her immigration examination, because she was unable to speak, read, or write English, and that she did not appear for reëxamination when summoned on three separate occasions. He therefore moves that her petition be denied for lack of prosecution. He makes half a dozen similar motions to deny petitions, and the Judge accordingly denies all of them.

"Your Honor, I now wish to present one hundred and forty-eight petitioners for naturalization," Mr. Roberts goes on. "These petitioners have all been examined, and it was determined that they all are eligible for naturalization. I therefore move that their petitions be granted and that they be admitted to citizenship upon taking the Oath of Allegiance. Of these petitioners, twenty-five have requested a change of name. The Service has no objection . . . and I therefore move that their requests for change of name be granted." He further moves that two of the petitioners be exempted from taking the Oath of Allegiance, on the ground that they are under fourteen years of age, and that a third petitioner be administered a modified Oath, on the ground that he is a conscientious objector.

The Judge, who sounds as though he were from the South, grants these motions, too. He seems to have a little flair: he manages to vary the routine replies, branching out from "The motion is granted" into "So granted," "I think I have no choice but to grant the motion," and the like.

The court clerk tells all of us petitioners who are to take the Oath to stand and raise our right hands.

"I hereby declare . . ." the clerk says, leading us.

"I hereby declare . . ." we respond.

"On oath . . ."

"On oath . . ."

And so he takes us through the Oath of Allegiance: ". . . that I absolutely and entirely renounce and abjure all allegiance and fidelity to any foreign prince, potentate, state, or sovereignty, of whom or which I have heretofore been a subject or citizen; that I will support and defend the Constitution and laws of the United States of America against all enemies, foreign and domestic; that I will bear true faith and allegiance to the same; that I will bear arms on behalf of the United States when required by the law; that I will perform noncombatant service in the armed forces of the United States when required by the law; that I will perform work of national importance under civilian direction when required by the law; and that I take this obligation freely without any mental reservation or purpose of evasion: So help me God." (The conscientious objector is later led through the Oath by himself, and does not have to agree to bear arms.)

I repeat the powerful, magisterial words of the Oath and am moved by them. At the same time, I feel that I can never altogether renounce the country in which I was born: never renounce my mother tongue, my Indian childhood, my Indian memories, my brown skin and distinctive Indian features—never entirely stop being an Indian.

"Fellow-citizens," the Judge is saying, in his sonorous voice. It feels strange to be so addressed. "It is a privilege to be the first to address as fellow-citizens those who have been admitted this morning to citizenship by the Oath just taken. It is also a pleasure and a privilege to welcome on this solemn and significant occasion the relatives and friends of our new fellow-citizens. I am sorry that our accommodations in this, the largest courtroom in the building, are not sufficient to provide a place to sit down for all of you. I observe with regret that some of you are obliged to stand. But my remarks will be sufficiently short so that you may be consoled by the thought that you will not be obliged to stand very long. First, you have all been found to be of good moral character. That means a lot. It means that you have, to this point in your lives, conducted yourselves uprightly and honorably. And, second, you have been found to be attached to the principles of the Constitution of the United States and well disposed toward the good order and happiness of the United States, and that is important also. We like to think on occasions such as this, when we are reminded of it, that this is a government of law, a government by consent of the governed, a government of, by, and for the people. When you go to Washington—and I hope that all of you will someday go to our capital city—I ask you to look at the beautiful white marble building of the Supreme Court of the United States, and, above the towering but graceful columns at the front of the building, read what is written there in only four words: 'EQUAL JUSTICE UNDER LAW.' . . . You have doubtless noticed the discussion and debate in the last few days over the refugees who have come to our country from Vietnam. It would be inappropriate for us to consider the merits of that debate and discussion. But you must have been struck, as most of us have been struck, by how often in this debate and discussion it is said we are a nation of immigrants. And it is true. We are a nation of immigrants such as you ladies and gentlemen who are before me as new citizens this morning. The United States has absorbed the strengths of all its immigrants, and this fusion of many different strains and virtues has greatly contributed to our present strength, and it has also greatly—indeed, essentially—helped to make democracy work. . . . We will ask the clerk to lead us all in a Pledge of Allegiance to the flag."

I am touched by the Judge's words. Yet I wonder what he can know of the inner life of each of the immigrants sitting or standing before him, of what each must have gone through to arrive in this court-room, and of what each must be feeling about this occasion at this moment. As we rise to say the Pledge of Allegiance, my young woman friend kisses me, and my writer friend shakes my hand and says, "Congratulations. This is great. My grandfather, too, was an immi-grant. He was from Poland."

As I pledge allegiance, I recall coming across some words of Learned Hand, who, swearing in another generation of citizens some thirty years ago in New York's Central Park, said:

We have some right to consider ourselves a picked group, a group of those who had the courage to break from the past and brave the dangers and the loneliness of a strange land. What was the object that nerved us, or those who went before us, to this choice? We sought liberty, freedom from oppression, freedom from want, freedom to be ourselves. . . . Liberty lies in the hearts of men and women; when it dies there, no constitution, no law, no court can save it. . . . The spirit of liberty is the spirit of Him who, near two thousand years ago, taught mankind that lesson it has never learned, but has never quite forgotten; that there may be a kingdom where the least shall be heard and considered side by side with the greatest. And now, in that spirit, that spirit of an America which has never been, and which may never be; nay, which never will be except as the conscience and courage of Americans create it; yet in the spirit of that America which lies hidden in some form in the aspirations of us all . . . in that spirit of liberty and of America I ask you to rise and with me pledge our faith in the glorious destiny of our beloved country.

After the ceremony, I go with my friends to have lunch at Fraunces Tavern, the inn dating from American Revolutionary times. We feast on New England chowder, spicy shrimp curry à l'Indienne with Major Grey chutney, and a bottle of Pouilly-Fuissé. "I am no longer a guest in your country," I say. "Now I, too, can sign petitions and march and protest in public when I feel like it, without worrying about abusing hospitality." One of my friends suggests that I wait until I have my certificate of naturalization in hand.

A couple of weeks later, my certificate of naturalization—No. 984 5165—arrives in the mail. It looks very much like an A.T.&T. bond, except that it has my photograph on it, and it reads, in part:

Petition No. 832653
Alien Registration No. A7 828 521.

Be it known that at a term of the District Court of The United States held pursuant to law at New York City . . . the Court having found that VED PARKASH MEHTA . . . intends to reside permanently in the United States (when so required by the Naturalization Laws of the United States), had in all other respects complied with the applicable provisions of such naturalization laws, and was entitled to be admitted to citizenship, thereupon ordered that such person be and (s)he was admitted as a citizen of the United States of America.

After using the certificate to obtain an American passport, I put it in my safe-deposit box, which I felt was an appropriate place for the deed to Learned Hand's hidden kingdom.

Originally appeared under the heading "Our Local Correspondents," as "Naturalized Citizen No. 984-5165" in The New Yorker, *August 29, 1977. First appearance in a book.*

SEVEN

The Benefactress

Late in November, 1952, I received a letter at college from my father saying that he had been in India for a month or so but was coming right back to America and hoped to see me soon. I was staggered. There was no hint in the letter of where he would get the money, what job, if any, he had landed, how he could think about flying from continent to continent as if he were a maharajah.

In 1947, we'd lost practically everything to Pakistan during the Partition of India and become poor refugees. In 1949, feeling that I should have the same opportunity for education as his six other children (meningitis had left me blind at the age of four), he had made it possible for me to come to America, at the age of fifteen, and my high-school education alone had cost him several times that of any of his other children. Still, he was employed during those years as a high-ranking official in the Indian government and received a good salary. But in 1951 he was forced to retire, having passed the government's mandatory-retirement age of fifty-five. After that, he got an assignment in Washington with the International Bank for Reconstruction and Development, but it was only for six months, and when he wrote the letter he had just finished a term as a visiting Fulbright professor at the U.C.L.A. medical school—essentially an honorary position. He had spent the rest of the summer in Los Angeles and San Francisco looking for something to do, but had found nothing. So in September, when I entered Pomona College as a freshman, he left California with no prospects for the future and few resources.

On the heels of my father's letter came another letter from India, this one from a Mrs. Ethel Clyde. She said that my father had been travelling with her as her "court physician" and was taking her back to New York in early December, and that she would like it if I joined the two of them in Miami over my Christmas vacation. She added that I could travel by plane or train, whichever was convenient, and she would cover all the expenses, because I would be her "guest." She said I could write to her at 52 Gramercy Park, New York City. The letter had a few words scribbled on it by my father, saying that he whole-heartedly approved of the plan.

I was overwhelmed. I had never met Mrs. Clyde, or even heard of her. The terms "court physician" and "guest" in the senses in which she used them were totally unfamiliar to me. Until her letter came, I had dreaded the approach of Christmas—dreaded battling the onset of depression as the routine of classes was broken, the residence halls emptied out, and I was left to walk around the echoing halls by myself. That is what Christmases at high school had been like for me, and I had had no reason to suppose that anything would be different at college.

Over the next few days, I must have written a hundred different letters of thanks to Mrs. Clyde in my head, but none of them sounded quite right, and before I managed to get one off to her a parcel from her arrived in the post, with a card saying that to help me with my studies she had picked up a little present for me in Switzerland, where she and my father now were. I tore open the parcel, and could scarcely believe what I found. It seemed like a toy typewriter, but it turned out to be every bit a real one, and more. Made in Switzerland, it was light, compact, and small, it had French-accent signs, and it responded to my fingers as if it had been specially made for them.

I typed out the following note to Mrs. Clyde on my new typewriter:

December 9, 1952

DEAR MRS. CLYDE:

It was indeed a delightful and pleasant surprise to receive your
very sincere letter and your practical gift. For you see this new
gadget will have a two-fold purpose. It will aid me in my studies,
and—sentimental and foolish though it may be—provide me with
a constant reminder of the greatness of a person whose thought-
fulness and generosity could extend itself to an individual she
hadn't even met, and place such faith and confidence in him. I
hope I will prove worthy of this confidence, and thus endeavor, in
my little way, to show my overflowing gratitude. Words actually
fail me in expressing my thanks to you, so please excuse this futile
attempt.

Surprises never cease. Because I had been expecting to spend a
rather dull yet perhaps studious Christmas, now seeing you along
with Daddy will be to me a great lift and will act as a stimulus to
my work.

Hoping with keen anticipation to see you. With my very best
compliments for the season and kindest regards.

Very sincerely yours,
VED MEHTA

After I posted the letter, I heard from Mrs. Clyde again, this time
from London. She wrote that, as it turned out, she had to spend
Christmas Day itself with a very sick friend, Ben Marsh, in Winter
Park, Florida, so could I meet my father and her a couple of days later?
I had planned to fly to Florida, but I now decided to take the train, as
a way of having something to do on Christmas Day.

On the eighteenth of December—I remember the date because it
was when college let out for the Christmas holidays—I got a telephone call from my father in New York. He and Mrs. Clyde had just
arrived on a transatlantic flight. I started asking him questions about
Mrs. Clyde, but he put me off, saying that there was a lot to tell—too
much to tell on the phone—and that we'd have plenty of opportunity

to talk when we met in Florida. Mrs. Clyde came on the line. I remember I groped for words, but she, although she restricted herself to amenities, was very fluent. I listened to her voice for some clue to her, to her life. It sounded ebullient, expansive, amused, almost boisterous, as if she were intoxicated by surprising me, talking to me for the first time, meeting me on the phone, making plans, putting them into effect. I remember hanging up and thinking that, compared with hers, many voices sounded stunted, shrinking.

The travel agent who was handling my reservations got me a roomette on the train. I didn't know exactly what a roomette was, and even when the porter showed me to it, I couldn't take it all in. It seemed to contain within its four walls, in a space exactly the size of a single bed, a world of comforts—a sofa, a washbasin, a toilet, a table, a bed, all fitted snugly together. When the bed was folded up into a wall, it became the back of the headrest of the sofa. When the tabletop was lifted and folded back, it revealed the toilet and washbasin. But the space was used so economically that the only way one could climb into bed was by stepping out into the corridor, and a stationary heavy curtain hung over the doorway, so that fellow-passengers wouldn't see one getting in and out of bed. The same curtain also helped to muffle corridor sounds once the sliding door was closed. The roomette was perfectly heated, and the windows were sealed against the soot and detritus that flew into Indian trains. In fact, it was as sanitary and well fitted as an American dream house.

"America . . . America . . ." I found myself mindlessly repeating the word, to the padded clackety-clack of the train, as I kept getting up from the sofa, moving out into the corridor with the curtain behind me, pulling down the bed, climbing onto it, getting down from it, folding it back, and sitting down on the sofa again—all the while trying to imagine how the rich passed the time in their cocoons, if this was how they travelled, and what my new-found benefactress was like.

That night, Christmas night, I changed into my pajamas and hopped into my bed. *America . . . America . . .* No sooner had I closed the door and got comfortable between the sheets and under the blanket than I felt that I wanted to use the toilet again. I slid back the door, got down between the bed and the curtain, folded up the bed and the tabletop, used the toilet, put the tabletop and the bed down, and got back into the bed. The bed must not have locked into place properly, because just as I was dropping off to sleep it slipped out of its lock and sprang almost shut, sandwiching me, head down, between bed and wall. I remember the blood rushing to my head, and my arms and legs, though actually paralyzed with fear, twitching frantically with violent phantom movements. One false move and the bed will snap shut, I thought. I'll suffocate. I'll be buried alive. In fact, I was sure that a mere jolt of the train would finish me off. (Whether or not it was actually possible for the bed to snap shut with me inside I don't know to this day. There certainly seemed to be enough space between the wall and the upended bed to seal in my thin body.)

Although I had no leverage, gradually and painfully, like a worm inching and feeling its way, I somehow slowly shifted my weight toward the top end of the bed, and at last I got the bed down far enough to jump out of it. Thereafter, I sat up on the sofa, benumbed, my heart thumping every time I thought of getting into the coffinlike bed, with its lid about to shut on me, and my pride keeping me from asking the porter for help. *America . . . America . . .* We travelled on and on, pulling into anonymous stations—I had no way of knowing what they were and where I was. I ran out of the little Braille material I had brought to read. Once or twice, I walked to the dining car and back, in the hope of striking up a conversation, but I didn't meet anyone. I looked at the hands of my watch again and again, trying to hurry them on. As we approached Tampa, where my father and Mrs. Clyde had arranged to meet me, I grew more and more worried that she would be disappointed in me.

On the day of our meeting, Mrs. Clyde wrote in her diary:

> We drove to Tampa and met Ved, who arrived from Pomona by train at 1:10. He has fitted right into our little group. What tragedy and what courage! Poor Ved and poor Mehta. It is a heartbreaking business!

She must have mistaken my fright for courage, because I remember that I was scared as I stepped off the train, carrying my suitcase and trying to force my eyes open, so that I would look as independent and normal as I could. Suddenly, a familiar arm was around my shoulder, and my father was introducing me to Mrs. Clyde. I put out my free hand to shake hers, and that caused some awkward confusion, for it turned out that she had to shift a cane from one hand to the other. (I learned later that she was seventy-three years old.)

Outside the station, her car and a driver were waiting for us. I remember that it was a big Packard, that Mrs. Clyde got in the front seat next to the driver, whom she introduced as Bruce Sweetland, and that my father and I got in the back.

"Bruce is from Huntington, Long Island, where I have a farm," Mrs. Clyde said. "He helps out with driving whenever I hit the road."

We drove toward Miami, Mrs. Clyde doing most of the talking, my father mostly murmuring agreement, and Bruce scarcely opening his mouth. She spoke of examples of meaningless suffering she had come across in the morning's newspaper. Someone's operation had been botched, and he had been left paralyzed. Someone else had starved. Each time, she asked rhetorically, almost provokingly, "To what end?" She mentioned Ben Marsh, the sick friend she had just visited in Winter Park. He was the founder of an organization in Washington, D.C., called the People's Lobby, which fought against social injustice, and which she had been supporting for years. He had a severe case of pleurisy, she said, and was on his deathbed. "To what end?" she repeated. "If your God exists, Mehta, he must be a fiend."

My father didn't rise to the bait. Instead, he said to me, "You see, Mrs. Clyde is a vehement atheist."

"But do you believe in God?" I asked him, remembering that he used to make fun of my mother for her superstitious religious beliefs.

"Not as such, but I certainly think there may be a power higher than we."

"But to what end, Mehta?" she asked, and then, turning to me, "Do you think such meaningless suffering could exist if there was a God?"

I wanted to say that I thought it could, but I wasn't sure of my ground. I couldn't make out exactly who Mrs. Clyde was and whether my father would have me speak freely with her. I kept silent.

"I think the best thing all the statesmen in the world could do would be to make one big bomb and blow the world up," Mrs. Clyde said.

I could hold back no longer, and, like the college freshman I was, jumped into the debate with both feet. "You can't possibly mean such nonsense. You're voicing a sort of death wish. A person may have the right to wish death for himself but not for the whole world. Even people who are miserable and suffer a lot would rather live than die." And so on. I liked the sound of my voice, and thought that my arguments were very impressive—the more so because she seemed to be giving me her full attention.

"But horses manage their affairs much better than we humans do," Mrs. Clyde said, with a laugh. She had a distinctive, hearty laugh. It erupted, and went on for a long time. She seemed to throw her whole self into it. I suddenly became aware that I wasn't getting anywhere with her, and felt crestfallen.

"The greatest compliment Mrs. Clyde can pay anybody is 'He has horse sense,'" my father said, as if to console me—to say that no one else could get anywhere with her, either.

"Horses don't have war or poverty or crime, and they live in harmony with nature, without clothes—without shame and guilt—as we human beings were surely meant to do, but don't," Mrs. Clyde said. "Can you tell me why we wear clothes?"

She laughed, and my father joined in, as if they had had this conversation before.

"To be decent, I think," I said.

"What's decent about clothes? Aren't horses decent? Aren't all animals decent? Would you be surprised if I told you I used to go to a nudist camp?"

I said I was surprised.

"You know, I've always been known as the black sheep in my family." She laughed and laughed.

"Mrs. Clyde believes that none of us should feel any more guilty than horses," my father said.

"My philosophy is that we do what we do because of our heredity, environment, and experience," Mrs. Clyde said. She asked me, "Can you improve upon it?"

I was nonplussed.

"Your father told me you're studying philosophy," Mrs. Clyde said. "You must have studied the problem of free will."

"Yes, I have. Different philosophers have different views on it."

"Well, I've got the answer in my book. Did you know I'd written a book?"

I said no, I hadn't known that.

"I'm not surprised—it's privately printed," Mrs. Clyde said. "The book is called 'Horse Sense in Poetry, Prose, and Song.'"

"There's a copy here in the car," my father said.

Mrs. Clyde went on, "It says, 'Man's actions are inevitably the same whether or not he believes in free will, since his actions are always and only the result of those things that make freedom of the will impossible.'"

"That's only one way of looking at it," I argued.

My father pressed my hand, and I desisted.

She laughed. "You can't help what you are. You are what you are. A criminal can no more help being a criminal than you can help being a student. That's why I think no criminal should be punished. He should be treated humanely and given a fresh chance."

"But what if he is a repeat offender?" I said. My father pressed my hand again, vigorously.

"I have an answer to that. Then he should be shot, so that society will be free of him."

I despaired of continuing the argument.

"Mrs. Clyde is really very tolerant," my father said.

"You should read him my poem 'Homosexual,' from 'Horse Sense,'" Mrs. Clyde said.

He turned the pages of the book and then read:

Have you ever asked yourself this:
What indeed it must mean
To have been born with instincts
That to most men seem obscene?

To be normally abnormal,
To be shunned, loathed and scorned
Though having been natural
When you did the things they mourned?

If the critics had been given
Those same instincts, are you
Certain they would be acting
Now just as today they do?

I wish that all men understood
That man cannot reject
Mother Nature's gifts to him
Although tragic their effect.

I was struck by her pithy versification of complicated themes. It's all so strange, I thought. In one way, she comes out with rigid, sometimes shocking statements. In another way, she seems to be the most accepting, enthusiastic, tolerant person I've ever met. Although she's broadminded, she's insistent about her opinions. I can't make her out.

"Feel free to speak Punjabi between yourselves," Mrs. Clyde was saying. "If I were in a foreign country, I would want to speak my own language. Go right ahead—don't mind us."

Immediately, I turned to my father and asked in Punjabi, "Why didn't you want me to discuss the free-will question with her?"

"You will see that the best policy is to agree with her, or, if you feel you can't do that, to be silent," my father said. "I know from experience that you cannot budge her from her view that everything is determined. You can argue the point with her until the cows come home, but she won't acknowledge any exception. If you don't agree that freedom of the will is impossible, you don't have horse sense, and if you don't have horse sense—well, you can't help it, because of your heredity, environment, and experience. Around and around the circle you go."

I had never known my father to be in any way hypocritical, and I felt a little uncomfortable talking about her in this way behind her back. I said as much.

"Then you'll have to learn by experience," he said.

"But why are we here with her, then? What are we doing here?"

"It's a long—a very long—story."

That night, we stayed at the Casa Grande Hotel in Coral Gables, on the outskirts of Miami. After dinner, as I lay on the edge of my bed in the room my father and I were sharing, I asked, "How long have you been together?" I had so many questions that I scarcely knew which to ask first. "How did you meet? She was in India with you, so you must have been together for over a month." I told him that I was struck by how he constantly tried to make his views chime with hers—how he agreed with her about nudist camps, for instance, when I knew he thought they were silly. "How do you stand it day after day, week after week? Ever since I can remember, all our relations have deferred to you, looked up to you, as if they expected you to give them the lead. I have never seen you defer to anyone before. But here you are agreeing with her about everything, saying yes to everything. And I can't get used to your calling her Mrs. Clyde, as if she were your employer, and her calling you Mehta, as if you were her employee. It irks me."

"Patience—have patience," he said. "I'll explain it all to you, but a step at a time."

The windows were open to let in the Florida breeze, and outside, against the night silence, the sound of the crickets seemed to recede. I lay very still, with my hand under my cheek, listening to my father.

The road to Mrs. Clyde began with the Watumulls, he was saying. In the summer, before he left Los Angeles, he had gone to a dinner party at the home of Mr. and Mrs. G. J. Watumull, an Indian-American couple known for their philanthropy, and had met Margaret Sanger there. He had long admired her work for family planning, and she had wanted to meet him ever since the year before, when she had read, as a judge, an essay he had written about population growth and entered in a competition sponsored by the Watumull Foundation. His essay had won first prize. Mrs. Sanger and my father didn't have much of a chance to talk at the dinner party, but she invited him to spend a couple of days at her home, in Tucson, Arizona. On his way to New York, he stopped off in Tucson. She gave him an earful about free love, abortion, and the contribution of the suffragists. He had not often heard women talk so frankly about such matters. Then she told him that though she was in her seventies and in poor health she was determined to go to an international conference on population control to be held in Bombay from November 24th to December 2nd that year.

"Mrs. Watumull is going, and I'm very eager that you should also attend—in fact, take up the cudgels for our cause in your country," she added.

"I know about the conference," he said. "Mrs. Watumull, too, has urged me to attend. I myself am very eager to go and help wake India to the cause, but I am a retired man, and I am in no position to volunteer my services, like you and Mrs. Watumull. I don't even have the wherewithal to go to Bombay and stay in a hotel."

She lost no time in pressing into his hand a check for six hundred dollars toward his expenses, and then wrote for him letters of introduction to several people in New York: Mrs. Dorothy Brush, the secretary of the population-control conference; Miss Georgea Furst, the private secretary to the Doris Duke Foundation, which had been contributing money to the cause for years; and Mrs. Ethel Clyde, who had got the Doris Duke Foundation involved in it in the first place. "You should call on all three of them when you get to New York," she said. "They are all good friends of mine. But, of the three, Mrs. Clyde is the only one who might actually give you another check. She's been a big contributor to Planned Parenthood, to the Presidential campaigns of the Socialist Norman Thomas, and to a hundred other causes."

"I'm not in need of more money for my expenses at the conference," he said. "I'm looking around for a paying job."

"You'd enjoy meeting Mrs. Clyde—she's a friend of Mrs. Roosevelt's. Who knows? Maybe you can persuade her to come to the conference."

In New York, my father looked up Mrs. Brush and Miss Furst, and they filled him in on details of the population-control conference. Then he telephoned Mrs. Clyde. She told him that she was feeling abominably tired but would like him to come to tea that afternoon.

When he arrived at her apartment, on Gramercy Park, the door was opened by a large woman with brown eyes and plenty of silver-gray hair, done up in little curls, which came down to her nape. She had an expressive face and a pleasant smile. She was colorfully dressed—in a red dress, with flat shoes that exactly matched it—but the clothes looked simple. She introduced herself as Ethel Clyde and led my father into her living room, shuffling rather than walking.

He looked around. The apartment appeared to be two apartments made into one, but instead of seeming luxurious it had a homelike feeling. There was a lot of old, worn French-looking furniture, and innumerable objects apparently picked up all over the world. Above the piano hung a painting of a tall old man with a white mustache and a pointed beard. He had classic features and a broad forehead.

"That's my father, William Clyde," Mrs. Clyde said. "After I was widowed, I took back my maiden name—keeping the 'Mrs.' because I had two children. But I brought them up as Clydes."

"Your father is a very distinguished-looking man," my father said. "He must have been a banker or an important business executive."

She laughed, in her explosive, resonant way. He had never known a woman to laugh that way. She is brimming with more vitality than many young women in India, he thought.

"He was the president of the Clyde Steamship Company, which my grandfather founded."

"A very famous line," he said, and he told her that when Mahatma Gandhi first went to England he sailed on a ship called the S.S. Clyde.

"I don't know anything about that," she said. "I never took any interest in the business."

His eye wandered to some amateurish unsigned watercolors on another wall. "Oh, I did those," Mrs. Clyde said, with her laugh. "I do some painting."

He liked best a watercolor of flowers hanging between a snow scene and a landscape, and he complimented her on it.

"Oh, that—that one was done by my teacher," she said, with another laugh. She was quick to laugh, and seemed to laugh at everything. She had him sit next to her on a sofa, and asked him directly, the expression in her eyes turning noticeably hard, "What can I do for you?" She picked up a handbag from a corner of the sofa.

He remembered what Mrs. Sanger had told him about the ease with which she wrote checks. Fund-raisers must come calling on her every day, he thought. She probably gives each one a check and sends him away.

"What can you do for me, personally?" he asked. "Nothing. I am an old physician from India. I just completed a short assignment for the U.C.L.A. medical school. I'm harboring an ambition to settle in London and set up a medical practice there one day."

She laughed. "I took you for a fund-raiser," she said.

He thought that perhaps he had sounded too comfortable, so he told her about his straitened circumstances—about the Partition and his retirement.

She listened to him, sitting back and studying him, but with friendly eyes. "How do you happen to know Margaret?" she asked at one point.

He told her about the population essay and their common interest in birth control. "I was Deputy Director General of Health Services in India, and I could have done much for our population problem, but my hands were tied. My misfortune was that my Minister, who was a very powerful person in the government, was a devout Christian, and she didn't believe in birth control."

"What a terrible thing!" Mrs. Clyde said. "I thought Nehru was a good Prime Minister. You should have told him to get rid of her!"

"That's not the way things are done in our country," he said. "Anyway, she was a very special disciple of Mahatma Gandhi, and Gandhiji believed that children were gifts from God, and that while each child came with a mouth to feed he also came equipped with hands and feet, to work for his food."

"Which God?" She proclaimed, almost boastingly, "I am an atheist."

He was genuinely surprised. Except, perhaps, for Margaret Sanger, he'd never met such an outspoken woman. She had the manner and tone of a gracious, almost stately lady, but now he was seeing another side of her—that of a freethinker.

"How did they think you could stop people from reproducing like rabbits, then?" she asked him.

"You are right about the rate of reproduction. Even as we have been sitting here, hundreds of new mouths to feed have been born in India."

"I thought Gandhi was humane, and wanted to help your country. He must have had some notion of how to stop people from reproducing. Or did he want your people to die of hunger?"

"The only means of birth control that Gandhiji and his followers approved of was abstinence, and yet abstinence cannot work as a method of birth control in our country."

"Why not?"

"Frankly, sex is about the only diversion most of our poor people have."

Eventually, my father raised the possibility of her attending the population-control conference in Bombay. "Mrs. Sanger is going, and she wants me to attend," he said. "She thought you might like to go, too."

"I went to your country in 1925, and I never want to go near it again," she said. "There's so much poverty and misery there." He thought her reaction childlike and typically American, but she suddenly added, as if on an impulse, "Still, if Margaret is going I'll think about it."

"I myself am not a good example of the population control I preach," my father went on, with his usual twinkle in his eye. "I have seven children, and whenever my children complain that we have too many I ask them, 'Which one could we have done without?'"

Mrs. Clyde laughed. "But I'm a good example," she said. "I have only two sons, and they are now middle-aged, and between them they have just one child, my Toby."

They had a good laugh about the size of their families. Then he looked at his watch and, realizing that he'd stayed for almost two hours, got up to say goodbye. As he was leaving, she asked him where he was staying, and he told her the Commodore Hotel, on Forty-second Street.

"I enjoyed our talk," she said. "I hope we'll meet again."

He said he would like that very much.

Outside on the street, the light was fading fast, and he hurried along toward the hotel. If Partition hadn't happened, I might today still be in Lahore, he remembered thinking. I might be stopping by one of my clubs, playing a little tennis, seeing old friends, joining a table of low-stakes bridge—living the life of a retired man who has done well by his family and the government. Every little corner of his Lahore came back to him with a rush. A man is nothing but a bundle of associations, and an old man is best off passing his waning days among the landmarks of his childhood, he thought. What opposites were this New York and that Lahore! Who could have imagined that he would be made a refugee in his own country, like some human flotsam, cut loose from the moorings of his family and ancestors, who had lived in the Punjab for hundreds, perhaps thousands of years? As so often happened, an apt Urdu couplet came to him spontaneously:

Light of my memories, let them stay with me.
Who knows down which lane the evening of my life shall pass?

No sooner had he reached his hotel room than the telephone rang. It was Mrs. Clyde. "Tomorrow, I'm going to Old Fields, my farm, with my doctor, Coda Martin, and his wife, Kitty," she said. "If you're free for the weekend, I would like to take you along. The farm is in Huntington, Long Island."

Even before the phone call came, he had been telling himself that he was a lucky man to be out and about in the land of his dreams, healthy and vigorous for an Indian man of his age. He could never be sad for very long. Whenever he felt low, an optimistic thought soon swept over him. He had always dreamed of coming out to the West after retirement, and now here he was, in America, in New York, being invited for a country weekend. He began looking forward to the companionship of a new friend and also of a fellow-doctor, who might suggest some means of employment. Who knew where this acquaintance with Mrs. Clyde might lead? In any case, he had no plans for the weekend; he was just going to stay in the hotel, read, and write some letters—something he could do in the country as well as anywhere else. He accepted the invitation with alacrity.

"My doctor and I will be driving out there," she said. "We'll pick you up at seven in the morning at the back entrance of your hotel— that's on our way. Would you wait for us outside?"

"I'll be standing out there five minutes before seven," he said. "I'm one of those Indians who are punctual to a fault."

On my second day in Florida, we drove to Miami Beach for a swim. In the car, Mrs. Clyde reopened the discussion about free will. I threw myself into it, arguing that we did have some kind of choice, however limited it might seem. "Look, I can raise my arm. That's my choice. That's free will."

"But the choice is made for you by your heredity, environment, and experience."

I went on trying to argue with her, saying that her schematic, generalized formulation almost seemed to preclude discussion, but I felt I was in a ring boxing with shadows. Besides, I felt constrained. She was the benefactress and I was the beneficiary. She was seventy-three and I was eighteen. Still, I persisted. "Can you give me an example of what you mean by heredity?" I asked. "Can you be specific?"

"Heredity is heredity. Don't you know what it is?"

My father pressed my hand and said innocuously, as if to change the subject. "The sky here is certainly nice and blue, but I myself thrive on the gray fog of London. I find that climate very bracing."

"How can you like the English climate?" Mrs. Clyde asked. "The English don't get any sun. I don't like England."

"Some of us like it very much," my father said.

"That's because you come from a hot country," she said.

He protested, saying, "Some of us like the English climate for its own sake."

Mrs. Clyde repeated his statement, worried it, challenged him to justify it, debated it, and would not rest until he had acknowledged that his view reflected his heredity and his experience of living in the environment of India.

"You always win, Mrs. Clyde," he finally said, laughing.

I had to laugh, too. For all his admonitions not to argue with her, he had fallen into the same trap I had.

"And would it surprise you to know that I never graduated from high school?" she asked me.

I said I was indeed surprised.

"I took some classes with my son Bill when he was going to Columbia. I took courses from John Dewey and Edward Hodnett, because I didn't want my sons to be so much smarter than I was that I wouldn't be able to talk to them. Can you imagine mother and son sitting in the same class? We created quite a stir."

She certainly is unusual, I thought. She doesn't fit into any mold.

"I never graduated, but one of my interests is 'educating the educators.'"

"Any time a cartoon, a newspaper story, or some fact Mrs. Clyde comes across strikes her as important, she sends it to a mail-order house with a note that every president of a college, or dean, or professor of history—whatever—should receive a copy, with her compliments," my father said.

I was much impressed, and felt that she and I shared a thirst for knowledge and a faith in education.

At the beach, Mrs. Clyde liked the looks of some beach shirts a vender was offering, and bought three, for Bruce, my father, and me. When my father and I went into a cabana to change into our swimming trunks and the shirts, I said to him, "I know these shirts are supposed to be salt-water-resistant, but I don't like their rubbery feel."

"I myself don't like them," he said. "They have pictures of sailboats and fishes on the back. They're something teen-agers and clowns would wear at home. But mum's the word."

The part of the beach we were on was fairly empty. Bruce rode far out into the sea. My father, an experienced swimmer, went beyond the breakers to swim. I wasn't much of a swimmer, and hadn't been in the ocean since I was a child, so I just waded in again and again, ran after the waves as they were going out, and ducked as I felt them coming in, to allow myself to be carried back. I was surprised at how warm and gentle the sea was, and in my heart I thanked Mrs. Clyde for bringing me to it.

When Mrs. Clyde's car pulled up in front of the back door of the Commodore Hotel at seven o'clock in the morning, my father was waiting. He slipped in beside Dr. Martin, who was behind the wheel. Mrs. Clyde sat in the back, alone. "I was looking forward to meeting your wife," my father said to Dr. Martin.

"My wife couldn't come," Dr. Martin explained. "She had to stay back to look after Jimmie, our dog, who's very old and sick."

Dr. Martin had a pleasant manner and bearing, and he was well spoken, but he was dressed in a gray suit and came across as a businessman. My father had trouble imagining him in the striped trousers and long white coat of an English doctor.

While Mrs. Clyde dozed, Dr. Martin drew my father out, quizzing him about his medical training. My father thought that Dr. Martin was trying to find out if his training was comparable with that of an American doctor, and wondered whether Dr. Martin might have a job for him up his sleeve.

"This was one of the first prefabricated houses to be built on the East Coast," Mrs. Clyde said when they pulled up to her country house an hour or two later.

"It could be a mansion," my father said, genuinely surprised. "This is a wondrous country, where such a house can be sold and bought, perhaps from a picture in a catalogue. The grounds, too, look very big."

"They're fields, not grounds," Dr. Martin said. "About forty acres' worth."

Mrs. Clyde told Dr. Martin and my father that they could do what they liked until lunchtime. A man called Berni, a German, who seemed to be a resident chauffeur cum butler, showed each of them to an upstairs bedroom with its own bathroom, while Mrs. Clyde went to sit in the sun on a glassed-in porch attached to her room.

My father went downstairs and knocked some balls around on a billiard table. He went out on the lawn and sat in a chaise longue and watched birds and rabbits dart about. He sauntered along a road, shaded by poplars, that seemed to lead into the village. He was used to doing things with my mother and the rest of us, and he missed our company, thinking how much fun the weekend would have been if we had all been there with him. He came back and went into the kitchen and made friends with the housekeeper, Mrs. Armer. She was a short woman with a plain but amiable face and a weak chin. What was most noticeable about her was a hearty working-class English accent.

My father asked after her husband.

"He's gone back to England to live, sir," she said. "He's always liked the English way of life better than the American. He's a private man, and now that he's getting on in years he likes his quiet. But I have to live here, because this is where my job is."

"My wife and I, too, have to live apart," he said. "I'm trying to make a living, and she's back home in India. And I, too, love England. I like its quiet and rhythm of life best of all. I would like to settle there." They commiserated with each other, and soon my father was telling her how to make *bhurji,* his favorite Indian dish, of scrambled eggs, onions, and chilies.

Mrs. Clyde came downstairs dressed in shorts. He was taken aback, but then reminded himself that, like Margaret Sanger, she was an outrageous rebel, even if she was also a gracious Victorian lady. "Let's go for a walk," she said, picking out a cane from a collection in a stand. "I'd like to see what's doing in the fields."

The day was crowded with many new impressions, but what he later remembered most clearly was that Mrs. Clyde talked to him and conducted herself with him as if he were an old, close friend rather than someone she had met only once before.

The next morning, as Dr. Martin and my father were sitting at the breakfast table and eating *bhurji*—Mrs. Clyde hadn't come down yet—Dr. Martin asked my father abruptly, "Would you be interested in travelling with Mrs. Clyde to India if she goes to the population conference?"

"I'm going to the conference anyway," my father replied. "I would be glad to accompany her and show her around."

"Well, she needs more than that," Dr. Martin said. "She told me that she would like you to take charge. If you're interested, we'll talk about her medical history when we get back to the city." He added, "I think she would make it worth your while to be her 'court physician.' She's very rich, you know."

" 'Neither their friendship is good nor their enmity,' as our Urdu couplet has it," my father said. Then, realizing that the couplet might be off-putting, he added quickly, "I would certainly be interested." He had never heard the term "court physician" before, and didn't know what that might involve, but the prospect of having a job, any job, and especially one connected with his profession, was tantalizing.

"She has the unmentionable disease," Dr. Martin announced. "You know what I mean."

My father didn't know what he meant, but decided to keep his own counsel for the time being.

"My opinion is she shouldn't travel without medical attendance, and she can well afford it," Dr. Martin said.

"Perhaps you would be interested in accompanying her yourself," my father suggested.

"It isn't easy for us American doctors to just pick up and go like that," Dr. Martin said, perhaps implying that Mrs. Clyde had told him about my father's straitened circumstances and that he took it for granted they would make my father willing to entertain such a proposal.

On the particular night of my Christmas holiday when my father told me about that conversation, it didn't occur to me to ask what "the unmentionable disease" was. Just hearing the words made my teenage heart race. After Mrs. Clyde died, at the age of ninety-eight, in 1978, I asked my father if professional ethics would allow him to tell me what the disease was.

"Oh!" he exclaimed. "There is no great stigma attached to it nowadays. It was epilepsy." He went on to say, "But I have to confess that when Dr. Martin first volunteered the name of the disease to me, in

New York, in those early days, I was thrown. My medical knowledge of epilepsy was very rusty. I don't think I'd read anything about it since the twenties, when I was a student—when it was indeed an unmentionable disease. I had to read up on it in the library. I learned that a lot of progress had been made. Dilantin kept it mostly under control. Mrs. Clyde took that medicine, but she must have had seizures in public when she was a child, before Dilantin was available, and she lived in constant fear that she might have a seizure in public again. You might say her doctors had to minister to her fear of the public manifestation of the disease rather than to the disease itself. The few seizures she had while I was with her were very easily taken care of. The picture was a little complicated, however, because she had a heart condition. She had to take digitalis. I remember at one point her fear of having a seizure in public started keeping her awake, and I consulted a specialist at the Columbia-Presbyterian Medical Center in New York, and added to the Dilantin a quarter of phenobarbital. This combination became her standby."

The evening following the weekend that my father and Dr. Martin spent at Old Fields, Mrs. Clyde told my father that she wanted to have a serious talk with him. She had asked him to come and see her, and they were again sitting in the living room of her apartment. She had in her lap a legal pad, her diary, and her checkbook, and various papers were spread about her on the sofa. "I had the brain wave to go to India with you as my court physician when I realized you weren't a fund-raiser," she said. "Now that Coda has discussed the whole subject with you, let's get down to business." Her expression, usually pleasant and receptive, abruptly became hard and challenging. "I'd like to go a month or so before the conference and do a little travelling. I'll pay all your expenses when we're travelling. What salary would you like?"

He suddenly woke up to the fact that he was actually going to be paid a salary. So being her "court physician" will be an assignment, like the Fulbright and the International Bank job, he thought.

"My last real job was with the International Bank," he said. "I was getting eleven hundred and fifty dollars a month."

"Then I will pay you the same," she said, almost as if she were clinching a deal.

"But that included a daily allowance of fifteen dollars for expenses. My actual salary was seven hundred dollars."

"Well, then, I'll pay you seven hundred dollars, since I plan to pay both your travelling and daily expenses as my guest," she said immediately. The salary seemed very fair. It was even princely by Indian standards.

"But Mrs. Sanger has already paid me six hundred dollars toward my expenses in Bombay." He was prompted to volunteer this fact because, after all, Mrs. Sanger had given him the money for a designated purpose.

"Then I'll deduct that from your expenses—from the cost of your plane ticket," she said, noting down the amount. "In America, you will be my guest, like all my other friends, so I will pay you a salary only when you are travelling with me. Anyway, my tax people tell me that since you're not a citizen of this country and don't have a green card I can pay you only when we're abroad."

It never occurred to him to protest. She, of course, had her own doctors here, and technically he would be on duty only when they were travelling. He nodded.

"Hurrah!" Mrs. Clyde cried. "Then it's settled! The plan is very advantageous to both of us."

And my father recited to himself an Urdu couplet:

In this ocean of destruction, the boat of life sails along.
Whichever place the boat happens to run aground, that is your
    shore and home.

In the afternoon, my father and Mrs. Clyde went to 125 East 72nd Street, where Dr. Martin had his office. Mrs. Clyde got a vaccination against smallpox and injections against cholera and typhoid, all of which were required for travelling to India. Then she visited with Kitty in the Martins' apartment, which was in the same building, while my father stayed in the office and Dr. Martin filled him in on Mrs. Clyde's medical history. After telling him about various vitamins, sedatives, and medicines she took, he said, "She's no spring chicken, you know. You have to be careful that she doesn't fall sick. When she's travelling, she has to stay in first-class hotels and eat in good restaurants."

My father finally had an inkling of what it meant to be a "court physician": he was being asked to attend on some kind of American queen.

"What financial arrangements have you and Mrs. Clyde arrived at?" Dr. Martin asked, without any preliminaries.

My father told him.

"An American doctor of your standing might have asked for four or five thousand dollars a month, and got it," Dr. Martin said. "She can well afford to pay, and, after all, you're going to be on call twenty-four hours a day."

My father felt a pang for having been so open and spontaneous with Mrs. Clyde—for carrying his heart on his sleeve, as usual. "At least, it's all found," he said, laughing it off. "Seven hundred dollars a month is all that the services of a retired Indian doctor are worth."

"You certainly shouldn't allow her to deduct six hundred dollars from your air ticket."

Mrs. Sanger's six hundred dollars would have come in very handy, he thought, while it can make no difference to Mrs. Clyde. But he felt he had no choice, and said as much. The subject was dropped.

When Mrs. Clyde and my father left Dr. Martin's building, she suggested that they walk for a few blocks before getting a taxi. As they made their way along, people turned back to look at them, smiling a little. She had on her flat, comfortable shoes and was carrying her cane, and that day she was wearing a cape. It was cut very loose, and, draped around her, it emphasized her largeness. The shoes, which, she had told my father, were handmade for her on Cape Cod from the leather of cows that had died a natural death, seemed a little incongruous on the city sidewalk, and so highlighted her eccentricity. The cane was almost a practical necessity for her, but it also gave her walk a certain dignity, verging on imperiousness. And there was my father at her side, in complexion so light, in bearing so distinguished that he could have been taken for an Italian nobleman. She looked so old and he looked so young that they might have been a mother and son who had just stepped off the boat from Europe.

Without a preparatory word, she stopped on the street and pulled out of her bag a few ten-dollar bills and tried to press them on him.

He drew back. "What is that for?"

"I'm tired. Let's get a taxi."

"I have money. Anyway, a taxi ride is only a few dollars."

Right there on the street, she explained to him that whenever he was with her he was her guest. Wherever they went, whatever they did together, and even wherever he went alone on her behalf, she must pay. That had been her practice ever since she could remember, and everyone who was her friend knew and accepted it.

It will be one thing for me to settle our hotel accounts with money from her when we are travelling, he thought, but it's quite another thing to accept cash directly from her. The money was still waving in her hand, so that any passerby could snatch it, and he found himself saying, "I'll keep a record. You can give me the money later." He tried to hail a taxi.

"But I don't like carrying money," she said. "I want you to carry my money, and I want you to pay for everything, because you're the man. You ask Coda Martin. Whenever he and Kitty and I go out together, I give him the money and he pays for everything."

People were beginning to stare at them, as if they were having a family quarrel. He wanted to put an end to the argument, to hurry her along, get her into a taxi. He looked up and down the street, but no empty taxi was to be seen.

"While we are preparing to go, there will be many little expenses—passport fees, travellers' checks, restaurant bills—that you'll have to take care of," she was saying. "There may be times when I don't feel like going out to lunch, and you'll have to eat alone and pay for it. Since you're my guest, you should have money in your pocket. That's why everything will be so much easier if you'll just agree to be my banker. I make all my companions my bankers."

The term "banker" assuaged his feelings somewhat, but he saw his job with Mrs. Clyde in a new light. It wasn't like the International Bank job or the Fulbright at all. It was personal—that of a courtier. He took the money, emptied the inside left pocket of his jacket, and stuffed the bills in. From that day on, he treated that pocket as Mrs. Clyde's "bank."

Over the next fortnight or so, my father went with her in taxis or in her car, driven by Berni, to doctors' offices, to the homes of her friends, to shops, to her tailor, where she had herself fitted for a new cape. He accompanied her on expeditions outside the city, here to see a sick friend, there to investigate the efficacy of hypnosis or of the single-tax movement, and, on a longer trip, to drop in on her invalid brother. Will, and her sister, Mabel, who lived together in the May-flower Hotel in Washington, D.C. He took most of his meals with her. Everywhere, he was her "guest," paying from her bank in his pocket. She told him that it would make her very happy if he would give up his room at the Commodore and stay in her guest room, but he resisted, clinging to a vestige of economic independence. When-ever he stopped to think about his new life, his new job, his new friendship, he recited to himself the Urdu couplet:

God knows what happens after death.
At least the present passes in tranquillity.

The few days I was Mrs. Clyde's guest in Florida, I was bowled over by her restless energy. We would "hit the road" in the morning with-out knowing where we would be spending the night. She seemed to go anywhere, do anything that came into her head. We went from Miami to Palm Beach and on to West Palm Beach, St. Petersburg, St. Augustine, Jacksonville; from hotel to hotel, restaurant to restaurant, tourist attraction to tourist attraction, auto camp to auto camp.

I had never spent a whole day in a rich person's company, and I couldn't get over Mrs. Clyde's complicated attitude toward money. She would choose simple, unostentatious restaurants, and she balked at tipping more than ten per cent. Yet an extra zero on the check she was writing for our hotel rooms seemed to make no difference to her. It was as if she worried about pennies but didn't care about dollars. She booked into hotels without comparing rates with other hotels or asking what a room would cost. If something caught her fancy in a shop, she bought it, without stopping to think whether she needed it or could use it. She made long-distance telephone calls to her friends from hotel rooms without worrying about what the calls would cost. Indeed, just when a phone conversation seemed to be finishing, she would start it up again, not once but a dozen times, without seeming to be aware of the expensive seconds and minutes clicking away. We could never have dreamed of a life like hers.

All the time I was with her, I tried to persuade her that I didn't need a separate bed in my father's room—that I could sleep on the floor.

"Why?" she asked.

"You can save some money by having us stay in a single room instead of a double."

"And have you, child, uncomfortable?" She laughed and laughed. "You are my guest."

It seemed there was no way to recompense her except through talk and argument.

My father and Mrs. Clyde arrived in London on the way to India on the morning of October 21st, and he started telephoning hotels from the airport. It was part of his job to make all the travel arrangements, and before leaving New York he had visited the offices of Thomas Cook & Sons and American Express. He had found the task uncongenial, and, moreover, he had been staggered by the prices quoted to him, perhaps because on the few occasions when he stayed in hotels in London he had sought out cheap bed-and-breakfast places, and had often been able to use his personal charm to get the landlady to make additional concessions. The travel agents had assured him that rooms in London were plentiful at that time of the year, so he had put off making hotel reservations until he and Mrs. Clyde reached London and he could personally visit the hotels, thinking that that way he might be able to get lower rates. But now, when he telephoned, he discovered that he and Mrs. Clyde had arrived in the middle of automobile and agricultural exhibitions, and it seemed there was not a room to be had in the entire city. After a great deal of telephoning, he was able to secure two single rooms, without private baths, at the India Service Club, on South Audley Street, in Mayfair.

When they arrived at the club, it turned out that Mrs. Clyde was the only woman guest in the place, and he was able to prevail upon another guest to trade his single room with private bath for her room. When Mrs. Clyde was shown to it, she shrank back but bravely said aloud, "It will be fun." She seemed very sporting and understanding about his failure to make prior arrangements. "How could anyone possibly have known that all the hotels in London would be taken over by trade shows?" she said.

But the next morning, when she and my father started down to breakfast, they caught sight of the back of a big fellow walking out of his room in an undershirt and a pair of baggy drawers, and with hair hanging wildly down his back.

"What kind of place is this, where a half-dressed man with dirty long hair can walk around in full sight of everyone?" she asked. "I wouldn't object to him half as much if he were in the nude, and lived in the open, among birds and trees."

"He belongs to the martial religion of the Sikhs," my father said. "Ordinarily, his hair would be in a topknot under a turban, but he must have just got up."

"What is he doing wearing his hair like a woman? Hasn't he ever heard of a barber?" She laughed. Even when she was irritated, she saw the humor in things.

"Keeping long hair and a beard is part of the Sikh religion."

"Why haven't I heard of that religion? What is he doing living in England? He's not English."

"There are a lot of people living in England who are not English. They are immigrants."

In the dining room, the waiter came to take their order, and she ordered a sizable combination of Indian and Western breakfasts. She's wonderful, my father thought. She has a healthy appetite and is very adventurous. No wonder she has so much energy.

"I thought your country was hot. Those Sikhs must sweat like anything. I thought you said your people were clean."

"I don't remember the context in which I said that, but we Hindus are known for being clean in our personal habits, for bathing frequently."

"But no one would say that that Sikh upstairs was clean."

"He was probably going for his wash. Sikhs bathe and wash their hair regularly."

"I thought India was dry and poor, and you had to conserve all the water you could for the crops."

"But it doesn't take much water to wash hair. Our women keep long hair."

"Maybe your country would be better off if you cut off the hair of Sikhs and your women."

"For the Sikh men and our women to wear long hair is a very old tradition. Indeed, we Hindus think that long hair is a woman's crowning glory."

"What good is hair and glory if you've got people starving to death?"

"Not everyone in India is starving. Anyway, it's our culture—our religion, our society."

She looked skeptical.

He searched for some comparison that might make sense to her. "Sikh men are like the Biblical hero Samson. Their hair is a symbol of their power and virility."

"If Samson were living today, he would cut his hair," she declared, and added, laughing, "He would certainly not go around in an English hotel with his hair flying about wildly. Why, the whole floor smells of sweaty hair. You know, I have a nose like a dog."

My father laughed, too.

Breakfast was served, and she attacked it vigorously, but that didn't slow her talking—or, rather, asking question after question about Sikhs, Hindus, India. Asking questions seemed to be her way of carrying on a conversation. "My middle name is Question Mark," she said. He tried to make the conversation personal, thinking that that way she might be able to have more sympathy for the Sikhs. "By the way, my grandmother was a Sikh," he said.

"Then why don't you have long hair?" she asked.

"I'll try to be clearer," he said. "Many Punjabi Hindus have Sikh relatives but remain Hindus. Sikhs are converts from Hinduism—they belong to a different religion."

"How can any thinking person be religious after Darwin?"

"Why not? There are plenty of thinking people who are religious."

"Science tells us religion is superstition. You're a doctor. You're a scientist. How can you not be an atheist? It's all heredity, environment, and experience."

He tried to argue with her, saying that for believers religion was as objective as the table he and she were sitting at.

"They're all barking up the wrong tree."

Mrs. Clyde and my father were at the breakfast table long after everyone else had left. It seemed that whatever he said met with a swift riposte, and that she made no effort to understand his point. She took his most casual remark literally and repeated it to him later out of context. The more he tried to end a subject, to extricate himself by giving short, evasive answers, the more tenaciously she pursued it. In New York, some of her enormous energy had been diverted onto her other friends and onto Mrs. Armer, Berni, and maids, and he could escape to his hotel, leaving her with other people. Now she had no one but him, and he had nowhere else to go, so he had to bear her firepower alone. He felt cornered. As a rule, he was full of energy himself, and very resilient, but talking with her was such an exhausting experience that he had come to feel flattened. I've now known her for three weeks, he thought. However bighearted she is, however eager she is to learn, when it actually comes down to it she has difficulty seeing any point of view different from her own. That may have something to do with the fact that she is rich, and that the rich are not used to having their opinions contradicted or challenged. She behaves as if we were equals, as if we were friends, and encourages me to say whatever comes into my head, but she is my employer, and there is no way I can be her equal. I have to be on my guard and try to please her at all times, however much it goes against the grain. In her presence, I will have to conduct myself according to Bhabiji's saying "First weigh what you're going to say, and only then say it." (Bhabiji was his mother.)

"I hate this hotel," she said suddenly. "I don't want to spend another minute here. I want to move right now."

They had planned to spend only two nights in London, and he attempted to persuade her not to move, since there was just one more night. The time would go very fast, he said. But once she had taken something into her head it was very difficult to get her to change her mind. So he said he'd go out and look for another hotel, and asked her for exact specifications.

She said that she would like them to have two rooms next to each other, possibly with a connecting door, so that if she suddenly sensed a fainting spell coming on and called him he could rush to her side. She wanted each room to have its own attached bathroom, with a shower. If possible, her room should have a balcony or a sitting room with a lot of sunlight. "You know from Old Fields that I'm a sun worshipper," she added.

He realized he had no choice but to do her bidding, and immediately set out to find new hotel rooms, while she went upstairs to her room to try to work on her watercolors. He stopped in at a travel agency, got a list of hotels, and canvassed them on foot. In due course, he took her to see the rooms in a hotel he liked, so that she could judge for herself. But she stepped into the lobby and said she didn't like the look of it—she would never stay there. He couldn't get her to go in any farther. Finally, he caught on to the fact that she would not be satisfied with anything less than a five-star hotel. Hang the expense, he thought. It's her money, and she has the right to spend it as she likes.

He took her back to the club, and, remembering that all the most important Indian princes used to stay at the Savoy, he went there. Apparently, the farmers and automobile dealers of the trade shows had not been interested in staying in such a grand place, and rooms that more or less met Mrs. Clyde's specifications were available. He took them, and by teatime they had moved in.

"The rooms are perfect," she said, and he felt relieved.

Mrs. Clyde didn't want tea in the Savoy, however, because it didn't have "tea music," such as she was used to hearing on visits to Germany. He took her to the Regent Palace, in Piccadilly, which he remembered for its waltzes, and she enjoyed her tea very much. She nodded to the rhythm of the violins playing "The Blue Danube" and ordered a second round of sandwiches and pastries.

They laughed about the pastries they were eating, the Sikh in the club, my father's Sikh grandmother, and why he liked women with long hair, and about how she had such thick hair for her age that most acquaintances didn't believe it was natural until she had them pull it. It dawned on him then that she was just a joyous, outgoing creature, who enjoyed everything—enjoyed her food, enjoyed talking, enjoyed asking questions. He recalled that she had sat in on a couple of philosophy classes at Columbia. She had perhaps learned about the Socratic method there and concluded that it was a stimulating form of conversation. Now that he thought about it, if anyone else had talked about the Sikhs and Hindus the way she did, it might have sounded disrespectful or mean, but with her it was the insatiable curiosity of someone trying to learn new things. He himself was known for being curious about everything, and he could sympathize with her. Maybe everything in her life fell into the category of travelling to new places, having new experiences, having spirited adventures. He reacted the way he did because of something in him—something in the Indian tradition—that made the whole world a system of subservience and dominance, as if, no matter how high you reached, there were always those higher, whom you had to defer to, and defer to completely.

Probably her American friends were able to talk to her as equals, in a spirit of fun, but he would always be careful and worried in front of her, fearful of offending her. There was nothing he could do about it.

The waiter brought him the bill, and he paid it, feeling flush. He was in his London, living at the Savoy, having tea with oh-so-familiar music at a place he ordinarily couldn't afford to go to, and with plenty of money in Mrs. Clyde's bank.

My father and Mrs. Clyde got to Bombay almost a month before the population conference was to begin, so that she could see something of India, as she had planned. But on the way from the airport to the Taj Mahal Hotel, where my father had reserved rooms for them, she saw from the taxi a sight that never stopped haunting her: whole families living in abandoned sewer pipes in a swamp. She kept repeating in the taxi that she wished she'd stayed away from the "poverty, filth, tragedy, hell, heartbreak" that was India. When she reached her hotel room, she choked up with tears in the middle of a sentence and collapsed into a chair. "Those poor people living in sewer pipes!" she sobbed. "To what end? To what end? I don't know why they should be allowed to survive."

My father tried to console her, alternately sympathizing with her point of view and trying to put the poverty in some kind of understandable context for her. "The poverty here is terrible," he said. "But at the same time you should know that the sixteen-mile stretch from the airport to the hotel has some of the worst squalor in India. Not all India is like that."

"It's so hard to bear," Mrs. Clyde said. "I want to go home. I wish all the nations on earth would help to build a great big bomb to blow up this miserable world!"

She had often made this statement before. Still, he was shocked by it all over again, and tried, as he had previously, to tell her that life, with all its joys and sorrows, was better than extinction. But she kept on weeping and shaking her head, saying, "To what end? To what end?"

"Before you run away, we should go and see the beauty of the Moghul monuments, and the boat and mountain life of Kashmir, as we planned," my father said. "India is rich in scenic treasures and spiritual heritage. There is more to the country than what you've seen."

She wiped her eyes and started looking her cheerful self. "It would be wonderful to get out of this hell and see something else," she said.

He thanked his stars that Mrs. Clyde had come to India in October, one of the three or four best months, for a combination of Indian heat and Indian poverty might indeed have driven her back to the United States. They started making plans to leave Bombay after a day or two of rest, my father writing out an itinerary for her and explaining to her the geography of Kashmir, and of Old and New Delhi, where some of the Moghul monuments were situated.

She said she was getting hungry, and he reminded her that, from London, they had arranged to have Om come to lunch that day. Om, my older brother, was studying marine engineering in Bombay. She seemed eager to be finally meeting one of the members of my father's family.

When he saw that her mood had improved, he remarked that he didn't enjoy going anywhere without his wife, his "one and only," and that he was arranging to have my mother join them in Delhi and travel with them in India.

She made a face. He had half expected that she wouldn't cherish the idea. He had noticed that on the whole she did not get along with the women he had met when he was with her, but sought out the company of men, as if she considered women a bore and felt she could have serious discussions only with men. Perhaps women of her class at that time were not interested in serious things, he thought. Perhaps that was why she was drawn to unorthodox women like Margaret Sanger. Still, as a family man, he had always assumed that his wife was welcome wherever he was welcome. And didn't Mrs. Clyde accept the company of Kitty Martin as a matter of course? My father had even hoped that she might be curious about my mother and eager to meet her.

"How can you possibly pay for her?" she asked. "I thought you were a poor refugee."

"It's true that I can't afford to have her with me in Europe or America, but from what I'm earning from you now I can easily pay for her travels here. Anyway, two can live as cheaply as one in the hotels."

She made a face again but said nothing.

She's so literal-minded that she takes my being an impecunious refugee to mean that I am without any resources, he thought. He recalled that in London she had insisted on paying for a scarf he needed against the cold, saying he should save every penny of his salary or he would starve to death, like many of his countrymen. It is almost impossible to get her to understand that I'm capable of taking care of my needs, the needs of my family, he thought—that, having lived most of my life with a good salary, I cannot suddenly behave as if I were an indigent, with no confidence in the morrow, as if I had no earning power. At the same time, he didn't want to do or say anything to give her the false impression that he was not in any need, and so jeopardize whatever help she might be able to give him. He tried another tack. "The idea of a man going about with a lady who is not his wife will not be understood in India," he said. "A Hindu can travel with a woman at his side only if she is his wife."

She laughed, as if he were making a sociological joke. "Mehta, I'm old enough to be your mother. I'm an old lady and you're my doctor. What's so difficult for anyone to understand about that?"

"But this is India," he said. "My children, in-laws, and relations will certainly not be able to understand our situation."

She was silent.

He pressed home his advantage. "I have not seen my wife for almost a year, and she must be with me."

"But she can be with us only as long as we are in India," she said firmly.

Since his financial situation made the question of my mother's travelling with them abroad academic, he said nothing.

Om arrived for lunch, and spoke of being impressed that his father was staying at the Taj Mahal Hotel.

Mrs. Clyde laughed with pleasure. She seemed her old, ebullient self. They could have been in a luxury hotel anywhere in the world. The three of them went down to one of the hotel's many restaurants and had lunch together. She ordered Indian dishes, ate heartily, and asked Om a lot of questions. When she learned that his real interest was acting and singing, and he had been pushed into marine engineering, she was horrified.

"People have to subordinate their passions and inclinations to the necessity of earning a livelihood," my father said.

"At home, people do what they like and earn a good living," she said.

"But America is very rich. India is very poor," my father said.

"Well, then, Om should come to America," she said.

"But how?" my father said. "You know our resources."

She looked pained, as if she were upset that Om couldn't follow his dream, like an American.

"Also, the American immigration laws are very tough for us Indians," he said, to shift the discussion from something personal to something abstract. "Indians wait for years to go and work there."

She seemed to feel better, and they changed the subject.

We were in a cabin at an auto camp in West Palm Beach. "Your mother . . . Mrs. Clyde . . . and I arrived back in Bombay . . . a few days before the population conference," my father said haltingly. His voice grew fainter and fainter; he was obviously drifting off to sleep.

I lay very still. I should let him sleep, I thought. But our time is so limited. I have to know what Mamaji made of Mrs. Clyde, what Mrs. Clyde made of Mamaji, whether Mrs. Clyde saw anything about India besides its hellish poverty—whether she came to like India.

"But you haven't told me yet what you did in India the month between your two stays in Bombay."

"Sightseeing . . ." He was fast asleep.

In spite of several conversations in Florida about that month, my father never really succeeded in evoking it for me. Perhaps we didn't have enough time, but I now think it is more likely that for my father Mrs. Clyde in India had been a little too much to cope with. It was one thing for him to be "Mehta" and her attendant in New York and London, and even in Geneva and Cairo, where they had stopped on their way to India, for in those places he was nobody. It was quite another thing for him to be in that subservient position in India, where he was the head of the Mehta clan—the lord of his manor, as it were—and where he had a vast network of friends who admired and respected him, and where he had been master of a huge government department. I didn't get a full picture of what that month had been like until long after Florida, when, some months before Mrs. Clyde died, she allowed me to copy the pages of her diary concerning the time she spent with my father, and gave me permission to use them. (She kept a diary most of her life, but her executors, in accordance with her wishes, destroyed it.) Those pages have proved invaluable in reconstructing this narrative.

29 October
Maiden's Hotel, Old Delhi.
　　We took the 8:30 A.M. plane for Delhi, arriving at 12:30 P.M. Shanti, Mehta's attractive wife, dressed in Indian costume (they are Hindus), has joined us at Maiden's Hotel. His charming daughter Umi and her nice husband came to call on me in my suite, and I kept them to dine with us.

31 October
　　A wonderful day full of the beauty, charm, and horror of India. Mehta, Shanti, Umi, and I drove to Agra (4 hours) starting about 8:45 this morning. Part of what we passed looked as though we might be back in Bible days. We saw bullocks (white) in a field, walking up and down a ramp pulling water from a well in a bucket made of a water buffalo's hide. This was emptied into a narrow trough, which ran to where a man irrigated the field by throwing the water about from a broken water pitcher, the kind carried on the head. I photographed the ramp, etc.
　　We had a rest after a good luncheon at the hotel. Then we went to the Taj Mahal at sunset. Had another rest before a good dinner. Returned to see the Taj in the moonlight before starting the long drive back to New Delhi. Very few were at the Taj at the time. I was able to sing one note under the dome and had it taken up and elaborated, as if by an angel chorus. It is uncanny indeed, and only works well if the note is a high one. Mehta tried, and his note carried on up higher, higher, higher.

1 November
Nedou's Hotel, Srinagar, Kashmir.
　　We walked to Dal Lake and took a very comfortable ride in a sort of river taxi called a *shikara*. We reclined on a short mattress with a straight back at one end and were propelled by a paddle through a tangled mess of houseboats, *doongas,* and other craft, between appall-

ing banks covered with all manner of dwellings unfit for human habitation.

2 November

Unfortunately, I have what is called "hill diarrhea." I understand that the majority of those that come here are bothered with it. Am eating light. This is the best and only hotel—has practically no view. The toilets flush only spasmodically; there is very little light anywhere in the evening, due to insufficient current. It is cold at night and there is no heat in the outer dressing room or bathroom. When water runs out of the basin, it runs into an indentation on the floor under the tub, as does the tub water, and from there out through a drain! The towels one would prefer not to touch, and the beds are far from comfortable, with hard pillows! During the day, when the stoves are lit, they give off too much heat.

We took a drive this morning and I made a rough pencil sketch at the lake.

5 November

Maiden's Hotel, Old Delhi.

Am immensely enjoying the comparative luxury of this hotel after the one at Srinagar.

7 November

Imperial Hotel, New Delhi

Shanti had two teeth extracted this morning, and, to my surprise, was able to come to the dining room and eat luncheon with us.

11 November

This morning, I went to the People's House [Parliament] with Shanti and Mehta. An interesting experience. Nehru spoke, but the acoustics there are non-existent.

13 November

Hungry early. Had breakfast in my room. Thomas Cook's and shopping this morning. Wrote Ingles [a doctor who was taking care of Ben Marsh] a brief note.

After luncheon, we got our visas for Indonesia, and I saw the garden where Gandhi was killed when he went there to pray. The spot is marked by a simple stone on which is carved the date and "oh, Ram" in Hindu [*sic*]. That is what he said when he was shot—his last words. (Ram is the name of a god.) The people quietly came to this place and removed their shoes before approaching the stone. One prayed, another picked red blossoms from the hedge nearby, to sprinkle on the stone, as others had done. I saw no woman come, but a small boy came with a man. Such simplicity, respect, reverence, and, I think, affection. I believe it would have pleased and touched Gandhi.

Had made a beautiful dressing gown out of half a bedspread I bought this morning.

14 November

We went to an Indian movie for a while—simple, unsophisticated, and boring from American standards. The music here is so different that I am not able to appreciate or enjoy it. It seems to me to be about halfway between ours and the Chinese.

16 November

Early this morning, Mehta, Shanti, and I drove to Qutb Minar, the famous minaret Tower, one of the architectural wonders of India. It has been called the most perfect tower in the world. It has stood about a thousand years. Afterwards, we visited an Indian village. Mehta and I took a variety of photos, among them ones of "holy men" who were truly appalling.

Aside from Bombay and the trip to Agra, Mrs. Clyde went only to Delhi and Srinagar, but on the whole the Indian pages of the diary bear the stamp of a person who makes a business of being on perpetual vacation. Much space is devoted to straightening out reservations bungled by travel agents; getting visas; going out to airports, for which a lot of extra time is allowed, in case the car has a puncture or there are long lines at the ticket counters; settling into hotels; confirming air tickets for the next leg of the journey. At one point, she decides that she wants to travel home via Thailand, Fiji, and Australia. Reservations have to be applied for, waited for, checked. Some are not available. Then she hears that Bangkok is hot and humid and full of mosquitoes. She decides that she never wanted to go to Thailand anyway. Now a new itinerary is drawn up, via Rome, Geneva, and Nice, Bermuda and Florida. That, too, is revised, and the trips to Florida and Bermuda are put off until after a rest in New York. New reservations have to be made. And, whichever way she goes, there is always the question of hotel accommodations. Throughout, she observes and comments on the hotel service, the food, the beds, and what she sees on the street below.

From what my family members recall of her visit, her daily routine while travelling was fairly simple. When she wasn't doing watercolors, writing postcards, or shopping, she was taking snapshots of scenes such as porters standing at train stations and men on the roadside cleaning people's ears or performing cataract operations. She looked through American newspapers when they were available, and enjoyed following the adventures of comic-strip characters. She sometimes fell asleep during the day with the newspaper open in front of her, but she stayed awake at night—a night owl, she called herself. She had a friend or two in every port of call. Most of the friends were Americans involved in some kind of "humanitarian" work. She enjoyed surprising them. She hardly ever accepted hospitality from them—it was simpler for her to have them for a meal at her hotel. The talk at such meals was about other friends or about her guests' financial, medical, or family problems—very rarely about what was happening in the world. Letters were forwarded to her from other friends, concerning similar problems, and in response, as often as not, she sent a check, usually earmarked for a specific thing—new dentures or eyeglasses, say—because she liked to feel she was alleviating a particular need. She began confiding in my father and discussing with him the little, specific needs that her guests and other friends, consciously or unconsciously, brought up. He was careful not to curb by word or gesture any of her generous impulses.

One day, he told me, he drove Mrs. Clyde in his car, an old Vauxhall, to see the house he was building. The second story was being worked on at the time.

"How can you afford to build a house?" she asked. He admitted that he didn't have enough money at the moment to finish it, and she started scolding him for building a house in the first place. He explained to her that because of the way he had obtained the land from the government it was cheaper in the long run for him to build a house than to rent one, and that anyway without a roof over one's head in India one could very easily be sucked down into a vortex of poverty.

She then noticed a man who was camping out on the property to keep an eye on the construction, and my father told her he was the one servant the family still had in its employ.

"What extravagance!" she exclaimed. "A man in your position shouldn't waste any money on such luxuries."

"Here we do not have labor-saving devices like vacuum cleaners, dishwashers, and washing machines, or conveniences like hot running water, supermarkets, and good public transportation—all of which are taken for granted in American cities," he said. "For a man of my class, you might say that a servant, like this car we are sitting in, is almost a necessity."

"But you're a poor refugee."

He couldn't get her to see that, however poor he was, he still had ambitions for his children and family.

"I don't like being here at this house," she said. "Why did you bring me?"

He recalled then that expeditions she made with him to his club and his office, which he had thought would help her to picture his life before retirement, had made her equally impatient. It was almost as if she wanted him to be an orphan, without a family, without a former life, and without ambitions—to be completely dependent on her. He felt discouraged, and quickly drove her back to the hotel.

Later that day, however, when he mentioned the expense of my education, she seemed very sympathetic. He realized that she had to be able to understand a situation and take an emotional interest in it in order to respond to it—that her sympathy was more easily engaged for someone who was sick or handicapped, who had a particular problem that she thought could be solved with money, than for someone who, like him, was struggling to keep his head above water and to make something of his family.

Throughout her travels in India, Mrs. Clyde was careful to speak to my mother, who knew very little English, slowly and in simple sentences, and frequently complimented her on her small store of English words and phrases. At one point, she admired my mother's Kashmiri shawl and wanted to get one like it. My mother took her shawl off and presented it to Mrs. Clyde. At first, Mrs. Clyde resisted, but then she put it around her shoulders as if she meant to keep it as a souvenir of their friendship. Nevertheless, it was hard to imagine two women more different. My mother remembers that when Mrs. Clyde saw her knitting, sewing, or embroidering in the sitting room of a hotel suite she would ask how she had the patience for such things. When she saw my mother eating pickled chilies in the restaurant, she wanted to know how she could bear to eat such hot food. But her questions were rhetorical. My mother, for her part, found Mrs. Clyde and her ways completely mystifying. Except for her cane, she seemed never to have anything in her hands—no knitting or sewing needle, no embroidery frame. She was supposed to be rich, but she wore costume jewelry, like a poor woman, and, what was worse, it *looked* like costume jewelry. She had creases in her aged face, but she seemed to wander around the world as if she were young. She lounged in the sitting room, not only with her head uncovered in front of the menfolk but also while she coiled strands of her hair around small cylinders—the like of which my mother had never seen—until her whole head of hair was bunched up tightly around her scalp. Then, when she removed the cylinders, she had little curls all over her head, like a schoolgirl. She talked to my father as an equal—as if she were another man—and she talked and talked and talked, seemingly without taking a breath, as if she never stopped to think.

When my mother aired some of her bewilderment to my father, he tried to explain to her that women in the West tended to be more interested in intellectual pursuits than in domestic ones, and did not attach the same importance to gold and silks that women in the East did; that the fairer skin of Westerners tended to wrinkle more, and Mrs. Clyde was, after all, seventy-three; that women in the West, instead of covering their heads, took pride in showing off their hair to men. But he had to acknowledge that when it came to talking he had met few people—women or men—who were Mrs. Clyde's equal.

Between meals and after meals on that Christmas trip in Florida, in the car and in hotels, whenever my father and I could snatch time for a conversation, he continued the remarkable story of himself and

Mrs. Clyde. They returned to Bombay and the Taj Mahal Hotel a few days before the opening of the population conference, on November 24th. My mother was with them, and before they had even settled into the hotel my sister Nimi arrived, covered with soot, having come straight from her job and endured a thirty-hour train journey from Jamshedpur. "The more the merrier," Mrs. Clyde said to my father, as if she felt that with just my mother and my father there she was a third party but with more members of the family around them she could be part of a whole, large Indian family. She greeted Nimi with genuine warmth. Informal, as always, she suggested that Nimi shouldn't stand on ceremony but feel free to unpack and wash up.

When Nimi went off to her room, my father told Mrs. Clyde that he and my mother had just heard through the family grapevine of a boy in the military who was looking for a wife and who happened to be in Bombay just then. "It's very auspicious that we should all be in Bombay at the same time," he said to Mrs. Clyde. "Who knows? I might be able to arrange for her marriage, and so shed one more responsibility from my shoulders."

"What do you have to do with her marriage?"

"This is India. As parents, we are responsible. In fact, we'd better hurry up. She's almost twenty-five."

"Why, I got married when I was twenty-eight, and I've known women in America who got married when they were forty!"

"Our first daughter, Pom, and our third daughter, Umi, were married by the time they were twenty. That's the usual age for girls from good families here to marry. And Umi has been married for three years now, though Nimi, as an older sister, should have married first. She's already at a great social disadvantage."

"But you told me that she has an M.A. and is self-supporting. Why does she need to get married at all?"

"It's true that she has a job as a social worker, but it is no future—no housing, no benefits. Even as it is, she wouldn't be able to do it without some help from us. This is not America, where women are part of the work force. The Western tradition of single women making their way independently in the world is unknown here. A girl who isn't married remains a lifelong liability to her parents."

"Well, she looks to me to be a perfectly bright, healthy young woman. Why should you have any trouble finding her a husband?"

"I'm no longer in the swim of things. My retirement and my travelling make it hard for me to come to know of boys in the market. And then the boys here nowadays demand big dowries. As refugees, we can't offer much."

Mrs. Clyde listened to him, incredulous. Despite his repeated explanations, she couldn't be made to see why any girl in India first consented to get married, then succeeded in finding a partner, and then went on to contribute so prodigiously to the population growth. She wanted him to denounce the custom at the population conference and launch a campaign to dissuade Indian girls from ever agreeing to an arranged marriage. "Can you think of a better way to control population growth?" she asked.

It took him some time to get her to see that Indian girls and their parents were so deeply conditioned to the custom that the kind of campaign she had in mind would be futile. "Girls are such a burden in our society, and people are so poor, that they marry their daughters off as young as possible," he said. "That's how it is that many women in our country produce children through all their childbearing years."

"Does Nimi know about this military officer?" Mrs. Clyde asked abruptly.

"Yes, we've informed her, but she doesn't take it seriously. That's another problem Shanti and I have."

"Let's invite him to tea here. I would like to have a look at him and see for myself how this whole business works—or doesn't work." She laughed her rich, childlike laugh.

My father arranged for the military officer to come to tea at the Sea Lounge, one of the hotel restaurants, that very afternoon.

At tea, it was quite clear from a few hints the officer let drop that he was looking for an Army wife—one who would fit into the life style of an Army officer. That meant getting along with the wives of his brother officers as part of an official family and living away from him for months at a time, looking after his home and the schooling of his children, while he roughed it in the barracks on the frontiers. What he was looking for was a woman who was as socially graceful as a convent-school-educated girl, which Nimi was, but as self-sacrificing and resigned as a Hindu widow, which Nimi was not.

Although custom dictated that Nimi sit demurely and look pretty and malleable, she took an active part in the conversation, and even made fun of the military officer for his contradictory expectations. "You want a modern, educated girl to take to functions and parties, but you don't want her to be intelligent. That combination is impossible to find."

My mother tried to turn the conversation to the delicious things they were eating, but Nimi, abetted by Mrs. Clyde, pressed on. She didn't see why she should sacrifice her career for him, she said, but perhaps he was prepared to come and live with her among the laborers in the steel plant.

They started discussing Nimi's job, and Mrs. Clyde said that she'd always preferred the Russian economic system to that of the United States, and that what she'd seen in India only confirmed her in her opinion.

After tea, my father escorted the officer downstairs to a taxi. "Are your daughter and the American lady Communists?" the officer asked.

"I don't know about Mrs. Clyde," my father said, "but my daughter is no Communist—she's just a fiery young woman."

When my father returned to the Sea Lounge, my mother, Nimi, and Mrs. Clyde were still discussing the officer.

"He was as stiff as a board, and very conservative," Nimi was saying. "I don't think he'd ever heard of modern, independent women. He's the last person I would ever marry."

Mrs. Clyde laughed and laughed at her outspoken reaction, and said, "You're a girl after my own heart." It seemed that the more outrageous and rebellious someone was, the more Mrs. Clyde liked that person.

My mother quietly remarked that she thought the officer was very handsome, and suitable in every way. He was of the right caste and subcaste, very well positioned to rise in the ranks of the military.

"There's no use building him up," my father said. "I don't think we'll ever hear from him again."

But they did hear from him, for he followed up his visit with a formal proposal. Nimi turned him down flat. My father didn't try to talk her out of it, because inwardly he shared her opinion of the young man. All the same, he worried about the responsibility of marrying her off. He was, however, consoled by Mrs. Clyde's praise of Nimi's stand: it was all part of her increasing emotional involvement with the family.

Most of the time in Bombay, my father, my mother, Nimi, Om, and Mrs. Clyde went around like a happy family. My father sometimes felt that he was looking after his widowed mother, just as he had actually done for thirty-three years. At a special table my father had secured in one of the Taj Mahal's restaurants, they ate, laughed, and talked about Mrs. Clyde's Indian experiences. Everything about the strange country and its strange customs and attitudes—the condition of the poor, the position of servants, the caste system, the antagonism between Muslims and Hindus, the effects of the Partition—had to be repeatedly explained to her. Whatever her questions, whatever their answers, she always ended up laughing, as if she had never known adversity, as if she asked questions for the sake of asking them. Her laughter touched off laughter in the others. It seemed that the whole point of talking was to try to bring everyone around to her benign point of view—to what she called her "philosophy." She would often finish a discussion with one of her verses from "Horse Sense":

Forgiveness! What nonsense! There's nothing to forgive.
Our thoughts and actions are not free one moment while we live.
Heredity, environment, experience, these three
Give all the freedom that there is on earth for you and me—
Freedom from responsibility

Or

What is sin? Now at last 'tis known
That what man does he *must*.
Heredity, environment, experience—then dust.

Then Mrs. Watumull, Margaret Sanger, and Georgea Furst arrived for the conference, and my father had to divide his attention between them and Mrs. Clyde. Mrs. Watumull did not like her room. My father, who had made friends with the manager, got him to change it. Mrs. Sanger had had two heart episodes on her way to the conference and needed some medicine, and he got it for her. She also needed some of her notes typed, and he found her a competent Goan typist. (People from Goa, perhaps the most Westernized part of India, tended to have an excellent grasp of English.) Miss Furst didn't know that there was a total prohibition in Bombay, and asked for a drink. My father took her on a wild search through the offices and bazaars, in an attempt first to get her a drinking permit that foreigners were entitled to and, when that failed, to get her an unadulterated bottle of gin from a bootlegger.

Finally, the conference started. They all attended the sessions and listened to the reports of delegates from various parts of the world, but Mrs. Clyde was visibly bored. It was soon evident that she was not interested in speeches or in the fine points of population control. The conference was just an occasion to travel and to support the cause of a friend. Still, she did like to be in the middle of whatever was going on.

At one point, Mrs. Watumull was having tea with Mrs. Clyde and my father at the Sea Lounge after a conference session, and she happened to mention his prize-winning population essay.

"I think you told me about your population essay, but I have never read it," Mrs. Clyde said. "I want to see it." She added, "Now is the accepted time."

My father didn't have a copy of the essay in Bombay, but Mrs. Watumull did, and she fetched it.

Mrs. Clyde closeted herself in her room for an hour, then emerged with the essay, saying, "It's wonderful. I have a brain wave." "Brain wave," my father had realized, was her term for a dramatic inspiration, and he prepared himself for anything—anything at all. She went on, "I must have a copy of this essay in the hands of every conference delegate by tomorrow morning."

"Now, now, now," my father said. "That is out of the question. It's almost seven o'clock now."

"There has to be a way," she said. "In this big city, there's bound to be a printer who will help us out."

Once she'd had a brain wave, there was no stopping her. The only idea he could come up with was to take her and the essay to the newspaper offices of the *Times* of India. A man in charge informed them that the printing section was closed, and said they should come back the next day. She was disappointed, but the mere act of having gone there made her feel that the project was under way.

In the morning, my father was tied up with the conference, but Nimi returned to the *Times* with Mrs. Clyde. The manager of the printing section told them he couldn't do the job in a hurry, and directed them to the printing shop of the Commercial Printing Press. It undertook the job.

Back at the hotel, when my father heard the price Mrs. Clyde was paying—a hundred and sixty-six rupees—he said he thought it was exorbitant.

"What is thirty-five dollars?" Mrs. Clyde said. "In America, it would be ten times that."

He guiltily remembered a poor tonga wallah in Srinagar who had taken them from the airport to the hotel and, seeing that one of the passengers was a foreigner, had demanded two rupees. My father had given him a rupee and eight annas, the customary fare, and dismissed the tonga wallah's grumbling as disappointment at not being able to take advantage of a foreigner. But now he felt sorry for the fellow. The extra eight annas would have bought him an evening meal, while it could have meant nothing to Mrs. Clyde. He decided that in future he would be more generous with the money in "the bank," and not try to pinch and save as if it were his own.

The pamphlets arrived the following morning, beautifully printed. My father and mother, Nimi, Mrs. Clyde, and Miss Furst carried the bundles down to the conference, and Mrs. Watumull had them distributed. Mrs. Clyde was very happy. She felt she had made a valuable contribution to the conference, and was confirmed in this opinion when delegates started lining up to get my father's autograph.

On leaving Bombay, my father and Mrs. Clyde went to Rome, Geneva, and Paris, and then back to London and the Savoy. There he redoubled his efforts to find something else to do, for Mrs. Clyde had paid him his salary and he had some foreign exchange to help get him established. He still had it in mind to move the family to London. Indeed, in New Delhi he had got his friend the British High Commissioner to stamp the passport of each member of the family "For Immigration to England." His Indian medical degree was registered with the British General Medical Council, and its number, 969424, was almost as familiar to him as his telephone number or his club-membership numbers. He now scanned the *British Medical Journal* for advertisements of medical practices for sale and studied the real-estate pages of newspapers. Practices in areas of London like Earl's Court, Islington, and Notting Hill Gate were selling for between twenty-five hundred and three thousand pounds, and houses in those areas for about the same amount. He would require additional money to get himself established, but he thought that by selling everything in

India and with some borrowing he should be able to manage. He went to Lloyd's Bank in Pall Mall to explore the possibility of getting a loan. The manager assured him that that would not be a problem. He bought a gray coat, a blue suit, black shoes, a new felt hat, and a new umbrella, and walked the familiar London streets in his new clothes, imagining what it would be like to be a London doctor, with my mother perhaps serving as his receptionist and nurse.

A friend introduced him to an Indian doctor who was looking for an assistant. The Indian doctor at once offered him the job, but the doctor's clinic was forty miles outside London and he wanted my father to begin immediately. My father told the doctor that he wasn't a young bachelor who could just get a room somewhere and start working—he needed time to get Mrs. Clyde back to New York and to go home to Delhi and wind things up there. He had no opportunity to explore other opportunities. After three days in London, he and Mrs. Clyde were on a plane bound for New York.

In New York, Mrs. Clyde wanted him to stay on with her as her guest through Christmas and the New Year. She wanted to do some travelling around the country—to see her brother and sister in Washington, to "motor" down to Florida to see how Ben Marsh was doing. My father asked her if he could fly to California and spend Christmas with me. She reminded him of her brain wave of inviting me to Florida. He wanted to revise the plan. He longed to spend some time alone with me, and help me to sort out my college experiences. He wanted to have a "holiday" from her, because he was feeling the strain of her constant company and the subordination of his will to hers. He was eager to get back to London and set things in motion there. Above all, he wanted to reclaim his independence, to be his own man. He felt he had spent a lifetime pleasing bosses. But he agreed to her proposal, and arranged to move into her guest room while he was in New York, because it turned out that she had no one else to spend the Christmas holidays with. She said she had to see Ben Marsh, who was so sick he might not survive into the New Year, and she said she would be grateful for my father's company. He felt that to say no to her under such circumstances would be letting her down, for he had begun to feel that he wasn't worth what she was paying him, that his medical training was almost irrelevant to his job with her. To compensate, he tried to do more and more for her, but the more he did, the less deserving he felt. It simply increased his sense of indebtedness. He consoled himself with the thought that by my spending Christmas with her in Florida he and I could see each other without his having to spend any money. More important, her meeting me might spark an emotional interest on her part in my education, and eventually lead to some kind of financial help, which would be a great load off his shoulders.

"What did you do after the weekend at Old Fields?" I asked my father in the course of that holiday in Florida. Eager though I had been before the Christmas break to discuss my college problems with him, when it came down to it I was unable to talk about them with him at all. Instead, I kept asking questions about Mrs. Clyde.

"We started out for Florida by way of Washington, and there we paid another visit to Mrs. Clyde's brother, Will."

"What does he do?"

"He doesn't do anything. When he was young, he used to dabble in horse racing and stocks and bonds, I believe. He just lives with Mrs. Hinshaw, his sister, and nurses, in the Mayflower Hotel. Mrs. Clyde had seven brothers and sisters, and he and Mrs. Hinshaw are the only ones still living."

"Are they like Mrs. Clyde?"

"Not at all. Mr. Clyde and Mrs. Hinshaw scarcely ever leave the hotel suite. I don't think that Mr. Clyde even gets dressed; he just stays in his dressing gown all day long. He has fibrillation of the heart, and is afraid of having a heart attack and dying. He doesn't have much energy, and Mrs. Hinshaw doesn't seem to be all there, although neither one of them is much older than Mrs. Clyde."

"Is Mrs. Clyde very close to them?"

"No, I don't think so. Before we went to see them, she noted down the points she wanted to cover. She hardly stayed with them twenty minutes, and after we left she asked me, 'Did I cover all the points?' "

The rich: in the houses we had visited during the summer to try to get scholarship money for me, and on the train that took me to Florida to meet Mrs. Clyde, I had kept wondering, What are they really like? At eighteen, I had a voyeur's interest in almost everything, and I pressed my father, asking, "How were they with one another?"

"I think Mr. Clyde was glad to see Mrs. Clyde, but he was equally glad to see her go. He drinks like a fish—Martinis, mostly—and he knows she disapproves of anybody who drinks or smokes. Mrs. Hinshaw doesn't approve of his drinking, either, and she has a very harsh, cracked voice. The atmosphere in the suite was far from peaceful."

I couldn't imagine that brothers and sisters would behave like that to one another, and I said something about their being very different from us.

"People like us, who don't have money, have romantic longings about it," my father said. "We say that if we had it we would do this and we would do that. But money can be a terrible thing, too. It can lead to drink and divorce and God knows what else. Look at us, father and son. In our society, children are considered continued growth of the parent. We are one and the same in spirit. That's how close we are. But I don't think Mrs. Clyde is very close to her sons, Tom and Bill. She doesn't see them much, and when she does, it's only for a meal or a drive."

Guessing that another long train journey would be hard for me to endure and that I needed to get back to college to study, Mrs. Clyde wanted me to return to Los Angeles by plane. But we couldn't get a reservation on any flight from Jacksonville to Los Angeles, so I ended up taking a train to New Orleans and a plane from there to Los Angeles. I was back at college by the beginning of the New Year.

It seemed that, for days after I left, Mrs. Clyde asked questions about me: How could my father possibly have allowed me to come alone to this country at such an early age? What would happen to me if I got sick? Who would pay the hospital bills? Who would look after me? How did he think I could possibly manage to keep up with my studies and compete with people who had eyes? What use would my studies be to me for earning a living? What would I do for my summer vacations? How could he possibly hope to pay for it all? When the questions were about my habits of work, she would be satisfied with his answers only until she could think up a new problem and a new question. When they were about finances, she couldn't be satisfied with his answers at all.

"What will happen if you should die?" she asked. "Who will take care of Ved? Where will he get the money even to fly home?"

"I'm not going to die."

"How can you say that? How can anyone say that? Look at Ben Marsh."

When she returned to Winter Park after leaving me in Jacksonville, she discovered that he had died just a few hours before. Although Mrs. Clyde had known for some time that he was on his deathbed, she burst into tears, and for many days afterward she would suddenly start to cry, thinking about him, and she did so then.

My father comforted her as best he could. "One has to look at the bright side of things. If I had thought negatively, I could not have raised a family at all."

"What's the bright side of having a blind child in college you can't pay for?"

"Something will turn up. It always does. Just a few years ago, who would have thought that we would have a roof over our heads again, and in New Delhi, or that I would get the bank job, or meet you and be on my feet again, so to speak?"

"But you could die tomorrow."

"I wouldn't enjoy living if I worried about dying all the time."

So the argument went on. Back in New York, my father made arrangements to sail for England on the S.S. United States and spend some time looking more deeply into the possibility of moving to London. The evening before he was to leave, as he was busy packing in Mrs. Clyde's guest room, she asked him to come into the living room for a "business talk."

When he entered the living room, he saw that she had spread all around her her diary, her checkbook, and an assortment of papers. As soon as he sat down, she picked up the legal pad that she usually had near her, and said, "I've had a brain wave. I'd like to make a contribution to Ved's education. Do you know of a nonprofit organization for the blind through which I could do it?"

He was thrilled, but also puzzled. The term "nonprofit organization" was unfamiliar to him, but as they talked he came to understand that she would make a contribution if she could get a tax deduction for it, and the only contributions that were tax-deductible were those made to nonprofit or charitable organizations. He mentioned the American Foundation for the Blind, with which I'd had some dealings.

She placed a call to Dwight Rogers, her lawyer and investment counsellor, and had a long conversation with him, then turned back to my father. "Dwight is going to look into it, and he'll have an answer for us by tomorrow," she said. "Now I want to turn to another matter. You know you are very valuable to me as my companion physician." The phrase, though less grand than "court physician," sounded more friendly to his ears. She said that it was too bad he lived so far away; she wished he could be in America all year round.

He said that if wishes were horses beggars would ride, but that, of course, he had a big family and a lot of family obligations in India. She said she was a little frightened about not having some kind of companion for her old age.

He brought up the name of her decorator friend Elizabeth Osteyee, who sometimes came and stayed with her. Mrs. Osteyee's sons were grown up, and she might be free to live with Mrs. Clyde all year round.

"You know, Mehta," she said, "I don't enjoy the company of women very much." Also, she said, she didn't want to make a permanent arrangement with anybody—she could die the next day, and then her estate would be encumbered.

It didn't seem to him a very convincing argument, but then he knew nothing about estates and American law.

"Besides," she said. "I don't want any one person to be living here all the time. I like variety."

As she talked, it became clear to him that she wanted a loose arrangement with him for a good portion of the year. He very diplomatically told her that that would be impossible for him, because he still hoped to practice medicine in London. In truth, he had come to realize that three or four months on the job with her was the most he could ever spend and still keep his mental equanimity. He could tell from her face that she was unhappy. She started looking through her papers, as if their conversation were over. But then she found a piece of paper on which she had jotted down some points, much as she had when she went to see her brother and sister in Washington.

"What about your coming back in June and travelling with me for two or three months?" she said. "I'm sure you'd be happy to get out of that terrible Indian heat."

"Indian heat is something really terrible," he said, recalling that in the British days he and the whole family had escaped as a matter of course to a cool hill station for the summer. But now he couldn't afford to go to a hill station, and the Indian heat took such a toll of his health that he often worried about its shortening his life. Coming out in June would be a godsend, in more ways than one.

"You know, Mehta, every summer I get hay fever. This summer, I'd like to try out the Swiss Alps and the spas and baths in Germany to see if they help in keeping it under control. Maybe going to Bermuda or Hawaii would help. You could accompany me as my companion physician, on our usual terms."

"Whatever you say goes with me," he found himself saying. "But what about my wife, my one and only?"

"What about her?"

"She doesn't like being left alone."

"I thought you said she was looking after the education of your younger children and keeping your home going."

That was true. Someone had to stay at home to look after things. "But she says at our age we should live together."

"How can you? I thought you needed to save money. How can you pay for an air ticket for her, and pay for her hotels in Europe?"

He thought of saying, "Two can live almost as cheaply as one," but then he realized that that was not true in the West. Of course, Mrs. Clyde, as a rich woman, could have invited him and his wife, and if he had been an American doctor he might have insisted that his wife travel with them. But an American doctor would have had some reserves at his back. He would have negotiated from a position of strength. My father had no reserves, nothing at his back, and so he didn't feel he was in a position to insist. He was beginning to realize that his friendship with Mrs. Clyde was of such a nature now that if she said she needed him he could not say no, any more than a practicing doctor can refuse to treat a patient—even a hypochondriac—who comes to him for help. After all, she was just arranging to pay for some of my education. (Years later, when I learned about this conversation from my father, I was horrified at the connection between her offering to give me help and her asking him to work for her. But my father reassured me, saying that if I'd been a witness to the conversation I would have realized that she had already decided to contribute toward my education and was treating the two matters as separate issues— that it was not in her character to make one arrangement dependent on the other.)

"If you agree, I can write a check right now for your return ticket to New York," she was saying. "Now is the accepted time."

"Whatever you say goes with me," he said. As it happened, after a great deal of struggle he had landed himself two lecture assignments. One, with the Associated Clubs of Topeka, Kansas, was a lecture tour of its "knife-and-fork clubs" all over the country from mid-October to mid-November, and the other, with the University of Minnesota concert-and-lecture service, was for a series of lectures from early January to early February of 1954. He had been hesitating about accepting these engagements, not because they would involve a frantic schedule of travel in small planes and buses but because most of the fee of fifty or sixty dollars a lecture would be swallowed up by the airfare from New Delhi to America and back, and he would have no place to stay, nothing to do, between the two lecture tours. He now discussed the whole subject with Mrs. Clyde. She decided that the minimum time he should work for her abroad was three months, and told him that he could stay with her as a guest whenever he was at loose ends in America. Now his airfare to America would be paid, and his board and lodging between the lecture tours would be taken care of. He would be able to save much of the lecture money. It would mean perhaps postponing the London-practice idea. But it was a bird in the hand.

"I may often go to Europe," she was saying. "But I don't want to make any commitments for more than a year, because who knows? I could die tomorrow. And how would my executors know what my arrangements were? Anybody could come and make any claim. I don't want to burden them."

"That suits me very well," he said. "I want to remain a free agent."

She picked up her checkbook to write him a check for an air ticket, but he told her that he could not accept a check from her, because no Indian was allowed to keep dollars in India. It was settled that in the spring she would cable him an open return ticket. She would arrive in Geneva on June 24th, and he would arrange to arrive a day or so earlier, so that he could receive her at the airport.

On the day my father was to sail for Southampton on his way back home, the telephone rang in my room at college. Instead of just my father calling to say goodbye, as I had expected, both he and Mrs.

Clyde were on the phone from New York. My father said in an excited voice that Mrs. Clyde had something to read to me.

"Yes," Mrs. Clyde said. "Your father and I and the lawyers and nice Mr. Barnett, of the American Foundation for the Blind, have been busy working on a letter that will be going out tomorrow. The letter is about you, and I thought you'd like to know what it says." She read the following letter in its entirety:

Old Fields
Huntington, Long Island
New York
January 15, 1953

American Foundation for the Blind, Inc.
15 West 16th Street
New York 11, New York

Att: Mr. Robert Barnett

Gentlemen:

I have today asked

City Bank Farmers Trust Co.
640 Fifth Avenue
New York, New York
Att: Mr. John Press

to segregate from my account and hold subject to your orders 80 shares of Montgomery Ward common stock. This is a gift to the American Foundation for the Blind which I hope you will use to assist blind students from India to obtain an American college education.

In using these funds I would be glad if you would help Ved Mehta finish his college education. He is a freshman at Pomona College, Claremont, California, where he is making a brilliant record. He is in great need of financial assistance to that end.

I would suggest that no beneficiary of this fund be given more than $1,500 a year in semi-annual installments. It would be perfectly satisfactory to me if you take no responsibility for disbursing the funds beyond making payments to the Dean of any college where such a student is in residence, considering it compatible with your ideas on this subject, that a receipt from the Dean should be a completely satisfactory accounting for the disbursement of the funds.

With many thanks.

Sincerely,
MRS. ETHEL CLYDE

I no longer remember what words of thanks I stumbled through, but I do have a clear impression that she didn't invite thanks in any way. She almost brushed them aside, as if the act of doing something for others were sufficient thanks in itself.

Originally appeared, under the heading "Personal History," as "The Benefactress" in The New Yorker, *May 9, 1988. Reprinted in "The Stolen Light," W. W. Norton & Company, New York, and Collins, London, 1989.*

EIGHT

In the Force and Road of Casualty

While I was an undergraduate at Oxford, most of my friends and I felt that we were living through some of our happiest years. One reason for this feeling no doubt had to do with the nature of Oxford itself. It was small and intimate, and yet very worldly. Practically every scholar or man of letters we studied, it seemed, had gone to Oxford or Cambridge. It had a mystique: even its spires were said to be "dreaming." Another reason had to do with our youth. However confident a persona each of us put on, our inner lives were full of *Sturm und Drang*. We craved certitude and order, and Oxford gave us both. All those of us reading in a particular school (a subject or combination of subjects) studied the same prescribed texts, often the same books. (I remember that some of my friends found their fathers' notes helpful, if their fathers had read the same subject.) Furthermore, it seemed that some of the best minds in Britain and the world beyond had been gathered at Oxford and Cambridge by a process akin to natural selection. Everybody had survived one open competition after another from childhood on. Indeed, there was a hierarchy among British schools, which competed for places and scholarships at Oxford and Cambridge, and a hierarchy among Oxford and Cambridge colleges, which, in their turn, competed for the best schoolboys, and the boys were awarded scholarships according to their performance on the entrance examinations. There was a similar hierarchy among undergraduates, who competed for the best degrees. (It was understood that one who got a First became a scholar or went into the Civil Service or the Foreign Office; one who got a Second went into a profession or became a writer or a journalist; one who got a Third settled for business or one of the other greasy trades.)

As we grew older, we discovered, of course, that many of these supposed certainties did not always hold true even in England, to say nothing of the larger world. Moreover, there was a definite closing in of options for clever men, and one could sense a creeping gloom among top undergraduates as they approached the end of their Oxford years; it sometimes made them reactionary in politics and out of sympathy with the mass culture that was taking shape around them. (Now that the mass culture has arrived, some people at Oxford speak of it as the New Dark Age.) They felt that they were misfits in their own country and culture. Many of them settled for an academic career, doing so not because they were natural teachers or because they felt there were certain books that had to be written but because there was nothing better to do out there. In contrast, like many good students from America, I had come to Oxford in the hope of perhaps becoming an academic, but I was beginning to doubt my abilities. I felt I could never be as good as, say, the Greats men (those who work toward a degree in ancient Greek and Latin literature, ancient history, and ancient and modern philosophy), because I had long since missed the bus for learning the ancient languages thoroughly. Nor could I comfort myself with the thought that I was as knowledgeable about Indian culture as they were about Judeo-Christian culture. I did not, for example, know Sanskrit. Almost all my education had been in the West. If I ended up living in the West, I felt, I would always be a second-class citizen. At the time, in my heart of hearts I wished that I had been born an Englishman and that I had all the intellectual equipment, with the accompanying symbols of privilege and power, of the best of the English.

Yet in later life I could never forget the fact that some of the best undergraduates I knew came to have troubled lives. I am thinking here especially of three of my friends: Roger Scott, who came up in my year as a scholar to New College to read Greats; Alasdair Clayre, who came up, also in my year, as a scholar to Christ Church to read P.P.E. (Philosophy, Politics, and Economics); and my Balliol friend Richard Snedden, a scholar two years ahead of me, who was also reading P.P.E. They had all been scholars at Winchester College, which in my day was spoken of, together with Eton, as the best public school in Britain. There were then some five hundred boys at Winchester, of whom about seventy were scholars—the academic crème de la crème—and lived in what was known as College, an austere, monastic six-hundred-year-old building.

I once asked Maurice Keen what Roger, Alasdair, and Richard had been like in school. Maurice had been at Winchester with them, but he was a bit older than they were and had come up to Oxford to read Modern History a couple of years before I did. (A star pupil of the distinguished medieval historian R. W. Southern, he later succeeded him as Fellow and Tutor of Medieval History at Balliol, our Oxford college.) He was a friend of all of us.

"Roger, Alasdair, and Richard were all head boys," Maurice told me. He went on to explain that a head boy was always a scholar in his last year of school, chosen by the headmaster in consultation with the second master. Such a boy was supposed to represent the highest values of the school—indeed, of public-school education generally. He had to be an all-round golden boy—not only have academic abilities of the highest order and be good at sports but also enjoy the esteem of both the staff and the other boys. In addition, seniority could play a part. If someone sufficiently qualified stayed on for an extra year—generally boys were at Winchester for five years—he would be preferred as head boy to someone a year below him, however "golden" the younger aspirant.

"Were you a head boy? Could Jasper have been one at his school?" (A close friend, Jasper Griffin, was a star Greats man.)

"No. Neither of us is any good at sports."

I asked him how Roger, Alasdair, and Richard had all managed to become head boy.

"They were a year below me, and theirs was, by any standard, a golden year. I left after five years, but, as it happened, one of my contemporaries, Leo Aylen, stayed on for a sixth year and was head boy for all of it. If he had not stayed on, Roger and Alasdair—but not

Richard—would, by all contemporary reckoning, have been strong contenders for the office. Anyway, both of them decided to stay into a sixth year, I suspect partly because each quite fancied the head-boy entry on his curriculum vitae. Roger became head boy for that Autumn Term, then left school. Alasdair succeeded him for the Spring Term, then left. Richard had also stayed on for the sixth year, less surprisingly, because he had come into the school unusually young—at twelve and a half. He decided to stay the whole year, and therefore was next in line for the office when Alasdair left, and so became head boy for the Summer Term—no doubt keeping out of office the most golden of the next year down, whoever that may have been. After Winchester, Roger and Alasdair went on to spend two years doing their National Service before coming up to Oxford—just as I had done—while Richard came straight up from school."

At Oxford, Roger, Alasdair, and Richard all seemed to be destined for great things. Yet the later lives of all of them were sad. I was left wondering whether the turns in the fate of all three were a coincidence or were in some way a consequence of their fast-lane education. It certainly seemed to me that their almost overbred intelligence could have developed only in the milieu of a British public school and the Oxford and Cambridge of the day. (Even people who had stable afterlives, in a way my friends did not, seemed to have been oddly affected by their school experience. One Balliol friend was so shy that during a conversation he would actually try to climb the wall—hoisting himself up onto a mantelpiece or the top of a bookcase and perching there like a frightened bird. He did other odd things, too, like walking up to a piano in a room full of people, striking one key, and then looking around to see what effect the "ping" had had on people. He had come up to Balliol just after he turned eighteen, and it seemed that his mind had been forced far ahead of the rest of him.) Nevertheless, they mastered their shortcomings sufficiently to become distinguished scholars, even if they never managed to—and, it may be, never wanted to—overcome a certain unworldly, eccentric attitude toward life.

Of the three, Roger was perhaps the handsomest and had the most dignified bearing. The legend of his school glory had preceded him to Oxford, and when he arrived he was taken up by several prominent

Winchester dons, like John Sparrow, the Warden of All Souls. However, they soon realized that he was not what they had thought he would be. He was oversensitive, fragile, and ruthlessly honest, and he seemed to be in constant spiritual turmoil. Perhaps because I had come from America, at Oxford these very qualities drew me to him, but some of the high-powered Winchester, or Wykehamist, dons saw them as a social handicap, and dropped him. He took their rejection of him very hard, and he left Oxford after a year or so, in the middle of his studies. I remember thinking at the time that talented people everywhere have difficulty, and perhaps take longer than ordinary people to make their way in the world.

Hardly anyone saw Roger after his departure. In 1970, he published a novel called "Downfall."

Alasdair was an especially close friend of mine at Oxford, but I didn't see much of him after I came down. One of my vivid early memories of him is from an evening at the Royal Opera House, in Covent Garden. The father of Rose Donaldson, one of my readers, had just become a director of Covent Garden. Rose, a jolly, well-connected young woman, had the opportunity to take a couple of friends to a production of "Boris Godunov" and had invited me to go. As bidden, I dressed in my dinner jacket and met her at the Oxford railway station. I was enormously delighted to find that her other guest was Alasdair, a man who would have stood out in any company. He had fine, well-defined cheekbones, dark hair and eyebrows, and, always, a lively, interested expression. He made the air sparkle with his conversation.

Alasdair entertained us all the way to London, talking about operas he had seen and singing snatches from them; the other passengers in the compartment fell as much under the spell of his gaiety as we did. At one point, he launched into "Boris Godunov," singing the part now of the scheming monk, now of the distraught czar, now of the chorus of peasants, and also singing the ringing of church bells. Sometimes his imitations fell flat, but he pressed on, totally unselfconscious. He had a lovely lilt to his voice.

At Covent Garden, we were seated in the Royal Box; Rose explained that this was one of the perquisites of a director when royalty was not present. The box was a spacious room with heavy curtains on the stage side. When we arrived, they were closed. Here Rose's parents, John and Frances Donaldson, presided over a dazzling party, which included Sir Isaiah Berlin and several people I didn't know—a merchant banker and his wife, and another couple, who, it seemed, had an estate near that of the Donaldsons. I was so intimidated by the company that I could scarcely find my tongue. Alasdair, however, went right up to Sir Isaiah and started talking to him. I was struck by the similarity of their voices: both were energetic and quick off the mark.

As an undergraduate, Alasdair was often compared to Sir Isaiah, as if people expected the younger man to lay claim one day to the older man's mantle. Like Berlin, Alasdair enjoyed chasing ideas and attaching them to thinkers, and puzzling out why those men had thought and acted as they had; like Berlin, he was a natural synthesizer. (Berlin, it seemed, couldn't mention Kant without mentioning Fichte and Hegel, as if he always saw connections among thinkers.) Like Berlin, he was passionate about music. And then there was Alasdair's shout, which sounded as if he had picked it up from Berlin. When I first met Alasdair, I thought that it was part of the hearty English manner, and imagined that many people at Oxford shouted like him. Later, I heard it said that Alasdair had learned his particular shout from Berlin, who, in turn, had learned it from Sir Maurice Bowra, another great Oxford figure. But the differences between Alasdair and Berlin were equally striking. Berlin seemed to have a sombre side, while Alasdair always seemed to be in high animal spirits. Berlin seemed set in his ways, while Alasdair was free.

As we were all standing and chatting, champagne glasses were pressed into our hands, and the waiters kept topping them up. A dinner table materialized, complete with damask cloth, silver, and crystal. There was still some time before the beginning of the opera, and the Donaldsons seated us as if we were in their dining room, Alasdair and I being on either side of Rose. We were served a smoked-salmon course—with very special white wine—and demolished it to the sound of the orchestra tuning up. Just before the curtain rose, the table and the dining chairs were carried out and comfortable arm-chairs carried in, transforming the private dining room into a ringside parlor, and the thick curtains of the box were drawn back.

Between acts, over more courses, with appropriate wines—and ap-propriate switching of furniture—almost everyone commented volubly on the voices of the singers and the quality of the sets; on Boris Christoff, the lead, and Rafael Kubelik, the conductor; on this production and others that people had seen. I knew the opera only from a set of records I owned. Although that allowed me to follow the story and the singing, more or less, I felt that if I opened my mouth I would only expose my ignorance, yet it would not do to continue to be silent. I resorted to the time-honored American technique of posing questions, asking at one point how Mussorgsky's opera was different from the Pushkin drama on which it was based, and whether anyone knew the differences between the earlier and the later versions of the opera.

Berlin was fast with answers, but Alasdair was not far behind. He was able to hold his own with Berlin on the subject of Pushkin. Indeed, I was floored by his knowledge and erudition. He was a year and a half younger than I was; I already had an American college degree, obtained while he was doing his National Service. How, I wondered, had he managed to learn so much? Was it Winchester or the English culture? I told myself there was no way to explain the springs of talent. After all, Pushkin, perhaps the greatest Russian poet, had died at the age of thirty-seven.

"What a silly way for Pushkin to go," I said now. "If Pushkin hadn't died in a duel—"

"The 'if's and 'can's of history!" Alasdair broke in. "What if Marlowe hadn't been stabbed to death in a tavern? We might have had a poet as great as Shakespeare."

The dining chairs were almost pulled out from under us, so that the parlor could be reassembled for the last act.

Since Alasdair and I were in different colleges, we didn't run into each other as a matter of course. We would arrange to meet by sending each other notes through the colleges' messenger service: there were several pickups and deliveries per day, so we could write to each other in the morning and meet a few hours later. He would usually come by Balliol, and we would go around the corner to Cornmarket Street and either lunch at La Roma, a cozy Italian restaurant, or have morning coffee or afternoon tea at the Cadena Café, to the strains of a live orchestra. (Auden's patronage added a touch of poetry to the atmosphere.) Alasdair was quite a university figure, yet there was nothing patronizing or pretentious in his manner. Almost from the start, he made me feel like an old friend, although there were a number of people he knew better, from school, from National Service, and from P.P.E. studies.

One recurrent topic in our conversation was Oxford philosophy, and whenever we talked about it I felt particularly sad that I wasn't a philosopher. In the nineteen-fifties at Oxford, the linguistic analysis of many chestnuts in the philosophical fire was causing a revolution in Western philosophy. Being an Oxford undergraduate at the time and not taking part in this revolution was a little like being a worker in Paris in 1789 and sitting out the storming of the Bastille. I relied on Alasdair to bring me up to date on the latest bulletins from the barricades. Not only was Alasdair a regular at the lectures of J. L. Austin, Elizabeth Anscombe, Gilbert Ryle, Stuart Hampshire, and other Oxford philosophical luminaries but he also saw many of them socially; his natural brilliance, his good nature, and his charm attracted dons and undergraduates alike. Many of us saw our dons outside lectures and tutorials—Oxford fostered the feeling that we all belonged to a community of equals—but Alasdair got more out of such friendships, because he had both the Winchester passport and the intellectual ability. (In due course, as everyone expected, he became a colleague of his former dons.) He was also lighthearted, even to the point of being a marvellous gossip. It was as if his high-minded principles found release in animated chitchat. After all, Oxford undergraduates and dons were like a big family, whose quirks, preoccupations, and habits were a perpetual source of amusement and entertainment to its members. To hear Alasdair talk about the philosophers was rather like being the proverbial fly on the wall and watching them wrestle with their ideas.

Some years later, I found myself writing a book much of which concerned Oxford philosophers, and I realized that a large part of what I knew about them I had absorbed from my conversations with Alasdair. Like a good teacher, he had imparted knowledge to me in such an informal way that I had the impression I'd picked it up on my own. I wanted to acknowledge his help in the book, but didn't want to embarrass him by associating him with it and making him a party to what might be controversial or might ruffle the feathers of the people

I was writing about, who were his friends and were now also his colleagues. When the book came out, I fully intended to thank him, but I never did. I expected him to say something about it, but he never acknowledged its existence. Almost without knowing it, I took his silence to be a sign of disapproval, and felt wounded. Rather childishly, I responded to his silence with a silence of my own. From a distance, he seemed so successful in the intellectual world that I felt as if our relationship of equality had ceased with my Oxford years. Sustained silence was so out of keeping with our easy undergraduate rapport that I was confused. The thread of our friendship was broken, and the explanations I gave myself for that—for instance, that it was difficult to maintain a friendship from opposite sides of the ocean—were insufficient. Years went by before I realized that his judgment of the book had nothing to do with my gratitude to him. By then, it was too late. On January 10, 1984, around eleven o'clock in the evening, he killed himself by jumping under an oncoming train in the Underground station in Kentish Town, North London.

I remember that when I heard the news I thought of many things, and especially of the death of Anna Karenina, for the novel was a favorite of ours, and we'd often discussed it. But there could be no comparison between a death near midnight in a gloomy station in the Underground and the death under the wheels of a pounding nineteenth-century Russian train, in a bustling, crowded provincial railway station—and, more important, no comparison at all between Alasdair's hurling himself out of this world without abiding faith and Anna crossing herself and begging God's forgiveness with almost her last breath.

The tremor that Alasdair's death created in the English intellectual community is still palpable. In fact, whenever his friends meet, they— that is, we—are apt to remark upon his absence and fall to discussing his manifold gifts, seeing in one aspect or another of his life a reflection of our own. Perhaps I should mention that one of his friends, Peter Jay (a former British Ambassador to Washington), who had been a scholar at Winchester and Christ Church a year behind Alasdair, still refuses to accept the idea that Alasdair committed suicide. He maintains that Alasdair probably fell under the train in a drunken stupor. (In later years, Alasdair was drinking a lot—wine, whiskey, just about anything.) Suicide, however, was the finding at the inquest, where the motorman, who was sitting at platform level, testified that he saw Alasdair actually throw himself under the train.

Alasdair was born on October 9, 1935. He was the youngest son of John Clayre, a doctor in Southampton, whose original surname was Christensen, and who was Danish by birth. For several generations, the Christensens had been doctors and lay missionaries, and it was by way of Australia that John Clayre had come to live in England. He seems to have had a great love for the Scots—for their robust yet puritanical character—and he gave his children, three sons, names with what he thought had a Scottish flavor: David and Iain in addition to Alasdair. Dr. Clayre died when Alasdair was in his teens, and his widow, Doris, settled near Winchester.

Alasdair was particularly close to his mother, a forceful, energetic, inquisitive, determined woman, who, like many women of her generation, hadn't received much formal education. Apparently, because he was both the youngest and the cleverest of her children, she favored him, and after he became a scholar at Winchester she invested ever more pride in his achievements, although his brothers were also intelligent, even if they did not win scholarships to great public schools. (Iain did engineering at Cambridge and has settled in Canada. David is a schoolteacher in Denmark.)

At Winchester, Alasdair was a great favorite of the headmaster, Walter Oakeshott, and, as it happened, Oakeshott left to become the Rector of Lincoln College, Oxford, a couple of years before Alasdair came up. Because of Oakeshott, when Alasdair came to Oxford, after doing his National Service, he had a leg up, and quickly became acquainted with many dons of various colleges. He was soon well known at Oxford in his own right, however, through a column he wrote for *Isis,* an undergraduate weekly. Even people who sneered at the pretensions and frivolities of the "rag" looked out for what Alasdair had to say. In fact, there was a marked disparity between Alasdair's thoughtful pieces and the silly headlines the editors put on them, such as "Clayre Soup" or "Clayre Out." The pieces had a certain kind of intellectual seriousness and political engagement, without the doctrinaire left-wing ideas so characteristic of under-graduate publications then. As a columnist, he seemed to enjoy manipulating abstractions, and forming moral judgments upon the whole social spectrum of England. In one column he attacked the language in which the social sciences were couched. In another, instead of adding his voice to that of the Campaign for Nuclear Disarmament in purely emotional and moral condemnation of "the bomb," he advocated an empirical approach to British unilateral nuclear disarmament, inviting those who airily espoused pacifism to consider its consequences: it might involve renouncing "our trade, our standard of living, our position in the world, our political independence, even our lives." In a third column he reviewed Roy Jenkins's book "Sir Charles Dilke, a Victorian Tragedy," and discussed the Victorian moral code, which if it was publicly violated could spell the ruin of an eminent figure. (Dilke's career was ruined, just when he was on the verge of coming into a high office, by charges of adultery levelled by a self-proclaimed mistress; she was probably prompted to make them by Dilke's apparent actual mistress, who, as it happened, was her mother.) In a fourth he reflected upon the relative uselessness of writing and thinking, his particular métier, compared with the usefulness of building bridges and manufacturing goods, the job of the worker. In looking up the pieces recently, I was pleasantly surprised to find how clearly I recalled them.

In 1959, Alasdair was awarded a congratulatory First in P.P.E.—that is, his papers were so brilliant that the board of examiners specially commended him in person—and that autumn he was elected one of three new prize Fellows of All Souls. As a Fellow, Alasdair became one of what were then sixty select, self-electing, self-governing, self-perpetuating Fellows of one of the richest colleges at Oxford, which had no students—indeed, no obligations of any kind. At All Souls, he was ensconced in rooms, panelled in mahogany, that are some of the most comfortable in Oxford, and in a setting that is, in its way, as exquisite as that of Winchester or Christ Church—indeed, of any in England. The college, which was founded in 1438, has great physical beauty. Its northern quadrangle, designed by Nicholas Hawksmoor and completed in 1734, ranks as one of the finest examples of eighteenth-century architecture in Britain, and on a clear day its high twin towers and, beyond them, the outlines of the Radcliffe Camera, which is a library in the shape of a rotunda, and the spires of the

Bodleian Library provide a striking vista. It was here that Alasdair was left alone to think and write. In "A Room of One's Own" Virginia Woolf, while bemoaning the social exclusivity of British higher education, says, "Intellectual freedom depends on material things." Alasdair was now provided with those material things as a result of his success in a series of competitive examinations, beginning, in effect, when he was eleven. (Competition, like flogging, had, of course, been one of the principal values that built and sustained the empire.) He used to say that as a sinecure for intellectuals All Souls had few, if any, equals anywhere in the world. An All Souls Fellowship was an unparalleled passport to almost any establishment position. Indeed, traditionally, many of the Fellows had not gone into academic life at Oxford but had held such positions in London—in the Civil Service, in banking, in publishing, in Parliament—and had visited the college only on weekends. Over the years, the college had played a very important part in British politics. Between the wars, for instance, it boasted such London Fellows as Curzon, Chelmsford, Halifax, Simon, Dawson, and Sir Arthur Salter. Some of the most important, if misguided, decisions of the period were substantially made in its common room: not to bring down Mussolini, not to help the Republicans in Spain, not to collaborate with Russia, not to defend Czechoslovakia.

In the early years when I saw Alasdair at All Souls, he seemed to take to the college as if it were his birthright. (I remember one garden party he gave at the college as perhaps the most dazzling Oxford party I ever went to.) A passionate, outspoken Marxist, John David Caute, was elected the same year as Alasdair, but he soon began to bridle at the old-fashioned comforts of the place. In fact, he and some other young fellows took it upon themselves to try to reform the college and bring it into the modern world, by making it, at least in part, into a graduate school—with actual students, and a new building to house them. Their plans eventually fell through, and Caute was so indignant that he made a public issue of this life of privilege by writing an article about it in the British monthly *Encounter*. In his article Caute fastened the blame for the failure of the reforms on John Sparrow, the Warden of All Souls, charging that he was clearly offended by the atmosphere of modern intellectual life, since he preferred gentlemen amateurs to professionals, classical discipline to practical subjects, bachelor dons to married dons. (Once, it is said, Sparrow quipped that nowadays young fellows were giving up "All Souls for one body." He himself was a bachelor.) Caute also charged that Sparrow found distasteful such notions as a college's accountability to the state and the opening up of higher education to greater numbers. (Caute resigned his Fellowship, because he no doubt felt it would be inconsistent and dishonorable to go on benefitting from it while attacking the college in print.) Caute was silent about which side Alasdair had taken in the affair, and Alasdair was too discreet to violate All Souls' code of confidentiality. I do remember, however, that Alasdair was torn by the row, and his distress made me think he might have had a foot in each camp. Caute, who had been brought up by his mother, like Alasdair, had gone to a public school, and he had garnered certain marks of Oxford success: as an undergraduate, he published "At Fever Pitch," a novel, and also got a First in Modern History. Sparrow, like Alasdair, had been a Winchester scholar, and, unlike Caute, was a pillar of the establishment: he had read Mods and Greats—Mods being the first part of the Greats degree—at New College, taken his mandatory Firsts, been elected to All Souls, been called to the bar, and become an important figure at Oxford. Alasdair seemed to see their clash as a family feud, and to be pained by it.

At All Souls, Alasdair took advantage of the international standing of the college, and the social and intellectual groups it opened up to him, but he never settled down to any particular line of work. While most of us marched purposefully toward a goal, he was constantly jumping from one thing to another, picking up things, making a success of them, and dropping them, as if he were trying to prove himself in different fields—in effect, continuing on the road of competition. One sensed a certain tension in him, as it seemed that he was increasingly drawn out of the cloistered, cozy world of Oxford, an extension of his Winchester life, into the larger, glamorous world of London.

Perhaps taking a cue from the philosopher Wittgenstein, he worked for a time as a gardener for the writer Richard Hughes, who was a friend of his. He took up architecture, and was awarded a scholarship to study the subject at the Architectural Association in London for five years, but he abandoned it within a year. He tried his hand at fiction, publishing a novel, "The Window." (The *Times Literary Supplement* review of the book began, "Mr. Alasdair Clayre has written a book about faith, hope and love. He is not able to cope with these high themes in terms of character; and there are difficulties of feeling that he does not approach.") He also published a volume of verse, "A Fire by the Sea, and Other Poems." He produced television programs and delivered lectures over the air for the Open University—a non-residential university for students of all ages (often employed), in which television is used as a teaching aid. He wrote a book, "Work and Play," in which he considered the ideas of philosophers on work: borrowing an analogy from Simone Weil, that the worker is like a rejected lover, he discussed the value of work that is fulfilling; and, drawing upon verbatim quotations from workers, he argued that the problems posed by repetitive industrial work can be solved not by more pay and fewer working hours, as is generally assumed, but by less industrialization, since tedium kills enthusiasm for leisure. At one time, he fell for Scientology, and was taken with its idea that one could maximize one's production and creativity by joining the community of its adherents; he was especially attracted to the commune style of living that some of its adherents had adopted. Members were required to turn over their money. Alasdair had no money to give, and after a few months the scales dropped from his eyes, and he escaped. Escape proved much more difficult for friends of his who had followed him into the movement; one of them had made over to it a good part of his substantial wealth.

For a while, Alasdair was a folk singer. He published a collection of his songs, and performed them on a couple of records. The liner notes on one record were written by the novelist Iris Murdoch. The notes on the other were by the writer and critic John Wain; he described Alasdair's songs a little in the manner of Polonius—as in turn "lyrical and elegiac," "purely satirical," "satirical with an undertone of pathos," "argumentative-satirical," and "philosophical and lyrical." Actually, Alasdair's songs were often fatalistic and had about them something of the troubadour, perhaps his most famous being "Adam and the Beast," in which Adam asks God, "Is it among the hunting beasts that I belong?" Some of Alasdair's songs were also recorded by a Persian folk singer, a young woman named Susha Guppy, who had immigrated to England from Iran.

I met Susha once. "I was introduced to Alasdair in the late sixties or early seventies," she told me. "In those days, he and a friend were running a very successful night club. I did an evening of singing there, and that launched my career in Britain. Alasdair's songs were perfectly all right—as a typically sixtyish poet's songs. It was as if he were trying to be Bob Dylan, but the songs were not as good as Bob Dylan's, so he thought that they were no good."

Like his professional life, his private life was turbulent, and was notable more for its conquests than for its stability. "When we were undergraduates, I once saw Alasdair near the sports field," David Pryce Jones, a friend of ours, recalls. (Alasdair had always been very good at football.) "As I was driving away, I saw Alasdair just hustle a girl into a ditch. I can still see her little feet going up in the air. This was the first time I had seen such an approach to courtship, and I think it was symptomatic of the way he set about things with women—I mean, he simply got on top of them. In the early years after we came down from Oxford, when Clarissa and I were living in our little matchbox of a house in the Knightsbridge area"—David was among the first of us to get married—"at least four broken-hearted girls must have come to the house to talk to Clarissa. All of them had been shattered by their experience with Alasdair. I remember having a conversation with him when he had got two of them pregnant at the same time. He was ashamed of it, but also proud of it. You see, he was a great moral figure, but had something wolfish about him, too. As he grew older, he got hold of younger and younger girls. Sometimes the wives of his close friends had to worry about the virtue of their daughters. He was a little like the Minotaur waiting for the next shipment of virgin flesh from Greece."

Alasdair's mother began to fret that her son would never get married and settle down, but Alasdair seemed unconcerned about the delay. He was the first to admit that he had trouble committing himself to one woman. And he once pointed out to me, "After all, Isaiah didn't get married until he was forty-seven." In October, 1974, however, when Alasdair was thirty-eight years old, he married Felicity Bryan. They had been living together for two years. Felicity, a literary agent, was the twenty-nine-year-old daughter of Sir Paul Bryan, a Conservative member of Parliament. (He represented the constituency of Howden from 1955 to 1983.) The wedding took place in the crypt of the Houses of Parliament, another of the old and beautiful settings that had formed Alasdair's experience. They remained married for six years, but during the last two they lived apart.

Alasdair's final piece of work was a twelve-part survey of China, for television, entitled "The Heart of the Dragon," and an accompanying book that bore the same title. The series, in a sense, had its origin in his friendship with Peter Montagnon, his former boss at the Open University and a longtime, distinguished producer for the BBC, whose credits included the series "Civilisation," with Kenneth Clark. In 1979, when Channel 4, a new commercial station, first began broadcasting, Alasdair and Montagnon formed a television-production company and called it Antelope—because, Montagnon explained, "we thought the animal smelled good and it was able to run pretty fast when required." One of the few conditions of the partnership was that sometimes Montagnon would be the front legs and Alasdair the back legs, and sometimes they would change ends; another was that they would work only with people they liked. Although it was clearly in Alasdair's interest to work with Montagnon, it was not so clear why Montagnon wanted Alasdair as an equal partner. He once said that he thought of Alasdair as heir to the late poet Louis MacNeice, and as being in the tradition of the Third Programme, for which MacNeice had done some of his best work. The BBC's highbrow Third Programme had carried the banner for international high culture in Britain until 1970, when it was discontinued, to the accompaniment of an enormous storm in the British cultural establishment. Montagnon, while recognizing that Alasdair would be an anomaly in popular television culture, apparently looked to him to bring to it a touch of the Third Programme.

Alasdair wrote the proposal for the China series in consultation with China scholars, to whom he had access through his All Souls connections. On the basis of that proposal and Montagnon's reputation, Channel 4 funded the entire project. Alasdair then scouted for locations—a job that meant travelling extensively in China, ahead of the film crew.

In the course of the work on the series, Montagnon often found Alasdair an extraordinarily joyous and extroverted collaborator, and suggested as much in this entry in his diary, dated October 23, 1981, which he shared with friends after Alasdair's death. It was written when they were in Turfan, in western China: "Last night there was a grand party given by the chief of 'the Foreign Office' in Turfan. He comes from a minority group; a Vega. Alasdair saved our bacon; we had to perform after the local girls and the local bands had just given over with their dances and songs. He was fast asleep in the front row. We dug him in the ribs, and whispered 'Alasdair, you're on.' He leapt up and into the breach, and sang two of his own songs brilliantly, then topped it by doing a Scottish reel, much admired by us, the locals and a visiting herd of American tourists." At other times, it seems, his work habits showed a different, rather anxious side of Alasdair. According to Montagnon, he would often stay up all night, going through a couple of dozen drafts of a chapter, and in the morning his colleagues would find him unshaven and surrounded by the debris of a sleepless night.

Alasdair spent three years on the series and the book. They dealt with China's history, culture, and economic conditions, and, together, perhaps constituted his longest-sustained piece of work. The date of the publication of the book was January 10, 1984, twenty days before the first installment of the series was to be broadcast. As publication day approached, Alasdair's friends noticed in him signs of anxiety; it seemed to them that he didn't want to expose himself to the criticism of reviewers, as though that would interfere with his sense of perfection. It was on that day that he killed himself.

A memorial service for Alasdair was held in February, 1984, in St. James's Church in Piccadilly. It fell to Felicity to organize it; neither his elderly mother nor his brothers, living abroad, knew who his friends were. The task was none too easy, not only because Felicity had remarried and had three small children but also because since the divorce many of Alasdair's closest friends had ignored her or seemed embarrassed to acknowledge her. "It is very frustrating to run into people you know—at the opera or the theatre—and have them simply pretend that you don't exist," she told me.

Among those attending the service were some of the most notable figures in British intellectual and social life. David Pryce Jones, Peter Levi, and Peter Montagnon—three of Alasdair's close friends—spoke, with Levi giving perhaps the most moving eulogy. "He was in the tradition of Diderot and Voltaire, except that he was shouting with laughter," Levi said. "He made philosophy as comic as it was serious. . . . He made a walk across a quadrangle feel like a wild intellectual adventure. . . . He even made All Souls sound like an endless opera by Mozart—not a usual view. . . . Alasdair was one of the few moral philosophers who understood the fundamental importance of pleasure, and, of course, its tragic nature. He did as much as anyone to infect our entire generation with liberalism, a love of liberty. . . . He was one of those minor characters in Shakespeare who make the whole play live. He died after weeks of severe strain, in a moment of desperation, by an unconsidered act of desperate courage. 'Against the leaf, that is violently taken with the wind, thou showest thy might, and persecutest dry stubble.' "

Felicity now lives just outside Oxford, with her second husband, Alex Duncan, who is an agricultural economist. In 1988–89, when I was a Visiting Fellow at Balliol, my wife and I saw something of them; they came to us, and we had dinner with her and Alex at their house, in the village of Kidlington. Naturally, one of our topics of conversation was Alasdair. In fact, she and Alex had become romantically involved when Alex was working in Gambia and she went to visit him for the Christmas of 1980 to recover from the final breakup of her marriage to Alasdair. (She and Alex had first met almost ten years earlier, when she was twenty-six and he was twenty-two, after her mother died and her father married Alex's mother.)

One day, Felicity came to lunch at the college, and we had coffee in my room. The subject of suicide was very much on my mind. That Michaelmas term, two undergraduates had committed suicide—one, Darran Walters, by taking cyanide crystals, and the other, Adam Lal, by jumping out of a fourth-floor window. It was reported that Oxford and Cambridge had higher suicide rates than any other universities in Britain, and, apparently as a precaution, many gas fires in college rooms had long since been replaced by electric ones.

"Was Alasdair prone to depression?" I asked Felicity.

"Not in the early years of our marriage," she said. "His troubles had more to do with his fear of settling down, and his wish to remain perpetually youthful. When he wasn't running around after very young girls, he was often involved with quite aristocratic, fashionable women."

"Were the two of you happy together?"

"We certainly had a very sociable life. In the early years, we had a lovely time. We travelled a lot. Though we did once go to America, and once to Denmark, to visit Alasdair's relatives, who were very jolly, we mostly went on little jaunts. On Friday, he would get the idea of going to France for the weekend, and within minutes we would be on the road on his motorbike. He was deeply committed to his motorbike, had it long before he married me. He liked it because he could go anywhere with it—put it on the train or ferry. We would go to Waterloo, take the train to Southampton, and go over to Le Havre, and we'd be in France. We would stay in a small hotel in Paris, look at things, have good meals, stay up late talking and drinking, and come back on Sunday. Then, in London, too, we were always going to parties on the motorbike. It made him feel fancy free. There was a bit of the gypsy in him. Alasdair was a very interesting mixture of the reclusive and the gregarious. He preferred dinner parties to cultural evenings, but we did go to some plays, and I used to drag him along to operas—I'm a great opera fan."

"Alasdair couldn't have been a very easy person to be with," I observed.

"When we first got together, he was trying to write for six months of the year; for the other six months, he was working for the Open University. I think it's a difficult thing for an agent to be married to a writer, and particularly a writer who doesn't feel he's doing very well, so we didn't share our work, and that made things easier. He never wanted me to read his writing. I never even read 'The Window.'"

"That's surprising," I said.

"I suppose he didn't feel proud of it and therefore didn't want me to read it. We did do a lot of work together, though, getting his records off the ground. We also used to sing a lot together. He had a lovely tenor voice."

"As you know, I didn't keep up with him during the years you were married," I said, "but it seems that he found settling down to a particular kind of work very difficult."

"Yes, though he was always involved with the media—especially television. At one point, he left the Open University and started working for the BBC in Manchester on a sort of television magazine program. He saw it as a chance to get out of academic television and do something more general, but the program was not a success, because it was the first time he had had to work like a reporter, and he didn't come off very well. He tried to go back to the Open University, but he'd lost his slot there. Then he worked for the *Economist* for a time. He had done some long essays for the magazine, and the editor, Andrew Knight, had the inspired idea to have Alasdair do a political column. He tried his hand at it, but it wasn't a success, either, because it meant that he had to hang around the lobby of the House of Commons and talk to politicians. Reporting just wasn't his line."

"I wonder why he didn't stick to the academic life," I said. "He was so well suited to it."

"He did, of course, have his room in All Souls, in the tower, as part of his Fellowship, and he would disappear there. But he didn't seem to have any really close friends there of the sort he could confide in. Anyway, Englishmen of his upbringing often have trouble talking about their feelings, particularly with other men. In fact, I think that's why some of Alasdair's closest friends were not English. Also, he was fearful of judgment by his All Souls colleagues. He felt that he had already let down so many people who had put a lot of faith in him. You see, he felt he was a failure. While we were married, 'Work and Play' came out, and he didn't enjoy its publication at all—he was so fearful of reviews."

"You lived mostly in London?"

"Yes. We lived in a flat, which he had bought before I knew him. It was on Mill Field Lane, half way up Highgate, West Hill, and from its roof terrace one had a lovely view of the Highgate Ponds, on the Heath. Alasdair was very much attached to it, because it was unusual and out of the way. It was a delightful walkup for a bachelor, but it had only one big room, and that doubled as his study and our living room. As far as I was concerned, it wasn't an appropriate place for a couple. Moreover, it was isolated and inconvenient. The entire time we were married, I tried to get him to move to a house—get more settled, have children—but he resisted the idea."

"Was that why you broke up?"

"Yes, although the immediate cause was my finding out that he was having an affair. He continued to have the affair, and was very much involved with the woman, but he couldn't see why that should get in the way of our marriage. We went to a marriage counsellor who was a Jungian analyst. I think she was recommended by Montagnon's wife. I found the whole process of therapy incredibly tearful and difficult. The hour would completely knock me out. Then Alasdair and I would have lunch together, and have a bright and jolly time, but there was no way to save the marriage, because he wouldn't have children. Just before I remarried, he invited me round to a splendid house he had bought in St. John's Wood. I couldn't stop crying. It seemed to me extraordinary that he should have got this big house—just the sort of house I'd always wanted for us—after I left him."

"Still, you kept in touch?"

"He came to see me at our house in Oxford just after we moved there, in 1983. I'd recently had Max, my second child, and Alasdair had just returned from China. I was eager to hear his impressions of China, but he kept saying, 'This could have been us. This baby could have been ours.' He seemed to want to start the marriage over again. I imagined that it was seeing me with my baby in our beautiful old Oxford house that had upset him. I tried to change the subject to 'The Heart of the Dragon,' but he kept saying that he was very, very lonely—that an American girl he was involved with had left him and gone back to the States. 'But how is the series going?' I persisted. He said that he wasn't sure how it would do—he considered it a secondary, rather than an original, work and dreaded the prospect of seeing it reviewed. All kinds of people were against him, he said. He sounded very paranoid. Toward the end of his life, he was telephoning me regularly. Generally, he would stay on the line for about an hour. There was no way I could calm him. One day, he called me and he just went on and on, and I put the phone down on him. I'd just had Ben, and I was breast-feeding him. I was very tired from having had three children, one after another. He phoned back. Alex picked up the phone and said, 'Alasdair, will you please stop phoning Felicity—it upsets her too much.' After that, we didn't speak until the Christmas before he died, when he phoned me at the office to say that he had lost his driver's license. He said that he had been caught speeding by the police and discovered to be over the alcohol limit. He thought he was going to be sent to prison. I assured him that he wasn't—that he had only lost his license. That was the last time I spoke to him."

"Did he talk about anything else?"

"He talked obsessively about money problems. That was ironic, because he died quite well off. After all, he owned the flat and the house, both substantial residences. And then Antelope went public some time after he died, and did extremely well. I often felt guilty about that last telephone call, and I often thought of him, but I didn't really mourn him until I got the news that 'The Heart of the Dragon' had won the Emmy—it was really extraordinary that an English television series should have won the Emmy. I burst into tears, and for a whole week I found myself thinking of him and crying. I felt that the Emmy was a symbol of success that would have meant a great deal to him, that would have given him self-esteem."

"But he had so many symbols of success much grander than the Emmy."

"But he needed a new one each time he did something."

Richard Snedden, the third of my Winchester friends and the only child of Sir Richard and Lady Snedden, came up to Balliol two years before I did, when he was eighteen years old, as a scholar. In contrast to Alasdair, Sned was a self-contained chap, who epitomized a certain kind of conventional British attitude and attention to style. He seemed to be comfortable only in his gang of public-school men, and for him people were either "in" or "out." Because he had gone to Winchester and was a scholar, I imagined that he would end up in the exclusive Foreign Office. As an undergraduate, he was particularly interested in holding offices—in societies, in the Junior Common Room, or J.C.R., in anything at all. He seemed to be fascinated by the trivia of the elections, like a child with an all-consuming hobby. In my first year, he was elected treasurer of the J.C.R., a student office out-ranked only by the offices of its president and secretary. The next year, he stood for president against Peter Davison. Peter was an outsider—he was a Canadian, and the only undergraduate at Balliol reading Theology—and he was very personable. Sned was perceived as a stiff, establishment candidate, and he lost. (Sometimes it seemed as though Americans and Canadians were the only people who could get elected to any office, because the public-school and grammar-school boys wouldn't elect each other.)

The only reason I got to know Sned at all was that both of us were members of the Leonardo and the Arnold and Brakenbury, or A. and B. One was a society of fifteen self-selecting, high-powered undergraduates who met every second Friday in term to read and discuss papers on the sciences or the arts while drinking a lot of mulled claret; the other was a college debating society with about thirty also self-selecting members who met every second Tuesday in term, also drank a lot, and delivered themselves of formal but irreverent and ironic speeches. At most other colleges, I would probably not have been taken into such select societies, and would never have crossed the path of someone like Sned. But Balliol had a tradition of nonconformity and openness, which threw people from different worlds and backgrounds together. At meetings of the Leonardo, when a paper was being discussed Sned was usually silent, or would let drop an enigmatic remark about extrasensory perception, or, if he did not like something someone had said, would groan—"Ugh." He shone only in private meetings. There he would be free with pranks and suggestions. Once, he proposed that the Leonardo invite Lord Hailsham, who was then the Deputy Leader of the House of Lords, as a guest speaker from London. People protested that such a grand personage would not deign to journey up to Oxford just to entertain fifteen self-important undergraduates. Sned maintained that if one summoned "the fellow" by telegram, rather than the usual formal letter, he would grasp the importance of the invitation, and hotfoot it to Oxford. Sned, on his own initiative, did send the telegram, but Hailsham never appeared.

Sned really came into his own in the frivolous A. and B., where he held many offices, in addition to that of president. He once made a speech on the subject of his habitual silence, and punctuated it with long pauses. Another time, he somehow got hold of a deck chair, brought it into a meeting, stretched out in it, and conspicuously fell asleep. Someone surreptitiously set a match to the canvas from underneath. Sned awoke, crying out "Dean! Call the Dean!" Christopher Fildes, then the president, ordered Deputy Constable Jake Broadley to extinguish the smoldering fire. John Albery, one of the most brilliant and versatile undergraduates, was singled out as the culprit, but, upon his expressing contrition, was forgiven. The president then called upon Toby Jessel, who held the office of both auditors, to help. The meeting concluded with Toby pretending to rock Sned in the charred chair while crooning Brahms's "Cradle Song." Sned took great delight in all the commotion.

Ray Ockenden, in a valedictory speech as ex-president of the A. and B., mocked two of Sned's conspicuous habits—feigned napping and secret telephoning. He was always rushing off to make a telephone call at the porter's lodge. We imagined that he must be telephoning his parents overseas—Sir Richard Snedden was a big wheel in shipping and travelled a lot. Ockenden's speech was in the form of rhymed couplets:

And who's this, creeping wanly from his bed?
Well, well, well, if it's not me old mate Sned.
Like all great diplomats a firm believer
In enigmatic phone calls to Geneva.

The Arnold and Brakenbury and the Leonardo Society were anathema to the sporty types, like football players, who affected such working-class customs as eating fish and chips off newspaper; to Christians in the college, like the members of the Oxford Inter-Collegiate Christian Union, who were against all societies that were not religious; and to socialists, who thought public schools and public-school ways antediluvian and deeply corrupting. Yet Oxford was full of select societies, many of them steeped in romantic lore. In the university at large, there was the Bullingdon, which had no fixed premises, and whose membership was restricted to twenty, but which was renowned for its bluest-of-the-blue members, who went on to play important roles in British society. They would hunt once a week, and in the evening, after riding their horses to the club's livery stable, would try, as one member at the turn of the century had put it, "to crack their hunting crops on undergraduates in the Quad"—usually unsuccessfully. Perhaps even more famous was the Gridiron, which was exclusive—at one time or another, the Prince of Wales, the Crown Prince of Norway, and Prince Paul of Serbia had been members—but boasted past intellectual members, too, among them Aubrey Herbert, Ronald Knox, and Harold Macmillan.

Within Balliol, there was the Annandale Club, which had no intellectual pretensions but was notorious for its upper-class excesses. For instance, one of the after-dinner amusements of the club's members some fifty years earlier had been to throw large quantities of college crockery down the hall steps in a ritual waterfall. Their high spirits were matched only by the tolerance of the authorities, who simply billed the members for the damage the morning after. But if those members—many of them Etonians—were wild, they also included some of the most brilliant Balliol men ever. Even A. D. Lindsay—their contemporary, who later became Master of the college—though he was repelled by their debauches, admired the natural brilliance of some of them, like Aubrey Herbert, who was perhaps identified even more closely with the Annandale than with the Gridiron, and who, though he was rusticated from the university for a time, went on to get a First in Modern History and to play an adventurous role in Parliament and in the First World War. (John Buchan used Herbert as the model for the hero of his novel "Greenmantle.") The Annandale members of my day—they included Snedden, Christopher Fildes, and Denis Cross—had style, if a prodigal style. They would get dressed up in tailcoats with silver facing on a gray collar (the club colors were black, silver, and gray) for no other purpose than to dine together in the Massey Room. And there were no more than ten Annandale members at any one time.

"What goes on at an Annandale dinner?" I once asked Sned.

"We have ananas Annandale."

"What's that?"

"A pineapple with its insides scooped out, and filled up with pineapple, ice cream, and kirsch."

"What else happens?"

"We hold a sweepstakes on the number of leaves on the pineapple, and the president usually wins. Our sconcemonger is called upon by a member to sconce the president for some failure or solecism in dress, like not wearing shirt studs in the club colors." In hall, if anyone commented on the silver or the paintings, or quoted Latin, or mentioned the name of a woman, he could be sconced—that is, given a flagon of beer or wine, which he had to drink without stopping. If he drank it all, the challenger, or sconcer, had to do the same, and so it went until one of the two fell down. The point of the ritual was to teach unmannered louts the art of polite conversation. "As part of the Annandale sconcing ritual, the president is brought a large silver pot of champagne, and he does his best to drink it," Sned went on. "The silver pot is then passed around, and the members become considerably rowdier. It's not all that different from A. and B., except that we do a little throwing about of things, in such a way that the Dean will ban the club for a term or two. But why are you asking? Dining societies only suit Englishmen of a particular kind. They are not for you wogs and frogs."

There was more jest than insult in his last remark, and I couldn't help smiling, reminded, as I was, of the Duke in "Zuleika Dobson," whose club was so exclusive that he could tolerate only himself as a member.

I didn't tell Sned that, even as the puritan in me disapproved of dining clubs, the bon vivant in me was envious of the members of every last one of them; that I, as an outsider, found Annandale members fascinating, and felt they were almost visionaries, in the sense that they imagined the real world to be like the Annandale, with rigged sweepstakes and with champagne on tap, as it were; and that it seemed to me that to be a foreigner in England and not to belong to at least one dining club was like missing out on the elixir of the English experience.

Still, my own friendship with Sned was unexpected indeed. At the time, I could not have explained it, but in later years I thought of many reasons for it. He was part of a group that one would have immediately picked out as being among the most interesting of the college groups. Though he himself did not put out much energy, I was drawn to him anyway, because he and his group had a certain style, natural elegance, and air of superiority, because I saw winning their acceptance as a kind of challenge, and because I wanted to feel that I was fully in the stream of English life. Besides, not only was I drawn to eccentrics, which I imagined Sned, among others, to be, but I also believed in eccentric relationships, which I saw ours to be.

Sned and his handful of hard-drinking, poker-playing, hell-raising Annandale cohorts perpetuated certain antiquated college traditions. One of their capers was to get "tight" at the club dinner, in the Massey Room, dash over, in their tails, to the east wall, which separated Balliol from Trinity, a college known for its social pretensions, and make a spectacle of themselves. They would line up at the wall, urinate on it, and belt out the old anti-Trinity song, competing to see who could sing the loudest:

> If I were a bloody Trinity man,
>   I would, I would,
> I'd go into a public rear,
>   I would, I would,
> I'd pull the chain and disappear,
>   I would! I would!
> Bloody Trinity! BLOODY TRINITY!

One could hear them going back from the wall to the Massey Room singing "I Would Honor Yet the School I Knew" or "Lloyd George Knew My Father." No doubt when Lloyd George was Prime Minister one's father's being known to him must have opened all kinds of doors for one, but now those doors were supposed to yield only to merit. It was one thing to sing this song, a staple of all college dining societies, in the privacy of the Massey Room but quite another to sing it in the quadrangle, in the hearing of undergraduates, who, by and large, disapproved of privilege.

Sned got a Third in P.P.E. People had expected him to do better in Schools, or final examinations, but then again members of his particular set generally aspired either to a First or to an even rarer Fourth, which was just above failing—to either extreme, as opposed to a middling result, which was the lot of most undergraduates. After going down, he spent two years in the R.A.F. There he was assigned to the Department of the Air Ministry, and worked as a scientific adviser. Afterward, he got a job with the Bank of England. We thought he was selling himself short, since in those days an Oxford graduate from a great public school who was going into finance would have been expected to go into the much classier world of merchant banking. After a couple of years at the bank, Sned left it and started working for I.B.M., U.K. He eventually became product planner for the company in the Netherlands. In the late sixties, he returned to England as the company's market coördinator, and went to live with his parents, in the village of Boars Head, in Sussex. They lived in a Victorian house called Aldwick Grange, built in 1873.

Sned had always felt inadequate beside his distinguished father, Sir

Richard, born in 1900 and educated at George Watson's College in Edinburgh, at Edinburgh University, and at Middle Temple Inn, had been called to the bar in 1925. He served as a director of numerous companies, like Consolidated Gold Fields, but his main interest was shipping. In 1929, he joined the Shipping Federation, a business organization of shipowners, as assistant secretary, and by 1957 he had risen to become its director. He was then well known as a labor negotiator, perhaps because he was ruthless to anyone who opposed shipping interests but, at the same time, was sincere in his concern for the sailors' welfare, and so enjoyed the confidence of both the shipowners and the leaders of the seafarers' societies. In 1951, he was knighted for his work in industrial relations. As a person, he was said to be delightful and amiable, quick and shrewd. Though he was a quiet speaker, when he thought that right was on his side both his material and his delivery could be devastating.

On Friday, March 6, 1970, Sned, then thirty-four, came home from work seeming confused and upset. He had been depressed for some time, and particularly since the death of his mother, at the age of sixtynine, about six weeks earlier. He had been very close to her, and in recent years had confided to his friends that his father mistreated her. It was hard to tell whether his perception was correct, especially since he himself had a history of psychiatric disorders, dating from at least 1965. In that year, his mother had found him with a loaded gun between his knees, as if he were intending to shoot himself, and he had spent three months in a mental hospital.

Father and son passed the weekend of March 6th together. Whatever Sned's own feelings of inadequacy, his father was very proud of him. Indeed, there was said to be a bond of deep affection between them.

But, as was later reported in the newspapers, on Monday morning Sned went to the garage, got an axe, and walked into the drawing room, where his father was sitting, reading a book. With the axe, he struck his father two heavy blows across the forehead, fracturing his skull.

Then he went into the dining room with the axe, and said to Miss Winifred Lyall, who had been the family housekeeper for twenty years, "I couldn't stand Daddy worrying about me anymore. I hit him with this. You can kill me now."

Miss Lyall screamed. She feared that he was going to kill her, too. "It was the right thing," Sned said, putting down the axe. "You're all right. You can kill me."

Miss Lyall told him to call the police. He dialled 999, the police emergency number, and said, "I think I have killed my father." He couldn't continue.

Miss Lyall took the phone from him and told the police what had happened.

When the police arrived, Sned gave himself up, saying, "Oh God, what have I done? He was suffering because of me. I wanted to kill myself as well—but I didn't have time. I have been a burden on my father for a long time. I thought I would end it all, killing him and then killing myself."

Sir Richard was found slumped in his chair, the book in his lap. He was rushed to Pembury Hospital, near Tunbridge Wells, in Kent, and he died there that same day.

The murder made headlines not only in the popular tabloids but also in the intellectual papers. On March 9th, at a special Magistrates Court in Mark Cross, in Sussex, Sned was charged with murder and remanded into custody. On May 14th, he was tried at Lewes Assizes, in the county. He pleaded not guilty by reason of insanity.

Mr. Basil Wigoder, Queen's Counsel, who was prosecuting, gave an account of the circumstances of Sned's crime, from which it emerged that on the day before the patricide he had decided to go back into the mental hospital, and had consulted the family doctor, John Elliot, about it. He had told Dr. Elliot that he might harm himself, and that, because this would worry his father so much, he might also do him harm. During the meeting, the Doctor had noticed that Sned's moods fluctuated from deep depression to euphoria, but thought that he had calmed down. After extracting a promise from Sned not to do any harm to either himself or his father, Dr. Elliot had felt sufficiently reassured not to commit him immediately to the hospital.

Dr. Jack Hobson, senior physician in the department of psychological medicine of Middlesex Hospital, who had visited Sned in prison, testified that for a period after his father's death he was certifiably insane, and said of his mental condition at the time of the murder, "Snedden did not know . . . he was doing wrong. He felt it was the only right thing to do."

Sned was acquitted by the jury of the murder of his father, and the presiding justice said that, by court order, Mr. Snedden should be "detained in a hospital specified by the Home Secretary." He was thereupon sent to Broadmoor Hospital.

The British law that a person who has committed murder or manslaughter cannot benefit from the estate of his victim does not apply when that person is found to be insane. Therefore, Sned inherited nearly a hundred and forty thousand pounds. His inheritance, though not large, was adequate for his needs, and was administered for his benefit by the family solicitor, Arthur Prothero.

Sned survived his father by only a little over five years. I thought of visiting him in Broadmoor, but I was not sure he would want to see me. After all, I was not a school friend or an Annandale friend, and I had not met his parents or received confidences from him about them. In fact, I later learned that hardly any of his friends visited him. By his heinous act, it seemed, he had put himself outside the pale. His Annandale cohort Christopher Fildes was an exception. He went to see Sned both in jail before the trial and in the hospital afterward. "In jail," he told me after Sned's death, "it was just like Evelyn Waugh's 'Decline and Fall' when the chaplain comes to see Captain Grimes and asks him if he is all right with God: ''Course I wasn't, told the fellow so.' That was just the kind of meeting I had with Sned. At Broadmoor, we had only a brief conversation. I seem to remember he was wearing the standard scruff order of an undergraduate—an old tweedy jacket, flannel trousers, a soft shirt, and a tie. 'Fildes,' he said. 'You know what? My friend over there and I went to the management yesterday and complained that the radiators were talking to us. We made quite a song and dance over it. Then James, a party to our practical joke, broke in, saying, "Don't pay any attention to *them,* they're both absolutely out of their minds. It's ridiculous for them to say that the radiators were talking to *them,* because they were talking to *me.*" You see, Fildes, you have to do something to keep sane in this place.' Even in Broadmoor, old Sned had style."

In "The Merchant of Venice," Aragon, one of Portia's suitors, delivers a memorable speech while examining the golden casket. He rejects it as the choice of

... the fool multitude, that choose by show,
Not learning more than the fond eye doth teach;
Which pries not to th' interior, but, like the martlet,
Builds in the weather on the outward wall,
Even in the force and road of casualty.

I was one of that "fool multitude" who didn't always find it easy to look beneath the surface glitter of Oxford, or, as Anthony Trollope put it, in "The Bertrams," to look beneath the eating of much pudding and the making of much noise at the young heart. But the casualties, no less than the victors, of the complex system of British education were witnesses to its enigma.

Originally appeared, under the heading "Personal History," as "Casualties of Oxford" in The New Yorker, *August 2, 1993. Reprinted in "Up at Oxford," W. W. Norton & Company, New York, and John Murray (Publishers), London, 1993.*